THE NATURE OF
AFRICAN CUSTOMARY LAW

The Nature of African Customary Law

by

T. OLAWALE ELIAS

Q.C., B.A., LL.M., Ph.D. (London)

*Federal Attorney-General and Commissioner for
Justice for Nigeria;
Of the Inner Temple, Barrister-at-Law;
Sometime Simon Research Fellow in the
University of Manchester*

MANCHESTER UNIVERSITY PRESS

© 1956

Published by the University of Manchester at
THE UNIVERSITY PRESS
316–324 Oxford Road, Manchester M13 9NR

Second impression 1962
Third impression 1972

ISBN 0 7190 0221 4

Printed in Great Britain by
Butler & Tanner Ltd, Frome and London

PREFACE

THIS book is intended primarily as an introduction to African legal theory within the wider framework of general jurisprudence. Accordingly, it is concerned, not with a comprehensive description of the various customary laws of the African peoples, but with an analysis of the basic concepts underlying African law and the interpretation of these against their social and juridical background.

The comparative approach is often adopted whenever it is thought that this will illuminate the text or point a parallel in the familiar fields of English (or any other type of) law. But it is not so much an exposition of a new theory as a synthesis of existing evidence, supplemented here and there perhaps by my own personal views and inferences. The general thesis it seeks to establish is the simple one, that African law, when once its essential characteristics are fully appreciated, forms part and parcel of law in general. It is thus no longer to be set in opposition to what is frequently but loosely termed ' European law ', and this notwithstanding a number of admitted differences of content and of method.

Practical problems of the legal administration of African colonies have except in Chapters XIII and XIV been touched on only incidentally, as this is a book of basic principles of law, not a handbook for the solution of current administrative conundrums. But it is hoped that what has been here attempted will be found of interest as well by colonial administrators as by students of African law generally. Amidst the prevailing dearth of legal literature dealing with general legal principles it should supply some of the sorely-felt need of the jurist and the sociologist. It can at least be offered as an essay in comparative jurisprudence.

The book has been written during my tenure of a Simon Research Fellowship in the University of Manchester. Part of that time was spent in paying study visits to parts of West and East Africa, with a view to obtaining first-hand information as well as correcting perspective or confirming impressions of African customary law *in esse*. The purpose has been to reduce to a minimum the chances of wrong inferences or generalisations to which a too rigid adherence to books and monographs alone might so easily lead. The aim throughout has, therefore, been objectively to assemble, to weigh and to assess all the available data bearing on each of the topics discussed in this book. The reader must judge for himself how far it has been achieved.

I wish to thank the authorities of the University of Manchester not only for financing my study visits to Africa but also for granting a subsidy towards the cost of publication. I would also like to thank Professor B. A. Wortley and the other members of the Faculty of Law for their friendly co-operation during my stay among them, and Professor Max Gluckman of the Department of Social Anthropology who, in addition to his many acts of personal friendship and kindness, allowed me to take part in the work of his Postgraduate Seminars on Social Anthropology, to which I was privileged to give a number of papers.

I need hardly add that, as no part of this book has previously been published, I hold myself responsible for all its shortcomings. Suggestions are welcome from readers for its improvement.

T. Olawale Elias.

The University.
Manchester.
May, 1954.

CONTENTS

vii

TABLE OF CASES

TABLE OF (BRITISH) STATUTES

TABLE OF COLONIAL ORDINANCES

CHAPTER I

PROBLEMS AND AIMS

IT would be both presumptuous and unwise to attempt within the compass of such a short work as this an adequately comprehensive study of the laws and customs of the polyglot peoples inhabiting the vast continent of Africa. There would be about as much wisdom in making such an effort regarding Africa as there would be in an attempt to issue even an abridged edition of the various systems of law and bodies of customs of the diverse peoples of modern Europe. The difficulty in the latter case would not be so much the lack of adequate materials as the resistance to such treatment of the bewildering quantity of available documentary data. The writer of such a book would be hard put to it to collate the various rules and conventions, already so well studied and minutely analysed and recorded, in the several constituent states of Europe. The Codes which form the bulk of the laws of Continental countries are not always susceptible of exact analysis or comprehension even by those trained in the Civil Law systems. But even if we suppose that the task of reducing European laws and customs to an orderly body of theories and principles were feasible, it is at least doubtful whether the product would be either very intelligible or very readable.

Far greater than these are the problems that beset the path of the writer on African laws and customs. The immediate trouble here is the obvious lack of material with which to build. In the first place, the extant available studies of the African situation are few and far between. Many areas of Africa are still virgin fields for research in so far as the social, political and cultural aspects of African life are concerned. These inadequacies make the writer's task somewhat unenviable when compared to that of his opposite number saddled with the compilation of European laws and customs ; since it makes the African writer's statement of principles and methods so much more open to challenge by any single discovery contrary to the generalisations which he must perforce indulge in at this stage of his enquiry. This naturally places a special burden of responsibility on the writer on African

I

customary law, if he wishes to fulfil his obligations to scholarship and to Africa itself.

The second problem which has to be faced is that, by the very nature of customary laws anywhere in the world, the numerous rules of behaviour, as of social control, remain largely *unwritten* except, of course, in those areas of Africa that have at one time or another come under the permanent influence of Islamic invasion. In these areas there exist codes of the various schools of Islamic law which are often in recorded form. The rest of the African scene presents, as far as written records are concerned, a rather bleak prospect, and one's vision of the landscape is still more dimmed by the lack of uniformity among many groups of the polyethnic societies of Africa. But such divergences as there are can easily be exaggerated, as Hilda Kuper has so rightly warned : [1] ' . . . in the vast continent of Africa there are hundreds of tribes, each with its own history and way of life. . . . This cultural variety is important but it must not be exaggerated. It underestimates the tremendous effect of past contact and over-emphasises African conservation. Moreover, the piling up of ethnographic detail produces an impression of chaos where there is in fact only variations on a few themes.'

There seems to be, however, one other redeeming feature : the facility with which traditional norms of behaviour are recalled by the Africans themselves when questioned about particular rules is nothing if not remarkable, especially when the party giving evidence of customary rules has no motive to misrepresent the facts. Modern research has indeed revealed the existence in some communities in Africa of certain types of professional persons trained in the art of playing the role of spokesman of what is the customary rule of law on a given matter before the traditional courts. Were the task of enquiry into African laws to be confined to evidence gleaned from such sources, and should such individuals be always available, the writer's task would be immeasurably lighter ; but that is far from being the case.

The legal writer has in the face of such overwhelming odds necessarily to depend upon miscellaneous sources of information : e.g. (i) social and anthropological studies which, though often very valuable for the light they throw on dark spots, are nevertheless

---

[1] See *The Listener*, Aug., 1952, p. 293 (a broadcast talk by her, entitled ' Cultures in Transition ').

sometimes too fluid for purposes of legal analysis ; (ii) the great wealth of information often contained (one might almost say, buried) in the various reports of Commissions of Inquiries [1] set up from time to time by the various Governments responsible for these territories, for the purpose of investigating local life and habits ; (iii) the increasing volume of recorded judicial decisions of statutory courts established in many areas of the Continent— by far the most reliable source of information for the legal theorist no less than for the professional lawyer. It is from such quarries as these in the African landscape that the legal theorist must hope to mine the various seams of indigenous African ideas of law and order, so as to fashion them into usable materials of contemporary juristic thought. It is not that the picture is at all always clear or exact but that, if a general conspectus is ever to be made of African laws, some such start ought to be made if only as an intelligent groping for the distant light.

Lest one should get the impression that the situation defies any attempt at a reasonably workable systematisation of such legal ideas and customs as are discernible from extant sources, one might hasten to add in extenuation that there are surprising similarities, at least in important essentials, in bodies of African customary law as divergent as those of the Yorubas, the Bantus, the Sudanese, the Ashantis, and the Congolese. It may be pertinent here to recall this observation about East African laws of Mr. C. Dundas (as he then was) : ' In all these tribes I observed a similarity in their conceptions of law and practice which suggested to me that certain principles might be common to all Bantu of these countries. I was fortunate enough to find in German East Africa a number of German writings concerning other tribes of which I have little or no personal acquaintance, and in these also I found a great deal of information which coincided with my own observations.' [2]

---

[1] Such, for example, as (i) Report of the Northern Nigeria Lands Committee—Cmds. 5102, 5103 (1910) ; (ii) Report of the Land Tenure Committee for Northern Rhodesia (1943) ; (iii) Reports of the Conference of Law Officers, 1926 and 1933, Nairobi ; (iv) Commissions of Inquiry in Kenya, Uganda and Tanganyika (1933)—Cmd. 4623 and Col. No. 96 (1934) ; (v) Report on Visit to West Africa in 1926—Cmd. 2744.

[2] C. Dundas, in an article, in the *Journal of Royal Anthropological Institute*, Vol. 51 (1921), pp. 217–78, entitled ' Native Laws of some Bantu Tribes of East Africa '.

It is these broad outlines of the examples and features of the various societies in Africa that it is proposed to analyse and summarise in this work. No doubt, further light will be shed in the future on many points of detail which may confirm or confute some of the generalisations we are about to attempt here. Such a situation will not be new to the African case, it being a common phenomenon in the general history and evolution of law. It is sufficient here that a start is made in what will undoubtedly be a long and glorious adventure into this hitherto uncharted field of legal theory.

The increasing economic and social importance of the Continent for our time, the emergence of political consciousness among the indigenous peoples in various parts of the Continent, and their aspirations towards recognition in the various fields of human endeavour, make it all the more urgent that an attempt should be made to give expression to the immanent ideas of the African peoples in the rapidly changing circumstances of their modern life. Another excuse is that although there is a growing body of literature on the social and economic sides of life on the Continent, largely inspired by the increasing desire of Europeans to open up for the benefit of the world at large its enormous but as yet almost untapped resources, there seems to have been no parallel need for an effort to study, and disseminate in a readily accessible form, the foundations of the legal ideas of the indigenous peoples of Africa, without a knowledge of which the orderly and peaceful government of the producing territories would sometimes prove difficult.

This attitude of indifference to a seemingly academic issue is understandable in view of the fact that it is often assumed that it is the business of the administering Powers to undertake the task of what is after all a proper incident of their administration of the various territories. In fairness to the latter it must be said that they have made or caused to be made numerous piecemeal studies of problems of local government and a few manuals or digests of customary laws ; but it is also true to say that the various Governments have yet to launch a wholesale campaign for the encouragement of the comparative study of the various customary laws and established customs. As Major Order-Browne has remarked : ' Prolonged research will produce various official reports which bear to some extent on the subject, while much useful information may be gleaned from numerous ethnological and sociological works ; in most cases, however, the material is incidental and scrappy, while it is also confined to the condition existing in some particular country or area ; very little attempt seems to have been made so far to deal with the whole problem of the African in contact with white man's law, while even the material and practical aspects of the subject have received but slight attention.' [1]

Yet a third reason for undertaking the present work is to make a plea for a change of heart and of attitude on the part of Western jurists towards the indigenous laws and customs of Africa. All too often, one finds that the majority of persons in the legal world of Europe and America entertain curious notions regarding African legal ideas and institutions, varying from the vague scepticism of those who think that there were no such things as laws in Africa before the advent of Europeans to those who, while admitting that there are such laws, yet demand a wholesale eradication of what exists and the substitution therefor of imported European legal concepts. This narrow attitude stems from the approach which judges everything African in terms of European standards and values and which dismisses out of hand anything that does not conform to such patterns. It is the aim of this book to try to discredit this mythological approach to African laws and customs.

If by what is here attempted European and African readers alike—and there are some Africans who share these European prejudices—may be made to appreciate the relativity of the social values which underlie all systems of law, and by which the genius of every people has always designed rules for the regulation of social behaviour in the community, then one's effort will not have been in vain.

From the point of view of comparative jurisprudence the present work is intended as a contribution to the literature on general legal theory. It is possible that some of the points here made

[1] Major G. St. J. Orde-Browne, ' British Justice and the African ', in *Journal of Royal Afr. Society*, Vol. 32, No. 127, April, 1933, pp. 148–59 ; p. 150. Even as far back as 1921, Lowie pointed out in his *Primitive Society*, in the chapter on ' Justice ', p. 404 : ' There is no one source that adequately describes African jurisprudence ; accordingly, it will be well to summarise the mutually complementary data from several areas.'

B

may serve the purpose of inducing a re-assessment of some of the controversial subjects of accepted Western legal philosophy, particularly on the thorny problem of the definition of law. It need not be emphasised that the reader will discover for himself how not very unlike the known legal ideas elsewhere are those of the African stated here : it will be only one more proof of the unity of all human knowledge and experience. Fortunately law, apart from differences in social environment, is no respecter of race or tribe, and the problems it has to solve are everywhere the same, namely, the resolution of conflicts in human society and the maintenance of peace and order.

It should probably be added that we are not unaware that Maine in his *Village Communities* and *Early History of Institutions* deals chiefly with ' ancient Law ' against the background of his Indian experience, that Diamond in his *Primitive Law* is concerned with a general enquiry into early law and, again, that Robson's *Civilization and the Growth of Law*, considers law in the stage of becoming. Julius Lewin's monograph, *Studies in African Native Law*, mainly based on his South African material, seems more concerned with problems of policy and administration than with detailed analysis of legal concepts, although very useful light is often thrown on some of these. All these studies have some relevance for the kind of examination of African legal situations such as it is proposed to make in these pages ; and we propose to make good use of these. Current legal theory has yet to take full account of the African interpretation of the juridical problems with which law must grapple in a given society. An intellectual adventure into African legal conceptions should enlarge our horizon, if it does not enrich our knowledge, of the function and purpose of law in the modern world.

It seems necessary to indicate, if only in a general way, the scope of operation of the customary law we are about to discuss. While we will state in all relevant contexts the modifications already effected in certain rules of customary law, we wish to give here the limits within which what is later described applies today.

Almost all African Colonial Ordinances provide that customary law should primarily apply :

(1) in all matters relating to marriage, land tenure, inheritance,

succession, testamentary dispositions,[1] and, of course, chieftaincy,[2] and similar traditional offices and institutions ;

(2) in all other disputes where (*a*) both parties are African, and (*b*) the subject-matter is neither subject to English law [3] nor expressly made so subject by the parties themselves.[4]

(3) where, although one party is an African and the other party is not, it would be unjust to either party to apply English law [5] ;

(4) where an alleged rule of customary law is not contrary to any existing statutory enactment or to ' the principles of natural justice, equity and good conscience.' [6]

Finally, it should be noted that the field covered in the ensuing pages is confined to indigenous Africa south of the Sahara. Accordingly, the Mediterranean fringe from Morocco to Alexandria, and even Ethiopia, must be left out of our present account, however relevant to these territories some of the principles enunciated for the remainder of the Continent might be. Similar considerations of strictly un-African characteristics must exclude from our purview such regions as Egypt, the Islamic area of the Sudan, and Zanzibar. At any rate, it is thought that the laws and customs of these territories are already familiar to European readers.

Also, the Union of South Africa will not be dealt with in any specific way, as detailed studies already abound on the African customary law there. But, for the purpose of general legal theory, relevant references will be made to it in appropriate contexts.

[1] So far as these are not varied by act of parties ; e.g. succession may be made subject to rules of English law by a testator, or marriage may be contracted according to English law under the Marriage Ordinance. See also, e.g. s. 17(1) of the Supreme Court Ordinance, No. 23 of 1943.

[2] E.g. *Eshugbayi Eleko* v. *Nigerian Government* (1931), A.C. 662, p. 673.

[3] Thus, modern commercial transactions like the sale of goods, the functionings of incorporated companies and of partnerships etc., are all governed by English law as embodied in local Ordinances. Similarly, English criminal law as expressed in the Criminal Codes has virtually superseded the customary laws of crime in almost all territories.

[4] Subject to the legal impossibility of applying English law to certain situations exclusively governed by customary law—e.g. the right of an individual in family land cannot be turned into an English fee simple ownership—parties to any customary legal transaction can stipulate that English law shall be the proper law.

[5] E.g. s. 17(2) of the (Nigerian) Supreme Court Ordinance, No. 23, 1943.

[6] E.g. s. 17(4), *ibid.*

CHAPTER II

THE NATURE OF AFRICAN SOCIETIES

LAW and politics are closely allied sciences, and it would be convenient to describe briefly, in the present chapter, African political organisations as a necessary preliminary to the subsequent enquiries into the nature of African laws and customs. Bound up with this interdependence of law and politics are the wider problems of legal philosophy such as (i) the great issue as to whether law precedes the State in order of priority or *vice versa*, (ii) the question whether law is the command of the political sovereign of a particular community of people, and (iii) the argument as to whether the legal rights of the individual are derived from the State, or whether the individual has no rights at all apart from the duties imposed upon him by the State. As we shall have occasion later to examine these and other issues, it is not intended to enter upon them here. What we are more immediately concerned with is the delineation of the various types of African societies and of such features of these as are vital to our understanding of the subtle workings of the various customary rules and conventions.

It is not to be expected that, amidst such a diversity of peoples and in such a considerable land area as the African Continent, any uniform and invariable pattern of society should exist. The African peoples are, as much by the accident of history as by numerous geographical handicaps, at varying degrees of political, cultural, and economic development. Since law is inevitably interlocked with all these phases of social life, it naturally manifests itself in different ways and conditions and so we sometimes get variation of details, if not of essentials, as we pass from one society to another.

But, in spite of this diversity, we have to bear in mind the strong evidence of general similarities which writers who have studied Africa at first hand, and appreciatively, have vouchsafed to us. Writing on Nigeria, Dr. C. K. Meek, for example, observed : ' It is clear that throughout Africa most kingdoms were modelled on the same principle. The Jukun state is of the same pattern as that of Bornu or Songhai in ancient times, and does not differ much from that of Benin or Oyo at the present time.'[1] M. Delafosse writes to the same effect, though his view is more general : ' Whatever be the degree attained by the political institutions of the African negroes and whatever aspect the civilisation of their various States presents, their organisation and functioning, everywhere and always, offer the same essential characteristics.'[2] A recent estimate is that of Hilda Kuper :[3] ' In Africa south of the Zambezi, one traditional pattern predominates—each tribe revolves round a hereditary chief. African societies can be broadly classified into a limited number of economic and political types. . .'. All these testimonies relate to chiefly societies, but the same general similarity in cultural and political patterns will be found to exist among the chiefless ones. The two main types will be described a little later.

A brief peep back into the historical antecedents of certain areas of the Continent would throw a flood of light upon how the political systems now existing have come about. It is a recorded fact that from at least the fourth century (circa A.D. 300) onwards there have flourished various African empires and kingdoms in West Africa such as the Ghana, the Songhay, the Mali, the Walata Empires,[4] and, at a much later date, the Kingdom of the Congo ;[5] in the south-east, the Zulu Empire; in Central Africa, the Kingdom of Monomotapa with remains still surviving to this day ; and in East Africa, the ancient Bunyoro Empire and the Buganda Kingdom.[6] Thanks to the graphic accounts of Spanish–Arab scholars[7] some of whom were eye-witnesses of what they described, we now know something of the glories as well as the comparative splendour that were once these African empires and civilisations.

---

[1] A Sudanese Kingdom, Ch. VIII (on Government), p. 346. For a fruitful comparison of Jukun with Buganda, ibid, pp. 336, 345–7.

[2] Negroes of Africa (1931), translated by F. Fligelman, p. 144.

[3] See her broadcast talk, ' Cultures in Transition ', in The Listener, Aug. 21, 1952, p. 293.

[4] For an account of these empires and kingdoms, the reader may consult Lady Lugard, A Tropical Dependency (1905) ; also Ibn Battuta, Travel in Asia and Africa (1323–54).

[5] F. Pigafetta, History of the Kingdom of Congo (Rome, 1591).

[6] Roscoe, The Baganda, Chaps. 7 and 8.

[7] Notably El Bekri and Ibn Battuta (Travels). See Tarikh-es-Sudan and Tarikh-el-Fettach, both compiled in Timbuktu in the fifteenth century. A straightforward account is contained in M. Delafosse, The Negroes of Africa.

We also learn of the various waves of Arab invaders and, centuries later, of the European slavers, who from a strange mixture of religious fanaticism and commercial cupidity, harried, sacked and disrupted the African empires and principalities. It is only in comparatively recent times that these have been reorganised, though slowly and sometimes ineffectively, by the Africans themselves. But ill fortune continued to dog most of the steps taken to consolidate and improve some of the political organisations and systems of government, because the European slave trade followed closely upon the devastations of the warring Arab hordes and so contributed towards the disintegration of African societies in most parts of the Continent. Let it be said at once, in the interest of historical accuracy, that the African rulers themselves played their by no means glorious part in this inhuman traffic in their fellow human beings, and it is a question whether most of the indigenous institutions and culture might not have been preserved had the African emperors and kings themselves thrown the whole weight of their military might and personal influence against the foreign invaders of their territories.

Nevertheless, the extant relics of these ancient glories would seem to warrant the inference that some of these kingdoms and principalities must have enjoyed spells of comparative peace and tranquility in which such ancient arts and crafts as those of Ife and Benin,[1] and of Ashanti,[2] or the wonders of the Zimbabwe culture,[3] could have flourished. Geology and archæology have also in recent times thrown up innumerable relics of the past of the African peoples all over the Continent, which cannot but be regarded as the cultural remains of peoples whose ancestors must have seen better days.

We have sketched in this brief historical reminiscence only as a pointer to some aspects of our coming discussion of the otherwise inexplicable manifestations of political and legal precocity which sociologists and anthropologists sometimes stumble upon nowadays in odd places in Africa.

[1] Read and Dalton, *Antiquities from the City of Benin.*
[2] R. S. Rattray, *Ashanti Law and Constitution.*
[3] See Caton-Thompson, *The Zimbabwe Culture.*

A. POLITICAL ORGANISATION

It has been suggested in a modern work of authority [1] that indigenous African societies can be classified into two groups. The first group consists of those with a centralised authority, administrative machinery and judicial institutions, while the second is composed of those societies with a very rudimentary political arrangement, without any strong centralised authority, administrative machinery or judicial institution. Societies of Group A are represented by the more advanced communities, culturally heterogeneous and consisting of units bound together by common interests and loyalty to a political superior, usually the Paramount Chief or the King-in-Council. Examples given are the Zulu, the Ngwato, the Bemba, the Bayankole and the Kede. Societies of Group B, on the other hand, have no one single centralised authority enjoying a concentration of political, judicial or military power capable of controlling by direct decrees the activities of members of the group. Examples given are the Logoli, the Tallensi and the Nuer.

This twofold view of African societies implies the existence of the following four principal differences:

(*a*) In Group A there is the incidence of *organised force* which is the principal sanction in a society based upon cultural and economic heterogeneity [2] corresponding to distinctions of wealth, privilege and status: whereas in Group B there is a notable absence of these features.

(*b*) Group A societies are usually amalgams of different ethnic groups, since there is a limit to the size of the population that can hold together without some kind of centralised government. Group B societies lack what is usually denoted by the term *government*, since cultural as well as ethnic homogeneity is the rule. The part played by the lineage system in the political set-up is that it primarily regulates the relations between territorial segments which obviously constitute the essential framework of the political organisation in such societies. By the lineage system is meant the ' segmentary system of permanent, unilateral descent

---

[1] M. Fortes and E. E. Evans-Pritchard, *African Political Systems*, p. 5.

[2] The Zulu and the Bemba seem to be exceptions in this respect. They each have cultural homogeneity. (*Op. cit.*, p. 9.)

groups ', while the kinship system consists of ' the set of relationships linking the individual to other persons and to particular
social units through the transient, bilateral family '.

(c) In both Group A and Group B societies can be observed an
underlying territorial framework, though its functioning in each
is different. This difference is due to the dominance of an administrative and judicial apparatus in the one type of social organisation and its absence in the other. In the first group political
rights and obligations are territorially delimited ; in the second
group, however, the territorial units are local communities
based on the size of lineage ties and bonds of direct co-operation.

(d) In Group B societies the only step in the direction of an
organised judicial system is the recognition of certain elders as
traditionally qualified and entitled to participate in the adjudication of disputes, such recognition being usually based on their
seniority as members of the social unit.

The purpose of the above analysis will be appreciated when we
come to deal at a later stage of our enquiry with the more immediate problem of the impact of British rule upon the two sysetms of
society. One observable feature of this is the loss by societies of
Group A of the right to exercise organised force and the consequent diminution of the traditional authority of their kings and
chiefs, who now find themselves having to play the equivocal role
of being, on the one hand, the agents of European governments
and, on the other, the representatives of their peoples. The
indirect-rule system helps to foster and to maintain this chiefly
state of precarious equilibrium with all its modern implications
from the point of view of the administration of such societies.[1]

The response of Group B, on the other hand, has been in the
opposite direction, also with its attendant difficulties. The lack
of centralised indigenous authorities has led to the employment
of all and every body who can be assimilated to the stereotyped
notion of an African chief as administrative agent of the new
government. The sorry tale of the political blunder in creating
these ' Warrant Chiefs ' is that unprecedented authority was conferred upon persons who had not the slightest shadow of a right
to such prerogatives, bolstered up as they were by the authority
of the new British governments. But these mistakes have been

---

[1] Some of these problems are briefly discussed at pp. 15–16, *op. cit.*

largely corrected, and the way is open to bolder experiments in the architectonics of modern local government. These are perhaps possible in the more politically advanced communities of Group A. Some of the other associated problems will be discussed in later chapters.

B. SOME OBSERVATIONS

The above description of the constitutions of African societies represents a definite advance upon previous studies of the nature of African societies. It shows unusual penetration as well as understanding of many aspects of indigenous African political systems. But its generalisations can only be taken as being approximately accurate, since there are some other vital features of these systems which seem to have eluded the vigilance of the anthropological experts. For example, it is thought that the analysis of African political systems into only two major groups [1] does not take sufficient account of the peculiarities of the political organisations of African societies subject to Islamic rule, e.g. Northern Nigeria, Northern Territories of the Gold Coast, most of the Gambia, some areas of Sierra Leone, the Sudan, Uganda, Zanzibar and some other communities of East Africa. One common characteristic of all these Islamic African societies is that they are *theocracies*, i.e. political systems of government with strong centralised administrations which are permeated through and through by Islamic theology and law. The heads of these political entities more often than not tend to be autocratic, and the power and authority which they wield are generally feudalistic. It will thus be seen that these constitute a third major group in addition to the two already described, even though they partake of the general nature of Group A in most respects. But religious law clearly plays a far more important part here than in either of the other two types.

[1] In fairness to the editors, it should be mentioned that they recognise a *third* variety of political organisation—namely one in which even the largest political unit embraces a group of people all of whom are united to one another by ties of kinship, so that political relations are coterminous with kinship relations and the political structure and kinship organisation are completely fused. Unfortunately, this type of society is not described in the book (p. 6–7). Also, Prof. D. Forde has recently suggested for West Africa *three* different types of political organisation. See *Civilisations*, Vol. III, No. 4, 1953, pp. 471–89.

Moreover, for the purpose of closer analysis we ought to sub-divide each of the political systems which we have denoted respectively as Group A and Group B above.   In Group A are to be found two types of political set-up : (*a*) strong centralised *kingdoms* such as those of the Yorubas, the Ashantis, and the Baganda, the territorial units of which are more or less closely knit together by ties of kinship, cultural affinities, and local contiguity ; (*b*) a conglomeration of kingdoms loosely united together for purposes of administration under the paramountcy of an accredited overlord or emperor.   Diversity of ethnic groups and variations of culture characterise this form of political organisation in which allegiance to a common head is dictated largely by the factors of necessity and security.   Again in Group B it is important to observe that while the societies lack centralised authority, administrative machinery and judicial institutions, they nevertheless have a rudimentary political arrangement whereby authority is sometimes wielded by a chief, who may be the head of the most important family in the local community and who probably enjoys seniority among the other family heads, or who may be an important religious officiant. In such communities one must look for authority in the person of a ritual functionary rather than in that of a political leader as such. So that Group B should be properly described as consisting, on the one hand, of those societies with some measure of political organisation having a kind of functionary as head and, on the other hand, those societies that have not.

While, however, we must keep it in our mind that these varieties of each group do exist, it seems better in subsequent chapters to refer only to the two dominant Groups, A and B.

C.   AFRICAN THEORY OF GOVERNMENT

As the learned editors of *African Political Systems* have observed in their admirable introductory essay, it seems no useful purpose would be served by attempting a hypothetical reconstruction of African societies of the dim and distant past.[1]   If one supports this attitude it is not because whole African communities have not been known to spin theories about their ancestry (e.g. the so-called *myth of the original ancestor*), or about the legendary founding of

[1] Our earlier reference on pp. 9–10 to the ancient African empires and civilisations cannot be said to fall into this category.

their settlement by an eponymous hero ; this figure is conceived of sometimes as having suddenly emerged from the earth at some revered spot within their territory, sometimes as having migrated as a break-away individualist from some other pre-existing community,[1] while at other times he is an all-conquering ruler and protector of the people. But whatever the theories held regarding the origin of particular African societies, they probably have as much validity for scientific purposes as have the equally sterile European theories of the ' social contract '.

It will be remembered that in Western political and legal thought various theories have been put forward as to the origin of political society. For example, John Locke believed [2] that, originally, men came together with a view to realising the purpose of social existence by entering into two main types of pact : [3] (a) the *pactum unionis* and (b) the *pactum subjectionis*. By the former, they all agreed one with another to form themselves into a community, since as social animals they could not possibly pass their individual lives in isolation ; while, by the latter pact, they next decided to appoint one of themselves as head, who should be an overseer in charge of the various activities of the group. This position the chief or king would retain only so long as he should remain acceptable to the community. Locke was definitely opposed to the Stuart claim to the ' divine right ' of kings. Thomas Hobbes, on the other hand, had taught [4] earlier that, historically, men were essentially selfish and wicked and that necessity and reason alone led the earliest human species into forming only one pact—the *pactum subjectionis*—by which they formally agreed to surrender all their private rights to a divinely-appointed head. No revolt on the people's part against the king would be at all possible since the head could, like Plato's philosopher-king, be relied upon always to behave like an honest man. At any rate there was no second pact between the people and the ruler by which the latter could be held accountable to the people. Rousseau's espousal of the cause of ' the common man ' led him to a conclusion diametrically

[1] In either case the emergent or migrant hero would be credited with some kind of following, without which social existence would in any case have been impossible.

[2] In his *Of Civil Government*, Bk. 2, ss. 96–9.

[3] Or, as Pollock points out in his *Introduction to a History of the Science of Politics*, Locke at least recognises two stages, if not two pacts.

[4] In his *Leviathan* (1651), Ch. xxviii ; also Chs. XII–XV.

opposed to that of Hobbes—namely, that there was from the beginning only a *pactum unionis*, the sovereignty always residing in the *volonté générale* of the ordinary people.[1] He denied that there ever was any voluntary transfer to an almighty sovereign of the people's inalienable and imprescriptible rights. Those, therefore, who were appointed to carry on public affairs could only be agents executing the sovereign will of the people, to whom they must accordingly be accountable for their actions. Understandably, Thomas Paine had no difficulty in embracing this doctrine in his *Rights of Man* (1789). Grotius had employed [2] the fundamental postulate of the maxim *Pacta servanda sunt* as the justification as well of the validity of international law as of the absolute duty of the people to their ruler. He would, therefore, seem to acknowledge not only that there might have been pacts—although he did not say how many—but also that the people, once they had surrendered their rights to the ruler, must accept even his misgovernment. Strangely enough, however, Grotius allows that the ruler is bound, nevertheless, by natural law to govern justly and that this is so even without any specific promise on his part to that effect.[3]

The purpose of this all too brief summary of the ' social contract ' theories is to demonstrate (*a*) their specifically political role in attempting to explain the relations between a ruler and his subjects, and (*b*) their general sociological role in an attempt to explain the existence and beginnings of human groups everywhere. In the latter instance they are historically untrue, if only because they are purely hypothetical and, as Fortes and Evans-Pritchard rightly assert,[4] it is pointless applying to contemporary African political systems, which are observable living organisms, these hypothetical reconstructions of the origin of human societies.[5] But it seems that this is not a sufficient reason why the learned editors should have eschewed all proper comparisons of the relations between Africans and their rulers, on the one hand, and Europeans and

[1] See his *Contrat Social*, Bk. I, Ch. VI.
[2] See his *De Jure Belli ac Pacis* (1625).
[3] See, generally, W. Friedmann, *Legal Theory* (2nd edn.), pp. 37–45.
[4] *African Political Systems*, pp. 4–5.
[5] That is why Plato was a better political philosopher than Rousseau if only because in his *Republic* he dealt with the political organisation of his contemporary Greek city-states, while Rousseau contented himself in his *Contrat Social* with romantic speculation about a non-existent political society.

theirs, on the other—at least in so far as these are common problems of political and legal theory. To isolate African ideas about these matters from the general problem of political philosophy would seem to be to fall, no doubt unconsciously, into the kind of error against which Radcliffe-Brown so pertinently warned earlier in his preface when he wrote [1] that modern European ' sovereign states ' are only one type of political system and that ' political theory and political practice (including colonial administration) have often suffered by reason of this type of system being set up, consciously or unconsciously as a norm '. That the learned editors did not intend the absolute divorce of African from European ideas on this matter for any purpose other than the achievement of scientific objectivity is obvious from the unusually lucid and penetrating account they give in the pages that follow.[2]

What, then, are African ideas of Government or, in ordinary language, of the relations between the ruler and the ruled ? This at once prompts the question : but how does one know what these ideas are, seeing that there is scarcely any large-scale theorising by the Africans themselves about such matters ? Yet, though their approach is often functional and pragmatic, it is nevertheless obvious that ' they would be unable to carry on their collective life if they could not think and feel about the interests which actuate them, the institutions by means of which they organise collective action, and the structure of the group into which they are organised '.[3] How can it be otherwise when such universal problems have to be tackled as tax collection, payment of tribute, organisation of the regional divisions of the State and their relation to the central authority, the reciprocal rights and obligations between the ruler and the ruled, and the mechanism for securing proper maintenance of accepted values and standards. Naturally, these issues affect hierarchically-graded societies but are absent in those which have little or no territorial divisions by reason of their being made up of segmentary, equalitarian and often economically homogeneous units. With the peculiar problems of social and political adjustments in such societies we shall deal presently.

In Group A societies, a chief is the administrative and judicial head of a given territorial division, having final economic and legal

[1] *Op. cit.*, p. xxi.
[2] *Op. cit.*, particularly pp. 5–14.   [3] P. 17.

control over all the land within his jurisdiction. In other words, the head of the State is a territorial ruler. In societies belonging to Group B, however, there is no administrative system, the territorial units being the local communities in which lineage ties and co-operative economic activities supply the framework of political organisation. But no territorial jurisdiction accompanies the distribution of political power.

Let us now look more closely into the indigenous methods evolved for the application of checks and balances to the exercise of political power in the two types of African society.

In chiefly societies the central authority of the king or chief is usually buttressed by such factors as his control of the national regiment, his power of appointment to and removal from regional administrations of subordinate chiefs (whether kinsmen or not), and the mystical qualities attributed to his office in popular imagination. But, so that this arrangement may not result in monarchical absolutism and political tyranny, there have been evolved such mechanisms as the king's council of chiefs, the queen mothers' courts, sacerdotal officials with a decisive voice in the king's investitures, powerful secret societies in which the king is only *primus inter pares*,[1] and the inevitable devolution of authority to the regional and local chiefs. All these as well as the intangible but effective factor of public opinion serve to protect law and custom by controlling the arrogation of royal power.

The principle, therefore, is that if a king abuses his powers, subordinate chiefs have the right to secede from the commonwealth or, in the alternative, depose him. In Yorubaland (in Nigeria) he would in former times be requested by his chiefs to ' open the calabash ', i.e. to commit suicide by voluntarily taking poison or to go into voluntary exile.[2] Similarly, if subordinate chiefs become tyrannical to their people or insubordinate to their

---

[1] See F. W. Butt-Thompson, *West African Secret Societies.*

[2] Note also, P. C. Lloyd, ' The Integration of the new Economic Classes into Local Government in Western Nigeria ' in *African Affairs*, Oct. 1953, Vol. 52, No. 209, pp. 327–34 ; at pp. 329–30 : ' Most Yoruba towns are still governed in fact by their tribal kings and chiefs. . . . The tribal system of government was essentially democratic. . . . The king was usually chosen from the lineage whose ancestor was the founder of the town. In most towns it seems to have been the custom for the members of this lineage to select candidates for the kingship and for the chiefs of the other lineages in the town to make the final selection.'

overlords, the latter can with the co-operation of other subordinate chiefs remove them from office and then punish them. Such co-operation will be forthcoming only if the king's or the people's case against the offending chiefs is considered just and necessary. According to Lord Hailey, there are also recognised means by which the community can exercise a check on arbitrary action on the part of Fanti and Akan chiefs.[1]

This scheme of constitutional checks and balances, especially that of devolution of central authority upon regional chiefs, is not a mere administrative device. It involves the vital principle that all sections of the people as well as all major interests (e.g. the West African 'secret societies') in the community are enabled, in the final analysis, to have effective say in the ordering of public affairs.

According to African notions of constitutional government, the territorial chiefs represent the central authority in relation to the people in their districts ; but they also represent the people under them in relation to the central authority. By the same reasoning local councillors and the principal ritual functionaries represent the community's interests in the preservation of law and custom by seeing to the due observance of the rites and ceremonies designed for the welfare of the local group. No king or local chief can disregard their voice in such matters. Other specialist organ-isations[2] exist for the protection of particular values of a public character and these must be duly consulted by the central or local authority if certain proposed measures are to be valid. It will thus be seen that all power and authority in a given society are composite. Their various components are lodged in different offices, and such subsidiary powers and privileges clearly serve as constant checks upon any excessive or arbitrary arrogation of power by either king or chief.

In another sense, it may be said that government in an African State implies a delicate balance between power and authority on the one hand, and obligation and responsibility on the other. He who wields political power and influence necessarily incurs cor-responding obligations and responsibilities. That is, the familiar

[1] *Native Administration in the British African Territories*, pp. 192–3. See also J. B. Danquah, *Akan Laws and Customs*, pp. 226–7.

[2] E.g. the Ogboni Society among the Yoruba of Nigeria often served as a bulwark against tyrannical chiefs. (See P. A. Talbot, *The Peoples of Southern Nigeria*, p. 756).

French maxim *noblesse oblige* can equally well describe the African idea.   Again, to quote Fortes and Evans-Pritchard : ' The structure of an African State implies that kings and chiefs rule by consent.   A ruler's subjects are as fully aware of the duties he owes to them as they are of the duties they owe to him, and are able to exert pressure to make him discharge those duties.' [1]

So far, we have been discussing the system of checks and balances in Group A societies.   Group B societies display a different kind of balance.   The conquest theory, by which centralised societies generally extend their territory and influence over less organised neighbours, does not apply to these, as there is no need for one culturally co-ordinate segment to subjugate another. All the segments are of equal rank and more or less parallel interests.

Accordingly, there exists a political framework based upon divergent local loyalties as well as conflicting lineage and ritual ties.   In the absence of a superordinate military or administrative authority, such divergence is indispensable to the maintenance of the political order.   It also means that there is no central political authority to exploit divergent local loyalties for its own ends, or to keep in check any inter-territorial conflicts.   Any conflict between two or more local segments is also a conflict between the two or more component lineage segments, since they are all closely interlocked.   Particular interests are protected against common interests and values by these inter-segment conflicts.   The mutual desire of the equivalent units for social and political equilibrium is the really stabilising factor.

A council of elders almost invariably replaces the chief or the chief-in-council of Group A societies.   There are also certain traditional, ritual functionaries whose role differs but little from that of their opposite number in centralised societies so far as it concerns matters of community rites and ceremonies and, as we shall see in subsequent chapters, even political and judicial matters. And title-societies and age-grade associations are important facets of the political order among these atomistic, equalitarian, and democratic societies. Professor W. M. Macmillan's *Africa Emergent* has described African democracy as ' a negative equality due to lack of opportunity '.   This is not so.   Opportunities exist for individuals of character and ability to achieve personal differ-

[1] *African Political Systems*, p. 12 ; see also p. 197, *infra*.

entiation and influence and to be accepted as leaders in particular departments of public life.[1] There is no room, however, for the demagogue or the incompetent in office. Leaders are made and unmade according to deserts. The people are the final arbiter of the democratic ideal as understood in these communities.

We can therefore see that, whether the society is a monarchy or a gerontocracy, one common denominator is the constant aspiration towards the democratic principle in constitutional government. Lord Hailey has recently described the position in these words : [2]

' African sentiment attaches special importance to the due observance of the procedure by which all members of the community concerned are able to have some voice in determining issues which are of major interest to it. It is rare to find in British Colonial Africa any instance in which the indigenous form of rule previously in force could be described as autocratic, and there are not many cases in which it could be described in a strict sense as authoritarian. It was a prevailing characteristic of the indigenous system of rule that whether power was vested in the hands of individual chiefs or of a ruling class, these had (unlike the absolutist regimes of a certain stage in European history) no machinery by the use of which they could enforce obedience to their orders.'

Subject to the qualifications we shall be making presently, this is a fair estimate of the vast majority of indigenous African societies. The representative character of their political institutions is well brought out and their constant pre-occupation with the goal of democracy in popular government is duly emphasised. Nor does the writer lose sight of the important fact that in African societies, as indeed in European or any other societies, theory does not always accord with practice. Thus, among the few cases in which the traditional (not indigenous) form of rule could in a strict sense be described as authoritarian, he mentions in another place the instance of the Islamic oligarchies such as formerly existed in parts of Northern Nigeria : ' The regime of the Emirates is by tradition authoritarian.' [3] To this

---

[1] See pp. 99, 107–8, 197, *infra*.

[2] *Native Administration*, Pt. IV, p. 2.

[3] *Native Administration*, Pt. IV, p. 23. Cf. D. A. Pott (a Senior District Officer) : ' Progress Report on Local Government in the Northern Region of Nigeria ' (1953), para. 37 (in part) : ' Much criticism has since the war been aimed at the status of the " Sole " Native

C

might be added such ' pagan ' instances of authoritarianism as the former military empire of the Dahomean kings or of King Shaka of the Zulu.   But such is the indigenous constitutional mechanism that the tyrant is ultimately dislodged by popular uprising on the part of chiefs and people alike.   As for the alleged lack of machinery for the enforcement of orders, however, the learned author would seem to overlook the many African societies with an administrative, judicial and military machine and the effective play that those in control make with it in the day-to-day problems of government.   And, even in the case of those societies that lack a centralised authority, instances of effective police arrangements abound for ensuring compliance with decrees and orders issuing from duly constituted councils of elders.

Further, it has to be remembered that it is not the possession of sheer force alone that secures obedience to a king's or chief's orders.   The African ruler is regarded as endowed with all the attributes of worldly power so that he can promote the well-being of his people in the ways and to the extent acceptable to them. His is not the role of a masterful overlord who can by arbitrary exercise of power impose his will upon the masses.   And this is so even although he is clothed with the aura of mystical majesty. But reverence for authority, whether it be of the king or of the established order, is ingrained in the African.   Even in chiefless societies the group of interlocking but mutually balancing segments retains its social cohesion and political structure by this sense of tradition and by an innate instinct for a practical, demo-cratic ideal of orderly existence.

One recalls here, again, the shrewd analysis made by Fortes and

Authority.   Its name smacked of absolutism and gave the ignorant or ill-intentioned the opportunity of labelling such authorities as totalitarian in practice as well as in title.   The Joint Select Committee gave its opinion that prior to the British Occupation " the traditional authority of a Chief . . . was exercised with the advice and support of an equally traditional council ", and considered that " both by tradition and by current practice the relationship between Chiefs and their Councils would be more accurately described by the phrase Chiefs-in-Council ". Accepting this opinion and on the motion of the Sultan (of Sokoto), the House of Chiefs in February 1952, unanimously approved a motion that " . . . every Sole Native Authority in the Northern Region should be known and described as a ' Native Authority in Council ' and that such legislation as may be necessary to carry out the foregoing instructions be introduced ".   Legislation giving effect to this motion has been passed. . . . '   (See also, *ibid.* paras. 8 and 9.)

Evans-Pritchard of the importance of the apparently intangible factors of myths and symbols in the maintenance of the social order : ' Myths, dogmas, ritual beliefs and activities make his social system intellectually tangible and coherent to an African and enable him to think and feel about it.' [1] It is these mystical values that evoke acceptance of the social order, and not the obedience exacted by the secular sanction of force. [2]

Finally, let us note the point often made that there is only one theory of government in African societies. It is true that when there is a political upheaval, the object of rebellion is not to change or abolish the established form of government, but only the occupant of the kingly or chiefly office. Even when sub-chiefs revolt against the king they do so only in defence of the values violated by his abuse of power.

This issue must not, however, be pressed too far. Cases are not unknown when, either as a result of conquest by a more power-ful foreign ruler or in mere imitation of more prosperous neigh-bouring chiefly communities, a once chiefless African society adopted a chiefly system—e.g. the Basoga under the Baganda conquest, or the territories overrun by King Shaka of the Zulu. Nevertheless, it has to be admitted that such voluntary and delib-erate change from a chiefless to a chiefly system, [3] though obvi-ously natural, has not been sufficiently frequent to be widely recorded so far. It is unthinkable that either form of society emerged just in that form from the earliest times and has remained so ever since. Equally, there is probably no recorded instance of a reverse change from a chiefly to a chiefless system, from a monarchical to a republican constitution. Such a change, even in Europe, is a comparatively recent phenomenon in the history of constitutional ideas.

The purpose of the foregoing reflections should become clear when we come to deal in detail with such problems as status and the individual in African society, [4] or what law is, [5] or why law is

---

[1] *African Political Systems*, p. 17.
[2] See Ch. V, *infra*, for a detailed elaboration of this.
[3] One such has been recorded by R. C. Abraham in his *The Tiv People* (2nd edn.), p. 101 : ' The Tiv (of Northern Nigeria) had originally a democratic (i.e. chiefless) organisation which became absorbed in the rule by Drum Chiefs who, after a series of progressive initiations, reached the highest grade when they were known as Full Chiefs '.
[4] Ch. VI.   [5] Ch. IV.

obeyed [1] by the people.   The first is naturally related to the rights and duties attaching to various groups and individuals in the legal organisation of the community, while the second directly raises issues such as whether the exercise of political power by the human sovereign in chiefly societies alone secures obedience to customary rules or whether the apparent lack of this in chiefless ones justifies us in assuming that there is consequently no law worth speaking about in these societies.

It is sufficient here merely to indicate these issues and to leave their discussion to a fuller treatment in the appropriate contexts later.   It is only if this sketchy and necessarily incomplete theoretical description of the African ideas of political government is grasped that the basic legal concepts we are about to discuss will become intelligible.

We will now go on briefly to dispose of certain popular misconceptions about African customary law.

[1] Ch. V.

CHAPTER III

COMMON ERRORS ABOUT AFRICAN LAW

THERE have been various views as to the nature of African customary law or even as to whether such law really exists. It may accordingly be useful to consider briefly the evidence for the conflicting opinions on the subject before we come to analyse the general theory of the nature and function of law in human society, together with the problem of the relation of African to other types of law. We will for the sake of convenience classify and examine the four principal schools of thought as follows: (1) The Missionary's; (2) The Administrative Officer's; (3) The Social Anthropologist's; and (4) The Judicial Official's.

1. *The Missionary*

The missionaries, especially those of the older generation,[1] are accustomed to regard African law and custom as merely detestable aspects of ' paganism ' which it is their duty to wipe out in the name of Christian civilisation. This attitude no doubt arises out of the conscious or unconscious identification of law with religion, and, in particular, of Christianity with Western civilisation. In so far as African culture is thus looked upon as an undifferentiated mass of customs, rituals and inhuman practices,[2] there is little that could be said for its recognition as part of the social order. African customary law must be bad for the new religious dispensation and ought for that very reason to be abolished *holus bolus*.

Sir T. Morison, formerly a District Officer in Kenya, once wrote: [3]

' I soon found myself struggling with graver questions of policy,

---

[1] For there are notable exceptions like Dr. E. W. Smith, who by long sojourn in Africa and by deep study of Africans, has acquired an unusual grasp of, and due respect for, their laws and customs.

[2] It will be remembered that Sir Henry Maine initiated this fallacy of attributing law, morality and religion to a common origin. Later jurists, notably Dr. A. S. Diamond in his *Primitive Law* (pp. 49–53), have disproved Maine's theory and shown that law has more often than not been independent of religion or morality.

[3] In an article entitled ' The Wachaga of Kilimanjaro ' in *Jnl. Roy. Afr. Soc.*, Vol. 32, No. 127, April, 1933, pp. 141–2.

the questions which go down to the root of tropical administration. Should we override native customs, some of which are in conflict with our Western standard of ethics ? . . . The missionary, of course, has no difficulty in answering these questions. These, he says, are pagan customs, his duty is to destroy them and substitute a higher law. . . . Some of them, especially in the past, have gone much further and have acted as if they believed that the manners and customs of the English middle class were part of the Sermon on the Mount. The District Officer cannot follow this simple line of conduct. In theory, the District Officer says that his policy is the sublimation of native custom so that it may approximate more nearly to what we believe to be a higher standard.'

2. *The Administrative Officer*

Lest we should get the impression that the District Officer, because of his more enlightened approach to African law, is always more satisfactory than the missionary, we would do well to remember that the author of the passage just quoted, went on in the next sentence to poke fun at the average District Officer's much-vaunted theory of ' sublimation of native custom ' and to show how difficult it is to put into practice. He was of the opinion that ' many of the current explanations or reasons given for native customs are incorrect ' and that his own experience of the African,[1] made him ' very sceptical of anthropological theories '.

Now, our author's assumption of the inaccuracy of general information on African customary rules is undoubtedly true, but his scepticism of ' anthropological theories ' is less than fair either to the importance of the subject of study or to the better-informed sociologist.[2] The anthropologist, as a trained scientist of human societies and institutions, is often far more adequately equipped for the proper study of the totality of culture than is the District

[1] The author's observation at p. 144, *op. cit.*, is, however, understandably accurate : ' The ignorant African is shy of giving his real reasons to the supercilious white man ; he may be laughed at, he will not be believed ; this is the sort of subject the white man does not understand, so he may as well give him an explanation that he can take in.'

[2] Sir T. Morison was not alone in his sneaking disregard of anthropologists. Another colonial administrator who attacked ' many anthropological fallacies ' was Mr. J. H. Driberg, at least before he himself became a professional anthropologist. See his article entitled ' Primitive Law in Eastern Africa ' in *Africa*, Vol. I, pp. 63–72 (1928).

Officer whose knowledge of the African is generally empirical, often intuitive. The purpose of administration is usually considered to be served once some kind of rough-and-ready justice has been thereby achieved.[1]

One of the defects of the administrative officer's approach to African law in general is that he seems pre-eminently occupied with problems of criminal punishment. His obsession with the administration of criminal justice is understandable, seeing that much the most important part of his duties is concerned with it. What is not so easy to excuse is the tendency to give the impression that African law is all criminal [2] and that, because certain criminal offences are recognised and punished by English law in ways often different from those of African law, the two systems are necessarily poles apart in all other respects.[3] This view obviously does not present a balanced picture of African law, whatever may be its value for the administration of criminal justice in Africa.

3. The Anthropologist

When we turn to the anthropologist we find him definitely more

[1] It is true, of course, that the District Officer, who has wisely turned anthropologist, is often a better administrator of justice ; e.g. Mr. J. H. Driberg, formerly District Commissioner in Uganda and in Sudan, later became Lecturer in Ethnology in the London School of Economics and Political Science.

[2] We shall deal more fully with this point in Chapter VII.

[3] This over-emphasis on Criminal Law and Procedure in Africa may be appreciated by considering the notoriety given to Royal Commission Reports like Criminal Justice in East Africa (Report on the Administration of Justice in Kenya, Uganda and Tanganyika, Cmd. 4623) ; see also ' Criminal Justice in East Africa ' by H. G. Bushe (an Address based on the same Report in Jnl. Roy. Afr. Soc., 1935, Vol. 34, pp. 117–128) ; also, a lengthy review of the Report by Sir Robert Hamilton and an Ex-District Officer in Jnl. Roy. Afr. Soc., 1935, Vol. 34, pp. 7–26.

Again, the theme of Major G. St. J. Orde-Browne's article ' British Justice and the African ' in Vol. 32, No. 127, April, 1933, pp. 148–59, and No. 128, July, 1933, pp. 280–93, was penal administration in Africa. Melland and Young's book African Dilemma (1937), has Criminal Law as its main theme ; similarly, F. Hives in his Justice in the Jungle (1932), about Nigeria.

Even a lawyer in the Colonial Legal Service like the late Mr. C. C. Roberts, in his book Tangled Justice, merely harped on the same chord.

In short, there has scarcely been any writing by administrative or judicial officials on African law dealing with any other topic apart from crime and its punishment.

percipient than either the Administrative Officer or the mere lawyer who has never studied African customary law and is, therefore, prone to nurse the most imaginary notions about its nature. An example of such a lawyer's misguided opinion is this one of Mr. R. T. Paget, K.C., M.P. :

'Thought in tribal society is governed not by logic but by fetish. To the tribe, trial by fetish is just and trial by reason is unjust. . . . It is futile to seek a reason in tribal justice, as it is not rational.' [1]

Without further comment on this statement, let us quote these words of Lord Porter in the recent House of Lords case, *Best* v. *Samuel Fox & Co. Ltd.* : [2] 'The common law is a historical development rather than a logical whole, and the fact that a particular doctrine does not logically accord with another or others is no ground for its rejection.' This accords well with the famous observation of Oliver Wendell Holmes : ' The actual life of the law has not been logic ; it has been experience. The felt necessities of the time, the prevalent moral and political theories, intuitions of public policy, avowed or unconscious, even the prejudices which judges share with their fellow-men, have had a good deal more to do than the syllogism in determining the rules by which law shall be governed.' [3]

But though the anthropologist has better understanding of his

[1] See *The Observer*, July 8, 1951, where this eminent lawyer was attempting to justify the then Labour Government's policy in banishing the ex-Regent Tshekedi Khama from Bechuanaland. Mr. Paget has yet to answer the challenge to his statement offered in the July 15 issue of the same paper by Dr. M. Gluckman, Professor of Social Anthropology in the University of Manchester, who, *inter alia*, remarked : ' It is a pity that Mr. Paget does not quote any authority for this sweeping condemnation of African people and their courts and political councils. No authority for it can be found in the *Handbook of Tswana (Bechuana) Law and Custom* which Professor Schapera compiled for the Bechuanaland Administration. The word " fetish " does not occur, while reason and logic are quite apparent.'

J. H. Driberg, in *The Savage as he really is*, strenuously argued in disproof of the notorious fallacy of Professor Levy Bruhl's theory of ' the prelogical mentality of primitive races ' in these words : ' The savage starts from different categories, but there is nothing wrong with his logic. Everywhere logical processes are the same, but the categories of thought must be affected by a variety of factors, which we may label environment, using the term in its broadest sense.'

[2] (1952) 2 T.L.R. 246, p. 247.

[3] *The Common Law*, p. 1. The same idea is reiterated by him at pp. 213 and 312.

African material, yet his lack of systematic legal training is often a handicap, leading to two types of mental attitude :

(i) That of the older anthropologists—happily a dying race— who, basing themselves upon current Anglo-Saxon law concepts with which they happen to have some nodding acquaintance, see little or no law in African societies and are emphatic that ' custom is king '.[1]

The implication of this in the present context is that everything is custom, that it is not possible to differentiate rules of social conduct into law and custom, and that the African at any rate does not make any such distinction. Without going into any great detail, one may quote a few examples in refutation of such a specious argument. Thus Miss M. M. Green writes : ' We shall see when we consider the judicial function that in this society *law* is distinguished from *custom* in the sense that it is enforced, directly or indirectly by the community, and that this distinction is recognised by the people.' [2] In the same way Sir Donald Cameron, formerly Governor of both Tanganyika and Nigeria, warned all those who would lump African law and custom indiscriminately together against ' the confusion of mere ceremonial practices with the essential requirements of the law ; for instance, dances and drumming at a Native wedding are the invariable custom, but they are not, like the payment of a dowry, essential in Native law to the validity of the marriage.' [3]

The usual practice of coupling the two words together in the expression ' African (or Native) law and custom ' should not be allowed to mislead one into thinking that law and custom are synonymous. They are two quite distinct concepts in African, no less than in English, or any other system of law.

(ii) That of the more modern group of social anthropologists [4] who, with their knowledge of comparative institutions and of

[1] See, e.g., S. Hartland, *Primitive Law* ; L. H. Morgan, *Ancient Society*, and L. T. Hobhouse, *The History of Social Development*.

[2] *Ibo Village Affairs*, p. 78.

[3] See his ' Memoranda No. 2 on Tanganyika Territory Native Administration and Native Courts '. For a similar distinction among the Nyakyusa, see G. B. Wilson's article ' Introduction to Nyakyusa Law ' in *Africa*, Vol. X, 1937, pp. 16–36, at p. 31.

[4] E.g. Schapera, *A Handbook of Tswana Law and Custom* ; Meek, *Law and Authority in a Nigerian Tribe* ; Rattray, *Ashanti Law and Constitution* ; Cory and Hartnoll, *Customary Law of the Haya Tribe* ; Howell, *A Manual of Nuer Law*.

current juristic thought, are prepared to say that African law is law though there are understandable differences between some of its provenances and those of other types of law, differences rooted in the social environment and economic milieu in which it has had to operate and to evolve all through the ages.

To this class belongs even so early a social anthropologist as Dr. R. H. Lowie, who makes this interesting observation :

'Among the Negroes of Africa primitive jurisprudence attains its highest development.   In precision and scope their code rivals that of the Ifugao, but unlike the Ifugao the Negroes have almost everywhere an orderly method of procedure before a constituted tribunal.   They display a remarkable taste for juridical casuistry and a keen enjoyment of forensic eloquence.' [1]

This follows logically from the author's earlier assertion [2] that most African political organisations are on a larger scale than those of other ' primitive ' peoples.   Generally, there seems to be little doubt that the degree of sophistication attained by the judicial organs of a given community is directly related to the stage and form of its social organisation.   African societies with a strong centralised political system tend invariably to have a more advanced body of legal principles and judicial techniques than have those with a more or less rudimentary political organisation.   In the former, there are usually hierarchically-graded courts ranging from the smallest chiefs' to the kings' courts, with well-defined machinery for the due enforcement of judicial decisions.   In the latter, *rules* rather than *rulers*,[3] *functions* rather than *institutions*, characterise the judicial organisation of these societies.   The apparent informality of the legal arrangements does not mean that the actual situation is chaotic, since the mechanism of choosing the adjudicating elders for the settlement of disputes, as well as that of enforcing their decisions, follows a clearly recognised pattern, even if the means adopted appear casual to the unwary observer.

Nevertheless, it remains generally true to say that the judicial institutions of the more highly organised political societies display the operation of legal principles in a more noticeable manner than do those of the less politically centralised societies.   It is, how-

[1] *Primitive Society*, p. 404.
[2] *Ibid.*, pp. 355–6 ; also pp. 367–8.
[3] Cf. Aristotle's remark to Alexander, Philip of Macedon's 14-year-old son : ' We Greeks do not accept as our ruler a man, but only the Law ' (see K. Freeman, *Paths of Justice*, p. 163).

ever, a difference only in the details of the social organisations of
the two major types of African society ; for while *institutions* may
differ, *processes* tend to be everywhere the same in all forms of
human societies.

In this connexion one recalls Professor Gluckman's observation
on the Adat law of Indonesia :

' What strikes me, as an anthropologist whose special province
is negro Africa, is the fundamental similarity between Adat law
and African law. It does seem as if the limitations of primitive
economics, and the organisation of small local communities on a
framework of kinship ties, produce similar legal rules.' [1]

Accordingly, it is highly doubtful whether one can say, as does
Professor Evans-Pritchard about the Nuer, that an African society
can be so small in its scale of social organisation that it may be
said to have no system of law : ' In a strict sense Nuer have no
law. There are conventional compensations for damage, adultery,
loss of limb, and so forth, but there is no authority with power to
adjudicate on such matters or to enforce a verdict.' [2] Kinship,
it is true, plays among the Nuer a far more important role in the
arrangement of the social order than it does in larger political
groupings. But, even among the members of the autonomous
household, one finds that disputes do occur in the matter of personal possessions of the individuals no less than in that of their
numerous rights to the family inheritance. These must often give
rise to rules being laid down for the regulation of the conflicting
claims of the members. [3]

If the foregoing is true of the members of a family, it must be
truer still of an aggregation of families such as the Nuer tribe.
Indeed, on his own showing, Professor Evans-Pritchard seems to
be denying the name of law to the Nuer legal rules only because
he failed to discover there courts and law-enforcement officials on
the modern British pattern. When the learned author later found
himself applying the word ' law ' to the Nuer, he hastened to
explain with this revealing statement : ' We speak of " law " here
in the sense which seems most appropriate when writing of the
Nuer, a moral obligation to settle disputes by conventional

---

[1] *Jnl. of Comparative Legislation*, 3rd Series, Vol. 31, p. 60.
[2] Evans-Pritchard : *The Nuer*, p. 162 ; also in *African Political
Systems*, pp. 293-4.
[3] This point is further elaborated in Ch. VI on ' Status ', below.

methods, and not in the sense of legal procedure or of legal institutions.   We speak only of civil law, for there do not seem to be any
actions considered injurious to the whole community and punished
by it.' [1]

Nor are his difficulties made any the easier by his further admission that there are sanctions,[2] that ' the basis of law is force ',[3] that
disputes do occur as to the ownership of cattle [4] and that ' chiefs
sometimes prevent fights between communities. . . .' [5]   Moreover, although comparisons are often said to be odious, nevertheless we know as a matter of sociological reality that communities
with even a much more rudimentary political organisation like that
of the Comanche Indians [6] or of the Ibos of Umueke Agbaja [7] or
of the Ifugao,[8] are known to have a definite system of law.[9]

It is, therefore, more in accord with the facts to jettison the all
too common assumption that African law is either no law or a

---

[1] *Op. cit.*, p. 168.   [2] P. 150.
[3] P. 169.   [4] P. 165.
[5] P. 173.   The learned author's admission that there is a political
system of the Nuer worth speaking of and that there is a kind of *civil*
law at least would seem to involve him in contradictions.   It seems that
what he really wanted to say was that, contrary to popular expectation
of the predominance of *criminal* law in early societies, he could not
find any criminal law among the Nuer—which in itself is, as we shall
see in Ch. VII, a debatable point.

As Radcliffe Brown has observed (*African Political Systems*, p. xviii,) :
' In seeking to define the political structure in a simple society we have
to look for a territorial community which is *united by a rule of law.*
By that is meant *a community throughout which public sentiment is concerned with the application of direct or indirect penal sanctions to any of
its own members who offend in certain ways, or with the settlement of disputes and the provision of just satisfaction for injuries within the community
itself.*' (The italics are mine.   Author.)
If the Nuer society fulfils these conditions, then we cannot but admit
that it has a system of law, in however strict a sense we conceive of
the word.   See, further, the next two chapters.

[6] See pp. 45–65 of E. Adamson Hoebel, ' Law-ways of Comanche
Indians ', in *Memoirs of the American Anthropological Association*, No. 54,
1940, published as supplement to *American Anthropologist*, Vol. 42,
No. 3, Pt. 2.

[7] See M. M. Green, *Ibo Village Affairs.*

[8] R. F. Barton, ' Ifugao Law ' (*University of California Publications
in American Archaeology and Ethnology*, Vol. 15, pp. 1–127 (1919)),
particularly at p. 9 : ' . . . of political organisation the Ifugao has
nothing—not even a suggestion.   Notwithstanding, he has a well-
developed system of laws.'

[9] It is interesting to note that *A Manual of Nuer Law*, by P. P. Howell,
has recently been issued by the O.U.P.

totally different kind of law from that to which Western society is accustomed. There is need to insist with Culwick : [1] ' It may possibly be surprising to some Westerners, and it certainly is a fact of great practical significance, that the basic social duty of the Bantu code differs from the basic social duty of their own society, if at all, in degree and not in kind.' Since certain fundamental conditions must subsist for human life to be possible in any part of the world, the task of African law as of English or any other law cannot differ very much, however widely their modes of opera-tion may differ.[2] And Gluckman's testimony [3] is even more definitive : ' I have studied the work of African courts in Zululand and Rhodesia, and found that they use the same basic doctrines as our courts do. African legal systems, like all legal systems, are founded on principles of the reasonable man, responsibility, negligence, direct and circumstantial and hear-say evidence, etc. African judges and laymen apply these principles skilfully and logically to a variety of situations in order to achieve justice.'

The two chief functions of law in any human society are the preservation of personal freedom and the protection of private property. African law, just as much as for instance English law, does aim at achieving both of these desirable ends. In this con-nexion, Lucy Mair reminds us : ' Rules of conduct towards his parents, consort and children, towards other relatives, towards religious or political authority, bind the member of an African tribe as they do the subject of a European State. The conduct prescribed may differ, but the end of orderly social co-operation is the same. Respect for property, for human life, for the sexual code enjoined by the society, are principles of African law as of ours.' [4] To this evidence as regards East Africa may be added Dr. Meek's with respect to West Africa : ' The mentality of primitive peoples does not differ essentially from our own, as any European knows who has lived at close quarters with " natives " It is not to be expected, therefore, that their norms of conduct

[1] At pp. 27–8 of his ' Good out of Africa ', *Rhodes-Livingstone Paper*, No. 8 (1942).

[2] *Ibid.*, p. 2 : ' The African and the European both have ideas of good, and often enough the broad moral principle on which they act is one and the same though their ways of applying it to their respective cir-cumstances may be poles apart.'

[3] In his letter in *The Observer*, July 15, 1951, to which we have referred earlier on p. 28 n. 1.

[4] Dr. L. P. Mair, *Native Policies in Africa*, pp. 270–1.

should diverge very profoundly from ours. And so what are crimes or torts to us are for the most part crimes or torts to them. We may even go further and say that their " gentlemen " are ours and ours are theirs.' [1]

It is conceivable that the less developed African societies will reflect less faithfully than the more developed ones the essential similarities between African legal ideas and those of the European. There is, however, no reason why that fact alone should obscure our view of the organic character of human law. Lord Hailey puts the issue into its proper perspective when he writes : ' The law of the ancient Babylonians, Hebrews, Romans and the Saxons had close analogies to what we see among the more primitive of the African peoples. If there is any peculiarity in African legal institutions, it is less one of intrinsic character than of the time at which they present themselves, for they exhibit to the modern world some of the scenes in a story which must have been enacted five thousand years ago in parts of Mesopotamia, and at later dates in Rome, Germany and Britain.' [2]

We will now conclude the anthropological evidence concerning the nature of African law with these words of Professor E. E. Evans-Pritchard : ' There can be no separate discipline which restricts itself to a study of primitive societies. It would be pointless to try to interpret the religious cults of primitive peoples except in terms of a general theory of religion. A theory of the fundamental nature of law must clearly cover the laws of both civilised and savage peoples.' [3]

4. The Judicial Official.

Having dealt with the evidence afforded by the missionary, the administrative officer and the social anthropologist, we must now consider the views of judicial persons who have direct knowledge of African law. For the purpose of legal analysis, which is our objective in this book, this must carry most weight.

Sir James Marshall, formerly Chief Justice on the Gold Coast and in Nigeria, after having served as Judicial Assessor to 'Native' Chiefs, is thus reported in The Times of July 17, 1886, :

[1] C. K. Meek, Law and Authority in a Nigerian Tribe, p. xiii.
[2] An African Survey, p. 265.
[3] At p. 12 of his ' Social Anthropology '—an Inaugural Lecture delivered before the University of Oxford on February 4, 1948.

' His testimony as to the efficiency with which the natives administer their own laws is very striking. He has sat beside native judges, and witnessed with admiration their administration of justice. These people have their own laws and customs, which are better adapted to their condition than the complicated system of English jurisprudence. The adoption of them would, it is maintained, be more conducive to the best interests of all than the present system. Everyone who has resided in any of our West African Colonies must be familiar with instances of natives who in education and intelligence have attained the European average. There are black Judges who might well be entrusted with the administration of County Court business, at least . . .'

But perhaps the most authoritative judicial pronouncement on African law is the following passage from the Privy Council judgment in the celebrated case *Re Southern Rhodesia* : [1]

' Some tribes are so low in the scale of social organisation that their usages and conception of rights and duties are not to be reconciled with the institutions or the legal ideas of civilised society. . . . On the other hand, there are indigenous peoples whose legal conceptions, though differently developed, are hardly less precise than our own. When once they have been studied and understood they are no less enforceable than rights arising under English law.'

It should be noted that the first part of this dictum does not deny the name of law to the obligatory rules of conduct among less developed African communities ; it merely points out that their legal ideas and processes bear little resemblance to the accepted forms and standards of more developed societies. In other words, the difference that it is intended to show is the familiar one which we have shown between the two major types of African political and social organisations. [2]

A similar parallel was recorded for Uganda by H. R. Hone, a former Attorney-General of that territory, in these words : [3] ' It must be recalled that the various native races of Uganda appear always to have acknowledged some system of law and justice and to have been amenable to some form of court. In

---

[1] (1919) A.C. 211, pp. 233–4.
[2] See Ch. 2, *supra*.
[3] *Uganda Journal*, Vol. VI, No. 1, July, 1938, p. 2, in an article entitled ' The Native of Uganda and the Criminal Law ' by H. R. Hone, M.C., K.C., LL.B., Attorney-General of Uganda.

Buganda, at the time of the arrival of the European, the native system of administering justice was found to be in a surprisingly stable and advanced state, as was the whole organisation of that country ; at the other extreme was the ill-defined and primitive dispensation of justice among the Nilotic tribes of the North. But whatever the degree of development the germ was there.'

But the reader should not think that a discordant note has not been sounded on occasions even by former occupants of the judicial bench in parts of Africa.   It is pleasant to relate, however, that they almost invariably fall into self-contradiction.   Let us consider this one of the late Mr. C. C. Roberts : ' In the first place, European conceptions of law and justice have to be discarded ; they have nothing in common with African cultures ; they are alien in growth and sentiment, and cannot be used to explain the basis of primitive legal theory.' [1]   As against this dogmatic averment we have our author saying a little further on : [2] ' That there is a recognised code of law founded on principles of justice is apparent if we examine the native laws affecting murder, adultery, theft, and many others. . . .   As to the laws governing inheritance, ownership of children, property or mortgage we find much resemblance to those in force in European countries.'

Instead of attempting to fly in the face of the available evidence that African law is law, it is probably wise and reasonable to admit that, where differences occur between aspects of it and those of more developed systems of law, they are differences of degree and not of kind.   H. R. Hone has put the point thus : [3] ' At first one is apt to say that it bears no relation or resemblance to our system.   While there is no doubt that, in external appearance, there is a complete lack of similarity, the fact is that the one is the other at a different stage of development.'

We have now had sufficient introduction to a study of the general character of African law to enable us to go on to the next stage, which is that of trying to find out what law really is.   Some understanding of this most controversial word in the whole history of men's ideas about social phenomena should make for a unified theory of law, of which African law forms part and parcel.

[1] See his *Tangled Justice*, p. 63.   [2] *Ibid.*, p. 79.
[3] Article in *Uganda Journal* (p. 6), cited at p. 35 n. 3.

CHAPTER IV

WHAT IS LAW?

IN view of the evidence of opinions examined in the preceding chapter it must be apparent to the reader that the question whether African customary law is law or not, can best be answered only when we know what law is. To help us to do this properly, we naturally want to be told what jurists mean by law. Now, probably the most difficult problem with which jurisprudence has to deal is that of evolving a valid description of law; it may with truth be said that its chief task begins and ends with trying to find out about the nature and purpose of law in human society. But there always has been much disagreement among jurists and sociologists about the nature of their subject.

A. LAW AS DEFINED BY JURISTS

There is perhaps no better starting-point than the work of John Austin, the reputed exponent of the analytical theory of law. According to him, law is ' a rule laid down for the guidance of an intelligent being by an intelligent being having power over him '.[1] This view implies the existence of a political sovereign whom people in an organised political society are in the habit of obeying, on pain of punishment. If, for a moment, we accept this ' command ' theory of law we shall find that African societies of the Group A type would satisfy Austin's requirement of political sovereignty as the basis of law ' properly so-called ', but that African societies of the Group B type would not, since these would not be politically ' organised ' in the Austinian sense —that is, they would be ' men living in a state of nature '. Of course the great jurist denied the name of law ' properly so-called ' to all the forms of customary law then known to him—the conventions of the British Constitution, Public International Law and, by necessary implication, even the English Common Law as ' the common custom of the realm '. It is clear that African customary law would have been even more rigorously excluded.

[1] *Lectures on Jurisprudence* or *The Philosophy of Positive Law* (1885), (5th edn.), Vol. I, pp. 316–7.

No doubt, Austin was primarily concerned about Western legal systems, and in particular the English system, where the King-in-Parliament is the final legal authority. Salmond was probably the first to point out that Austin only defines ' a law ', an English Act of Parliament—not ' law ' in its general connotation, and that Austin is right so far as his actual standpoint is concerned. Salmond further argues that certain of Austin's followers alone are to blame for wrongly extending his original concept to cover all forms of law in general, thereby exposing his theory to a good deal of criticism. Even so, the responsibility must be Austin's for taking such a limited view of the law and of what an ' organised political society ' should be. Strictly interpreted, this term excludes all but the Group A type of the African societies we have already considered.[1] His excuse would possibly have been the very restricted state of knowledge about human social organisations so prevalent in those pre-Darwinian days ; he certainly might have changed his mind about customary law had he lived to learn the later teachings of social anthropology. He would then have discovered that a human society is not necessarily in ' a state of nature ' (i.e. lawless) merely because it lacks a sovereign commander, an army of uniformed policemen and an imposing prison-house.[2] The mechanism for securing law and order in a given society need not be so highly institutionalised in order that the rules of human behaviour may be regarded as law.

Austin's pre-occupation with how laws are enacted has, therefore, led him to conceive of law as a command issued by a determinate human superior to determinate human inferiors. In order to avoid the weakness of such a position, Salmond and Gray —both being essentially Austinians—would shift the emphasis from *enactment* of the law to its *enforcement*. They prefer to define law by reference to a court. Basing themselves on Mr. Justice Oliver Wendell Holmes's *dictum* that ' the prophecies of what the courts will do in fact and nothing more pretentious are what I mean by the law ', they argue that law is only what is recognised and enforced by the courts.

[1] See Ch. II, *supra*.
[2] The view of those who hold (as we have seen in the preceding chapter) that certain African societies have no law has largely been coloured by the Austinian theory. We shall soon see, later in the present chapter, how it has also affected definitions of law by certain sociologists.

Salmond defines law as 'the body of principles recognised and applied by the State in the administration of justice'. In other words, the law consists of the rules recognised and acted on by the Courts of Justice.[1] Gray is even more radical in his reliance upon the courts for his conception of law ; he denies the name of law even to a statute until it has been used as a basis of decision by a court. His definition is : 'The law of a State or of any organised body of men is composed of the rules which the courts—i.e. the judicial organs of that body—lay down for the determination of legal rights and duties.' [2] The absurdity of this view of the law is that while it recognises precedents as a source of law it refuses that name to statutes and customs until both become precedents by being embodied in judicial decisions. The logical conclusion, then, is that precedents alone are law.[3]

From all this insistence on the court as the basis of their definitions of law, it seems to follow inevitably that societies like our Group B ones without formal systems of courts must be regarded as having no law. Such a position is clearly indefensible for at least two reasons : (a) because much depends on one's conception of the word ' court '—whether it is a special building in which a robed judge and wigged barristers dispense justice, or whether it is any sitting at which disputes are settled and the social equilibrium of the community is restored by its accredited functionaries ; (b) because many conflicts between individuals even in civilised societies with formal courts are in fact usually resolved without their ever reaching the courts.[4]

[1] J. Salmond, *Jurisprudence* (10th edn., 1946), p. 41. Salmond clinches his argument in this expressive epigram : ' Custom is to society what law is to the State.'

[2] J. C. Gray, *The Nature and Sources of the Law*, (2nd edn., 1921), p. 82.

[3] See A. L. Goodhart's article, ' Some American Interpretations of Law ', in I. Jennings (ed.), *Modern Theories of Law* (1933), pp. 1–20. Consider also Jerome Frank's claim in *Law and the Modern Mind* (1930), at pp. 46, 122–5, that law is simply a matter of judicial guesswork, or Cardozo's that ' Law never is, but is always about to be '.—at p. 52 of his *The Growth of the Law* (1924). So, too, R. M. MacIver : ' Law is the body of rules which are recognised, interpreted and applied to particular situations by the courts of the State.' (At p. 272 of *Society : Its Structure and Changes* ' (1932).

[4] Cf. Wade and Phillips, ' The rule of law can exist without a single system of judicature, provided that the essential requirements of justice are observed ' (*Constitutional Law* 3rd edn., p. 304).

It is, therefore, all the more surprising that even Diamond, who has done so much in recent times to advance the study and appreciation of ' primitive ' law, hardly goes beyond arguing on the whole that societies without courts have no law. After stating that there are rules of conduct which are invariably observed and which are compulsory in the sense that in the opinion of members of a community they must be observed, he contends :

' But it is not a rule laid down by any authority possessing power to declare law, for no such authority exists. . . . It is not therefore a satisfactory use of the term " law " to apply it to the rule of conduct which we have mentioned as being observable among savage peoples who possess no courts.' [1]

Diamond, however, goes on to say : ' There are, however, already in the savage societies which do not possess courts, a few rules that are in the direct line of the history of law ' ; he says that these societies clearly recognise offences such as theft, homicide, adultery, incest, witchcraft, and that they distinguish between civil and criminal law into the bargain. But, surely any human society that does these things must be regarded as having law ? Diamond would have been on firmer ground if he had avoided mixing up the establishment of courts [2] with the existence of law.

All the jurists we have so far considered, whether their emphasis is on enactment or on enforcement of a rule of law, are commonly styled the analytical positivists, with Austin as their leader. They concentrate on the detailed but careful analyses of legal concepts with a view to determining their logical nexus and function in a system of law. All ethical considerations must accordingly be excluded from any legal analysis : morals have nothing to do with law, and it is no business of the lawyer to

[1] At p. 191 of his *Primitive Law*, (2nd edn.). Also, at p. 203, he identifies law with court : ' The creation of legal rules of conduct has been identical.'

[2] But Diamond's idea of a court may be gleaned from this passage (at p. 194) : ' But even among peoples as early as the First Hunters, a practice begins to grow under which the elders, the heads of the community, discuss the guilt of the accused, and if necessary the nature of the punishment, in the presence of the people, hearing the accused and anyone else who has anything to tell them. Here are the beginnings of courts.' This is a mitigating attitude which somewhat serves to mark him off from Salmond and Gray in their view of courts and the law.

concern himself with the end or purpose of the law, which is peculiarly a function of the legislator.

However, Léon Duguit, a major jurist and a Frenchman, enunciates the principle of the *règle de droit* as the only true basis of the social order in any community.[1] Individuals owe it to themselves and to society to ensure the orderly progress of public as well as private affairs. To this end, the community may be regarded as two complementary segments—the rulers and the ruled—and their lawful behaviour is guaranteed by the principle of social solidarity. For a republican the sovereign monarch is out of the question; hence, the community is divided into (*a*) the governors—those appointed to run the affairs of State— and, (*b*) the governed—those who in the interest of the common weal give up part of their civic prerogatives to the governors. The relation is, however, not one of subjection such as is implied in the Austinian theory of sovereignty, but one of mutual inter-dependence inspired by a desire for *division of labour*. The conduct of the governors and of the governed is regulated, both as between the two groups and as between any two of their individual members, by the principle of social solidarity. This *règle de droit* of Duguit is, like Kant's imperative, a categorical postulate. Each and all in the community are bound by the inexorable operation of this vital principle. It is the duty of all members to maintain the absolute solidarity of their society. No claim to civil rights can be asserted by anyone except such as are derived from a strict obedience to this immanent principle. Any rule of social behaviour that conforms to it is a rule of law.

Accordingly, Duguit readily admits that customary law is law. Indeed, his sociological evaluation of human groupings as well as his theory of government are concepts which all the main types of African societies can claim for their very own. The king or chief and his council of elders are looked upon only as constitutional functionaries who must govern in strict accord-ance with the traditional norms of political and social behaviour. The chief is father of his people who, in their turn, are expected to maintain the social equilibrium by performing their civic duties. A recalcitrant and lawless chief, like any other member

[1] See *Law in the Modern State*; see also Laski's essay in Jennings, *Modern Theories of Law*, pp. 52–67.

of the community, was in former days eliminated, sometimes by banishment, sometimes by being put to death. No one, not even the king or chief, was allowed to disturb the social solidarity of the group.

But Duguit does not set any great store on enacted law. He even frankly proclaims the all-sufficient authority of French customary law, to the apparent disregard of the Code Napoléon. This is a fault, as is also his idea that the obligatory force of a rule of law lies in the possible incidence of a revolution in case of disobedience to the dictate of social solidarity. ' The rule of law ', says Duguit, ' is not a rule properly speaking, but is a virtual discipline which social interdependence imposes on all members of the group.' He then adds, rather ominously : ' There is a rule of law from the moment when the violation of this rule provokes a social reaction.' In other words, the general public determines what is a rule of law by means of a revolt against its breach. But here is a difficulty. This yard-stick of Duguit is almost as unhelpful as Kelsen's that war and reprisal give international law its legal character.[1] Our jurist's idea of social solidarity resembles the ' natural law ' thinking of the Middle Ages : that it is a criterion capable of deciding what is and what is not law.

In spite of these defects, Duguit dismisses Rousseau's *volonté générale* as mere sophism and, to that extent, succeeds in sweeping away the idea of the sovereignty of the nation so beloved of Rousseau and other Social Contract theorists. He deserves credit also for the emphasis he rightly lays on the function of law in society, for he believes that the purpose for which a rule of law is given alone justifies it.

It is perhaps appropriate at this stage, when we have been dealing with the theory of a jurist who expressly admits that customary law is law, to turn to a brief survey of the ideas of

[1] Hans Kelsen has propounded a ' Pure Theory of Law ' in *The Law Quarterly Review*, Vol. 50, pp. 474–98 (1934), and Vol. 51, pp. 517–35 (1935). See also his article, ' The Pure Theory of Law and Analytical Jurisprudence ' in *Harvard Law Review*, Vol. 55, pp. 44–70 (1941). He believes that law is an ' Ought ' and is based on an Initial Hypothesis, a *Grundnorm* ; this is the sanction of the municipal law of a country, just as war and reprisal are the sanctions of Public International Law. Also, like Austin, Kelsen would keep law and ethics separate ; but the choice of his ' Grundnorm ' necessarily involves a judgment of value, and this is a weakness.

the historical school of jurists. The analytical school founded by Austin, as we have seen, would have nothing to do with either the past or the future of law : the one and only task with which the jurist need concern himself is an analysis of what law is, here and now. The historical school, on the other hand, believes that however far back one goes into the past of a people one will always find some law governing them. Von Savigny is the leader of this school, and has given the most comprehensive account of its beliefs and tenets.

Savigny does not give a strictly formal definition of law [1] but merely describes it as an aspect of the total common life of a nation, not something made by the nation as a matter of choice or convention, but, like its manners and language, bound up with its existence, and indeed helping to make the nation what it is. The danger in this idea that institutions are not made but grow lies in its speculative optimism that whatever is becoming, or is continuously in a way to be, is best. But it is clear that Savigny's conception of law is definitely opposed to the glorification of individual reason, since his major preoccupation is with how law becomes, not whither it tends or whither enlightened effort may make it tend. Roscoe Pound's charge of ' juristic pessimism ' against him and his school is to that extent unfair. [2] Savigny's thesis is a direct negation of the idea of the unitary sovereign as the sole and inevitable source of law.

However, Savigny's theory that the true foundation of law rests on the inner consciousness of the people is subject to the following considerations :

(a) It has been objected, as for example by Gray, [3] that most people do not know the law and that it is rather difficult for them to have joined in founding the law. Gray thinks that there is a confusion here between the act of the people in its sovereign (corporate) capacity with the act of the people considered as individuals.

But it seems that Gray over-states the point somewhat.

---

[1] Unless, indeed, we take seriously his formulation (in s. 5 of his *System*) of law as a rule existing for the purpose of regulating the actions of the individual in the interest of the whole community ; if the people acting together can somehow frame general rules of action, then such rules are law.

[2] See R. Pound, *Interpretations of Legal History*, p. 66.

[3] *The Nature and Sources of the Law* (1921 edn.).

Savigny has obviously anticipated this objection by affirming that there is a class of experts who are part of the people and who are charged with the duty of making the law : ' For *all* are conscious of the justice of the rule, while only *some* get the opportunity of practising it.'   This is clearly a recognition of the fact that there comes a stage in the life of the people when popular consciousness can no longer manifest itself directly but comes to be represented by lawyers, who formulate on behalf of the people the technical legal principles.   Even then, the lawyer remains an organ of popular consciousness, confined to the task of bringing into shape what he finds in the social life as legal raw material. To Savigny the lawyer is accordingly more important than the legislator, as legislation is always a later development than law in any society.[1]

(*b*) Another criticism of Savigny is that if law is the popular consciousness of the community, what of the individual who breaks the law ? He is a member of the people ; but what of his consciousness ?   Probably Savigny's answer would have been that, since law is parallel to language, an individual who misuses language does not thereby cease to be one of the people whose consciousness that language, like the law he breaks, represents.

(*c*) The really fatal objection to Savigny's whole standpoint is the notorious phenomenon of ' reception ' of bodies of laws by some nations from others ; for example, the reception of the Code Napoléon in Egypt and Belgium, or that of the German Civil Code in Japan and Turkey.

Now, the French Code, was to a large extent based on such pre-existing French materials as the works of Pothier and others. The theory of the common consciousness (*Rechtsüberzeugung*) of the French people as thus embodied in the Code has direct validity.   But how explain why its reception by these alien peoples can ever make the French Code an expression of *their* popular consciousness ?   Can the Code Napoléon really be described as the emanation of the national will of the Egyptian or Belgian peoples ?   And yet systems of laws thus ' received ' have worked well in exotic social contexts.

[1] E.g. : ' Customary law may complete, modify, or repeal a statute ; it may create a new rule, and substitute for the statutory rule which it has abolished '—s. 18 of Savigny's *System*, Vol. I (Holloway's translation).

No, this nationalist conception of the basis of law is not sound, even if we concede that political nationalism was not Savigny's main thesis but was only incidental to his exposition of it. Its inadequacy is, for much the same reason as that given in the preceding paragraph, quite apparent in its failure to explain why English law has been received with varying degrees of adaptation, not only in America and the Dominions, but also in Africa, India, the Pacific Islands and elsewhere.

When these criticisms have been made we must acknowledge the value of the historical school as being, (a) the negation of the almighty sovereign as an indispensable foundation of law, (b) the assertion that however far back you go into the past, you will always find some sort of law governing the people, (c) the realisation that the form in which law is present to the people is not abstract, but that it is a living perception in the consciousness of legal institutions in their organic forms, and (d) the distinction between what is law and what is custom : that the common consciousness of the people must be distinguished from their *customs* which are merely one of its manifestations, since custom is merely the index of the law of a people.

Sir Paul Vinogradoff, who himself wrote two volumes entitled *Outlines of Historical Jurisprudence*, is however, not an orthodox member of the historical school. Rather, he believes that recognition, by the members of a given community, of certain rules of behaviour as binding upon them, gives those rules the stamp of law. In his view, law is not just what the sovereign commands nor what the courts will enforce, but a body of rules of human conduct recognised by the people as obligatory upon all and sundry. He accordingly defines law as a ' set of rules imposed and enforced by a society with regard to the attribution and exercise of power over persons and things '.[1]

Implicit in this idea of social recognition as a necessary ingredient of a rule of law is the element of cognoscibility—that is, that those who are subject to its sway shall know and be able to identify the particular code of social behaviour as one which all acknowledge to be inexorable in its operation. Vinogradoff's exposition seems to lead to the inference that recognition, uniformity and enforceability are the essential elements of law—a point of view that gets rid of the inconvenient assumptions of a

[1] At p. 59 of his *Common-sense in Law*.

precedent political sovereignty (Austin) and of the subsequent judicial enforcement (Salmond and Gray) as the criterion of law. It has the merit of being elastic enough to embrace practically all types of human societies, including the main African groups previously considered.[1] His historical studies have not restricted his views of the law to a mere consideration of its development or of its present nature. But he does not fully enter into his problem with sufficient intimacy of understanding, or he would have discovered that the attribution of power in society is not a simple process for legal purposes.

A glance back at the various theories of law so far advanced reveals the inadequacy of both the historical school and the analytical. Towards the end of the last century and early in the present one, a new feature has emerged in legal thought, emphasizing the social side of law—its end or purpose.[2] There has arisen a movement away from the traditional idea of law as something given which the judge or jurist has got to find out by the use of logic—a movement, again, from that complete separation of the legislator from the lawyer. The latter was characteristic of the nineteenth century as a whole, as we saw it characteristic of the English analytical school. Bentham's censorious jurisprudence had nothing to do with the lawyer, just as Austin's imperative theory had nothing to do with the mere legislator. So that juristic thinking had nothing to do with the purposive element in law. The legal categories of Kelsen[3] and Stammler,[4] no less than Savigny's preoccupation with the historical antecedents of the law, would separate the lawyer from the legislator. All with one voice proclaimed that it was none of the business of the jurist to speculate as to the end or purpose of law.

Before the end of the nineteenth century the evils of this attitude began to provoke the criticism of certain jurists, notable among whom is von Jhering. Rejecting the traditional jurisprudence of *concepts* in favour of the jurisprudence of *interests*, he advocates the view that the purpose or end of law is its most important aspect. Law does not only grow but can be made to

---

[1] He himself claims so much, *ibid.*, pp. 59–60.
[2] See, e.g., Stammler, *Theory of Justice*.
[3] See p. 42, n. 1, *supra*, and his *Society and Nature : a sociological Inquiry* ; also, J. Stone, *The Province and Function of Law*, pp. 97–8.
[4] See his *Theory of Justice*.

secure the social advantage of the community. A penetrating summary of his views is this one of Pound's in his famous article, 'The Scope and Purpose of Sociological Jurisprudence' : [1] 'Whereas the philosophical jurist considered that the principles of justice and right are discovered *a priori*, and the historical jurist thought that the principles of justice are found by experience, Jhering held that the means of serving human ends are discovered by experience and fashioned into law.'

It is only fair to say that, nowadays, the legislator is not to be set apart from the lawyer. Law is no longer the mere defence of society against violence, internal or external ; there must be a conscious desire to benefit the people generally. Salmond latterly held the same view. This ' social engineering ', as Pound calls it, is the purposive element of law-making. Speaking of the legal order Pound states this concept in these words : [2]

' It is one side of the process of social control. It may well be thought of as a task or as a great series of tasks of social engineering, as an elimination of friction and precluding of waste, so far as possible, in the satisfaction of infinite human desires out of a relatively finite store of the material goods of existence. Law is the body of knowledge and experience with the aid of which this part of social engineering is carried on.'

Roscoe Pound's definition of law is that it is ' social control through the systematic application of the forces of politically organised society '. Jurisprudence, to Pound, is the science of social engineering having to do with that part of the field which may be achieved by the ordering of human relations through the action of a politically organised society. This, however, is no authoritarian social machinery, as some critics have alleged.

Though difficult to classify, Pound is in a way a sociological jurist. He is no doubt a pragmatist in that he does not believe in any illusory ideas about an ultimate ' *summum bonum* ' in law. To the extent to which he refuses to be tied down to just one point, he is a pluralist, or, if we like, a relativist in law. Hence his famous simile of ' social engineering '. He gets into difficulties, however, when he constructs his tariff of the interests that are to be legally protected.

[1] See *Harvard Law Review*, Vol. 24, pp. 591–619 (1910–11).
[2] *Interpretations of Legal History*, p. 156. (The italics are mine.)

B.   LAW AS DEFINED BY ANTHROPOLOGISTS

Others besides jurists have also had to consider the nature of law in the context of their sociological study of non-Western communities.   Here, we have a fair chance of looking at law from an angle different from that to which jurists have all too long accustomed us.   Unfortunately, however, the sociologists have not permitted themselves that measure of independence of pre-existing legal theories which is necessary for an objective view of law as a social science.

Thus, Hartland, in his *Primitive Law*, considers that Austin's imperative theory is not broad enough to cover the so-called primitive societies and that a new definition of law is needed. So far, most people would agree.   But it is not easy to derive much comfort from this definition proffered by Hartland : ' In such communities law is not the act of a sovereign, whether an individual or a body of men : it is the traditional rule of the community ;   and it is enforced, not by a sanction prescribed *ad hoc* by the sovereign, but one that is involved in the beliefs and practices of the community.' [1]   This is not only unhelpful even as a description, but is also a crude form of Austinianism tinkering with sociological malobservation.   Earlier in his book Hartland makes the following pertinent comment :

' Hence, among civilised peoples who are accustomed to associ- ate laws with written documents, the rules obeyed by savage peoples have been refused the name of law and called only customs.   But customs that are fixed and generally obeyed are indistinguishable from laws.   In our own country, the judges of the King's courts have always recognised and given effect to them as laws, though prescribed in no written legislation. . . .   Both on the positive and the negative sides custom has been recognised as law.' [2]

It is, therefore, curious that he should later be found putting forward the definition we have just considered.   The pith and substance of it he reiterates in other passages [3] of which this is

[1] P. 137 (published 1924, London).   [2] *Ibid.*, p. 2.
[3] E.g., p. 8 : ' In these stages of culture, in the same way as the name is an essential part of the individual, the law is an essential part of the tribe.   It is no question of aim or utility.   Every portion of it is equally binding and has the same reputed origin. . . .   The law is a manifesta- tion of the tribal life, as individual as life itself.'

typical : ' Primitive law is in truth the totality of the customs of
the tribe. Scarcely anything eludes its grasp.' [1] It is equally
astonishing to see J. H. Driberg quoting this particular statement
with approval and saying that law ' comprises all those rules of
conduct which regulate the behaviour of individuals and communities, and which by maintaining the equilibrium of society
are necessary for its continuance as a corporate whole.' [2]

Writing a few years before Hartland, Hobhouse defines [3] law
as ' a body of rules enforced by an authority independent of
personal ties of kinship and friendship '. This tells us practically
nothing about the essential quality of a rule of law. It is too
much obsessed with how law is enforced and by whom. Marett
seems non-committal in that respect, for his own definition is that
law is ' the authoritative regulation of social relations '.[4] This
would appear to get rid of the difficulty that some means of
regulating social relations, though clearly entitled to the epithet
of ' legal ', are not always fully entitled to that of ' authoritative '.

It will be re-called that Roscoe Pound defines law as ' social
control through the systematic application of the forces of politically organised society '. This has received Radcliffe-Brown's
blessing in his article, ' Primitive Law ',[5] in which he treats
obligations imposed on individuals, where there are no legal
sanctions, as mere matters of social convention or custom but
not of law. This enthusiastic adoption of Pound's definition
has, however, led Radcliffe-Brown into difficulties, as when he
asserts that ' some simple societies have no law, although all have
customs supported by sanctions '. But one would have thought
that, using words in their orthodox sense, a *custom* supported
by *sanction* is law. Even in England, a valid custom has the
force of law if of immemorial antiquity, certain, not unreasonable, and obligatory on all those within its area of operation.
It is perhaps not without some significance that the English
common law has been defined as ' the commonsense of the
community crystallised and formulated by our forefathers.'

[1] P. 5.
[2] At p. 65 of his article, ' Primitive Law in Eastern Africa ', in *Africa*,
Vol. I, pp. 63–72 (1928).
[3] *Morals in Evolution*, p. 73.
[4] See his article, ' Law, Primitive ', in *Encycl. Brit.*, Vol. 13, pp. 781–2.
[5] See *The Encyclopædia of the Social Sciences*, Vol. IX, pp. 202–6,
1933, New York.

However, Radcliffe-Brown is right in insisting that law is not synonymous with socially sanctioned behaviour. He is certainly sounder here than the earlier anthropologists like Hartland who regard law as ' the totality of a people's culture '.

Unlike Radcliffe-Brown, however, Malinowski sees an obvious danger in regarding law solely as a process of control exercised authoritatively by the body politic. He accordingly rejects Pound's definition on the two grounds, (a) that it excludes such obviously legal institutions as exist in societies of our Group B type, which have no centralised politically organised authorities and do not therefore systematically apply force, and (b) that it denies the name of law to the rules by which social rather than political bodies like the kindred or extended family so effectively regulate their relations.[1]

Malinowski's own definition is as follows : ' " Civil law ", the positive law governing all the phases of tribal life, consists then of a body of binding obligations, regarded as a right by one party and acknowledged as a duty by the other, kept in force by a specific mechanism of reciprocity and publicity inherent in the structure of their society.' [2]   To this curious definition at least four exceptions may be taken : (i) Its attempt to define law in terms of reciprocal obligations or of the opposition of rights to duties ; (ii) Its inclusion in his definition of the idea—e.g. that of publicity—of how social norms actually operate in society ; (iii) Its very restrictive view of law, which leads to an equating of ' civil law ' with law generally, thus excluding criminal law from his definition altogether ; [3] and (iv) Its veiled assumption that law pervades ' all the phases of tribal life '. There is something essentially unjuridical about a view of law which sees all social phenomena as permeated by immanent legal principles : ' . . . law covers the whole culture and the entire tribal constitution of these natives.'[4]

C. K. Meek thinks that the only fault with Malinowski is that it is going too far to include as law every item of culture that

[1] We have seen this weakness in Hobhouse's definition. See pp. 48–9 earlier.

[2] At p. 58 of his *Crime and Custom in Savage Society*.

[3] In his revolt against those who regard ' primitive law ' as wholly *criminal* Malinowski is in danger of going to the other extreme of regarding it as wholly *civil*, though he denies this (p. 54).

[4] P. 49.

makes for order, uniformity and cohesion.[1] As we have just
shown, this is only *one* of the many faults of the great anthropologist and not just the only one.   Moreover, we cannot acquit
Meek himself of his victim's offence when, five years after the
publication of Malinowski's book, Meek wrote in his own *A
Sudanese Kingdom* : [2] ' For law covers the whole culture of the
people.' His criticism of Malinowski on this score must, therefore, be taken to imply a change of heart in Meek by the time
he came to write his later book [3] in 1937.   But he could, even
then, still say : ' It will meet our difficulty if it is understood that
the word " law " is used loosely to include modes of regulating
conduct which, at most, have only a quasi-legal character.' [4]

Nevertheless, it is a valid criticism of Malinowski's view of
law that he tends to include in it too much of the culture of
the people.   And it hardly helps matters very much for Malinowski to plead in self-defence : ' Thus, though in my survey attention has naturally been mainly focused on the legal machinery,
I was not intent on proving that all social rules are legal, but on
the contrary, I wanted to show that the rules of law form but
one well-defined category within the body of custom.' [5]   This
can only lead to the strange but inevitable conclusion that *law*
is embodied in *custom*.   Earlier and elsewhere, however, Malinowski had given this rather more cautious definition : ' A given social
norm or rule is legal if it is enforced by a direct, organised, and
definite social sanction.' [6]   What the nature of the sanctions he
had in mind was is not clear from this definition, which he seems
to have abandoned in his more famous and later work.

Malinowski's conceptualisation of the law, then, ultimately
reduces him into a position more or less the same as that of
Hartland and the rest, whom he originally set out to correct.[7]
This is not to say that he has not achieved more in the way of
better insight into and perception of the nature of ' primitive '

---

[1] See his *Law and Authority in a Nigerian Tribe*, p. xiv.
[2] P. 347 (published in 1931).
[3] I.e., *Law and Authority in a Nigerian Tribe*.
[4] *Ibid.*, at p. xv.   He was commenting, with approval, on Marett's
definition of law as ' the authoritative regulation of social relations '.
[5] P. 54 of *Crime and Custom in Savage Society*.
[6] *The Family Life of the Australian Aborigines*, p. 115.
[7] This criticism has also been made by W. A. Seagle in his article,
' Primitive Law and Professor Malinowski ', in *American Anthropologist*,
Vol. 39, Pt. II, 1937, pp. 275-90.

law than these others have done. For one instance out of many, one is bound to admit that for all Malinowski's rapturous over-statements he, like Radcliffe-Brown, properly emphasizes that rules of law are distinguishable from rules of mere custom. That, in the final analysis, he has to be put in such strange company, is only the result of the failure of an effort to claim too much for a good cause.

Finally, we may note briefly that just as Radcliffe-Brown seems to have been swayed by Pound and Malinowski, provoked by Austin and Maine, so it looks as if Schapera has been lured by Salmond, Gray and Diamond into making the court the touchstone of a rule of law. Thus he writes : ' We may, therefore, regard as a law any rule of conduct likely to be enforced by the courts if and when it is brought before them.' [1] But he is not unaware of some of the difficulties about this view, for he readily admits that his definition will be ' unsatisfactory to the jurist ' since it necessarily includes ' some rules the courts will not enforce if put to the test.' This, however, is not the only objection to an attempt at defining law by reference to a court, as the reader can see from what we have said earlier on the subject. [2]

C. GENERAL ESTIMATE, AND A SUGGESTED DEFINITION

It will be remembered that Eugene Ehrlich has also included in his view of law infinitely varied matter. [3] The vast number of human social relations and groupings within the State are governed by rules which are, in Ehrlich's opinion, just as import-ant and effective as are those enacted by the State. The normal lawyer takes notice of only ' norms for decision ' which may or may not be in accordance with the actual ' facts of the law '. But Ehrlich does not make any distinction between the two, and so his idea leads to a situation where everything is law. There should obviously be some limit to the content of law.

---

[1] *A Handbook of Tswana Law and Custom*, Ch. II.   [2] Pp. 38–40.
[3] See his *Fundamental Principles of the Sociology of Law*. In this connexion Bentham, who in his *Theory of Legislation*, p. 82, defines law as ' the will of the legislator ', also states at p. 90 of his *Limits of Jurisprudence Defined*, (ed. C. W. Everett) : ' Under the term " law " . . . we must include a judicial order, a military or any other kind of executive order, or even the most trivial and momentary order of a domestic kind, so that it be not illegal.' This is typical Benthamite rationalisation which, while well meant, is too widely stated.

The perennial problem of jurisprudence, however, is, firstly, to know where to draw the line between what is law and what is not and, secondly, to discover according to what definite criteria this line is to be drawn. Various suggestions have been made. The ' imperative ' school, whether of the Austinian ' sovereign's command ' type or of the ' judicial enforcement ' brand of Salmond and Gray, will recognise as law only what goes by that name in Western political systems. Duguit's ' social solidarity ', while not being so unreasonable in its attitude towards customary law, remains essentially an *a priori* approach to the fundamental problems of the law. Savigny's backward longing for the romantic past of the law, useful as it is in ensuring an honourable place for customary law in the scheme of legal thought, is handicapped as much by its speculative optimism as by its nationalistic interpretation of law. Nor is Pound's idea of law as a process of control exercised authoritatively by the body politic a universal criterion for determining what is a rule of law in any given human society ; its main purview, though greatly enlightened by the brilliant doctrine of ' social engineering ', is still limited to advanced societies of the Western type.

It is precisely because of the inadequacies of the current legal theories that Dr. A. L. Goodhart has recently suggested this definition of law. ' Law ', he says, ' is any rule of human conduct which is recognised as being obligatory.' [1] The former Professor of Jurisprudence at Oxford claims that his definition is in accord with Marett's definition of law as ' the authoritative regulation of social relations '. With respect, one might say that Sir Arthur Goodhart's legal affinity is more with his Oxford predecessor in the Chair of Jurisprudence, Sir Paul Vinogradoff, than with Dr. Marett, the former eminent Oxford Professor of

---

[1] See his article entitled ' The Importance of a Definition of Law ', at pp. 106–9 of *Journal of African Administration*, Vol. III, No. 3, July, 1951. This definition was first put forward in the learned jurist's contribution to *Interpretations of Modern Legal Philosophies* (1947), a volume of essays presented to Dean Roscoe Pound of the U.S.A. His own Essay is entitled : ' An Apology for Jurisprudence—Definition of Law ', and his definition occurs at p. 288. But at p. 293 is also offered this definition of *State* law : ' State law can, therefore, be defined as those rules of conduct, which are obligatory on the members of the State as such, just as the laws of the Worshipful Company of Bellow Menders consist of the rules of conduct, obligatory on the members of that society.'

E

Anthropology. As we have seen [1] Vinogradoff has in his *Common-sense in Law*, defined law as a ' set of rules imposed and enforced by a society with regard to the attribution and exercise of power over persons and things '.[2] Thus the threefold idea of a rule or body of rules, of its social recognition and of its obligatory character, are common to both jurists' definitions, while all that Marett stresses is the incidence of regulation or control, a faint echo of Pound.

Goodhart prefaces his definition with the remark : ' My definition of law is a simple one, and is intended to cover both law in a primitive community and in a highly developed modern State because I do not believe that it is either possible or desirable to draw a line of distinction between them.' [3] This, if we may say so, is the whole argument of the present and the preceding chapters. In this connexion it is useful to refer briefly to a controversy. When critics complain that Austin's definition does not contemplate the customary law of non-Western societies, Salmond makes an heroic effort to defend the great jurist by the argument that Austin need not define law in such a way as to include such customary law since one does not normally define man so as to include the anthropoid ape. There are, it is submitted, three fallacies in this contention. In the first place, Salmond seems to forget that, both biologically and morphologic-ally, Western and non-Western men are contemporary entities, which man and ape are not. In the second place, it is obviously a little disingenuous to compare law to biology in this way. In the third place, any attempt to compartmentalise such a science as law on the arbitrary basis of the accident of human aggre-gations, instead of taking an integral view of it as a universal phenomenon, can only present a one-sided picture of what is essentially an objective social reality.

The better view seems to be to regard law as a common, indeed an indispensable, attribute of all human societies. But the definition suggested by Goodhart would seem to require two qualifications : (*a*) Law is not merely *a rule* of conduct, it is

[1] See p. 45 *supra*.
[2] The late Sir Frederick Pollock, another veteran Oxford jurist, defined law as ' a rule of conduct binding on members of a common-wealth as such ' (*A First Book of Jurisprudence*, p. 29). By ' common wealth ' he seems to have meant any organised human community.
[3] *Journal of African Administration*, Vol. III, No. 3, 1951, p. 109.

a body of rules ; (*b*) Though it may sound a little trite to quarrel with the unintended neutrality of both the *recognition* or the *obligatoriness* in this definition, yet it may give sinews and even flesh to the somewhat dry bones here provided if some indication is added as to who are to recognise the rules or accept the obligation. It is, therefore, with some trepidation that one ventures to suggest this definition : ' The law of a given community is the body of rules which are recognised as obligatory by its members.' This recognition must be in accordance with the principles of their social imperative, because operating in every community is a dynamic of social conduct, an accepted norm of behaviour which the vast majority of its members regard as absolutely necessary for the common weal. This determinant of the *ethos* of the community is its social imperative.

This definition avoids the kind of difficulties involved in looking at law as the act of a sovereign or of a sovereign legislature, or as a system of categories, or even as a species of control imposed from above. It does not assume a particular type of political organisation or a special brand of social philosophy. It merely seeks to embrace all the known types of human social groupings irrespective of the pattern of their internal orderings or the degree of their several civilisations. It is not that these considerations have no bearing upon the character of law as such, but that they cannot be used to determine generally what law is—and this is the central problem of jurisprudence.

If order, regularity and a sense of social obligation are essential attributes of law, in Western no less than in non-Western societies, our definition can fairly well claim to satisfy these. It is not perfect. It can be criticised on many grounds ; nevertheless, it will be found to possess the merit of enabling us to regard African legal ideas as but an integral part of the general theory of law.

CHAPTER V

WHY IS LAW OBEYED?

THE analysis of the nature of law which we have just made naturally prompts the enquiry : Why is law obeyed in any community ? To this question have been given answers almost as diverse as the theories that have been put forward concerning the nature of law itself.

A. COMPULSION AS SANCTION

We see, for instance, that the element of compulsion enters into nearly all the definitions of law that we examined in the preceding chapter. It will be recalled that Austin erects his theory on the corner-stone of command by a political superior to subordinate political inferiors. He distinguishes between *general* and *particular* commands. The latter are the arbitrary and irregular behests decreed *ad hoc* to specific individuals, as when, for an example, a footpad points a gun at a person or group of persons and issues the peremptory order : ' Your money or your life, guv'nors ! ' This type of command lacks the virtue of being applied to the *bulk* of a politically organised society of persons by another or others having lawful authority so to apply it. Such particular commands cannot, therefore, be law. But a general command issuing from a properly constituted authority to whom or to which the majority of a given community *habitually* render obedience under pain of punishment, is a rule of law. This sanction, Austin explains, while being of the essence of any law, need not depend upon its quality or even quantity in order to compel obedience from those subject to the law : ' The smallest chance of incurring the smallest evil ' is enough.[1] Austin distinctly excludes the violence of the motive to comply. It is sufficient if it regularly obliges the generality of people to a line of conduct.

To the whole of this theory Bentham adds the significant

[1] See his *Lectures on Jurisprudence*, p. 12.

suggestion[1] that a reward offered to induce persons to confess or disclose the commission of crime should be regarded as also a sanction.[2] Austin, of course, soundly rejects this view of the idea of a legal sanction, accusing Bentham of doing violence to language by his bold inclusion of the idea of reward in its connotation; he said that Bentham was confusing *motive* with *sanction*.[3]

Again, Duguit's ' social solidarity ' is valid only if understood to be categorical in its operation : ' The rule of law is not a rule properly speaking, but is a virtual discipline which social interdependence imposes on all members of the group.' Hence it is that Duguit ultimately rests the validity of a rule of law upon whether its breach would provoke a social reaction.

When we turn from the *a-priorists* to the advocate of ' social engineering ' we find again that law is after all ' social control through the systematic application of the forces of politically organised society '. It will thus be noticed that whether we regard law as a command or as a categorical norm, or as what is authoritatively enforced, we find as a thread running through the entire fabric of the several theories, a constant imperative idea as the underlying assumption of legal rules.[4]

It is quite clear, however, that this fashionable way of regarding obedience to law as based on compulsion or force, whether physical or mental, is not altogether satisfactory.[5] Apart from the obvious fact that it does not afford any direction as to what the judge should do in any particular case before him, this

[1] *Principles of Morals and Legislation*, Ch. VII.

[2] Bentham would have derived not a little comfort from this statement of Malinowski in his *Crime and Custom in Savage Society*, p. 58 : ' These rules of civil law are elastic and possess a certain latitude. *They offer not only penalties for failure, but also premiums for an overdose of fulfilment.*' (The italics are mine.)

[3] See his *The Province of Jurisprudence Determined*, pp. 93 *et seq.*, also, *Lectures on Jurisprudence*, p. 13.

[4] Indeed, W. W. Buckland, in his little book, *Some Reflections on Jurisprudence*, holds that sanction based on force is indispensable to law. (See pp. 88–92.)

[5] Force or coercion has been thus defined by R. M. McIver in his *Society : Its Structure and Changes :* ' Whenever men act, or refrain from acting, in a manner different from that which they themselves have chosen or would choose in a given situation, because others deliberately limit the range of their choice either directly, through present control over it, or indirectly, through the threat of consequences, they may be said to be under coercion. (p. 35)

doctrine of sanction is psychologically inaccurate. Sanctions, if strictly interpreted, cannot on the Austinian or any other analysis enable a policeman to effect the arrest of a felon or deter persons from entering into illegal contracts. There must therefore be some other reason or reasons why people obey the law, besides the presence of mere force.

B.   PSYCHOLOGICAL SANCTIONS [1]

In his *Studies in History and Jurisprudence*,[2] Lord Bryce enumerates these *five* grounds of compliance with a rule of law : Indolence, Deference, Sympathy, Fear and Reason—in that descending order of importance.   In his view,[3] the greatest single factor which ensures the people's obedience is *indolence*, in the sense of sheer mental inertia. The majority always prefer to follow the line of least resistance and will willingly and loyally accept what is laid down for them as guiding principles of behaviour, since they are themselves too lazy to question either the rulers or the rules.   A second but less important cause inducing in the people generally a disposition to obey the law is *deference* either to the personal authority of the lawgiver(s) or to the impersonal authority of tradition.   It is bad form to flout authority and so disturb the basis of the accepted order of social life. Without feelings of reverence for the claims of immemorial and therefore well-tried ways and usages, stability is endangered and the sanctity of family life, upon which society is founded, becomes assailed.

Yet another reason for compliance with established law, Bryce finds, is that people feel *sympathy* for one another, the ruler for the ruled and *vice versa*, in the delicate task of social adjustments rendered necessary by the facts of a common political life.   Otherwise, human relations would become impossible because the principle of co-operation so vital to smooth social existence would cease to operate.   A purely individualistic assertion of personal

---

[1] The denomination of sanctions into *pyschological* and *sociological*, has been adopted as a classificatory device only and *not* as terms of art. For instance, the ' command ' theory of sanction has also its psychological as well as its sociological implications.

[2] See his Essay on ' Obedience ' in Vol. II (1901), at p. 463.

[3] The reader is warned that, in the elaboration which follows, the statement of Bryce's arguments as well as their accompanying criticisms is the present writer's.

independence by the members of any community would be incompatible with their very existence *as a community* or, if such selfish claim were made subsequently to the establishment of the body politic, would lead to its rapid disintegration. One suspects that the whole of Bryce's idea of ' sympathy ' as a legal sanction looks rather like Duguit's ' social solidarity ', by which the governors and the governed are equally bound in fulfilling the purposes of State law. We notice it also in Kant's principle of the categorical imperative, as we find it characteristic of Stammler's twin conception of the principle of respect and the principle of co-operation.

But *fear* is also, for Bryce, an important element of the obedience paid to law, though it is not the most important. Somehow, people obey the law from fear of punishment, whether by human authority or by divine intervention. They comply because they stand in constant dread of being mulcted for their transgressions against the law. The power of the State to penalise infractions of its laws, or that of the supernatural agencies to castigate for outrages against divine ordinances, often acts as a sufficient deterrent to would-be offenders. Unlike many others before and after him, however, Bryce thinks that the importance of fear as a ground for compliance with law can easily be exaggerated. One ventures to suggest here that fear of sanctions, legal as well as spiritual, is an emotion rooted in the psychology of the people and induced by specific mechanisms of the same evocative order ; but fear alone cannot always explain just why the law is so overwhelmingly obeyed. Neither the threat of force nor the dread of penalty can account entirely for the general habit of obedience to law, except on the part of the hardened criminal.

Of all the five grounds for compliance Bryce places *reason* last, as he seems to share with Max Weber the belief that law generally evolves from the irrational to the rational. Some legal rules are patently absurd and yet men follow them in the normal ordering of their daily life. But Weber's ' charismatic ' doctrine of legal evolution does not exclude the possibility of reason as a ground of obedience, especially where the *raison d'être* of a particular rule appears to make sense to those called upon to obey it. After all, men are rational beings, however irrational either their laws or the reasons for their observance may be. Rules of law that are neither reasonable nor plausible tend generally to be disregarded or evaded, until they fall into desuetude or are changed ; if they cannot be evaded, then flagrant breaches occur which may provoke a social reaction against their continuance. For the most part, however, men obey law because they consider it the reasonable thing to do.   It is unreasonable to defy the law. Reason dictates that law is essential to the achievement of the purposes of social existence and that in any case obedience pays.

For Bryce, then, these five grounds, taken either separately or together, represent the foundation of obedience to law.   Goodhart has recently added a *sixth* ground, namely, *the innate desire for order* not explicable solely on the ground of indolence.[1] This suggestion would seem to imply that there wells up in the breasts of most men an emotional yearning for regularity and system in the daily conduct of human affairs.   The majority, far from cherishing selfish ideals and pursuing the path of chaos, love peace and order.   They realise that the best policy of social insurance against anarchy is law, and are therefore prepared to obey it for that reason, if for no other.   While the learned jurist does not actually use this argument, so much seems to be implicit in what he does say.   But, in pointing out that the six grounds of compliance are ' the dominant ones ', Goodhart agrees that there may be others besides.

C.   SOCIOLOGICAL SANCTIONS

In the sphere of ' primitive ' law, in particular, other suggestions have been made regarding the issue of submission to law.   Thus, Radcliffe-Brown says[2] that both customs and laws are social norms and that they are not distinguishable on the basis of content but according to the type of sanction supporting the particular norm.   He then erects a tripartite system of categories, with subdivisions, of social sanctions.   A social norm, he says in effect, becomes legal if its infraction or neglect will be met by the systematic application of the forces of organised society.

[1] See p. 109 of his article, ' The Importance of a Definition of Law ', in the *Journal of African Administration*, July, 1951.

[2] See an article entitled ' Sanctions, Social ' in *Encyclopædia of the Social Sciences*, Vol. 13, 1935, pp. 531-4.

He is thus on the side of Roscoe Pound and his school. The logical implications of this idea can be seen in his statement elsewhere,[1] that in some societies penal sanctions hardly exist and that *education* is all that is necessary to induce the habit of obedience to law. In other words, in many well-organised societies in Africa, force is as much a sanction of the law as it is in Western societies ; whereas in societies not so well-organised, education sufficiently ensures spontaneous obedience. That this dichotomy is neither desirable nor necessary becomes obvious once we admit that law cannot be built on mere force or defined by reference to it alone.

A writer who is uncompromising in his belief that African customary law is supported exclusively by supernatural sanctions is Orde-Browne who wrote : [2] ' Since all laws were based on supernatural authority for their origin, the same power was relied upon to ensure the punishment of offenders ; human society need take no action when a far more dreadful and inevitable vindication of the outraged code might be expected from spiritual sources. . . . The enormous force of such a system must be obvious, far outweighing the European's reluctance to risk the pangs of conscience, the contempt of his fellows, or the action of mere human law.' This classic re-statement of an out-moded theory of the religious origin of law shows the writer to be oblivious of the elementary fact that the psychological motivation underlying moral conduct, fear of ridicule or of legal penalty is not peculiar to the European, and that African law does not so weakly abdicate its functions in favour of an all-pervading super-natural authority. Has not this writer fallen into some confusion in his one-sided view of the sanction of African law by making this grudging admission in a later passage ? [3] : ' . . . no trace of retributive action ; repair of damage done, with social and spiritual penalties to correspond, comprised the whole arcanum of punishments available ; only in serious and exceptional cases was an offender against the welfare of the community permanently eliminated from society.' So that there are, after all, non-religious penalties like payment of reparation for unlawful injuries

[1] *African Political Systems*, p. xv, edited by M. Fortes and E. Evans-Pritchard.
[2] See his article, ' British Justice and the African ', *Jnl. Roy. Afr. Soc.*, Vol. 32, No. 127, April, 1933, pp. 148–59, at pp. 151–2.
[3] *Idem.*, p. 157.

done to another as well as elimination (whatever this may mean) on the ground of the heinousness of the offence.

Some limitation to the operation of supernatural sanctions in an African society is indicated in this observation by Godfrey and Monica Wilson with regard to the Nyakyusa: [1] 'Supernatural sanctions were believed to be effective only against kinsmen, neighbours, and those with whom a man was in personal contact. No one feared witchcraft from outside the chiefdom.' This may not be the universal attitude towards religious sanctions in all African societies, but it should be a useful corrective to the exaggerated influence in legal matters often attributed to it by writers like Major Orde-Browne.

Dr. Meek adopts, understandably, a pluralist approach to the problem of sanction. He says : ' Religious awe acts as a potent legal sanction, and so do all social and economic regulations. The king, as the head of the religious and social life, is the supreme court of appeal, but normally all cases of breach of law are settled in a lower court, viz. the court of public opinion which casts ridicule on one who fails to conform to the recognised standard of social contract, or which condemns him to a punishment by supernatural powers for a breach of some religious taboo imposed for the protection of society.'[2] This mixed bag, when sorted out, will be found to contain these articles : religious awe, ridicule, social and economic regulations, and litigation—all of which are regarded as legal.

The more orthodox sociological interpretation of obedience to law in ' primitive ' society may be illustrated by this statement of Sidney Hartland : ' The general belief in the certainty of supernatural punishment and the alienation of the sympathy of one's fellows generated an atmosphere of terror which is quite sufficient to prevent a breach of tribal customs.' [3] The twofold factor of obedience, according to this view, is fear of supernatural punishment and of social ostracism. Dr. Rivers, however, believes that ' there is a group sentiment which makes unnecessary any definite social machinery for the exertion of authority ',[4] and he is here at one with E. Lambert, the French-

[1] P. 36 of their *Analysis of Social Change* ; see further G. Wilson, ' An African Morality ', an article in *Africa*, Jan., 1936, p. 91.
[2] C. K. Meek, *A Sudanese Kingdom*, p. 347.
[3] *Primitive Law*, p. 214.
[4] *Social Organisation*, p. 169.

man, who postulates the theory of the juridical sentiment of the people as the sole foundation of law in any society.[1]

Sometimes, we come across some such vague observation as this one of C. C. Roberts (a former judge in East Africa) : ' The sanctions underlying primitive law are so strong that the law is accepted and its principles are not questioned. . . . To rebel is to be cast out of the society in which he (the native) lives.'[2] In addition to the idea of expulsion as a legal sanction, we have here in embryo a statement of the doctrine of the willing and unquestioning obedience to customary law that is often supposed to characterise ' primitive ' societies. As good a formal statement of it as any is this one of Lowie's : ' Generally speaking, the unwritten laws of customary usage are obeyed far more willingly than our written codes, or rather they are obeyed spontaneously. . . . To become the laughing-stock of his daily associates for minor misdemeanours and to be completely ostracised for graver offences are terrible punishments for the native, and they have a deterrent force of which the infliction of penalties in our sense is often quite devoid. To this should be added the religious motive. Certain crimes are reckoned as sins, they are offences against the unseen powers of the universe and invite condign punishment regardless of any secular agency.'[3] Put in a nutshell, the idea is that obedience to law is automatic and spontaneous and that the factors making for this blind and passive acquiescence are ridicule, ostracism and fear of supernatural punishment.

Within the once fashionable theory of ' primitive communism ', Durkheim expounds the idea that all legal reactions are founded in the psychology of the group, never in that of the individual.[4] He therefore regards the religious sanction as a projection of the tribe since ' communism is in general existence in the domain of law '.[5] Freud, on the other hand, treats the religious sanction of unwritten customary law as a projection not of the tribe, but of the father. And Professor Gilbert Murray has assured us that

[1] See his ' Comparative Law ', an article in Vol. IV of the *Encyclopædia of the Social Sciences* (1931), pp. 126–9.
[2] *Tangled Justice*, pp. 63–4.
[3] *Primitive Society*, p. 384.
[4] In his *L'Année Sociologique*, Vol. I, p. 353 ff.
[5] See his *Division of Social Work* (*De La Division du Travail Social* (5th edn.)).

these two rather contradictory explanations of the automatic sway of custom can be reconciled. ' This is no real contradiction,' he argues, ' since in the patriarchal tribal system it is the father of the family who normally exercises authority and insists that the group law shall be obeyed.' [1] He is thus able to conclude that Durkheim's analysis in fact includes Freud's. Even if this were so, the theory of primitive communism or clan unity is, as we shall see in the next chapter, a patent fallacy.

In his well-known article,[2] Driberg sees the greatest point of divergence between African customary law and English law in the differing apparatuses for the judicial enforcement of legal rules, e.g. in the absence of prison and police force in the former. He does, however, regard some form of sanction as essential to both types of law. Accordingly, he enumerates these sanctions as ' universally valid in Africa ' : (a) Religious Sanctions ; (b) Collective Responsibility ; (c) Magical Sanctions, and (d) Ridicule and Ostracism. He prefaces this classification with the remark : ' Primarily the law is obeyed, just because it is accepted. Its acceptance and its position as an integral part of the social organisation are its own sanction. It is obeyed because only by obedience to the law will society function, and it is in everybody's interest to subscribe to its regulations. Law is not the act of a sovereign, it is not enforced by *ad hoc* sanctions, but by a sanction involved (as Hartland remarks) in the belief and practice of the community.' It follows that he thinks that law is obeyed, (i) because it is accepted, (ii) because obedience pays, and (iii) because it carries its own sanction as part of the whole cultural milieu. It also suggests a throw-back to the dogma of automatic submission of an earlier age. Nevertheless, argues Driberg, no community consists entirely of ' right-minded ' people and so other sanctions are necessary for social control through law.

Underlying everything is the *religious* sanction which is based on ' the theory that the clan is a continuous entity comprising both the living and the dead. The ancestors are just as much concerned as the living in the due observance of the law.' The dread of ' this terrific antiquity, remote but ever present ', operates

[1] *The Individual in East and West* (ed. E. R. Hughes), Ch. II, ' Group Law and Private Conscience ' pp. 37–8, contributed by Professor Murray.
[2] ' The African Conception of Law ', in the *Journal of Comparative Legislation and International Law*, 3rd Series, Vol. 16, pp. 230–46, at pp. 237 ff.

to compel an aweful obedience to law, besides introducing a religious sanction ' which is perhaps the most potent factor of all '. Driberg even permits himself the indulgence of marrying the theory of the religious basis of all law to that of automatic submission to custom, as when he writes : ' No compensation for an offence, no reparation, is complete without sacrifice. Every offence has to be legally compensated and ceremonially purged, and till both are done the offender and his community are in danger of spiritual retribution. It is this religious nexus which gives African law an authority sufficiently to dispense with the mechanics of enforcement.' But, later,[1] Driberg asserts that Africans do not scruple to abrogate harsh or inconvenient laws, even if that should involve resort to all kinds of fictions. What, then, becomes of the alleged grovelling cringe for their ' terrific antiquity ' if they can so wantonly tamper with the supernatural ordinances of which their entire law is said to consist ? Again, Driberg elsewhere devotes a fairly lengthy article to proving that ancestral worship is in reality more *social* than *religious* and that what are so often mistaken for supernatural observances are essentially secular.[2]

His second head of sanction is *collective responsibility*, which he regards as ' a potent factor in the prevention of crime and in the liquidation of the offence without extraneous pressure '. His meaning appears to be that all members of the group or clan are responsible for the actions of their fellows and the price of individual security is eternal vigilance about one another's doings. Also the knowledge that every damage or hurt inflicted by a group member upon an outsider can be avenged against *any* member of the offender's, acts as an effective deterrent to gratuitous wrongdoing. Finally, the group can by the threat of outlawry or by its actual infliction after the commission of an offence, deter its members, since such a denial of group protection to the offender means virtual death to him. He is thus put beyond the pale of tribal law.

Magical sanctions form the third category and are said to be analogous to the religious sanctions in that they carry an

[1] At p. 242.
[2] See his article ' Secular Aspect of Ancestor-Worship in Africa ' (in *Supplement to Journal of Royal African Society*, Vol. 35, No. 138, Jan. 1936).

automatic penalty in such offences as breaches of taboo and the neglect of certain religious ceremonials.   These sanctions recoil on the health and prosperity of the offender and his group. Similarly, the non-performance of funerary rites acts as a powerful legal sanction, since living members will thereby learn to conform to the established code as a means of securing this necessary passage into the world beyond.   Appeal to the ordeal in a judicial trial is also a legal sanction which differs from an automatic sanction only because it does not carry its own penalty ; it merely gives a verdict that ' leads to an automatic adjustment of the equilibrium '.   Driberg's one worry is that his automatic sanctions do not always recoil on the right person.   He is sure, however, that ' even the threat of witchcraft—generally anti-social, but used socially as a legal sanction—may be invoked to secure reparation from a recalcitrant individual '.   We shall see this conception of the legal character of sorcery again when we come to examine the ideas of Malinowski.

Like most of the other sociologists, Driberg includes *ridicule and ostracism* in his scheme of sanctions of African customary law. He puts them last in his list because he believes that they are effective minor legal sanctions.[1]   It is at least doubtful, however, whether the minor role thus assigned to ridicule and ostracism fits the facts presented by the writer.   For instance, he makes a great deal of the importance of status and prestige in African communities, pointing out that this is the reason why defamation is everywhere so heavily penalised by substantial compensations.

Driberg's analysis of the forces of conformity to law in African societies will thus be seen, on the whole, to be little more illuminating than any we have yet examined.   Despite his interesting observations on many aspects of social control and psychological habituation operating in these communities, he remains bogged down in the mire of older anthropological dogmas like the theory of the ' primitive ' man's automatic submission to custom or of the pre-eminence of supernatural auspices in legal matters.

All these Malinowski has effectively challenged in his famous *Crime and Custom in Savage Society*.   He begins by suggesting

---

[1] On the other hand, according to Rattray (*Ashanti Law and Constitution*, p. 372), ridicule is the most important sanction in Ashanti Law, with supernatural sanctions next in the array.   Rattray, however refuses to discriminate between supernatural and religious sanctions.

that, whether the society is ' primitive ' or ' civilised ', laws are obeyed ' willingly ' and ' spontaneously ' and that neither the threat of force nor the fear of punishment can wholly explain why this is so, except in the case of the recidivist. Malinowski adds : ' Again, there are a number of laws, taboos, and obligations in every human culture which weigh heavily on every citizen, demand great self-sacrifice, and are obeyed for moral, sentimental or matter-of-fact reasons, but without any spontaneity.' [1] Our perspective on law in ' primitive ' society is bound to be wrong if we think that it has to be obeyed spontaneously merely because of the absence of courts, policemen and a centralised political authority. It must be realised that the law is enforced not by any motive of fear of punishment or passive submission to tradition, but by ' very complex psychological and social inducements '. [2]

In order, however, to give form and substance to his ideas, Malinowski asks the crucial question : ' What is the motive force behind these obligations ? ', and his answer is : ' Every community has, therefore, a weapon for the enforcement of its right : reciprocity. . . . This is not limited to the exchange of fish for vegetables. As a rule, two communities rely upon each other in other forms of trading and other mutual services as well. Thus every chain of reciprocity is made the more binding by being part and parcel of a whole system of mutualities.' [3] While all this is true to some extent, it savours too much of a purely economic interpretation of legal sanctions. But he is too wise an anthropologist not to recognise that ' there are also other driving motives, besides the constraint of reciprocal obligations '. If reciprocity operates as a *legal* constraint, he sees the *social* constraint in the average individual's ' regard for the effective rights and claims of others '. [4]

When, however, he goes on to assert that other mental and social forces—the publicity given to ceremonies, love of pomp and generosity accompanying the making of gifts of food and exchange [5]—make certain rules of conduct into binding law, we feel bound to protest. As we saw him do by his inclusion in the definition of law of almost all facets of a people's culture, so here we find him in equal danger of mistaking the effect for

[1] P. 13.   [2] Pp. 15, 31–2.
[3] P. 23.   [4] P. 28.   [5] Pp. 29–31, 55.

the cause of obedience to law.   We would suggest that the public
way in which obligations are performed, in so far as such obligations are really legal rather than social, is indeed not the reason
why the law is obeyed but it is a manifestation of that obedience.
The acceptance of the binding nature of a legal rule must obviously precede any conscious effort to comply with its precept.
The trouble with Malinowski seems to be that, just as after
rightly distinguishing between law and custom he ends up by
giving a definition of law that fuses both, so here after showing the fallacies of the theory of spontaneous obedience to
law he tends to confuse purely *social* with intrinsically *legal*
obligations.[1]

Even *religious* obligations, such as the rites of mourning and
sorrowing for the dead, are said to be legal : ' Who, however,
would suspect a legal side to such religious transactions ?   Yet
in the Trobriands there is not one single mortuary act, not one
ceremony, which is not considered to be an obligation of the
performer towards some of the other survivors.' [2]   And he adds
in another place : ' The worship of ghosts, spirits or mythical
personages—they also have a legal side clearly exemplified in the
case of mortuary performances, described above.' [3]   Apparently
there seems to be no aspect of life in which Malinowski fails to
discover his legal sanctions.   He is only out of the wood when he
suggests that the reason why *economic* obligations are kept is fear
of opprobrium and social ostracism.[4]

In spite of his misplaced insistence that ' reciprocity ' is the
most important factor of obedience to law,[5] however, Malinowski
winds up lucidly in these words : ' The savages have a class of
obligatory rules, not endowed with any mystical character, not
set forth in " the name of God ", not enforced by any super-

---

[1] And this is still true, despite this his own feeble defence : ' I was
not intent on proving that all social rules are legal ' (p. 54).   This
denial is an implied admission or consciousness that he himself suspects
that he might be confusing the two !

[2] P. 33.

[3] P. 43 ; *sorcery* and *suicide* are also ' legal influences '.   Malinowski
seems to regard sorcery both as a genuine legal force and as an instrument
of crime (pp. 93–4)—an offender against the rule of exogamy is driven
to a ceremonial suicide ; sorcery may also be used in enforcing the rules
of tribal law, e.g. ' to destroy crops, to thwart a fisherman, to drive pigs
into the jungle.'

[4] P. 41.   [5] Pp. 31–2.

natural sanction but provided with a purely social binding force.'[1]
He continues, more shatteringly : ' The force of habit, the awe
of traditional command and a sentimental attachment to it, the
desire to satisfy public opinion—all combine to make custom be
obeyed for its own sake. In this the " savages " do not differ
from the members of any self-contained community with a limited
horizon, whether this be an eastern European ghetto, an Oxford
college, or a fundamentalist Middle West community. But love,
of tradition, conformism and the sway of custom account but
to a very partial extent for obedience to rules among dons, savages,
peasants or junkers.' This seems a sufficient answer to Seagle's
charge [2] that Malinowski is incapable of appreciating the theory
of the automatic sway of custom propounded by Rivers, Hartland,
and others. Rather, Malinowski is at pains to show that ' group
sentiment' and ' collective responsibility' are not the only nor
even the main sanctions of customary law ; ' esprit de corps,
solidarity, pride in one's community '—all enter into the situation
and are as indispensable to the maintenance of a ' high ' as they
are to that of a ' low ' culture.

Malinowski's summing-up is as follows : ' There must be in
all societies a class of rules too practical to be backed up by
religious sanctions, too burdensome to be left to mere goodwill,
too personally vital to individuals to be enforced by any abstract
agency. This is the domain of legal rules, and I venture to
foretell that reciprocity, systematic incidence, publicity and
ambition will be found to be the main factors in the binding
machinery of primitive law.' [3]

Now, consistently with his identification of ' primitive ' law
with *civil* law, Malinowski has chosen *reciprocity*—' the con-
catenation of the obligations '—as the most important criterion
of the law. But, as Seagle has rightly pointed out, reciprocity
is involved only in civil obligations, hardly in criminal ones,
unless one is prepared to accept Hegel's theory that the average

---

[1] P. 51. But he adds at p. 53 : ' There are also norms pertaining to
things sacred and important, the rules of magical rites, funerary pomp
and such like. These are primarily backed up by supernatural sanctions
and by the strong feeling that sacred matters must not be tampered with.'

[2] See ' Primitive Law and Professor Malinowski ', an article by
Seagle in *The American Anthropologist*, Vol. 39, Pt. II, pp. 275–90,
1937, particularly pp. 278 ff.

[3] Pp. 67–8.

F

criminal longs as much to be punished as the rest of us do to punish him. We may add that, even in civil cases, reciprocity does not often seem to be prominent since there is no exact equivalence between the breach and the reparation, e.g. in many instances of tortious liability.

In fairness to Malinowski, however, it seems that what he really means by 'reciprocity' is more or less the same as what jurists assume when they say that every right has a correlative duty. In the law of civil liability a plaintiff can only succeed if he proves that (1) he has some recognised legal right which (2) corresponds to some legal duty owed to him by the defendant and (3) a breach of which has resulted in damage to the plaintiff.

Understood in this sense Malinowski's idea of 'reciprocity' becomes useful as showing that, among the Trobriand Islanders at any rate, the forces of law and order are based on a recognised system of mutually balancing rights and duties. We get support for this view when we carefully examine the words of his definition of law (given earlier)—significantly enough, he uses 'rights and duties' as the key words.

The only fault here is that law cannot be conceived of entirely as a matter of rights and duties.

Again, reciprocity is seen best at work in societies with a system of dual organisation in which the community is divided into two mutually complementary segments, usually exogamous. This symmetry of structure which is the indispensable basis of reciprocal obligations Miss Green has also found among the Ibos of Umu-Eke Agbaja (in Eastern Nigeria), who are exogamous communities; [1] and it seems that similar discoveries are possible in other African communities organised on the basis of the inter-play of kinship bonds and of common locality, in which group solidarity is maintained by a system of mutually balancing seg-ments. Hoebel, in his article [2] 'Law-ways of the Comanche Indians', has, however, shown that, while reciprocity may play an important role in other primitive societies, it does not do so in his field: ' In Comanche society, reciprocity is not developed to an exaggerated degree, so that Malinowski's approach is even less applicable here than it might be elsewhere.' Other instances might be found to disorganise the theory of reciprocity.

[1] M. M. Green, *Ibo Village Affairs*, pp. 150 ff.
[2] *Op. cit.*, p. 32, n. 6, *supra*.

But Malinowski anticipates the existence of such inconvenient exceptions by postulating a general doctrine that the dual organisation was *originally* universal. Even so, this is a serious weakness in his whole theoretical position, not only because it involves him in wild generalisations as to social origins (a strange thing for someone who holds history in such contempt), but also because it admits by implication that there are societies today in which reciprocity has ceased to operate, if it ever did operate at all, as an effective social dynamic.

When all these criticisms have been levelled it remains to be said for Malinowski that he quite rightly emphasises the clear distinction which even the most 'primitive' communities do draw between the supernatural and the secular rules of conduct. Not for him the inane dogma of the 'confused savage categories'; not for him the specious theory that magic, religion and medicine are just lumped together in 'primitive pre-logical mentality'. Rather, he insists that it is only the religious or supernatural sanctions that are regarded as automatic in their operation in so far as this depends on the unseen powers, while secular sanctions are enforced by known human agencies. A time comes in the evolution of any culture when human intervention gradually encroaches upon the territory of the mystical, assailing the automatic process of the divine powers and converting the previously supernatural sanctions into the secular; and the latter become again differentiated into the social and the legal.

Seagle in his article previously referred to has charged Malinowski with having committed 'the pathetic fallacy of primitive jurisprudence'. But is his own substitution—and glorification —of 'publicity' for 'reciprocity' an improvement? Since he does, but Malinowski does not, believe in the existence of courts and of the formalisation of all legal transactions as indispensable to law, this is not a surprising accusation. Publicity, in his view, is far more important than reciprocity. But do people anywhere in the world really obey the law only because of publicity? One would have thought that Malinowski, inadequate as we have shown his theory of reciprocity to be, offers us a more rational explanation of the curious phenomenon of obedience to law than does his critic.

One scholar has made the interesting suggestion that the gist of the argument advanced by Malinowski in his book can be

summarised in these few words : ' Put shortly,' Dr. Mair wrote,
' a man obeys the rules of the society in which he lives, partly
because he has been brought up to take them for granted, partly
because, in the main, obedience pays.' [1] If only on account of
the succinctness of this epitome of the often provocative ideas
of Malinowski, the pupil is certainly clearer than her mentor.
Another Malinowskian, T. M. Culwick, has set out his own ideas
on sanction at somewhat greater length.   Thus he begins : [2] ' So
it is that we find a man's fulfilment of customary duties, so far
from being either automatic and unconstrained or induced by
purely supernatural sanctions, is clearly forced on him from without by sanctions inherent in the system of mutual rights and
obligations in his group.'   But he adds that the respect paid so
readily on all hands to the fulfilment of these obligations is
induced by fear—' this fear of hunger and misery is, we find on
examination, harnessed by society to compel respect for obligations '.   Thus we have a new interpretation of the idea of fear
as a legal sanction : it is no longer the fear induced by the possibility of punishment inflicted by the State or by supernatural
authority ; it is the fear, generated by economic necessity, of
being ' left out ', so to speak.   This, he says, is particularly true
of law in a closely-knit group ; but, as society advances, new
economic conditions weaken group solidarity, thereby strengthen-
ing the economic liberty of the individual.   He, then, arrives at
this further idea : ' . . . the effective sanctions of the tribal
code are *economic*, though it would appear that this is not always
the case ; e.g. in South Africa where powerful social sanctions
are said to operate against premarital pregnancy.   The truth is,
no doubt, that in every tribe both types of sanction are present but
their relative prominence varies.   In any case, it is only to be
expected that new developments in the economic life of the tribe
should have important consequences in its social life.' [3]   If we
like, we may say that all this is Malinowskian.   But we have to
admit that Culwick goes further than Malinowski in that his
economic evaluation of the role of sanction is not based on
reciprocity as such, but on the phased unfolding of the social
pattern of a given community, and the response that its members

[1] *Native Policies in Africa*, p. 271.
[2] At p. 30 of his monograph, *Good Out of Africa*.
[3] *Ibid.*, pp. 21–2.

are called upon to make to the recurrent problems of adjustment. But fear, as an underlying factor in the maintenance of mutual rights and obligations, is too simple as a legal sanction, and it is not rendered any the less so whether it is treated as a psychic, a psychological, or even an economic, phenomenon.

We, therefore, consider fear an inadequate explanation of why law is obeyed, and it does not matter whether the type of fear we have in mind is one of punishment, ridicule, ostracism or economic exclusion. We consider publicity, reciprocity or systematic incidence as equally barren of results in the maintenance of the social order. Collective responsibility, like automatic submission, is essentially a fallacy, the product of malobservation of the actual functioning of law in so-called ' primitive ' societies. Religious and magical sanctions play a disporportionately smaller role in securing compliance with rules of established law than their advocates would have us believe. Nor can we agree that law is obeyed on the grounds, in descending order, of indolence, deference, sympathy, fear, reason and innate desire for order, although they together constitute a formidable arcanum of sanctions. Finally, the imperative theory of law regards the use of force as part and parcel of the mechanism of ensuring obedience. Only societies possessing institutionalised courts, police, and prison-houses would qualify for these Austinian assignments, so inevitably bound up with a view of law as the command of a political sovereign.

We cannot accept the doctrine that obedience to law is the result of fear induced by the psychological pressure of force. This is not because African societies have nothing comparable to offer in the way of organised force as a means of law enforcement. In this connection we may add that Driberg, in the article already considered, also lists instances of unclassified sanctions. On the analogy, no doubt, of the established agencies of law enforcement in Western societies, he searches for similar mechanisms in African societies and soon finds these in many places. He observes [1] that, in West Africa, secret societies like the Oro and the Ekemeku, operate as sanctions for the observance of the law, that they are police societies acting as guardians of public morals and punishing offenders, and that in them he finds the nearest approach to the English system of punitive

[1] At pp. 237 ff. (See the citation given earlier at p. 64 n. 2.)

justice.[1]   Also, the Komo society among the Bambara exists for
social protection, punishing murderers, thieves or other wrong-
doers. So, too, the Ngi (gorilla) society among the Fang executes
the practitioners of black magic, besides punishing other evil-doers.
Driberg argues that ' these are really special tribunals of tribal
justice, carrying the sanctions of tribal law, and should not
be confused with the tribal associations . . . which dispense
associational laws to their members only : these societies, being
limited in membership, are in a sense extra-legal and should
only be considered as one of the sanctions of public law.' The
Poro society, probably the oldest in Africa, is ' the sanction for
all tribal institutions and is the apotheosis of their legal concepts.'
To the same category must belong the age-grade association of
Uke Ekpe [2] in Eastern Nigeria or the Ogboni societies [3] among the
Yoruba of Western Nigeria on the *judicial* side of their functions.[4]
Other instances of law-enforcement mechanisms exist in societies
with a centralised political authority, a super-ordinate, military
organisation and an administrative machinery. It is known, also,
that even those societies which are merely segmentary, atomistic
and politically unorganised communities have their own effective
arrangements for enforcing compliance with law. For example,
Miss Green has described [5] various ways in which pressure is
exerted by organised groups within the community to secure
obedience to law. She concludes : ' Among the Ibo penal
sanctions certainly exist.'

We have followed Driberg's excursions into all these agencies

[1] For some of the judicial uses to which these societies are put, see
pp. 212–222, ff. 262–7, *infra*.
[2] This is an age-set association of youths among the Afikpo people
of Eastern Nigeria, members of which perform such local police duties
as are delegated to them from time to time by the adjudicating elders
of the community—See S. Ottenberg's article, ' The Development of
Village " Meetings " among the Afikpo People ', in the *West African
Institute of Social and Economic Research* (*Conference Report*), March,
1953, at pp. 187–9.
[3] See, further, pp. 197–8, 216, 227–8, 266–7, *infra*.
[4] Incidentally, we may note that the Mau Mau, currently active in
Kenya (East Africa), is not an indigenous African ' secret ' society for
the maintenance of the legal order, but a political *movement* of recent
origin—see, e.g. Dr. L. S. B. Leakey's *Mau Mau and the Kikuyu* (1952) ;
also, Cmd. 9081 : Report to the Secretary of State for the Colonies
by the Parliamentary Delegation to Kenya, Jan. 1954, London, H.M.S.O.
[5] See her *Ibo Village Affairs*, pp. 79 ff., about Umu-Eke Agbaja, a
community of some 300 to 400 people.

of legal coercion, not because we agree with him that they are absolutely necessary to ensure obedience to law in African or any other society, but because we see in the mere statement of their existence in the present context a refutation of the fallacy that all sanctions are religious or that African law is entirely innocent of law-enforcement machinery in the Western sense.

There is a real element of truth in this observation of Hone : ' Ultimately the sanction for the enforcement of all laws is the consent of the people and the rate of development of any judicial system depends in the last extreme on the force of public opinion. But there are other factors which, though not perhaps in themselves of permanent and lasting force, give an impetus to development on the lines of natural justice and as such have a permanent and lasting value.' [1]

And against taking too sanguine a view of legal sanctions which might possibly deny that there are in fact effective sanctions in African customary law, we would do well to bear in mind this *caveat* of no less a jurist than the late Sir Frederick Pollock : ' Now what is felt to be wrong is felt to call for redress. This may be direct or indirect, swift or tardy ; but in the mere sense and apprehension of redress to come, however uncertain the manner of it may be, we have already some kind of sanction, and not the less a sanction because its effect may be precarious.' [2]

[1] H. R. Hone, ' The Native of Uganda and the Criminal Law ', in *Uganda Journal*, Vol. 6, No. 1, July, 1938, p. 7.
[2] *A First Book of Jurisprudence*, p. 26.

CHAPTER VI

STATUS AND THE INDIVIDUAL

A. GENERAL INTRODUCTION

THE role of the individual in a given society depends in the last resort upon his place in it. How he fits into that place is largely conditioned by the nature of the particular society. As a matter of legal theory the reason why it is important to determine the exact position of the individual in the social structure is that only by it can we assess the extent of his rights and duties, the range of social activities in which he may or must participate, and his opportunities for personal differentiation within his community.

Our concern here is mainly with those legal aspects of his social relations which affect his acts or omissions with regard to all others within his universe of daily activity. On what the exact criteria should be for determining whether or not an individual belongs to a group or class with limited rights and duties within a given community, jurists are still in dispute. Various attempts have been made by writers on jurisprudence to define the term ' status ' for legal purposes, but a satisfactory formula has yet to be devised. The trouble is that ' status ' is a word which has no very precise connotation.

Thus, with respect to English law, John Austin argues [1] that the term cannot be used with exactness, but says that ' where a set of rights and duties, capacities and incapacities, specially affecting a narrow class of persons, is detached from the bulk of the legal system, and placed under a separate head for the convenience of exposition, that set of rights and duties, capacities and incapacities, is called a status '. This implies that the grouping together of those persons who are said to have a status is a mere classificatory device of the law—which is true enough as a generalisation but which does not define how narrow the class must be or in what the rights and duties, capacities and incapacities must really consist.

[1] In his ' Lectures on Jurisprudence ' (ed. Campbell), Lects. XL–XLIV, particularly at pp. 699–700 and 710.

Salmond, finding Austin's formula too vague, proposes[1] the following four alternative meanings of status :

(a) legal condition of any kind, whether personal or proprietary ;

(b) personal legal condition, excluding proprietary relations ;

(c) personal capacities and incapacities, as opposed to other elements of personal status ;

(d) compulsory as opposed to conventional legal position.

Because all this is hardly an improvement on Austin's definition, Allen suggests that status should be taken to mean ' the condition of belonging to a particular class of persons to whom the law assigns certain peculiar legal capacities or incapacities or both '.[2] Status may arise from a variety of conditions such as sex, minority, and marriage, all of which are bound up with the problem of the family. Mental or bodily defect such as insanity or congenital idiocy may occasion legal incapacities or privileges, as may membership of a caste, profession or official rank. Criminality may curtail or destroy personal liberty, and bankruptcy may divest of property. Also, foreign nationality, race, or colour (where these exist) may cause the law to distinguish a group. It is therefore clear, says Allen, that status is not merely a basis for legal classification, but a matter of great political, legal and social importance.

Paton has recently offered[3] the following commentary on Allen's analysis : Firstly, status arises from membership of a class whose powers are determined extrinsically by law, rather than by agreement between the members. No member can vary the conditions thus imposed by the law ; for instance, the status of marriage is conclusively fixed beforehand by the law and cannot be varied by either party to the marriage.

Secondly, although an infant cannot choose whether or not to enter the status of infancy, it is nevertheless not always true that the membership of a status class is necessarily forced upon the individuals affected. Thus a mortgagor defines for himself his own rights and duties vis-à-vis the mortgagee and other persons interested in the mortgaged property. He may and often

[1] *Jurisprudence* (9th edn.), pp. 323-8.

[2] *Legal Duties*, p. 42 ; see also pp. 32-3, where Salmond's views are also criticised. Allen's admirable discussion of the whole subject will b found at pp. 28-47

[3] See his *A Textbook of Jurisprudence*, pp. 256-7.

does understand those rights imperfectly, but he must be presumed to know and to choose the legal consequences which flow from his act of agreement.   Also, a girl cannot be forced into the status of matrimony against her will ; but if she does marry, certain legal incidents attach to the marital status which do not depend upon the will of either party.   Thus, she becomes immune from actions in tort brought against her by her husband : she has a claim to support from her husband, and in cases of necessity a power to pledge his credit.   The status of marriage cannot be ended merely by the wish of the parties.   Graveson suggests [1] that the will of the party may affect the beginning or the end of status, but never both.   Marriage illustrates freedom at the beginning, and the control of law at the dissolution, of the status. An ambassador can be made such only by act of the State, but presumably he can destroy his status by resignation.

Thirdly, Maine's argument that status normally arises nowadays because of a defect in judgment of the members of a status class is, however, not universally true.   It is not the desire to protect certain classes against their own weaknesses that determines their being given special treatment in modern legal systems. Thus, the law of every sovereign State gives a special status to ambassadors, not because they suffer from occasional defects of judgment, but for the better promotion of international comity.

Fourthly, membership of a status does not always result in restricted power.   Thus, while in the case of an infant or a lunatic, legal power is restricted, in that of an ambassador (for example) additional privileges are normally conferred.   It is,

[1] See his article ' The Movement from Status to Contract ' in *Modern Law Review* (1941), p. 261 ; also *Status in the Common Law*, pp. 128–36. The learned author's definition of status, at p. 2, is :

' A special condition of a continuous and institutional nature, differing from the legal position of the normal person, which is conferred by law and not purely by the act of the parties, whenever a person occupies a position of which the creation, continuance or relinquishment, and the incidents are a matter of sufficient social or public concern.'

Most of the difficulties about this definition are, however, implied in the explanation of the expression ' the normal person ' which the author himself immediately proceeds to give (pp. 2–3).   But one serious point of weakness in it is the failure to indicate the sufficiency or otherwise of the ' social or public concern ' that should mark off a status condition from other conditions.   This weakness, it may be pointed out with respect, is of the same order as Austin's failure to define the narrowness of the class or indicate in what the ' rights and duties, capacities and incapacities ' must consist (see p. 76, *supra*).

therefore, incorrect to imagine that only incapacities attach to status.

Fifthly, not all group membership gives rise to a status. Status arising from membership of a group inevitably affects a member's legal relations, or at least his power to enter into legal relations. There is no status of the blue-eyed or of bridge-players, for although both of these groups may be regarded as forming a class, that class has no precise legal significance. Paton suggests that the test is that status is a condition which affects generally, although in varying degrees, a person's claims, liberties, powers and immunities; e.g. in the case of a trustee, certain powers relating to the trust property are granted to him while duties are owed by him to the beneficiaries of the trust. We cannot, however, infer any special status from this fact of trustee-ship, since it does not at all affect the trustee's general legal relations.

On the other hand, when we speak of the status of infancy, we at once imply an absence of legal capacity which is not limited to one act in the law but extends to all his legal relationships with others generally.

Holland therefore asks : [1] ' Does the peculiarity of the personality arise from anything unconnected with the nature of the act itself which the person of inherence can enforce against the person of incidence ? ' If I am a mortgagee or a trustee of one particular transaction my other legal relations are unaffected. But if I am a lunatic so found, my power is gone and I cannot for the duration of the lunacy exercise any legal powers.

A very useful point made by Allen in his analysis of status, is his insistence that ' there is a clear distinction between capacity to acquire and exercise rights, and the rights which are exercised '.[2] Status is a *condition*, while capacity is a *power*. Allen accordingly emphasises : ' We must, then, distinguish three quite different things : *Status*, the condition which gives rise to certain capacities or incapacities or both; *Capacity*, the power to acquire and exercise rights; and the *Rights* themselves which are acquired by the exercise of capacity.' [3] Paton's own conclusion is : ' Using the terminology of Hohfeld, we would say that status is the condition of being a member of a particular group, which membership

---

[1] *Jurisprudence* (13th edn.), p. 143.
[2] *Legal Duties*, p. 46.　　　　　[3] *Ibid.*, p. 47.

affects generally claims, liberties, powers and immunities.' But even this does not solve our problem.

One of Sir Henry Maine's famous generalisations is : ' If then we employ status, agreeably with the usage of the best writers, to signify these personal conditions only, and avoid applying them to such conditions as are the immediate or remote result of agreement, we may say that the movement of the progressive societies has hitherto been a movement *from Status to Contract*.' [1] The four words in this statement that call for special comment are ' progressive ', ' hitherto ', ' status ' and ' contract '.

The application of the epithet ' progressive ' to societies in this context implies that there are those that are static, either because they lack the intrinsic quality essential for change or because they have generally remained unaffected by any extrinsic factors. Now, African societies, to the extent to which modern research has revealed their known character, are anything but static. It is true that the tempo of social change is slower in some African societies than in others, and that most of them have managed somehow to preserve the outward mechanisms of their social structure all through the ages. But this does not mean that *within* the societies themselves there has not always been a good deal of dynamism, making for change in interpersonal relationships no less than in inter-group contacts. We may therefore say that, if it were really the case that a human society could be regarded as eternally the same and unchanging, at least African societies exhibit all the marks of ' progressive ' societies as conceived by Maine.

When the great jurist framed his formula about the social progression from status to contract, he was careful to insert as a limiting factor the word ' hitherto ', although his followers have tended to assume that the statement without any such qualification has a universal validity. Basing himself on his study of Indian village communities and his researches into Roman and Greek societies, Maine saw [2] the gradual unfolding of the human spirit from the thraldom of tribe or group into the condition of a free-willing individual uninhibited by ties of kinship or group. The evolution of the law concerning the rights of the married woman shows a movement from status to contract, as does the

[1] *Ancient Law*, p. 174.
[2] *Ancient Law*, pp. 172 ff.

comparative freedom of modern man in contrast with the bondage of early man.

But it must have been apparent to Maine even in his own day that, because it became necessary to restrict freedom of contract in order to give real freedom to economically weaker classes, dialectical developments from contract back to status had set in in various departments of life : new relationships were already forming between landlords and tenants, mortgagors and mortgagees, employers and employees, and similar opposing groups members of each one of which look upon those of the other as belonging to new classes based upon status.[1] These are in essence the old medieval relationships between lords of the manor and their villeins, lenders and borrowers, owners of industries and their workers—all in new guises. The Industrial Revolution, while breaking down still further what Renaissance humanism left of the feudal organisation of society, created in its turn new but parallel social classes grouped around the opposing interests brought into being by this industrial civilisation.

It would, therefore, seem that status will always be with us. There is no doubt that the various communities of miners, factory workers and industrialists are not water-tight and that the individual members of any of them are in theory free to move from one community to another, but we also know that in practice the prospects for such movement are often dim. For a variety of reasons a miner's son, for example, who would become a lawyer without external aid must be prepared to face an uphill task indeed. The stratification of society into more or less organised classes seems to have been an inevitable feature of human existence throughout the ages, although the basis of the division has neither been constant nor the same at all times and in all places.

Maine also contends that ' ancient ' law is a jurisprudence of personal inequalities. In early societies, a man's whole legal position depends on whether he is bond or free, native or foreign, child or parent, male or female ; and these tests of legal standing are clearly matters which the individual does not decide for himself—they are accidents of birth and circumstance. The law

[1] But this use of the word ' status ' is true only in a loose sense, since membership of each of the opposing classes still leaves the individuals free in other respects.

has abolished many of the lower grades of society, and the tendency is to confine the creation of status to those cases where there is special justification. What were once the lower ranks begin to enjoy many of the privileges of their ' betters '. Nevertheless, as we have shown above, age, sex, and alienage are still indicia of status in ancient as in modern societies.

B.   STATUS IN AFRICAN LAW

1. *Group Status.*

When we come to consider the African situation, what do we find ? We are at once confronted with the popular fallacy that all members of a given African society, without exception, belong to one status only—the one generic status of the clan or tribe. Thus Hartland wrote : ' The unit is not the individual, but the kin. The individual is but part of the kin.' While this may be the broad social picture presented to the observer by the interplay of co-ordinate groups within the tribe or State, it fails as a theory of the legal unity of the clan. The trouble is that the myth of kinship communism, while making such great play of the ' pervading group-sentiment, if not group-instinct ', does not pierce the veil of clan corporateness in order to discover the tensions, the personal jealousies and rivalries, as well as the individual self-assertions that go on *within* the group itself. Anyone who cares to look into the actual social relations between the individuals who make up the group—whether this is family, clan or tribe—will realise soon enough that disputes do take place in all manner of situations.[1] For instance, the clothes of one individual are sometimes unlawfully worn or torn by another of the group ; hoes and cutlasses, bows and arrows, spears and traps, fishing rods and fishing baskets are freely borrowed by one individual from another and are sometimes returned damaged or never returned at all ; A may grab a portion or the whole of B's allotment in the family or clan holding : in all these constant inter-actions of social and economic forces within the group, the headman performs the function of ' guide, philosopher and friend ', and compensations and penalties are exacted and paid just as much as the Chief or council of elders deal with inter-

---

[1] Malinowski also made this point at p. 48 of his *Crime and Custom in Savage Society.*

group disputes, or even those intra-group ones in which the headman's decision is impugned by a member on the ground of partiality, or again those involving any two or more important personalities in the community.

This internal judicial administration accounts for the apparent placidity of clan organisation and the seeming solidarity of its members in relation to other groups. It is probably true to say that the ascription of unity to a clan is only valid as a fiction adopted by its members as a defence mechanism in the external relations of the clan to others in the community.[1] It is rather like the unity often claimed nowadays by a political party or even a State *vis-à-vis* other parties or States, though these are naturally on a much larger scale and with a more impersonal dependence.

2. *Primitive Communism.*

The individual certainly has fairly well-defined rights and duties within his group. It is true that land is held, not by the individual as in Western societies, but by a group, the family being almost invariably the unit of land-holding. But a close study of the actual arrangement within the family shows that there are specific assignments of plots to all the individual members of it who are old and able enough usefully to exploit the resources of the soil, or who have reached an age to claim a portion of the family house to live in, or of family land on which to build their house or hut. Such a portion of the house or land once allocated is always transmissible to the descendants of the original allottee *ad infinitum* and can be put to any kind of use which is compatible with the requirements of good house management or good husbandry. The only serious restriction is that land is inalienable by any individual member of the owning family unless (1) the prior consent of the family has been obtained thereto, or (2) the land has been partitioned among all the members entitled thereto and the individual is merely disposing of his own portion. With these two provisos, then, the individual is quite free to do what he likes with his own.[2]

Similarly, careful analysis of the rights of the individual in the products of the soil cultivated by the family group or the

[1] See, generally, Ch. X, later.
[2] This point is further elaborated in Ch. IX, *infra*.

catch from co-operative fishing discloses that his is not the case of someone without definite claims upon or mutual obligations towards the other members of the group. In most cases the proceeds of the common effort are shared among the participants according to individual deserts or by mutual agreement and, even when the necessity arises for garnering a fixed surplus as provision against a rainy day, the respective rights and obligations of members attach to it until ultimate distribution. If the products are sold all those who have contributed labour towards their provenance are entitled to share in the sale price.[1]

The head *as head*, whether of the family or of the co-operative group, may be allowed an extra portion for his additional responsibilities towards the younger members of the family, or on account of capital or labour contributed by him over and above that contributed by the others. But in no case is the individual treated as an unknown quantity who merely gives his labour to the group and thereafter remains entirely at its mercy in the matter of subsequent disposal.

The bargaining powers of the individual naturally increase as the co-operative unit moves away from a kinship basis towards a territorial alliance based on purely social and economic, non-kinship association. The rights and duties of the individuals within the family or clan are, by the inevitable economic and kinship ties, naturally more circumscribed than are those of party members or State nationals considered as individuals. Even in African societies these individual rights and duties vary with the type of social organisation and the degree of cohesion already achieved. Thus, kinship as a bond of social cohesion is more powerful in any society that lacks a developed political organisation than it is in one less heterogeneous or atomistic. Family and, to a greater extent, clan ties weaken as the blood span spreads out and group solidarity becomes of less account in the normal life of the members. The degree of interdependence of members depends, after all, upon the intensity of social relations, and these obviously vary in different societies no less than in the diverse organisations of the family, clan, or tribe. This is where Durkheim falls into serious error when he dogmatises [2] that intensity of social relations grows more and more as the

---

[1] This point is further elaborated in Ch. IX, *infra*.
[2] See E. Durkheim, *De la Division du Travail Social*.

group expands. He fails to appreciate the sociological fact that with the increasing social integration of the disparate clans or other kinship groups, there gradually develops a wide tribal loyalty or even national solidarity in place of the narrow one of the clan. In the end, tribal or national unity triumphs over the erstwhile unity of the clan. The family becomes absorbed into the clan which itself forms one of the aggregates making up the community ; the community finally turns into a society, which is just the name we give to the group of individuals with the least intensity of personal relations, that is, in which kinship ties are weakest and social and political solidarities are strongest.

Thus it is that in African societies which have achieved strong centralised political organisations, kinship affiliations are generally limited more or less to autonomous families made up of very close blood members. These acknowledge the usual economic and social obligations towards only the restricted few within their own immediate families and, often towards only their full brothers and sisters and their parents. In other types of African society with no highly organised social groupings, kinship plays an important, though not the only, part in human relations. The individual's behaviour is largely affected by his place in the kin-group, more so than in other forms of human association. But the group is not an independent self-contained unit ; rather it is made up of individuals who often re-act upon it and even sometimes change its character. Besides, there does not seem to exist in any known human society simply ' the ' group, but always a multiplicity of groups, the individual being a member whose rights and duties within such groups naturally differ according to the type of group.

In any group, however, psychological differences are sure to lead to inevitable differences in social valuations so that the group becomes an aggregate of individuals and not, as the doctrine of group solidarity would have us believe, a mere agglomeration of undifferentiated automata. As Marrett points out,[1] Morgan's discovery of the classificatory system of relationships, though useful in providing a clue to the study of the more rudimentary types of social organisation, yet tends to ' bring all those to whom the same relational term applies into one unwavering

[1] R. R. Marrett, ' The Individual in Primitive Society ', an essay in a book entitled *The Individual in East and West*, (ed. E. R. Hughes).

G

line as regards their rights and duties in regard to the remaining categories. As a matter of fact, however, a man not only knows his own mother apart from his merely tribal mothers, but treats her quite differently.' The admission by a clan member of the *sociological* paternity or fraternity of certain of his fellow-members does not mean that he equates either of these with the *physiological*, to which alone he feels immediately bound socially and economically.[1]

In conclusion, we may note that the theory of unity of the clan is further vitiated by such important factors as the following :

(1) It is necessary to bear in mind that there are few African communities that can claim tribal purity or homogeneity. Most tribes are in varying degrees heterogeneous : for example, war captives are being continually absorbed into the conquering tribe, and exogamous marriages usually imply the admixture with indigenous stock of foreign strains through women married from other clans or tribes.

(2) Inter-tribal economic co-operation in the form of trade or a joint enterprise like hunting may involve the individual in a new type of economic dependence which cuts across not only family or clan autonomy but also tribal exclusiveness.

(3) Again, puberty initiation rites tend almost invariably to aggregate the individual to wider groupings than those based purely on kinship ties of family or clan. This often results in stronger bonds of loyalty and therefore of disposition to help an associate at need. Age-grade associations, warrior classes, social clubs, secret societies—all these and more play their by no means insignificant part in increasing the range and widening the boundaries of the social and economic interests of the individual beyond the restricted ones of the family or the clan.

It is not unknown for secret societies and other large associations to operate over a number of unrelated neighbouring tribes, with the mutual adoption of one another's customs and the consequent forging of strong links of social and economic interdependence and of inter-tribal solidarity. According to Beaufaict, formerly hostile tribes like the Ababua, Abarambo, Mangbettu and the Azande formed associations known as the Nebeli and Ngobo Societies which, by bringing them into frequent contact with one another, succeeded in welding them together.

(4) Since the compelling reason for the normal closeness of

[1] Further developed in Ch. X, *infra*.

kinship groups is the economic dependence of the individual upon his family—joint exploitation of the family land until partition, joint rearing of the family herds of cattle, etc.—it follows that the marriage of a member and the new responsibilities of raising his own family all too often effect a loosening of the former blood bonds, and consequently of the claims of his relatives upon him for the usual economic help. It is also at this stage in his development that his orientation to wider social alignments impels his estrangement from the blood group.

Perhaps it should be emphasised here, if any emphasis were needed, that there is no legal restriction on the absolute liberty of the individual member of a family to set up house on his own as soon as he is old enough for it, or to join any association he likes so long as he complies with the relevant formalities.

Before we go on to examine the status of the individual, we may here touch briefly on another important aspect of the conception that only the group has status in African society, that clan unity is everywhere triumphant.

3. *Collective Responsibility.*

Arising out of the idea that the individual is merged in his group is the theory that the latter is collectively responsible for his offences against outsiders. The group pays all compensations for his private wrongs and answers for all his public offences. Such is the principle of group solidarity, according to this view, that a crime committed by one member of the group against another is no concern of anyone else but the group. Some say that in such a case the offender goes unpunished since it is hardly to be expected that the group would fine itself in order to appease itself. Others believe that the group would itself punish the offending member by expulsion from the group, which would mean that he thereby might be treated as an outlaw, as outside the pale of group protection and therefore anybody's meat. If killed thereafter by someone else his group would take no action either of revenge or of composition of a possible feud between his own group and that of his killer by the payment of *wergild*. It is said that in certain cases, the group itself gets rid of a persistently criminal member by expulsion or otherwise, as he is then considered a liability rather than an asset to the clan or family inheritance.

Durkheim is certain that all legal reactions like group responsibility or revenge are founded in the psychology of the group and not in that of the individual, who is a mere unit of the group whole.[1] From this has been deduced the further idea that when, for example, a member X of group A is killed by a member Y of group B, the whole of group A troop out to avenge X's death by killing in reprisal any member Z of group B if Y cannot be got hold of. Sometimes, group A may accept compensation in the nature of cattle or other forms of tribal currency ; at other times, member Y or another member Z is merely seized into group A as a substitute for the unfortunate victim X. Since social equilibrium is restored by such mechanical adjustment of the loss of one economic unit by its replacement by another or, in the case where the murderer or his group-member is killed in revenge, by the mutual diminution of both groups, there is nothing more to be done. If we may so express it, it is all a question of Group $A - X =$ Group $B - (Y$ or $Z)$, or Group $A + (Y$ or $Z) =$ Group $B - (Y$ or $Z)$. But either equation would be false as an explanation of the process of restoring the social equilibrium of the given community, not only because Group A is not necessarily always equivalent in quantity to Group B but also because even if cattle are substituted for X, Y or Z, the punishment does not fit the crime and this is bound to disturb the social equilibrium.

Apparently, this theory of group collectivity implies also that the process of redressing the balance is the same whether it is private wrongs (i.e. purely civil offences) or public wrongs (i.e. criminal offences) that are in question. So that if Y in the above illustration breaks X's borrowed hoe or fishing rod instead of killing X, the whole of Group A must at once engage in a free vendetta to secure just reparation from Group B or any of its available members. Of course, we know that this is not so. We need not go into all the other interesting ramifications often claimed for the doctrine of group responsibility. But what are the facts ?

Now, the so-called ' unity of the clan ' is an inaccurate description when used to explain why the clan pays for the wrong-doing of one of its members. As we have shown earlier, the paying group, where the group pays at all, is rarely larger than the

[1] E. Durkheim, *L'Année Sociologique*, I, pp. 353 ff.

family or occasionally the extended family of the offender; it never embraces all the hundreds or thousands with more or less tenuous blood relationships to the wrong-doer. It is true that a distant member, perhaps a wealthy cousin 'to the fortieth remove' of the offender, may sometimes offer to pay part or all of the latter's fine imposed by the court; but so may any unrelated but sympathetic neighbour of the offender's group. In most, if not all, African societies, playing the role of 'a good neighbour'—the good Samaritan—is a virtue highly valued and generally expected of the more fortunate members of the community, in times of stress or emergency, towards the less fortunate. Blood relations of the offender obviously feel a higher moral obligation to help their kin.

In all these cases of so-called group responsibility, the *legal liability* is without question that of the offending individual alone, but the discharge of that liability is very often the concern of all those close relatives of his whom local opinion regards as *morally* bound to succour him.[1] To this there are at least two exceptions, when there is a legal duty on the relatives to come to an offender's rescue: (1) The first is where the relative is father of or is otherwise *in loco parentis* to the offender who is yet a minor or a weakling for whose good behaviour the former is ordinarily responsible; (2) The second exception occurs if the offender has rendered services to the relative or the group of relatives now called upon to answer for his misdeeds, or if he has a recognised claim of right to contribution from or indemnity by the relative or the other members of the group. The basis of such a right is economic, and is usually the result of joint enterprise or co-operative labour activities carried on by the family or other social group as a scheme of social insurance. While parental obligation to answer for the 'debts, defaults or miscarriage' of a dependant is generally unlimited, the amount of contribution or indemnity to which the offender is entitled under the second head of exception tends to be proportional to the amount of his own just share of the common pool, unless indeed the others loyally concede to him more than his deserts. With regard to these two heads of exceptions, then, the foregoing analysis shows that the *primary* liability is that of the offender while the *secondary* liability is that of the parent or the group. This secondary

---

[1] See on this point what is said later at pp. 137 ff.

liability is of course a *vicarious* one.   In all other cases, the *legal* liability is that of the wrong-doer, although the *moral* responsibility to see that liability discharged is almost invariably that of the group.

What we have so far been considering concerns all private wrongs as well as such public wrongs as are susceptible of reparation in cash or in kind.   Where the penalty for an offender's public wrong is death, mutilation or any other corporal punishment, even the protagonists of the theory of group responsibility agree that the first and only person subject to the particular punishment is the criminal himself.   Only if he is unavailable either because his kin are hiding him and will not surrender him on demand, or because they have helped him to escape or again because the offender is party to a conspiracy for the commission of the crime alleged, is someone else, believed to be actively associated with the criminal or the crime, seized and punished instead.   Anyone who has reason to fear his being seized for another's offence has the legal right to seek asylum in one of the public sanctuaries or in a chief's palace until the proper determination of the issue.[1]   The choice of who is to pay for a crime in default of the actual criminal is thus seen to be not as arbitrary as is commonly alleged by lay observers.   It is precisely because those exacting the particular form of penalty follow some clearly accepted channels that vendettas are so comparatively rare on such occasions.[2]   And when the offender's group take the punishment appropriately inflicted by the other side without any retaliation, this is instantly acclaimed by the advocates of

[1] Thus, C. Dundas wrote of certain East African peoples that blood revenge was usually ' directed against the murderer or some near relative ', and that sanctuary was provided for the murderer who sought refuge with the chief to avoid blood revenge.   Blood revenge was restricted to the slaying of one person, but it naturally tends to further reprisals, and so to feuds or open warfare, which was not to the interest of the chief, sultan, or king, who thereby lost subjects, and consequently intervened.   And the degree to which such intervention was effectual was according to the power of these supreme authorities.   (See p. 236 of the *Jnl. Roy. Afr. Inst.*, Vol. 51 (1921), pp. 217–78, an article entitled ' Native Laws of Some Bantu Tribes of East Africa ').

[2] This is not to deny the incidence of feuds between some clans or tribes, or of the attempts often made to pay off old scores, sometimes after a long distance of time from that of the original offence.   It is only to emphasise that the incidence of feuds is strictly outside the sphere of law.

group solidarity as an illustration of the automatic operation of custom.

Both the civil and the criminal aspects of collective responsibility may be paralleled by analogous concepts of English law. Thus, to take random illustrations in English civil law, it is clear law that a master or employer is vicariously liable for all the wrongs committed by his servant or employee in the course of the latter's employment; an employer of an independent contractor is vicariously liable for the latter's wrongs to third parties while carrying out very hazardous activities; while only the father or legal guardian of a child under 21 can be sued for the latter's torts and contracts for 'necessaries'. In all these instances, the offender is also liable, of course. As for crimes one naturally recalls the medieval English law of *frankpledge* which, because of the lack of any organised police, was 'a system by which all free men of a tithing were responsible for the general good behaviour of its members'. But a closer parallel is afforded by the modern English rules governing the liability of 'parties to a crime'. These are four in number: (1) Accessories before the fact; (2) Accessories after the fact; (3) Principal in the first degree; and (4) Principal in the second degree. The first category means all those who counsel, procure or instigate the commission of the crime; the second, all those knowing that a crime has been committed, help the criminal to escape or aid and succour him—this class is to be distinguished, by the way, from another class of ancillary offenders who are liable to quite often heavy penalties for what is technically known as 'misprision of felony', i.e. knowing of the commission of a crime by another and omitting to report it;[1] the third category describes the actual perpetrators of the crime and they are of course liable as such; the fourth category comprises those who aid and abet the criminal in the act of committing the offence alleged. In heinous crimes called 'felonies', all four types are punishable equally with the criminal: paradoxically enough, only the one considered most guilty among the escaping criminal's relations is normally punished in the African situation. In misdemeanours, i.e. lesser criminal offences, the punishment varies according to the category under which the participants come.

Enough has now been said to disprove the fallacy of unity of

[1] This is now an obsolete offence : see R. v. Aberg (1948), 1 A.E.R. 601.

the clan, primitive communism or group responsibility, at least
so far as African societies are concerned. Status does not attach
only to the group and the latter is not the unit-bearer of rights
and duties. The individual member of the group is, in the final
analysis, the prime actor although, as we have pointed out, he
is not as independent of his fellows as is his opposite number
in a non-collectivist Western society. To appreciate fully the
actual role of the individual in an African community, two further
misconceptions must be briefly examined :

4. The ' Sheep ' Theory.

An extreme view is reflected in the saying ' custom is king '.
While this may express the authority of customary law, it certainly cannot be taken to imply that the individual is a slave
of custom, that he is bogged down inexorably by kinship ties
of family, clan or tribe, or that he just follows the line of least
resistance—a blind worshipper of tradition, a gregarious member
of the tribal flock. Hartland, for example, was emphatic that
' he never seeks to break forth '.[1] To this classic expression of
a widely-held view, Marrett retorts : ' But, as Freud points out,
such tyrannous prohibitions (i.e. taboos) would be unnecessary,
were there not rebellious feelings to be crushed into submission.
On the contrary, let us pay due attention to the spiritual effort
needed on the part of each and all to maintain the social energy
at the required pitch. Thus, on the one hand, the gerontocracy,
or whatever other government is responsible for keeping order,
must be equal to the constant strain. To deny individuality to
the successful functionary would be to overlook the fact that the
good workman finds himself in the competent execution of his
job.' [2]

Culwick, in his usually forthright way, also warns : ' We find
the tribal code is the code of a closely-knit group. No one in
that group is in an economic position which renders him wholly
independent of the goodwill of his fellows : none can therefore
afford to forego his privileges by ignoring his obligations. At

[1] *Primitive Law*, p. 138. Cf. ' A primitive people, virtuous by rote
rather than by reason, followed unthinkingly that principle of " mutual
service " which Aristotle held to be the natural bond of a well-ordered
community '—K. J. Spalding in his article, ' A Chinese Aristotle ' in
The Individual in East and West, p. 65.

[2] *Op. cit.*, p. 22.

the same time, the fact that he is economically and socially bound to his fellows does not rob him of his individuality, his desire to evade irksome and unpleasant duties if he can, his natural preoccupation with the needs and desires of himself and his immediate family, let what will happen to others.'[1]

It is therefore clear that the theory of automatic submission to custom cannot hold simply because the African rates the immemorial rules of his society probably no higher than Edmund Burke rated the traditions of the English people and the sacrosanctity of immemorial usage.[2] The regularity and apparent passivity with which he observes the norms of social and political life must not be taken as an indication that he cannot or will not do otherwise. We have had occasion to take this point much further when we dealt with sanctions (or, Why Law is Obeyed).[3]

5. The ' Peacock ' Theory.

At the other extreme are those who from their practical knowledge of the real nature of African society are anxious to show that, far from being the docile, sheepish creature of popular imagination, the African individual is a real peacock. He is nothing if not boastful, arrogant and self-assertive. His aggressive, equalitarian attitude makes him impatient of authority, truculent and insubordinate. Let us hear Malinowski speak :

' Take the real savage, keen on evading his duties, swaggering and boastful when he has fulfilled them, and compare him with the anthropologist's dummy who slavishly follows custom and automatically obeys every regulation. There is not the remotest resemblance between the teachings of anthropology on this subject and the reality of native life.'[4]

[1] *Op. cit.*, p. 30.
[2] Notably in his *Thoughts on the Cause of the Present Discontents* and *Reflections on the Revolution in France*.
[3] See Ch. V, particularly pp. 63–5, 73–5.
[4] *Op. cit.*, p. 30. But Seagle (in his article ' Primitive Law and Professor Malinowski ' in *The American Anthropologist*, Vol. 39, Pt. II, pp. 275–90, 1937), complained that Malinowski ' completely misunderstands ' the dogma of the automatic submission to custom : ' All that the remarks as to the *automatic* force of custom imply is that somehow, marvellous to relate, the savage recognises the obligatory character of his customs although they are backed by no specific judicial sanctions of a repressive character as in civilised society. In this sense the custom of the savage is certainly automatic, and while he may behave as if he were its slave, he is not a slave who never revolts.'

Other writers have been even more trenchant in their language, citing instances of some individualist African communities as evidence of the peacock theory. If that were so, there should be perpetual conflict between such rugged individualists,[1] and any African community would be a veritable Bedlam. The evil, selfish nature of man so specially remarked upon by Hobbes in his epigram : *homo homini lupus* (i.e. man is a wolf to man) would be a perfect description of African societies. The leviathan would jostle his fellow tribesmen out of existence every time he felt the impulse to assert his prerogatives. But, alas for the prospect of peace among the protagonists of the peacock theory, such a pessimistic view of human nature stands contradicted by the realities of African society.[2]

In sum, the truth is that the African individual is neither a robot nor a peacock. He is, like any other of the human species, a social animal. In that respect he has his life to live among his immediate kith and kin no less than among the other members of his community. The range of his relationships, as of his obligations, will of course depend upon the social set-up, particularly on the degree of intensity obtaining within the group or community to which he happens to belong. Whatever the character of a given society may be, however, close and informed analysis will disclose that the several members retain their individualities to a greater extent than is usually realised.

Nor is it accurate to argue, as does a *third* school of thought, that only the eccentric in an African group can claim any individuality. We have seen that there is more scope for self-realisation for the individual than one is led to believe possible in a normal African society. But, seeing that the member's margin of safety is too narrow for abnormal egotism to be fashionable, it behoves the individual aspiring to high office or craving the esteem of his fellows to curb his personal idiosyncrasies if he is to have any chance of success. No doubt, as will be shown later, intellectual endowments and character and courage are highly prized

[1] Well might the unbridled individualist, like Edmund in Shakespeare's *King Lear*, question—

> *Wherefore should I*
> *Stand in the plague of custom?*

[2] ' The extreme individualism often found in primitive communities does not favour universal anarchy '—Lowie, *op. cit.*, p. 384.

in African society, since lack of these in persons normally entitled to offices like those of war-leaders, chiefs, and family-heads, is often a legitimate ground for passing them over in favour of others endowed with these qualities. But this is far from saying that the revered intellectual or warrior is erratic, any more than is the wealthy member who defies the usual norm of generosity to his fellows in their hour of need. Yet, the possession of brains, brawn or wealth is an index of individuality. The eccentric has no place in the ordinary scheme of things in an African, as in any other, society.

C. STATUS OF THE INDIVIDUAL

Having disposed of the fallacy that status attaches only to the clan or tribe, we may now examine the nature of the status which we claim for the individual.

Driberg's conception of status is that of a layman to whom everything pertaining to an African individual in his relation to society is a mark of status. Thus, he says :

' Every individual is born into a certain status relative to all other members of his community. It is not a personal status, as it might be in an individualistic society, and does not imply rank, but reciprocal obligations and benefits which he incurs as a member of the community. All his conduct is conditioned by his status, which is not a permanent one but changes with his age and experience and may be affected by the decease of relatives and the inheritance of new responsibilities. (The principle of substitution is a correlative to status, since all of the same status in the community may at any time be called upon to act as a substitute for another member, a principle which, as we shall see, is of considerable importance in African legal theory).' [1]

Four aspects of this statement deserve comment :

(a) That every African is born into a status : In saying this Driberg is being better than his own argument ; indeed, he is expressing a truism with even wider validity than he knew. In an African, as in the European or any other society that we know of, birth always determines status—for example, the status of being a British subject or a Bemba, a Yoruba or an Ashanti. In

[1] P. 232 of his article entitled ' African Conception of Law ' in the *Journal of Comparative Legislation and International Law*, Nov., 1934.

short, birth as a determinant of national status is a universal factor
and is accordingly not a peculiar feature of African society.

(*b*) That this status ' does not imply rank, but reciprocal
obligations and benefits which he incurs as a member of the community ' : The difficulty here is to know what meaning to give to
' rank' in the present context.   Rank as a result of social differentiation may in its literal sense be a mark of status, as showing the
stratification of society into distinct groups with special rights and
duties.   But mere membership of a community considered as a
community cannot, as Driberg implies here, confer a status upon
the individual, unless indeed one accepts the otiose theory of
group status implicit in the so-called unity of the clan.

Of course, the status of being ' a citizen of the British Empire
and Commonwealth ' comprehends the one hundred and twenty
million odd souls who live in Great Britain and the colonial territories.   But when we employ the word status in talking about
the individuals in each country we usually refer to a special legal
condition implying peculiar capacities and incapacities.   Austin,
it will be remembered, would ascribe status only to ' a narrow
class of persons ' detached from the bulk of the community and
endowed with special ' rights and duties, capacities and incapacities '.

Perhaps the most workmanlike view is that of Allen who
suggests that status is ' the condition of belonging to a particular
class of persons to whom the law assigns certain peculiar legal
capacities or incapacities or both.'   Thus, to be said to have
a status in the legal sense, an individual must belong to a special
class within the community ; he may but need not be placed in
that group by the law, although he must not be able both to
' contract in ' and to ' contract out ' at his own free will ; again,
while a special status may be conferred on mental defectives or
other incapacitated groups, it is not every group that enjoys a
status in law.

(*c*) That it is not a personal status but that it is nevertheless not
permanent in that it changes with the individual's age, experience
and personal condition : This, to say the least of it, implies a
contradiction in terms—the status is not personal but it changes
with the change in personal conditions.   Moreover, Driberg
seems here to be confusing status with prestige.

In all African societies with no strong centralised political systems as well as in some with such systems, the institution of age-grades has important juridical functions. The puberty initiation rites, for example, may be the means in some societies of determining the legal capacity of the individual to marry, to become a warrior or to take part in certain other public activities of a social or legal character. Sometimes these rites are merely preparatory to some later public ceremony or display of certain personal attributes as among the Masai and the Zulu, on the successful performance or display of which alone may depend the conferment of a status requisite to prescribed forms of social participation.

Similarly, membership of such public institutions as the Ogboni (Secret) Societies among the Yorubas or the Poro (Secret) Societies among the Mende can and does confer authority upon its members to act as State police in certain circumstances and as courts of trial in others. On the other hand, there are innumerable other social groups which have no institutionalised legal functions of any kind but which either confer mere prestige upon their members or exist only for their mutual benefit. These cannot confer any legal status on their members, although the courts will protect their ordinary rights if otherwise infringed.

(d) That ' the principle of substitution is a correlative to status, since all of the same status in the community may at any time be called upon to act as a substitute for another member ' : It does not seem quite clear what Driberg means by ' the principle of substitution '.

Firstly, it may mean the same thing as one aspect of the theory of the unity of the clan, whereby one member may be seized to answer for the default of another in relation to other clans. We have seen, however, that this is not a case of the simple substitution of one member for another.[1]

Secondly, it may mean the limited practice among some tribes, notably the Masai, by which a married member of an age-grade association may have sexual relations with an unrelated wife of another member of the same age-grade group.

Thirdly, it may mean the widely-prevalent practice in African societies according to which a member of a family or extended family who shows special aptitude in that capacity is deputed to act in law-suits in which other family members may happen to be

[1] See also pp. 87-92, *supra*.

involved from time to time. This champion-at-law, concerning whom we shall hear more in the chapter on the judicial process, is the African version of the modern British barrister-at-law or advocate. But, surely, one does not ordinarily conceive of such legal representation as ' a correlative to status ' ? And yet it seems that this is the real sense in which Driberg employs his principle of substitution, for he goes on a little later to give instances of this practice amongst the Mangbettu and the Chagga.[1]

We now see that neither the group nor just any individual of a community *ipso facto* enjoys a status in the strictly legal sense. In an African society, just as much as in an English one, the law makes certain arrangements for treating some groups differently from the rest of the community in the matter of rights and duties, capacities or incapacities or both, though the forms and rules of the particular arrangements are not the same in both societies. Thus English law gives a special status to the Sovereign, ambassadors, infants, lunatics, married women, aliens, convicts and others. In African law, the main categories we have to consider are kings and chiefs, women, infants, aliens, slaves, and castes.

1. *The King or Chief.*

It may at first seem that in societies with a hierarchical system of chieftaincy and particularly those in which there are kings at their heads, the rulers must necessarily be despots. The institution of kingship or chiefship is, except among certain tribes,[2] generally regarded as sacred in African society ;[3] but no holder of either office is in the political thinking of the people above the law on that account. He has no divine right to dispense and suspend the law of the tribe, although there have been tyrants who have sometimes set the law at naught. But, by and large, an African king or chief is in theory at least a constitutional ruler. Thus Dr. Mair wrote :

' In most indigenous African societies, in the specific case of obedience to political authority, there were on the one hand recognised limitations to the exercise of authority—for the " abso-

---

[1] *Journal of Comparative Legislation and International Law*, Nov., 1934, p. 232.

[2] E.g. the Olubadans among the Yorubas of Ibadan, Nigeria, have never been regarded as sacred ; also, the chiefly office among the Mendes of Sierra Leone has no sacred character.

[3] K. A. Busia, *The Role of the Chief in the Modern Political System of Ashanti.*

lute powers " of an African chief extended only to his personal relationships, not to interference with what was traditionally established as the normal conduct of life among his subjects and on the other recognised ways of expressing dissatisfaction. Thus, situations in which authority could become so oppressive that the advantages which it gave in the organisation of security, offensive warfare, justice, provision against famine, and the like, did not compensate for the toll demanded of the subject in tribute or services, were rare.' [1]

Certain well-defined prerogatives often attach to the kingly or chiefly office, since the proper and effective exercise of authority would be impossible without them in any human society with a system of monarchical rule. But the council of elders and notables acting as a kind of cabinet ensures that the king's doings do not run counter to accepted standards of propriety; and a king or chief, who exceeds his legitimate powers and proves unamenable to such discipline, may be deposed, or is sometimes asked to commit voluntary suicide, or is put to death by the unanimous verdict of public opinion.[2] In these cases, the council of elders or some powerful secret society made up of the chief's coevals often acts as a court of trial before his execution.

It may be added that any individual in the realm can aspire to the highest office that is not strictly hereditary. Members of the established ruling ' houses ' are normally entitled to become chiefs, local or paramount; and also, war-chieftaincies are often created for those deserving of public distinction but who are not of the ruling houses. Even slaves are known to have become war-chiefs in many communities.[3]

---

[1] L. P. Mair, *Native Policies in Africa*, p. 271 ; also her ' Chieftainship in Modern Africa ' in *Africa*, 1937, Vol. X.

Sjoerd Hofstra, in his ' Personality and Differentiation in the Political Life of the Mende ' in *Africa*, Vol. X, pp. 436–57, stressed that the chief's authority largely depended upon a genuine respect for and a sense of loyalty on the part of the subjects, which varied according to the personal qualities of the particular chief.

Malinowski, in *Crime and Custom in Savage Society*, p. 46 : ' Even the chief . . . has to conform to strict norms and is bound by legal fetters. When he wants to declare war, organise an expedition, or celebrate a festivity, he must issue formal summons, publicly announce his will, deliberate with the notables, receive the tribute, services and assistance of his subjects in a ceremonial manner, and finally repay them according to a definite scale.'

[2] Pp. 18 ff.   [3] Cf. W. M. Macmillan's view at p. 20.

2. *Women.*

It is a notorious fact that women in African, as in even many a modern, society play little if any part in public life. Their place is in the home, looking after their husbands and children. This somewhat restricted sphere of a woman's social functions is not, as is often supposed, due to the fact that so-called ' bride-price ' is paid on them by their prospective husbands before marriage. Such a payment is not a purchase money for the woman, any more than the now obsolescent [1] English system of a prospective wife's father's dowry payment to the husband at marriage can be described as the purchase of a husband for her. Hilde Thurnwald, herself a European woman who had studied East African peoples, wrote :

' Considering these circumstances, it becomes obvious that the paying of the bride-price cannot be regarded in the same way as the rationalistic purchase of a commodity or be compared with the acquisition of a slave. The idea of such a " purchase " has been absent even in the previous epochs ; it is lacking in the modern times, too, when money is more often given for payments in kind.' [2]

The position of women can, therefore, only be the result of the particular mode of ordering social, economic and even military affairs in a given African society. Thus, the Amazons of Dahomey, redoubtable women warriors, left the care of the household chores to their effeminate husbands whilst they waged their

---

[1] Though it is still the case that Personalty Settlement under a Trust for Sale (ss. 23–33 L.P.A., 1925) often secures the same end in English law.

[2] R. C. Thurnwald, *Black and White in East Africa*, p. 147.

' The Africans rightly defend themselves against the assertion of superficial European observers that women are bought and sold by them. If it were so, the woman would be the slave of the man, which is true neither in law nor in fact '—D. Westermann, *The African Today*, p. 125. See also Pts. I and II of *African Marriage Survey*, ed. by A. Phillips.

' The position of women in African society has often been misunderstood. It has been assumed that a woman was merely a chattel with no rights and no authority of her own, and that *lobola* was, in the well-known words of Sir Harry Smith, " the sin of buying wives ". The matter is not quite so simple as that and the effective status of some women in certain tribes and of all women at certain times in all tribes is considerable '—Prof. A. V. Murray in ' Education under Indirect Rule ', pp. 227–68 of *Jnl. Roy. Afr. Soc.*, Vol. 34, 1935, p. 247

formidable wars of conquest against tribal enemies.[1] Even where women did not occupy such a dominating position, we find that their lot has never been other than reasonably wholesome. ' Woman's life is passed differently from that of the men and has its own sphere, but the woman's position among most tribes cannot be regarded as depressed or slavish. Indeed, the mothers, who possess a moral force as guardians of the tribal traditions, often wield considerable influence over the fate of their people.' [2]

In Uganda, for example, we notice the pre-eminence of the queen dowager of the Baganda who often reigns in her own court. The king of the Bakuba, although commonly regarded by his people as the incarnation of the supreme deity, yields precedence to his mother whose prerogative it is to address him first—a local etiquette denoting her temporal superiority.[3] In many African households the woman is usually, though not always, the mistress of the family.[4] Her predominance is unquestionable in those social organisations which have the matrilineal and matrilocal systems of kinship arrangement, since' the husband is then generally in a position of dependence upon the wife's family. The man's position is, however, often better where the kinship system is matrilineal but marriage is patrilocal (as among the Ashanti, for instance), although even here the woman retains and often embarrassingly asserts her independence of her husband.[5] The children of such marriages look upon, or until recently used to look upon, their maternal uncles as more important than their fathers.[6]

---

[1] Be it remembered, too, that the monarchs of Dahomey were notorious tyrants in many ways.

[2] Thurnwald, *op. cit.*, p. 172.

[3] Lowie, *Primitive Society*, pp. 335–6.

[4] For a recent account of the role of women in the Bamenda agricultural communities of the Cameroons under United Kingdom Trust, see P. Kaberry, *Women of the Grassfields*, particularly Chs. 5 and 6.

[5] Perhaps we may be permitted to draw here the analogy of the husband–wife relationship between Portia and Bassanio in *The Merchant of Venice*. The same Portia that knelt so meekly at Bassanio's feet declaring her love and accepting his overlordship—

> *Happiest of all is that her gentle spirit*
> *Commits itself to yours to be directed*
> *As from her lord, her governor, her king.*

could, on the proper occasion, round so superbly on Shylock in the trial scene or even on Bassanio himself for parting with her keepsake ring.

[6] Rattray, *Ashanti Law and Constitution*, p. 41 ; Danquah, *Akan Laws and Customs*, pp. 153, 183 ff.

H

But, as Lowie pertinently remarks, we must guard against the tendency to confuse the multilateral forms of a woman's social and legal relations within a given African community. ' First of all, it should be noted that the treatment of woman is one thing, her legal status another, her opportunities for public activity still another, while the character and extent of her labours belong again to a distinct category." [1] In the matter of status, then, a married woman can among the majority of African peoples hold a portion of the family land, particularly in such agricultural communities as favour farmwork for women. In urban areas, she is entitled to have a portion of the family house allotted to her so that she can reside there and otherwise deal with it as her brothers can.

Among trading communities, women are normally liable for their personal debts and other defaults to others ; and they may themselves sue others for these. But, for household or other family requirements, it seems that on the whole the husbands are usually held liable in their position as the breadwinners of the family. The husbands will, however, often deny liability for debts incurred by their wives for ordinary personal effects and may often suspect the suppliers (if these be men) of adultery with such wives : no man who is not a blood relation ought to furnish a married woman with such chattels without the knowledge and concurrence of the husband.

It appears, also, that except in matrimonial causes, such as divorce on the grounds of cruelty, adultery or impotence, husband and wife can hardly sue each other for the usual subjects of dispute between ordinary, independent individuals. Even in the matter of the repayment of the so-called ' bride-price ', it is usually the wife's parents or her lover who are or is sued by the husband. In any case, it seems extremely doubtful whether the traditional African courts will entertain ordinary suits brought by one spouse against another during the subsistence of the marriage.

3. *Infants.*

Infancy is a concept that has universal legal validity among all African societies, though the age at which it terminates naturally varies from one community to another. Particular ages entitle the individual to particular types of social participation in the

[1] Lowie, *Primitive Society*, p. 178.

various affairs of life, and legal capacity or incapacity accompanies certain ages. But almost everywhere one finds among the different societies the requirement that the attainment of puberty by the infant is the minimum condition for recognition as a member of his community. Thus, one sees that until the infant has performed the prescribed puberty rites, he or she is not legally entitled to get married ; also, only passage through the puberty school can initiate one into the various age-grades proper.

Now, puberty is normally attained at between the ages of 14 and 16 for girls, and 16 and 18 for boys.[1] But in point of fact most communities insist on their girls waiting at least a little longer ; while the compulsion to acquire the often high ' brideprice ' or to participate in some military expedition or, in some communities, to organise raids for the boys, generally requires that marriage must take place at still more advanced ages. Sometimes, the puberty initiation ceremony is only a prelude to yet more ceremonies which alone fix the legal and social status of the growing infant. For instance, among the Masai,[2] every infant is expected to advance from boyhood to bachelorhood and from bachelorhood to the elder's estate. But there is no implication of superior and inferior caste as the basis of differentiation of the age-grades among the elders. Initiation makes him a warrior ; two years later, he becomes an apprentice (a shaved one) ; at between the ages of 28 and 30 years [3] he figures as a full-fledged brave, gets married on leaving the bachelor's kraal, and so assumes the dignity of an elder. Similarly, the girls become known as ' novices ' after the appearance of their first menses ; a little thereafter, they are generally regarded as fully-grown women ready for marriage ; they however continue to enjoy a distinct rank until they attain their menopause.

Among the Chagga,[4] initiation of girls takes place usually when they are 16 or older, and they marry as late as 20 or even later. At any rate, in 1935, the average marriage age was between 18 and

[1] In Eire, Northern Ireland, Great Britain (until the 1929 Age of Marriage Act), and practically all European countries, the ages of marriage *are* 12 for a girl and 14 for a boy. Marriageable age in Great Britain is now 16 years (since 1929) for both boy and girl.

[2] Lowie, *ibid*, pp. 259, 265. Initiation involves circumcision for boys and clitoridectomy for girls.

[3] Among the Yorubas the age of marriage used to be 30 : see Johnson, *History of the Yorubas*, pp. 100 ff.

[4] Thurnwald, *Black and White in East Africa* (1935), pp. 144–7.

26 years.[1] We learn from our source also the interesting fact
that before the Lindi dynasty Chagga girls used to get married
at between 18 and 20 years of age but, when the Lindi family
imposed their domination after the middle of the last century,
they began to drag as many girls as they liked into marriage. The
only way of discouraging this habit was for parents to betroth their
girls very early, about the age of 9 or 10. After the fall of the
Lindi dynasty, however, the marriage age went up again until it
stood at 16 for 'pagan' girls. Early betrothal seems to have
taken place also among the wa-Shambala and the wa-Gogo;
and we are assured by Hilde Thurnwald : ' The girl's wish is
more frequently taken into account than generally conceded
as true. . . . The girl is expressly consulted and her wish
respected. . . . If not, the girl considers her self-respect im-
paired and may even commit suicide from loss of prestige.' [2]

Further instances [3] could be given of the practices among other
African communities but probably little useful purpose would be
served thereby. What stands out from the preceding analysis is
that for capacity to marry and perhaps to do certain other legal
acts, the attainment of puberty is a necessary minimum condition.
Infants often have to wait, however, before they are fully received
into adulthood. It may not be far wide of the mark to add that,
so long as they remain unmarried and attached to the parents'
home, they are for all practical purposes regarded as infants. The
parents are still responsible to others for their good behaviour
as well as for liabilities to others, though exceptional circumstances
may warrant a different inference. Where, however, they get
married but remain with the parents, the new status of matrimony
will usually mean the assumption of full legal capacity by the
infants.

It will have become clear by now that age plays at least as
important a part in African society as it does in the English or any
other human society. The means employed for social differentia-

---

[1] Among the Hottentots, the marriageable age was 18 : see A. W.
Hoernle, ' Certain Rites of Transition and the Conception of Nau
Among the Hottentots ' in *Harvard African Studies*, Cambridge, Vol. II
(1918), pp. 67–8.

[2] Thurnwald, *ibid.*, pp. 146–7.

[3] E.g. among the Basuto most men marry at about the age of 23 to 26.
The rich might marry earlier and the poor later. Women usually marry
at between 18 and 24. (H. Ashton, *The Basuto*, p. 62.)

tion by age varies, however, in different societies. The absence of official public records in traditional African societies has led to the formality of public initiation rites for groups of approximate coevals at various levels of the social strata. The public has always been the best witness to these age ceremonies on which the individual's social and legal standing in the community so largely depends. Without such symbolic acts of public testimony it would often have been difficult to ascertain when or whether an individual had reached the legal age to marry, to become a warrior, or to stand for election into such important public bodies as the so-called secret societies with definite political and juridical functions.

Although age-classes plays such an important part in social life, it would nevertheless be wrong to imagine that membership of every such group necessarily confers a legal status upon the individual.[1] The various coming-of-age ceremonies must, therefore, be carefully distinguished from those that are merely designed to celebrate the formal inauguration of cultural, religious or social clubs—all being forms of the social instinct for masculine gregariousness.

4. *Aliens.*

It has been frequently asserted with some truth that the African customary law of a tribe applies only to its members. Thus, Driberg emphasises : ' Law is the possession and privilege of

---

[1] One does not often realise how important age is in English law, for example, until one looks at some such facts as these :

(*a*) 3-year-olds must be paid for on public transport.

(*b*) 5-year-olds must go to school.

(*c*) 8-year-olds may now be prosecuted for crimes (below this age they are *doli incapax*).

(*d*) 14-year-olds may enter a ' public house ' but may not drink ; they now enter the category of ' Young Persons '. (For (*c*) and (*d*) see *Children and Young Persons Act*, 1938.)

(*e*) 15-year-olds may now leave school.

(*f*) 16-year-olds may get married, subject to parental consent ; they may also smoke in public, drive a motor-bicycle but not a motor-car, and be sent to Borstal.

(*g*) 17-year-olds cease to be ' Young Persons ', may drive a motor-car, and be charged and tried for offences in courts for adults.

(*h*) 18-year-olds may drink in public, may be conscripted into the army, navy and air force ; and may be hanged for treason or murder.

(*i*) 21-year-olds have full legal capacity—may marry without parents' consent, are responsible for own debts, and may vote at elections.

a restricted group.' He goes on to insist that the scope and protection of this law extend only to members of the group. But he
concedes that strangers are often assimilated with the group by the
rules of hospitality, the protection of friends, inter-marriage, and
inter-tribal associations, all of which generally make it possible for
members of the group to plead the strangers' cause in a vicarious
capacity. But, instead of going on to argue that African law is,
nevertheless, different from ' European ' law in this respect, what
Driberg might usefully have added is that most if not all customary
legal systems, as the English legal system, for example, make
their own legal arrangements for the formal incorporation of aliens
with the indigenous community.

The requirement in the African situation is that the stranger
must have been previously introduced to the chief or elders of the
district, must have resided with his host for such period as would
enable the elders to judge of his general suitability for membership
of the group, and should then be formally adopted by the chief
and his council of elders at a small public ceremony witnessed by
as many people as care to be present. Thereafter, he becomes a
full member of the community, subject alike to its law and custom
and to the normal privileges and responsibilities of its membership. This is, of course, the procedure for permanent naturalisation of stranger immigrants into the tribe.[1]

It does not mean that aliens on casual visits among the members
of a tribe are without legal protection. Indeed, so meticulously
observed are the rules of hospitality that persons from the king
down to the merest peasant in the community will go out of their
way to protect the life and property of all friendly aliens during the
sojourn of the latter in their midst. If they err at all, it is in their
over-anxious tendency to favour the foreigner in many disputes
with members of the host community. But he will be given no
quarter if he wantonly commits a flagrant breach of the laws of
hospitality or of tribal rules of a solemn character. The ultimate
fate which awaits him depends on the circumstances of his temporary visit to the group, his opportunities of knowing the enormity
of his crime and his general disposition before and at the
trial.

[1] Not entirely dissimilar in essence from the requirements of the
British Nationality Act, 1948, in the matter of application by foreigners
in the United Kingdom for Certificate of Naturalisation.

5. *Slaves.*[1]

In discussing the status of slavery in African society, a necessary distinction must be made between slaves who were captured in inter-tribal wars and those who gave themselves into the bondage [2] of creditors for unpaid debts either incurred by themselves or by a relative. In the latter case but not in the former, the bondsman or bondswoman retained the normal attributes of a member of the community except in matters likely to prejudice the creditor's rights to the recovery of his debt. In some societies the personal services of the bonded person were reckoned towards the eventual liquidation of the debt ; in others, they were not. But the creditor was ever under a duty to treat the bonded as he would a member of his own family, and the instances were numberless in which the bondage ended abruptly in marriage between a male creditor and a bondswoman or between a female creditor and a bondsman. Where marriage did not supervene the bonded person either worked off his redemption or was ransomed by a relative or friend paying his debt.[3]

In the case of war captives practice differs in the various African communities. Some bluntly refused to make slaves of fellow human beings merely as a result of the accident of war, and the captives were either immediately absorbed into the conquering community or immediately released to go where they listed. But many communities in East, Central and West Africa, took war slaves whom they usually treated rather less favourably than bondsmen, at least at the beginning. The relationship between master and slave was not one of abject degradation but one of keeping each other at arm's length until the slave's character and ability, or lack of these, should decide whether his future lay in assimilation into the master's household or whether he should, if still young and virile, be sold off. In nearly all cases they were on first acquisition given portions of their masters' family land for their personal exploitation, while they served the masters by

[1] This is an example of a word which has quite reversed its meaning, for the Russian ' slava ' means glory or fame and was applied to the peoples we now know as Slavs. But when captured by the Huns they became bondsmen, and so the word ' slave ' came into being to describe a servant without privilege.

[2] This is sometimes referred to as the Pawn System, and the bonded person is said to be ' pawned '. See further Ch. IX, B(2), *infra*.

[3] For further consideration of this subject, see pp. 170-1.

assisting in the cultivation of the latters' farms on a certain number of days per week.

The master's powers seem limited to reasonable chastisement of young slaves or sale of old ones if they could still fetch any money. Nowhere was there a legal right in a master to kill his innocent slave, although masters sometimes abused their powers. On the other hand, it was very frequent that slaves were adopted into their masters' families and, by dint of hard work and honest solicitude for the welfare of their masters and of the latter's families, they often became heads of such families in course of time.[1]   It was not unusual for slaves or their descendants to become chiefs in communities with a non-hereditary chieftaincy system. The position subsequently attained in society accordingly depended very often on his own innate resourcefulness, character and ability.

It may be remarked in passing that these two forms of customary slavery are now as dead as the Dodo in all the British territories in Africa, with which we are immediately concerned. They were formally abrogated, wherever they still existed, by means of several Abolition of Slavery Ordinances and Proclamations.

6. Caste.

It remains for us briefly to note the existence of a rare institution which had all the hall-marks of caste. Certain communities, usually of the non-centralised and atomistic type, regarded sections of their members as unclean pariahs with whom it was considered degrading to associate in the normal intercourse of daily life. Of course, marriage with them was completely forbidden. Among the Ibos of Nigeria they were known as ' Osu ',[2] and it is certainly strange that so democratic and equalitarian a people should have abandoned certain of their number to such an abject status. Among the Masai, where they formed guilds or sibs of blacksmiths, these were segregated from the rest of the community

---

[1] Lowie, *ibid.*, p. 336 : ' In Uganda a slave girl who bore children to a freeman became free together with her progeny, and sometimes, though not generally, her sons were permitted to inherit property.'

[2] Green, *Ibo Village Affairs*, pp. 23–4 ; Meek, *Law and Authority in a Nigerian Tribe*, pp. 31, 203–4.   Also, W. R. G. Horton, ' The Ohu System of Slavery in a Northern Ibo Village-Group ', an article in *Africa*, Vol. XXIV, No. 4, Oct., 1954, pp. 311–35, particularly pp. 316–17, 326–8, 334–5.

though such a martial community was to a great extent dependent on these untouchables for their weapons.[1]

By a strange coincidence, and this is as much as one can say in the absence of positive evidence as to a possible common origin, both the Ibo and the Masai social and political organisations have no strong centralised political authorities in the persons of kings or chiefs, but both have only spiritual functionaries who are more of tribal saints than rulers, and who rarely wield any judicial or other temporal power. Both place a premium on the dignity of the individual to a remarkable degree. But, strange to relate, both suffer in their democratic arrangements the existence of this curious phenomenon of caste.

It does not seem, however, that members of the caste in either type of social organisation are really prejudiced in many ways. They are quite free to pursue their trade, to acquire land and other forms of property, to get married among themselves and rear their own children, and generally to be left unmolested by their more fortunate but contemptuous fellow tribesmen. The one serious disability is the stigma of social inferiority which operates legally to forbid intermarriage between them and the rest of the community. The only opportunity for intercourse with the rest is the economic one forced upon the ' superior ' majority by the need for trade or purchase of the goods in the making of which members of the caste excel.

It should be interesting to know how disputes between the full citizens and these lesser breeds, which are bound to arise out of even this limited intercourse, are settled.[2] It is not difficult to imagine that the democratic instinct of the leaders of the community would dispose them to accord members of the caste in such disputes at least a modicum of their economic rights.

[1] Lowie, op. cit., at pp. 336, 368.
[2] We are told that, among the Ibos, the ' Osu ' are or may be a part of the mechanism whereby law and order are preserved ' and that ' a big strong osu of Umueke sometimes assumed, or was given, mild police functions '—Green, op. cit., pp. 50–1, 123. See also Ch. XII, pp. 221–2, infra.

CHAPTER VII

DISTINCTION BETWEEN CIVIL AND CRIMINAL LAW

A. DENIAL OF THE DISTINCTION IN AFRICAN LAW

THE assertion has often been made by writers on African law, at least by those of the older generation, that no distinction is ever made therein between civil and criminal wrongs as commonly conceived in ' European ' law.[1] The usual evidence cited in support is that offences like murder and theft, which are clearly criminal offences according to English law, are generally treated by many African societies as matters for private redress by the wronged party or group rather than by the State as the custodian of public safety and welfare. Now, while there is some truth in this way of thinking, it is certainly not wholly accurate.

Several factors appear to be responsible for the inadequacy of the prevailing analysis, and mention may be made of, *inter alia*, these important ones : (*a*) the great influence of Sir Henry Maine's writings ; (*b*) the tendency on the part of these writers on African law to forget, or perhaps to be unaware of, the historical evolution of the distinction made in modern English law ; (*c*) the common disposition to argue as if the classification of offences into criminal and civil were clear-cut and free from difficulties in European legal systems or even within the content of English law itself ; and (*d*) the all too ready desire to assume that African law in general must, by the very fact of being African, be irreconcilably different from English, indeed European, law.

Let us begin, then, with Maine. It will be recalled that he it was who first drew attention in his *Ancient Law* to what he regarded as the strange preponderance of criminal over civil law in ' *ancient* ' (identified for this purpose with *African*) law. Maine

---

[1] We have used the term 'European ' law here in its popular opposition to African law, particularly because even Continental writers on African law are in the habit of freely indulging the fancy that their own systems of law are at one with the Anglo-American systems in this matter. In the pages that follow we shall attempt to demonstrate the error of this assumption.

had stressed the primitive belligerency of the savage, who are supposed to be always at war with one another and whose daily life is, because of the prevailing social chaos, supposed to be dominated by crime.   Then he added this controversial point : ' Now the penal law of ancient communities is not the law of Crimes, it is the law of Wrongs, or, to use the English technical word, of Torts.'[1]   The qualification here implied of the theory of warring savages does not acquit him of the charge of responsibility for the fundamental fallacy.   Like some others of Maine's not so happy generalisations, this is very confused and confusing, even as a description.   It is apparently a contradiction in terms to say that a *penal* law is a law of *civil* wrongs ; but what the jurist really implied is that penalties for *all* wrongs are exacted by the affected individual or his clan as a matter of private vengeance or redress.

According to this view, there is no feeling of public sentiment, no principle of social solidarity in an African society capable of arousing the corporate ire of the community and expressing itself in some form of joint effort against disturbers of the social equilibrium.   Writers [2] who follow Maine into this species of speculative opinion must be taken to assume that all African societies are of a piece in never having evolved, politically, beyond the stage of the patriarchal or matriarchal family.   We know, however, that this is not the case and that there are many with centralised political authorities, administrative machinery, military and judicial organs, that do enforce law and order as understood in their several communities.   In societies with a rudimentary political organisation, it is usually the case that permanent and continuous guardians of the public weal are hard to identify, since very often these communities lack a regular system of chiefship or kingship.   But, unless these democratic and equalitarian human groups had always had the inevitable social instinct of fellowship and harmonious living together, their communities could not have endured thus far.   There must have been some standards of social behaviour, some irreducible minimum of collective public sentiment, a flouting of which by a swashbuckling member would provoke universal disapprobation, if not joint repressive action.

[1] Maine's *Ancient Law*, p. 379.
[2] E.g. Hartland, Hobhouse, Rivers.

B. SOME REFUTATION OF THE ARGUMENTS

It is against the placid acceptance of the Mainesque theory that ' primitive law ' does not discriminate between civil and criminal offences that Malinowski has so effectively protested in his *Crime and Custom in Savage Society*.   He is at pains to demonstrate that ' civil law, consisting of positive ordinances, is much more developed than the body of mere prohibitions ', and that ' a study of purely criminal law among savages misses the most important phenomena of their legal life '.[1]   While admitting that in the Trobriand Islands, with which he is immediately concerned, crimes ' can be but vaguely defined ', he insists that all ' primitive ' peoples have civil as well as criminal law.   Murder, theft, breaches of exogamy and sorcery, for example, are all crimes.   As for civil law, which Malinowski proclaims to be the dominant one in the Trobriand society he is describing, instances are marriage, inheritance, property, exchange by barter, and the innumerable social activities that so significantly characterise the life of the community.   We have had occasion to point out,[2] however, that Malinowski has allowed his revolt against the charge that primitive law deals only with crime to lead him to the opposite extreme of saying that it deals only with civil wrongs.

Talbot's verdict, in his voluminous study of the peoples of Southern Nigeria, is : ' The distinction between criminal and civil offences was not very definite, and the same act might be regarded as either, according to the tribe or clan.   It will be seen that, in the main, the classification was not very different to our own.'[3]   Dr. Meek, writing of the Ibos, has observed : ' . . . what are crimes or torts to us are for the most part crimes or torts to them.'[4]   Lowie is quite sure that ' primitive ' law does make a clear 'distinction between torts and crimes '.[5]   Diamond, the well-known authority on ' primitive ' law, is emphatic that it recognises a distinction between civil and criminal wrongs, at least at a certain stage.[6]   Lowie has recorded that among the Amaxosa and their neighbours ' a fundamental distinction is drawn between criminal and civil cases.   The former include political offences, sorcery,

[1] P. 31.   [2] See p. 50, *supra*.
[3] Talbot, *The Peoples of Southern Nigeria*, p. 625.
[4] Meek, *Law and Authority in a Nigerian Tribe*, p. xiii ; also pp. 208–28.
[5] Lowie, *Primitive Society*, pp. 385 ff.
[6] Diamond, *Primitive Law*, (2nd edn.), pp. 192–4.

and crimes against the persons of tribesmen ; they are prosecuted by the chiefs and the fines belong to them by inalienable right. All other cases are prosecuted by the plaintiffs and the chiefs have no claim to the award made.' [1]

Offences of a criminal character have also been discerned among, for example, the Kamba of Kenya. According to Pen-will,[2] ' when the " utui " elders felt that a crime was too serious to be atoned for by the fine of a bull, or by driving the culprit out ', they would arraign its perpetrator formally before the ' king'ole ' [3] as an ' undesirable member of the community '. If found guilty of the charges preferred against him, he might be executed in a bush rendezvous. An alternative mode of punishment sometimes ordered by the ' king'ole ' was for the man to be hanged by the neck from some tree in a public thoroughfare ' as a warning to other potential wrong-doers '.

We learn also that among the Bantu of North Kavirondo, homicide and theft are normally redressible by compensation, whereas incest and witchcraft are punishable as crimes ; that in cases of theft there is usually no need for the parties to a suit to give presents (in the form of cattle) to the judge in advance, since the latter expect that fines are forthcoming by law ; but that in cases of debt and ' bride-price ', such gifts are regularly made. This is evidence of a differentiation of procedure which is, at the very least, suggestive of the modern distinction between criminal and civil cases.[4]

Other instances of the public organisation of redress for certain private wrongs that are considered to affect the body politic can be cited. With respect to the Ibos, another example of a people without a strong politically centralised authority, Miss Green has described how offenders against the code of conduct enjoined

---

[1] *Op. cit.*, p. 409. Rattray has discovered the same distinction among the Ashanti, *op. cit.*, pp. 285–93, although he employs the infelicitous expressions of ' Sins ' (for crimes), and ' Efisiem ' (for civil cases).

[2] At pp. 88–90 and 94 of his *Kamba Customary Law* ; so, also, among the Nandi of Kenya : G. S. Snell, *Nandi Customary Law*, pp. 78–9.

[3] The ' king'ole ' consisted of ' the mass of the male population of a group of " motui ", the largest Kamba group that acknowledged a common institution. . . . It was a crude legislature, judiciary and executive, all combined ; the " government ", however sporadically and however seldom it might meet, of the area over which its jurisdiction was recognised ' (*ibid.*, pp. 88–9).

[4] See Wagner's essay, ' The Bantu of North Kavirondo ', in *African Political Systems*.

upon members of certain associations or even against what has been publicly decreed as binding rules are punished by collective action.[1]   She adds that ' the commission of an offence which is . . . forbidden—would seem to involve the whole community and not merely the individuals concerned.   The individuals who take action do so on the part of the community.   If there is any point in trying to apply the categories of criminal and civil law to Ibo judicial matters, then presumably offences against Ala and probably other such (*forbidden*) behaviour might be classified as criminal cases.' [2]   She elsewhere [3] describes stealing as ' the classic Ibo crime '.

On the other hand, we have writers like C. C. Roberts pontificating thus : ' Primitive law lays down rules for behaviour and its penalties are directed . . . towards the restoration of the equilibrium.   There is no distinction between civil and criminal law as we understand it.' [4]   Since this view is typical of those held by some writers who have had some connexion with the administration of law in parts of British Africa, we will pause for a while to consider what the distinction between civil and criminal law really is in English law, so that we may the better appreciate this insistence on the African divergence from the normal.   Let us take some authoritative examples of this school of thought.

C. ANALYSIS OF THE ISSUES INVOLVED

Now, three heroic efforts have been made to define the English (perhaps we should say, the Anglo-American) legal distinction between civil and criminal offences :

(1) The first is that of Orde-Browne who wrote that the conception of society taking vengeance on an offender was one quite alien to the African, while any reformative effect depended upon the application of the principle that law-breaking did not pay. The culprit was mulcted for the benefit of the sufferer, and it was

[1] See her *Ibo Village Affairs*, pp. 101, 226–30 ; also, Meek, *op. cit.*, 225–7.

[2] Green, pp. 101–2. (The italic is mine.)

[3] *Ibid.*, p. 223.

[4] *Tangled Justice*, p. 64, although the writer's description of the treatment of such offences as Murder, Adultery and Theft at pp. 79, 84–5, seems strongly to suggest that they are nothing short of criminal wrongs.

obviously not worth while to infringe the established rules.   But one may seriously doubt whether this is peculiar to African customary law, and whether it is a valid basis of distinction between it and other types of law.   Nevertheless, the writer felt able to draw this strange inference :

'Thus the law was civil rather than criminal, and all but the gravest and most unusual crimes were dealt with on a system which resembled arbitration rather than punishment ; so long as the harm done was as far as possible made good, society was not expected to take further action.'[1]

The learned writer then proceeds to consider the nature of crime ' according to European ideas ' as currently accepted.   He believes it to be evident that crime ' can be divided into two classes, real and technical offences ', that under ' British law ' both classes might be dealt with by the police but that there is usually ' a clear distinction between the two ' in that society adopts a different attitude towards them ; so that anyone found guilty, for instance, of riding a bicycle on the footpath would not feel the disgrace attaching to a conviction for theft.

After allowing for the fact that punishments nowadays are lighter in some ways but heavier in others than they were in his grandfather's days, the writer insists :[2] ' Nevertheless, there is always an underlying conception of the difference between a disgraceful action and one that is merely culpable ; and this forms the basis of the public opinion upon which all effectual law must be grounded.'   In advancing this curious argument it does not seem ever to have occurred to Orde-Browne that he is merely stating a truism about law in general.   Regarded as an attempt to lay down a logical basis of differentiation between African and European law, this argument does not bear a close analysis ; as an attempt to define the boundary between civil and criminal offences, even under English law, it is no more than an expression of the vague feeling of all those who pontificate on what they regard as African legal curiosities without having previously informed themselves sufficiently of the niceties of English law, a knowledge of which they often so dangerously take for granted.

[1] Major G. St. J. Orde-Browne, ' British Justice and the African ', an article in the *Jnl. Roy. Afr. Soc.*, Vol. 32, No. CXXVII, April, 1933, pp. 148–59, at p. 151.
[2] *Ibid.*, p. 152.

(2) The second is that of Hone who asserts [1] that a wrong which is ' an injury to society at large ' and the punishment of which at the same time proves to be ' a deterrent to all other members of the State ' and ' a corrective to the individual wrong-doer ' is what Europeans call ' a crime '. It is ' the duty of the State to detect them, to arrest the criminal and then to move the proper tribunal to exact an appropriate punishment and afterwards to carry it out '. Truthfully enough the learned jurist observes that the ability of a community to recognise certain wrongful deeds as crimes denotes a certain stage of development ; but he is in error when, writing of Uganda of all African societies, he argues that ' the conception is clearly an advanced one not to be generally associated with or expected from primitive communities such as flourished in Uganda before the advent of the European '. We shall see presently how he himself impliedly admits that even at that stage some Uganda tribes had already recognised between types of offences a distinction more or less similar to that between civil and criminal.

Again, like Orde-Browne, he soon becomes involved in contradictions. He expressed the conviction that where, for example, he found that the death penalty was in fact exacted in pursuance of customary law, ' the fundamental justification was retribution and the restoration of balance, rather than that the public conscience was shocked into the infliction of the extreme penalty as a warning and deterrent to lawless persons and as a protection to society at large '.

But such was the weight of the evidence surrounding him as he wrote these words that he hastened to add this important qualification of the pathetic fallacy : ' While the facts show this hypothesis as to the native conception of law to be a true one, there is, nevertheless, evidence that in parts of Uganda, some wrongs in certain tribes were already recognised as injuring society at large and, therefore calling for a penalty which stamped the disapproval of the State as such and was more than merely commensurate with the wrong done to the individual who primarily suffered.'

With respect to the Lango, the least organised tribe from the point of view of legal development, he warned that the clear evidence that then existed of indigenous conception of wrongs

[1] See his article, ' The Native of Uganda and the Criminal Law ', *op. cit.*

amounting to crimes must not be taken for what they really were :
' Thus, the exaction of the death penalty among the Lango, in
cases of patricide or fratricide is not to be quoted as an instance of
more advanced ideas ; it depended for its justification merely on
the *inefficacy of the punishment of compensation and the need for
restoring the balance of a life for a life.*' [1] This tendency of writers
to refuse to face facts and to attempt to explain away such inconvenient examples, so persistent in almost all the African societies
hitherto accurately studied, is not a little difficult to understand.

The case is still more perplexing when such bland denials of
a distinction by Africans between civil and criminal offences are
almost invariably followed in the same account by some such
grudging admission as this one, again by Hone. He wrote :
' Even among these primitive people, however, it was recognised
that three species of misdeeds were wrongs against society at
large for which there could be no appropriate remedy save the
complete removal of the offender from the ranks of the tribe by
immediate death. These offences were witchcraft, incest and
sexual offences contrary to nature.'

Of the more advanced tribes in Uganda and elsewhere in
Africa, this verdict is still tru_r.

(3) The third view is that of Seagle [2] who, after criticising
Malinowski for saying that ' primitive ' law also recognises a
distinction between civil and criminal law, goes on to admit that
' it is extremely difficult to distinguish civil from criminal law even
in mature legal systems. It can be done neither in terms of
procedure nor of sanctions. Criminal law is a breach of public
law but there is no absolute formal distinction between public and
private law.'

Had this learned jurist stopped there, all might have been well.
But he felt bound to specify a threefold basis of distinction
between civil and criminal law which should enable him to set
' primitive ' law apart from European law. He argues that [3]—

(i) ' the classic dualism is founded primarily in economic

---

[1] Italics are the author's. The learned writer's account was based
on Driberg, *The Lango* (pp. 210–15), which probably explains the
apparent contradictions into which he has fallen.

[2] See his article, ' Primitive Law and Professor Malinowski ' in *The
American Anthropologist, op. cit.*

[3] This numbered classification is entirely mine and has been adopted
for purposes of close analysis.

I

individualism.' Here, the writer develops the theme that the 'civil law' becomes associated with private rights and that there is really no civil law ' until there is a market in which things are exchanged as abstract commodities ' rather than as concrete object of use.

(ii) ' the criminal law betokens a State monopoly of force.' In both civil and criminal law what really happens is that ' the will of the State is objectified ', the only difference being that in the former the State is an umpire between two private individuals as litigating integers, whereas in the latter the State supplies the public prosecutor as one of the integers.

(iii) the award of the court differs, too, in that while in one case it is a ' commodity ', in the other it is a ' penalty '.

He therefore concludes : ' In the absence of both the State and the market the distinction between civil and criminal law, is altogether without fundamental basis.' By this interesting piece of dialectic our jurist is able to reach substantially the same conclusion as that of Hone, namely, that the drawing of a distinction between civil and criminal offences represents an advanced stage of intellectual and political orientation not normally to be expected of ' primitive ' societies. We have just shown how far this conclusion is valid.

It must be confessed, however, that of all the arguments usually advanced in favour of a scientific distinction between civil and criminal law, this economic interpretation is the strangest. We may well ask : What has the economic exchange of commodities got to do with the primordial problem of classifying legal wrongs ? Does the legal distinction between civil and criminal offences in, say, American law really turn upon whether material goods are exchanged on a system of barter or on a money-for-goods basis ? One would ordinarily have thought that such considerations were clearly irrelevant to the juridical issue involved ?

But, it is true to say, as does our jurist, that no distinction can be made between civil and criminal wrongs in terms either of procedure or of sanctions. Thus, to take two important examples of the classical English concepts, Blackstone defines crime as ' a violation of the public rights and duties due to the whole community, considered as a community ';[1] but Kenny, thinking this

---

[1] 4 Blackstone's *Commentaries on the Laws of England*, pp. 3 and 4. Another definition given by Blackstone in the same place is that a crime is ' an act committed or omitted in violation of a public law forbidding or commanding it '.

inadequate and adapting Austin's definition, suggests that ' crimes are wrongs whose sanction is punitive, and is in no way remissible by any private person, but is remissible by the Crown alone, if remissible at all '.[1]   It has to be said, however, that the difference between Blackstone and Kenny is not so much a fundamental disagreement about the essence of crime as a measure of the development that has taken place in legal ideas and processes in England between the eighteenth and the twentieth centuries. Neither the ' violation of the public rights and duties ' of the community nor the State's power of remission of an offender's punishment can entirely explain why certain offences are civil and others criminal.[2]   Accordingly, no absolutely satisfactory definition of a crime has yet been put forward by any jurist—so intractably subtle is the distinction between civil and criminal offences even in developed systems.   It is therefore surprising to find Mr. Seagle employing so confidently this economic theory as a basis for such a distinction.

D. DISTINCTION INTO PRIVATE AND PUBLIC LAW

We have now seen how the various writers on African law have fallen into unnecessary quibbles and contradictions in their several attempts to deny that a distinction—even such as can be said to exist at all in all legal systems—does exist also in African customary law.

Some jurists have despaired of the classic differentiation of offences into civil and criminal, and have sought to substitute for it one into *private* and *public*, as if these were themselves terms of art.   This revival of the Blackstonian ideal has been prompted by a desire to find some workable basis of classification of legal wrongs which would avoid the difficulties inherent in the now more popular but scarcely less imprecise civil-and-criminal

---

[1] See Kenny, *Outlines of Criminal Law* (15th edn.), p. 16.

[2] In spite of the valid objections to Blackstone's exposition concerning the nature of public and private wrongs, it seems on the whole a more practical, commonsense approach to the problem than the procedural test adopted in varying degrees by Austin, Salmond and Kenny.   In Bk. III, p. 2, Blackstone wrote : ' The distinction of public wrongs from private is that civil injuries are private wrongs, regarded as transgressions on the rights of individuals, while crimes are public wrongs, regarded as affecting the whole community'.

dichotomy. Thus Radcliffe-Brown has suggested [1] that the terms ' public delict ' and ' private delict ' would be more appropriate to describe the undoubted differentiation, which he discovers that ' primitive ' law makes, between categories of offences. Driberg, in taking up this theme song, has been even bolder in asserting that Africans do not understand the distinction between civil and criminal but that they do that between public and private law. His definition is : ' Private law deals with acts which disturb the equilibrium ; public law with acts or situations which negative those conditions which make the maintenance of the equilibrium possible.' [2] He continues to argue that only in offences which are held to be definitely anti-social is the public law invoked, and by anti-social is meant ' something much more than the disturbance of this or that equilibrium '. The anti-social crimes which he puts under public law are treason, witchcraft, incest and sexual perversions, and any of these is punished by death, ' because that is the only measure which can preserve society '. He even admits there and then : ' This is true also of nearly all the major offences in our criminal codes. . . .' [3] It is interesting to note also that Driberg, throughout the remainder of his article, continues to employ the terms civil and criminal in discussing African law.

Again, Driberg is in error when he regards as treasonable ' an act subversive of the conditions under which alone equilibrium can be maintained ' and as, therefore, coming within the category of ' public offences ' but nevertheless as ' not inflicted in retaliation for the offences *per se*, but because through the centralisation of authority in the ruler as representative of tribal interests these offences had come to be regarded as treason '. One would have thought that the whole tenor of the evolution of English criminal law has been a movement from the exaction of private vengeance by the injured individual to the monopoly of redress (for offences *contra pacem regis*) by the monarch on behalf of the community. Where is the fundamental difference between the African and the European concepts in this respect ? In certain of the more highly organised communities, the compensation paid in private suits goes to the ruler who may then give back part or all of it to the successful litigant. The common saying in homicide cases is

---

[1] In his essay in *The Encyclopædia of the Social Sciences, op. cit.*
[2] *Op. cit.*, p. 231.   [3] *Ibid.*, p. 236.

that ' all blood belongs to the chief ', and the legal implication is
that such offences are an affront to the authority of the chief or
king who is thereby entitled to avenge the wronged members of
the community.[1]

On the whole, therefore, one can see quite clearly that there are
about as many difficulties in distinguishing between public and
private offences [2] as between criminal and civil, and that either
method will not support the view that African law is necessarily
different from the European on that score.   It is suggested, with
respect, that what matters is not the name by which offences are
designated in a particular legal system but the extent to which
they are recognised and punished as such.   The recognition
accorded as well as the penalty imposed must depend ultimately
upon the classificatory device adopted by a given society for the
realisation within itself of peaceful and orderly existence among
its members.   On this basis it is further submitted that the
popular rough-and-ready distinction between civil and criminal
be retained for our present purposes and that, so far as it can be
said to be valid at all for English (or even European) law, it is
also valid *mutatis mutandis* for African law generally.

E. SUMMARY OF EVIDENCE IN FAVOUR OF THE DISTINCTION INTO CIVIL AND CRIMINAL LAW

In thus holding that African law, like any other law, differentiates between offences that must be publicly punished by society at
large and those that should be left to private redress, we are not
by any means suggesting that there is, therefore, no difference
between the African and a more developed legal system like the
English.   What we do affirm is that the basic attitude is essentially
similar, though not necessarily identical in all respects.   It would
be not only foolish but also absurd to ignore the obvious fact.
that the legal, no less than the other, arrangements of a society,
are affected by their sociological context.   What we have been
trying to say all this while is that a human society, whether

[1] Cp. ' Kafir criminal law rests primarily on the principle that the
persons of individuals belong to the chief '—Lowie, *op. cit.*, p. 409.   See
also *African Studies*, Vol. 12, No. 4, 1953, pp. 181–8.

[2] Sir Frederick Pollock, *A First Book of Jurisprudence*, p. 92, seems
to express the modern view that there is no satisfactory classification
of law into public and private.

hierarchically organised or horizontally aligned, whether European or African, has broad notions of what may be safely left to private arbitration or self-help and what ought to be made the concern of all as likely to imperil orderly social existence. Of course, such notions will vary as much, or as little, with the *mores* and the *ethos* of particular communities as with their historical and geographical conditions. Thus :

(i) The class of offences which English law regards as criminal is different in marked respects from that recognised by, for example, French law ; and the same is true as between Anglo-American legal systems on the one hand and Continental systems on the other. Even as between the English and American laws or as between one Continental country and another, there are noteworthy points of difference in the matter of classification of offences into the civil and the criminal.

For example, according to Gordon Westwood,[1] English law punishes homosexuality as a crime under the Offences Against the Person Act, 1861, whereas in most of the countries with penal systems based on the Code Napoléon such as France, Switzerland, Egypt, and China as well as some American States, homosexuality between two consenting adults is not even a civil offence, let alone a criminal one. Also, in French law, incest is not defined as a crime *per se*, and even in England where homosexuality has been a felony since feudal times, incest only became a crime in 1908. On the other hand, in practically all African societies incest and unnatural sexual behaviour have always, as far back as we can go, been visited with the severest penalties ranging from execution[2] of the offender to personal torture or a heavy fine.

Again, adultery is a crime under French law[3] and, as was formerly the case in the English action of ' criminal conversation ' against an adulterer, a wife's single act of adultery was sufficient to constitute a crime, but if an action were brought against the husband it had to be shown that his adultery was not an isolated

---

[1] *Society and the Homosexual.*

[2] It is a definite crime among the Shilluk, formerly punishable with death but now by a heavy fine, for any man to have sexual intercourse with their king's daughter who by Shilluk law must never marry : See *Report of the Wellcome Tropical Research Laboratories* (1911), pp. 218–19, under the title of ' The Cult of Nyakang and the Divine Kings of the Shilluk ' by G. C. Seligman.

[3] Ss. 491–503 of the French Code Pénal.

act and that it had been committed inside the matrimonial home. In the matter of penalty for the crime of adultery, the husband can only be fined, whereas the wife is liable to a term of imprisonment of from two months to two years.[1] Adultery in England was formerly punishable by a tort action for ' criminal conversation ' until the latter was abolished in 1857 ; [2] however, adultery is still the basis of a claim for damages.   But in many African societies, adultery is a civil offence,[3] although in some it may be treated as a crime : for instance, it seems to be a crime in parts of Nyasa-land,[4] and in Kenya it is made a crime against local law and custom when it is punishable by a fine of up to 40s. in addition to the customary compensation.[5]

It is not generally remembered in this connexion that within English law itself, the very same offence may be both a civil wrong and a criminal offence.   Instances are Defamation, Conspiracy and the various forms of Trespass to the Person—assault, battery and false imprisonment.   For each of these offences the injured party may of his own motion bring a civil action or the State may institute a criminal prosecution.   Certain offences that were formerly treated by the law as no offence at all or perhaps as civil wrongs have been subsequently turned into criminal offences by statute.

(ii) By English law, a breach of contract is a civil wrong involving the guilty party in liability for damages to the innocent party.   But, in parts of British Central and Eastern Africa, a breach by an employee of his contract of employment has been made a crime under the various Master and Servant Ordinances.

Occasionally, in English law, a predominantly criminal offence may be treated by the court as if it were civil, especially if the parties have kinship ties or where these are still vital in the locality. An example of how an English court would apply the human touch and waive technicalities is a recent case [6] between a Mr. Fairhurst and his niece, a Mrs. Sproson, at the Chester Assizes held on October 30, 1952.   It happened that while 71-year-old

---

[1] See also M. Francisque Goyet, *Précis de Droit Pénal Spécial* (6th edn.).
[2] I.e. by the Matrimonial Causes Act, 1857.
[3] H. Ashton, *The Basuto*, p. 255.
[4] See *R*. v. *Sidney and Emily* (1934), 4 Nyasaland Law Reports, p. 6.
Cf. *R*. v. *Robert and Aluwani* (1940), Nyasaland Law Reports, p. 2.
[5] See The Native Tribunal Ordinance, 1930, s. 13(a).
[6] See *The Daily Telegraph* of Friday, Oct. 31, 1952.

Fairhurst was living with his niece and her husband at Crewe, the niece stole £436 from her uncle's tin biscuit box placed in a trunk in which he had kept the sum of £500. Instead of causing a prosecution for larceny to be instituted, he sued for the return of the stolen money as for a civil debt and Mr. Justice Pearson gave him judgment with costs. Mrs. Sproson admitted that she ' went to uncle's box ' as and when she needed the money. The judge observed that the tin trunk was tied only with rope and that it was a very careless and unfair way for Mr. Fairhurst to keep his money : ' he had put the defendants in temptation '. Considering that this was a glaring case of larceny, we may ask why the judge did not order a criminal prosecution of the thieving niece instead of trying the case as one for the recovery of a mere civil debt. It is submitted that some such consideration as this will often be found to account for the tendency, so usually exaggerated, of African law to adopt the role of a domestic tribunal in many cases where a more developed body of law would apply the criminal sanction.

In those African societies with close kinship ties, many of the legal situations to be dealt with would generally be of the type dealt with in this unusual case of *Fairhurst* v. *Sproson*. It is not that Mr. Justice Pearson did not understand the definite distinction which English law makes between civil and criminal ; rather, it is that he preferred to lay aside legal technicality in order to achieve a harmonious result. Imprisonment might very likely have set niece against uncle, but that would have done no good to either side.

(iii) It will be recalled that the point often stressed by those who deny that African law differentiates between civil and criminal, is that murder is often a matter of compensation paid by the criminal or his kin-group to the relatives of the victim. We have shown that this has not always been the case even in the least developed of African societies, and that death is more often than not the normal penalty for unlawful homicide. We would none the less grant that the extreme penalty is often commuted into compensation where the circumstances of the murder are not really aggravating or do not vitally disturb the social equilibrium of the community. This, it is submitted with respect, does not sound too strange when it is remembered that death as a penalty for murder has been abolished in many developed countries of the world today, without social disaster.[1] And the murderer, far from being made to compensate his victim's dependants as African law would make him do, only goes to a not uncomfortable prison to be maintained at the expense of everybody else, including of course that of the unfortunate dependants of his victim.

Again, although English law still exacts the death penalty for unlawful murder,[2] nevertheless, it is a rule of the Law of Tort that 'the death of a human being cannot be complained of as an injury'. But the same rule has been eaten into by the Fatal Accidents Acts, 1846 and 1864 which provide that all the lawful dependants (including even an adopted child) of the victim of a killing not amounting to wilful murder shall be entitled to substantial compensation for their maintenance by the person responsible for the death.

(iv) It may probably aid our perspective in this matter to bear in mind this historical reminder sketched by Hone in the article [3] to which we have referred earlier :

'In England for a long time there was no distinction between criminal and civil cases, the underlying principle of the administration of justice was restitution and not retribution. Thus, compensation was the proper remedy for most wrongs committed and there were no police and no prisons . . . A criminal, however, caught red-handed was sentenced at once. Sentences of imprisonment were unknown ; the punishment for theft was mutilation or the payment of compensation, while murder was avenged by death and in other homicides by compensation.'

Lack of this indispensable background knowledge of the growth of English law itself has been largely responsible, if any one imponderable factor may be said to be responsible, for the

[1] In France, simple murder is punished by life imprisonment, but circumstances of aggravation may make it equivalent to 'assassinat' and therefore punishable by death. The status of the person killed (e.g. if a public official or a parent) may turn *simple* murder to aggravated murder (ss. 400–5 of the French Code Pénal).

[2] The Royal Commission on Capital Punishment has had suggested to it the abolition of the death penalty for all types of murder : See its Report (Cmd. 8932), 1953, ss. 13, 61–4, 605 ; although the Commission was not asked to consider the specific issue of abolition.

[3] *Op. cit.*, p. 6. One sincerely wishes that this able writer had remained true to the facts according to his own light and that he had avoided the temptation to be deflected from his juristic purpose by the confused theories of non-jurists about African law.

well-meant but often misguided notions that have been bandied about by people whose business it ought properly never to have been to lay down final theories about the nature of African law.

(v) While it must be conceded that the process by which certain species of civil wrongs come to be regarded as criminal offences is generally a mark of the development into a more complex political order, it is equally necessary to point out that, historically, most human societies have always made a distinction between, on the one hand, offences *mala in se* and, on the other, offences *mala quia prohibita*. Some wrongs like murder, theft, and unnatural sexual offences have been universally condemned by the whole human race as evil in themselves, while others have from time to time been prohibited by society as merely subversive of the social order. Since the latter category of offences springs from the practical needs of each society, it is naturally the subject of legislative regulations, a violation of which does not incur the same measure of opprobrium as attaches to a breach of any of the offences considered to be *mala in se*.

Dr. C. K. Allen [1] in discussing the problem of distinguishing criminal from civil wrongs, rejects the purely procedural criterion of Austin and Kenny and falls back upon Blackstone's view of crime in its public nature. He distinguishes the wrongfulness of offences into (*a*) intrinsic wrongfulness, and (*b*) social expediency. In thus regarding the criminal nature of an act as dependent upon its moral turpitude, Allen is relying upon this age-old division of offences into *mala in se* and *mala quia prohibita*. Although this cannot be made the basis of a scientific classification of offences into civil and criminal, nevertheless, daily experience supports the view that the common attitude towards offences considered evil in themselves is different from that towards offences which are the creation of express prohibition and which do not involve moral turpitude. Moreover, Allen's development of the principle of social expediency as a determinant for classifying offences has something to be said for it.

(vi) That African law recognises certain types of practice wholly foreign to modern English law must, however, be admitted. The practice of what has come to be known as ' ritual murder ', for example, has been retained too long in many African societies,

[1] *Legal Duties*, Ch. III.

whether highly organised or not.   It is hardly paralleled elsewhere in the Western world, although examples of similar practices
abound (or, until recently, abounded) in many Eastern countries.
This abominable custom has probably done more to strengthen
the hands of the detractors of African law than any other single
defect in it.

Also, African law permits the summary execution of the so-
called sorcerer or witch by the social group.[1]   Belief in witchcraft
is prevalent, since it is thought to be generally levelled at established institutions and important pursuits.   Therefore, the sorcerer or wizard must be summarily eliminated from membership of
the community, so as to prevent his ever getting a chance to disrupt
the delicate fabric of its social life.   This is indeed a pity, and one
must hope that the practice will soon disappear from those remote
areas in which it might still be thought permissible to kill persons
on the ground of witchcraft.

But, having said that, we must add that this curious belief in
witchcraft is not peculiar, in essence, to the African.   Even in
England, witchcraft was a capital offence until abolished by the
Witchcraft Act, 1735.   In Western Europe, a witch was legally
executed as late as 1782.[2]   But, although witchcraft has been
legally proscribed, belief in it is still strong among the rural communities of the greater part of the modern world.   One has to
look at the current ' witch-hunt ' for Communists and their so-
called ' fellow-travellers ' in contemporary America, in order to
appreciate how susceptible even industrialised and ' civilised ' men
can be to a certain psychological habituation, due to marginal
insecurity and spiritual dread of the unknown.[3]   The type-figure
seems to be still much in evidence today : the witch-doctor or the
black magician of ' primitive ' society has merely been replaced in
modern ' civilised ' society by the scientist, be he a psychiatrist
or a spiritualist medium.

[1] But the reader must take this subject to the fuller treatment of the
whole topic given at pp. 225 ff.

[2] Lowie, *Primitive Society*, pp. 405–6.

[3] Note, again, the present widespread belief in ' flying saucers ' in the
United States of America, the current vogue of ' science fiction ' all over
Europe, and the modern extensions of the Frankenstein legend in, e.g. ' The
Thing from Another World ', ' The Day the Earth Stood Still ', each
dealing with visitants from another planet.   Aldous Huxley amply caters,
in his drama, *This World of Light*, for the taste of millions who ' like
their universe draped in transcendental mysteries '.

The only peculiarity—and it is an important one—about witch-craft in Africa is that belief in it is still so pervasive.[1] The under-lying assumption of sorcery in African or European societies is, therefore, one of degree and not of kind. Let us add that, by the various Witchcraft Ordinances (in some cases dating back fifty years or more), it has been declared a criminal offence in all British-African territories to practise or pretend to practise witchcraft, and, conversely, to try or attempt to try anyone for witchcraft.

(vii) It is quite feasible that, with increasing economic and social changes in the modes of life of the African, his legal ideas in regard to crime will more and more approximate roughly to those of English law, especially in those fields where modern commerce and technology are fast revolutionising traditional attitudes and concepts. Thus, Bushe put his finger on the right point when he wrote : ' . . . apart from the provision which the law—Native and British—must necessarily make to provide for the safety of person and property and the exercise of personal rights (and at their simplest there is little difference in principle between the law of Bantu and Briton to this end), a modern government has to provide by statute or rule for a multitude of things unknown or scarcely known to Africa forty years ago—railways, post and tele-graphs, water supplies and electric light . . .'[2]

Regulations made to achieve these ends are on their first intro-duction bound to be little understood or hardly popular, but the process of assimilation and absorption should be easier if the right effort is made to correlate the new ideas with the old. The new offences thus created are what Major Orde-Browne has called ' technical crimes ',[3] as between which and ordinary crimes there is an understandable distinction drawn by the British people no less than by the African—which fact the learned writer seems to have overlooked. Only it is more so in the one case than in the other.

(viii) Finally, we will briefly dispose of the fallacy that English

---

[1] Cf. George Ordish (*The Listener*, Dec. 23, 1954, p. 1105): ' It seems the plant (i.e. the mistletoe) was particularly useful against witches, and as witches are very active in dairies—particularly in northern England and Wales—it was always hung in the dairy to give protection and, I believe, it is still used to some extent for this purpose there, as it is well known that nothing is so fatal to milk and butter as witchcraft.'

[2] H. G. Bushe, ' Criminal Justice in Africa ', *Jnl. Roy. Afr. Soc.*, Vol. 34 (1935), pp. 117–28.   [3] See p. 115.

(or even European) ideas of criminal law are incapable of application in Africa, because of the alleged incompatibility of the cultural and social attitudes of the African with the European. Quite apart from the fact that this argument disregards the inevitable changes, often phenomenal, which are daily taking place in Africa and which are thereby bridging the gaps between the rural (African) and the industrial (European) organisation of society, it conveniently ignores the similar phenomenon of adaptation that is taking place elsewhere.

To take a few examples, in South Africa and Ceylon, Roman-Dutch law has had to be radically recast on its criminal side and English criminal law adopted in order to meet the needs of a changed and changing social and economic order in these territories. The same adjustment has long been made in the Hindu and Moslem legal systems of India and Pakistan ; Burma is no exception. As we have shown earlier,[1] various countries of Europe, the Middle East and the Far East have at different stages of their development thrown overboard their native Criminal Codes and laws and have adopted either the French, the German or the English model.

There is, therefore, no reason at all to doubt that African law can and will make the same adjustment. It has, in fact, made encouraging progress in many developed communities in British Africa. English criminal law, often suitably modified to meet local requirements, is already operating there fairly successfully. It would, however, be rash to predict the exact character of the ultimate amalgam.

[1] See pp. 44–5.

CHAPTER VIII

PRINCIPLES OF LIABILITY FOR LEGAL WRONGS

HAVING shown that African customary law does make its own distinction between what are called criminal and civil offences according to English law, we may now go on to consider what notions of liability are entertained in the respective spheres of legal wrongs. First, let us examine the general ideas held about the aims of law in African societies before we attempt to analyse the basic concepts of liability for civil and criminal wrongs.

It is commonplace to describe African law as positive and preoccupied with the maintenance of the social equilibrium of the community, and English (or European) law as markedly negative. It has also been claimed for it that its chief aim is compensation for the wronged as opposed to the European ideal of punishment of the wrong-doer ; the aim of African law, so the argument runs, is restitution, not retribution. A third generalisation about African law is that it is restricted to a limited group, whilst European law tends to be all-embracing and comprehensive. A fourth contention is that the basis of its operation is communal, not individualistic, as it is in European law. This list of ' points of departure ' between the African and the European systems of law could be and are even added to, but it seems advisable to pause here in order to ponder the implications of those just stated.

Writers on African law are perfectly right to stress that its essential characteristic is the maintenance or restoration of the social equilibrium of the community and that this pervades the whole fabric of African law. But it is fallacious to make this assertion only with respect to African law, since that implies that English (or European) law therefore has an entirely different aim. Against this, we may recall here Lord Sumner's well-known *dictum* : ' The object of a civil enquiry into a cause and consequence is to fix liability on some responsible person and to give reparation for damage done.' [1] To the same effect is Roscoe

[1] In *Weld-Blundell* v. *Stephens* (1920), A.C. 956, p. 986.

Pound's recent statement : [1] ' What the law has been trying to do is to adjust relations and order conduct so as to give the most effect to the whole scheme of expectations of men in civilised society with a minimum of frictions and waste.'

We see, therefore, that whatever differences in other respects there are between African and European legal ideas, in both the ultimate aim of law in society is essentially the maintenance of the social order. Any attempt to restrict this function to African law fails to acknowledge that African law has its punitive as well as its compensatory side, and that such a dual feature is not at all inconsistent with the maintenance or restoration of the social equilibrium. Moreover, it confuses the civil with the criminal object of law and forgets that even in English law the aim of the law of civil liability is also compensation while only that of criminal liability is at all punitive.

Before we embark upon any detailed treatment of the ordinary ideas of legal liability for wrongs in African customary law, however, let us briefly note an important problem. It is true that (a) the belief in the influence of former existence on present life may sometimes operate to excuse individual responsibility for wrongs done, as the tendency then is to say that the wrong-doer cannot ' help himself '—it is no fault of his ; and (b) the attribution of certain events and occurrences to the action of supernatural agencies, such as that these have been brought about through the ire of an offended ancestor or a deceased kinsman,[2] often results in the attempted propitiation of the offended spirits rather than in vengeance against the living individual who has done a wrong.

While these are real difficulties in the way of any general claim that African law recognises personal liability for mundane wrongs, this impersonal view of cause and effect in such cases serves at any rate to assuage the passions so freely aroused by provocative behaviour in situations rendered explosive by excitable persons. In the interval of consulting a diviner or arranging an ordeal, passions will have cooled somewhat, so that the issues can now be more objectively appraised. The psychological basis of such device, and it is scarcely more than a device, to stave off the consequences of rash and hasty action, must not be overlooked.[3]

---

[1] *Justice According to Law*, p. 29.
[2] See, e.g. Evans-Pritchard, *Witchcraft, Oracles and Magic*, p. 63.
[3] This point is considered at some length in Ch. XII, later.

A full understanding of an African community would generally reveal the deep underlying assumptions of the whole concept which would belie this all too facile attribution of human conduct to the erratic whims of non-human agencies. It would be found that most if not all African communities with a belief in witchcraft, or even black-magic, normally attribute to supernatural powers natural occurrences (especially public disasters) to which no rational explanation, as conceived in the community, could be given by the people. A sudden and extraordinary invasion of locusts at harvest time, an unprecedented rainstorm accompanied by lightning and a few human casualties, an unexpected eruption of a long quiescent volcano—these and similar happenings must be the work of supernatural forces. In English law these might constitute the legitimate defences of 'Act of God' and 'Inevitable Accident', notions not essentially dissimilar to those we are discussing.

In private disputes between two individuals or wrongs done by one person to another, however, it would be noticed that people are less disposed to excuse personal failings not beyond the offending individual's power to prevent or avoid. And this is so in spite of any widespread belief that individuals could be bewitched into committing certain species of offences.

That the vast majority of wrongs are treated on the purely rational basis of individual responsibility should become obvious to the reader of what now follows.

A. CRIMINAL LIABILITY AND EXEMPTIONS THEREFROM

Over and above the criticisms just made, there are at least two main obstacles to the acceptance of the equilibrium theory as popularly postulated of African law : (1) the obvious disproportion between the offence and its attendant penalty in most African societies, and (2) the clear evidence we have that the motive or the intention of an offender is taken into account in awarding punishment or ordering the payment of compensation. Let us take each point separately :

(1) If, as is so often alleged, African law is positive, collectivist, and therefore concerned only to restore the *status quo ante*, one would expect that its main aim should be to make the punishment fit the crime. Restitution for theft or compensation for homicide restores the equilibrium, and there is an end of the matter.

This may be true of simple, pastoral communities of our Group B type, but with regard to the Group A variety, this hypothesis breaks down. But even in the less developed communities of the former type, instances can be cited of disproportionate penalties ; e.g. if a stolen article can be restored to its owner or replaced by an equivalent, it is all very well with the equilibrium theory ; but if not, an arbitrary value is imposed which may or may not be equivalent to that of the stolen article.

And while Hartland's statement, that with advancing civilisation in a primitive society the extreme penalty of death and mutilation is often mitigated or compounded for, is valid for the later stages in the process, he seems, nevertheless, to have overlooked the fact that there are in fact cases where the penalty imposed is out of all proportion to the offence committed. As clan independence disintegrates, giving way to a centralised political organisation, the old checks and balances weaken and, until a measure of political stability is achieved as in many West African States, the social equilibrium is sought to be maintained by these disproportionate penalties for offences likely to endanger society during the period of transition.

(2) This raises the controversial issue : Are motive, intention, negligence, accident, etc., relevant in African law ? Many writers have tended to deny this possibility. What about the punishment of *any* member of an offender's clan by the offended clan ? Motive is surely disregarded then, so argue the protagonists of this view. Also, strictly speaking, once it is admitted that the object of African law is merely to restore the *status quo*, intention ought not to enter into any consideration of the offender's liability. The offence has been committed and has to be adjusted, irrespective of the motive or intention of the offender or his victim.

But there is abundant evidence pointing the other way. Dr. Wagner has observed that the Kavirondo Bantu punish *intentional* wrongs by the imposition of double the compensation normally payable for *unintentional* wrongs. That is, the Kavirondo Bantu *do* distinguish between these two types of wrongs.[1] Again, Driberg records [2] that according to Colle, the Baluba distinguish between voluntary and involuntary homicide ; drunkenness is a mitigating circumstance among the Basonge. The Bashilange,

[1] A. Phillips, *Report on Native Tribunals in Kenya*, pp. 254-5.
[2] Driberg, *op. cit.*, pp. 225 ff.

K

the Chagga and others all make the same distinction. On the other hand, among the Awemba and some other tribes, accident or drunkenness appear to be discounted. But whether the offence is murder or manslaughter the penalty, which is death in the case of the former but compensation in that of the latter, is just as much a process of restoring the equilibrium. But there is no mitigation of the extreme penalty where the victim is a guest or a host, since this is a breach of the laws of hospitality on which the integrity of the community depends *vis-à-vis* its neighbours.

In the light of the foregoing argument it is somewhat surprising to come upon this conclusion of Driberg's : ' I think it is true to say that motive is only regarded in so far as it affects the whole community and prevents its proper functioning, or destroys those qualities which make for corporate harmony and equilibrium. With us, the motive, or the intention, is immediate and individual ; with the Africans it is not so much the guilty intention, but the effects of the intention on the community at large.' [1] It would be superfluous to try to argue that this strange distinction between group and individual motive as specific characteristics of African and European law, respectively, is demonstrably false.

We have shown earlier [2] how and why the glib assertion of the unity of the clan is misleading, particularly in the determination of legal rights and duties. It is not only that the institution of clanship is not a universal condition in African societies,[3] but also that the corporateness of social life in most of these communities normally allows for conflict and a measure of self-assertion within the group. This necessarily implies the existence of individual rights and duties, and the recognition of the concept of personal responsibility for any wrongs committed by a member.

As for the argument about the collective responsibility of the group for its member's delicts, it is interesting to find a scholar of the standing of Lowie write : [4] ' As might be inferred from the

---

[1] *Op. cit.*, p. 236.   [2] See pp. 88–92 *supra*.
[3] E.g. Prof. M. Gluckman has observed that the Lozi of Northern Rhodesia have no system of clanship or lineage but trace relationships through mother and father only—see Browne and Forde (eds.), *African Systems of Kinship and Marriage*, pp. 166–206. And Prof. S. F. Nadel has found paternal and maternal filiation combined, resulting in the absence of serious crime. (*Ibid.*, pp. 333–59.)
[4] *Op. cit.*, p. 387.

satisfaction of justice by the punishment of any member of the offender's group, criminal intent plays not nearly the same part in criminal law as it does in our own jurisprudence.' But the learned author then proceeds to cite instances of ' the care with which they discriminate between voluntary and involuntary deeds, and between those purely accidental and those resulting from carelessness '. Thus he observes that the south-eastern Bantu draw a highly interesting distinction between accidental manslaughter and accidental injury to property ; compensation must be paid to the chief for every homicide, irrespective of criminal intent ; but if harm is done to any property without premeditation, no indemnities are exacted. Of course, the writer admits that there are important qualifications to the trite generalisation that intention plays no part in determining liability in ' primitive law ', but insists that ' after all qualifications are made it remains true that the ethical motive of an act is more frequently regarded as irrelevant in the ruder cultures than in our courts of justice '.

Basing himself on Driberg, H. R. Hone said of the British advent in Uganda : ' What then was the native conception of law at this time ? Roughly, it was that all wrongs concerned only the individuals affected. If my goat is stolen I must find the wrongdoer and bring him to the chief ; my remedy is then either to get the goat back or to be compensated in money or kind so that I may be restored to my original position. In other words, the native conception of law extended only to retribution.' He found that homicide was normally settled by a payment of bloodmoney comprising seven head of cattle to the next-of-kin of the deceased ; it was only in the case of intra-family homicide that the death penalty was exacted since it was considered inappropriate to allow family cattle to be forfeited by one member to another as compensation.

We also learn that the Teso exacted blood-money where the murderer was apprehended ; but if he escaped, he was outlawed and the members of the deceased's clan were entitled to obtain their satisfaction by killing a member of the murderer's clan. Adultery and theft were compensated in cattle or goats ; if a hired thief were killed in the execution of his mission, his relatives were entitled to be compensated by his hirer.

The Basoga employed killing as the penalty for murder, and

fines supplemented by flogging were the punishment for most of the other offences.   Among the Banyoro and the Bagishu, accidental homicide incurred no penalty except the provision of a feast by the killer for the surviving relatives on both sides, those of the deceased attending as evidence that they harboured no malice against those of the killer.   If the killer was a member of the same clan as his victim, he was required to pay a fine equal in value to the marriage payment on a wife, and this was payable to the victim's father who might, if he wished, take a wife and raise another child to replace the victim.   Wife-beating was no offence and an adulterous wife could legally be killed by her husband ; her adulterer was liable to a heavy fine or, in extreme cases, might be killed by a husband who discovered him in the act.   The Baganda sometimes allowed the wife's relations to bring a case against a husband who had killed her, in order to find out whether the killing was justified in the circumstances.   Murder was sometimes visited with the execution of the murderer, though generally the penalty was the payment of blood-money.   An adulterer of the upper classes usually paid for his offence with his own life, since he was supposed to be a serious menace to the personal safety of his victim's husband [1] ;   he who violated a fellow peer's wife would kill him if he could, as indeed he metaphorically did by the very act of the adultery committed with his wife.[2]

By the middle of the nineteenth century ' a stage of development had already been reached in many tribes in Uganda, whereat a differentiation was made between a deliberate killing and any less culpable form of homicide, the former being dealt with by the infliction of the death penalty, the latter by compensation.   Here we have, in outline, the conception familiar to our law, of the difference between murder and manslaughter.'   This, if we may say so, is the only verdict that the former Attorney-General of Uganda could have reached on the evidence before him.   Hone then adds that, because of the prevalence of the principle of restitution, compensation was, nevertheless, usually payable even in cases of accidental death unaccompanied by negligence ;   that is, where in English law the killer would escape all liability, civil

---

[1] Also, among the Yoruba of Southern Nigeria, death was the penalty for adultery with chiefs' wives—Talbot, *The Peoples of Southern Nigeria*, p. 629.

[2] See p. 179, *infra*, in this connexion.

or criminal. His conclusion was that all these, far from being peculiar to African ideas of legal liability, could be paralleled by similar English legal developments in the Middle Ages.

On the other hand, Major Orde-Browne would seem to be repeating the outworn argument that African law was communal in these words : ' The second peculiarity of the old law was its communal application ; its decisions applied not so much to the individual as to a group. . . . Where the individual was so closely identified with the group, the working of the law was naturally facilitated, and recompense was almost always possible. When a murder was committed, the family thereby deprived of a useful member would receive compensation from the offender's relatives *if he himself could not pay.*' [1] One is bound to give thanks to this writer for the conditional clause which so appropriately supports the very point we have made before, [2] that, in spite of the complex web of kinship ties and agnatic obligations, the individual and not his kin-group is primarily and ultimately responsible for his acts in relation to other people. It is curious to note that a believer in the communal nature of African law can unwittingly admit so much.

More objective and direct is the evidence given by Fortes with respect to the Tallensi of the Gold Coast : ' As a member of a particular lineage a man has definite rights and duties and enters into a stream of social relations from which all who do not belong to that agnatic line are excluded.' [3] Later, in another connexion, the writer issues a necessary warning : ' But this does not mean that all Tale jural relations are based on the concept of collective responsibility. On the contrary, jural responsibility is precisely fixed on particular individuals or exactly defined corporate units. This is graphically summed up in many Tale maxims. Thus they say " A pipe sounds best in its owner's mouth . . ." that is, an action should be answered for by the person directly responsible for it.' [4] He goes on to cite [5] as a good illustration of his statement ' that collective responsibility is not a principle of Tale jural relations ', the liability of a debtor to reimburse, by an equivalent

---

[1] *Journal Roy. Afr. Soc.*, Vol. 32, No. 127, pp. 148–59, at p. 151. The italics are mine.

[2] Pp. 89–92.

[3] *The Dynamics of Clanship among the Tallensi*, pp. 134–5.

[4] *Ibid.*, p. 230.   [5] *Ibid.*, p. 245.

amount of property, a fellow clansman whose live-stock has been raided by a creditor from another clan as a means of the creditor himself paying. ' It is not the clan but the debtor himself who is responsible for his debt. Self-help is a technique for putting pressure on a debtor through the mechanisms of clan and lineage cohesion.'

Similar, too, is Miss Green's testimony regarding the Ibos : ' A case is normally regarded as between individuals and whether or not they are of the same village they have a variety of judicial possibilities open to them.' [1]

Also, Dr. Lowie, quoting Wagner's writings, records [2] that in Kafir law, if several persons took part in a brawl, the penalty for each person slain was imposed on all those engaged in the fight. The penalty for killing a male was seven head of cattle and that for killing a female was ten head of cattle, the difference being due to the property obtained by the latter at marriage. For assault and battery the fine ranged from one to five head of cattle and both parties were subject to a fine each, since nothing was considered sufficient to warrant one man striking another even in self-defence ; but it would seem that this was the case only in the absence of a reliable witness as to who started it all. In the case of abortion both the woman and her accomplice were each fined four or five head of cattle. Prior to 1820, a man caught in adultery with a woman could be killed with impunity, but King Gaika abolished this law and made the killer guilty as for other forms of manslaughter. [3] Adultery was treated as a civil case and the fine ranged from one to four head (of cattle) according to the husband's station in society ; the fine was raised from seven to ten head if it clearly resulted in pregnancy. Theft, mainly in the form of stock-raiding, was penalised by the exaction of a tenfold compensation if the property was not recovered. But wilful damage to property must be fully indemnified, while no damages were granted to a complainant for purely accidental injury.

The evidence of Dundas for the Wakamba, Wakikuyu, Watheraka and Wadigo of Kenya Colony and for the Wazegutia, Wapare

---

[1] Green, *Ibo Village Affairs*, p. 113.
[2] *Op. cit.*, pp. 410 ff.
[3] This principle is not unlike the *ratio decidendi* in *Holmes* v. *D.P.P.* (1946), A.C. 588. See also p.249

and Wachagga in the Tanganyika Territory (formerly German East Africa), seems somewhat as follows.[1] Blood revenge was usually directed against the murderer or some near relative, and it always ensued in all cases of premeditated and unprovoked murder arising out of beer drinks. In homicide cases accident was not always a mitigating factor, though settlement was then by payment of compensation : ' . . . . very convincing proof will always be required, and it may be said that the onus of proving that it was accident lies with the offender.' [2] Practice, of course, varied among these tribes, from the open recognition as lawful of killing in self-defence as well as of killing without intent, on the one hand, to the bland denial of either, on the other. In Ukamba and elsewhere an inquest of elders, including a searching *post mortem*, was very often held in order to discover any possible internal injury.

In reiterating the general proposition that the murderer's motive or intention was usually disregarded in awarding penalties for homicide, Dundas gave three reasons : (1) that any relaxation of this general rule would result in increased bloodshed ; (2) that its maintenance prevents fine distinctions being drawn between intentional and unintentional or negligent acts ; and (3) that it enforces care and restraint upon men's actions. But he soon proceeds to enumerate in scattered parts of his lengthy article the following (summarised) exceptions to the general rule :

(a) Among the Akamba, accidental killing was always compensated by only half the amount of blood-money for intentional killing. This is called *mbanga*, which is a word also used by the Akikuyu to signify the killing of a man by some article or animal belonging to another. Both the Akikuyu and the Akamba would award the article or animal causing the death to the deceased's relatives.[3]

(b) If two men killed each other in a fight, compensation was dispensed with by a kind of set-off ; and a man might, without

---

[1] *Journal of Royal Anthropological Institute*, Vol. 51 (1921), pp. 217–78, ' Native Laws of Some Bantu Tribes of East Africa '.

[2] *Ibid.*, pp. 238–9.

[3] One is reminded here of the former practice in English law whereby a personal chattel which was the immediate and accidental cause of the death of a human being was forfeited to the Crown as *Deodand* (*Deo* = to God, and *Dandum* = to be given). The practice was abolished by the Statute 9 and 10 Vict. c. 62 (1846).

paying any compensation, kill another whom he saw in the act
of killing his brother.

(c) So also, if a murderer refused to pay a duly adjudged compensation, it could be exacted by force, and if anyone should be
killed in the ensuing scuffle, no blood-money was payable.

(d) A person might refuse to accept any blood-money and
might instead kill the murderer or the latter's close relative.

(e) In all these East African communities a man might kill his
wife without being liable to pay any compensation,[1] but the
balance of any marriage payment must still be paid by such
husband to her father. All other cases of homicide involving
blood relations [2] must be compensated for by blood-money, which
varied from the full amount to a half or less, *according to circumstances* : 'The clan is excluded from any share, although it
contributes as in any other case of homicide. If a man kills any
distant relative or a clansman living in the same locality, he must
pay half the blood-money, but if he slays a clansman not residing
in his district he is liable for full blood-money. Cases of accidental killing were usually settled by arrangement between the
clan and the family of the victim.'

(f) Generally, the taking of the life of a stranger must be fully
compensated, even though he had stayed with his host for only
one day. The payment was always made to his host. But blood-
money for the murder of, or by, a stranger could only be claimed
if the stranger had already been fully adopted by the claimant or
if the stranger had previously entered into blood-brotherhood
with a member of the family.

(g) Provocation, particularly in cases of theft where the thief
was caught *in flagrante delicto*, was always and everywhere among
these communities a mitigating, nay an exonerating, circumstance.
But the right to kill in such a case was not frequently exercised in
practice. The usual penalty among the Kikuyu for stealing stock
was ten times the value of whatever was stolen, *plus* three sheep
for the elders sitting as judges. This was in the nature of a fine
imposed over and above the due restoration of the property itself.

---

[1] Possibly because he was the only person who was entitled to receive
any compensation that might be due on her life through another's
killing. Also the cow is given to a widow as her own property if her
husband was killed by another person.

[2] E.g. a man killing a brother, sister, mother or father had to pay
definite compensations to the others according to an agreed tariff.

Every person taking part in the theft must pay this penalty.   Any man who ate of the meat of a stolen beast had to pay three sheep. ' While almost every other offence is attributed to circumstances rather than to character, that of theft signifies to the natives an unpardonable nature.'

Against the common assertion of communalism in legal liability, Dundas finds that ' Even between the best friends and nearest relatives, compensation is paid which one might otherwise expect would be waived.'   And this, be it noted, among predominantly clan-ridden African communities in which the so-called ' unity of the clan ' ought to exclude such intra-group liability.   To cap it all, Dundas observes :

' Homicide seems to be the only offence affecting not only one individual.   A man who has committed such an offence goes to all his clansmen and *begs* contributions towards the blood-money ; this is done to the present day, and to refuse such *assistance* is regarded as shameful, and as equivalent to a denial of kinship. *Yet the clan will not commence the payment : the debtor must first say what he is prepared to pay, and if he is destitute of means the clan will not subscribe.'* [1]

Finally, the purification or peace-making ceremony of killing a goat and/or sheep after payment of compensation for murder is designed, either by itself or in addition to the taking of an oath, to effect lasting reconciliation between the two families of the murderer and the murdered.   Dundas is emphatic : ' Those who can attribute to a crime such direful results cannot be supposed to regard it as a trifling affair, and there must be an in-born horror of taking human life.   The native is, in fact, not often guilty of murder, as we commonly understand the term.   Of premeditated murder I have only known two cases, but ninety per cent. of the cases of people being killed may be said to be due to drunken brawls. . . .'

B. SUMMARY OF PRINCIPLES OF CRIMINAL LIABILITY

(1) There is a notion of *mens rea* in African law.   The reason why compensation is such a recurrent, indeed almost inevitable, feature of cases of homicide is that, as we have just been told by Dundas in the passage last quoted, about ninety per cent. of the

[1] All the italics are mine.

deaths were the result of unpremeditated drunken brawls. The theory in the African mind is then, that a person thus temporarily deprived of his reason was incapable of forming an intent, let alone a guilty one, sufficient to induce him to want to kill an innocent companion or stranger. A clear distinction between murder and manslaughter is implicit in this way of treating homicide cases.[1]

That the majority of homicides take place in circumstances of accident or want of premeditated malice is also borne out by the fact that, of the eleven cows included in the blood-money payment throughout the Machakos District of Kenya, the first cow is called *ng'ombe ya mbanga*, meaning the ' cow of the *accident* '.[2] But the same writer later said : ' Kamba law does not distinguish between murder, manslaughter or a death caused by accident. The blood-price is payable in each case. If a man were to fire an arrow at an animal and hit a man beyond, not knowing that he was there, he would be held fully liable.' [3]

This seeming paradox can be resolved if it is frequently borne in mind that here, as elsewhere with some other writers, there is a confusion between *liability* and the quantification of *damages*. There are varying degrees of liability as well as of damages in almost all other cases of injury to the person outside the category of fatal ones. In homicide cases, however, the elders naturally regard the consequences of the children and other dependants of the victim being suddenly left destitute as more important than the *manner* of the encompassing of the death by the killer. A death has suddenly occurred, the killer has been apprehended and has not denied his guilt ; the elders say : Let him compensate his victim's surviving relatives according to the customary tariff schedule appropriate to his case. This interpretation seems supported by Penwill's own later observation [4] that, while cases of petty assaults are expiable by the payment of a goat, those of serious bodily injuries are normally visited with severe penalties.

(2) On the other hand, death is almost always the invariable

---

[1] For the clear distinction drawn by the Ashanti in these matters, see Rattray, *Ashanti Law and Constitution*, pp. 296–303.

[2] Penwill, *Kamba Customary Law*, pp. 78 ff.

[3] *Ibid.*, p. 81. A possible explanation might be that the judges would consider that the man who fired an arrow in such circumstances had clearly failed to show the *exacta diligentia* expected of a reasonable man in his position at the time and place the incident occurred.

[4] *Ibid.*, pp. 85–6.

penalty for dastardly acts of wanton homicide—whether these proceed from motives of revenge, or of gain, or of sadism.

(3) The very existence in almost all the penalty tariff schedules of a graduated scale of compensation or fine for a single offence indicates, if it does not conclusively prove, that the judges do not just impose punishments automatically but that the culprit's liability is measured by the extent of the enormity of his crime and by certain extenuating circumstances, if any. All this might not be expressly stated by the judges as part of the award, but few among their audience at a trial would fail to realise the implied assumptions influencing particular declarations of penalties. It is seriously urged here that motive, accident, intention, etc., largely enter into nearly every considered judgment from which the incautious observer would apparently regard them to be absent.

(4) But, when all this has been said, it remains true that in view of the limited margin of security in small, often isolated communities and the tendency for passion to be easily inflamed by provocative behaviour, what would be deemed a good enough motive or intention in, say, English law, might not necessarily be so considered in certain types of African law.

(5) When people deny that motive, intention, etc., play any part in African law, they seem to be arguing from the particular to the general—from the single instance of homicide and its treatment to the whole of African law. They forget that all African law is neither homicide nor even crime in general, and that there are large areas of civil law in which these concepts (i.e. motive, intention, etc.) are fully regarded by the elders in their adjudication of disputes.

(6) Drunkenness produced by ordinary intoxication is generally no defence against a charge for any offence. The general idea is that, since the man drank of his own free will and ought to have exercised his own discretion to know when to stop and had failed to do so, he should suffer for not behaving like a reasonable member of society. On the other hand, if a man were made drunk by others and then put to some act or omission resulting in injury or harm to another, those responsible for his condition at the material time would be liable and not he.

In cases of insanity, the family of a madman were usually held responsible for all his crimes. If he was so out of his mind as not to know what he was doing at the time of committing the offence in question, his family should have given him all necessary medical treatment or at least kept him in confinement so that he did not go about injuring other people. Should they fail in their duty, they would be liable for any offence he might commit whilst so left at large.

(7) It may be that the legal arrangement above outlined may be truer of African societies with a centralised judicial machinery than of those having none ; and it may also be that a greater degree of sophistication is to be expected in the exaction of the blood-price. Clan feelings being less strong, if not entirely absent, and the organised force of the community in the person of the chief and his councillors being more readily available, notorious murderers are likely to be similarly protected against mob violence until their innocence or guilt can be established judicially. It is suggested that in the judicial process of such societies, the presence or absence of malice, accident, negligence and the like will be found to be more explicitly mentioned and considered in the judges' statements of their verdict than would be the case in the judicial process of less highly organised societies.

We must now examine the civil side of African law with a view to discovering its basic ideas as to legal liability. The questions here are : Is there a law of contract or a law of tort in African law, or is there just an undifferentiated and confused mass of obligations without any underlying assumption in both of legal principles ?

For the sake of convenience we will discuss the main issues under the separate headings of Contracts and Torts, so that by a fairly close examination of the relevant data we may discover the true nature of civil liability as conceived in African customary law.

C. CIVIL LIABILITY UNDER CONTRACTS

We may pose the problem here at once by quoting this significant but fairly typical opinion of Seagle : '. . . and it is doubtful whether " contract " as such exists, i.e. whether obligations are recognised as binding irrespective of mutuality or pre-existing obligation. However, the forms of the obligations are probably determined less by the elements of reciprocity than by the limitations of the legal system with respect to enforcement. In any event in both primitive and civilised societies reciprocity is entirely absent, at least in any economic sense, in the institution of the gift. Moreover, reciprocity is involved only in civil obligations.' [1]

A partial refutation of this may, however, be seen in this statement [2] by Driberg : [3] ' Every status has its own obligations to the community and the community never regards the individual unless he discharges his obligations. All benefits are dependent on duty : there is, and there must always be, a constant reciprocity between giving and receiving. A living elder assists the community with his advice and experience, and in return, whenever an animal is killed or a feast is prepared, a specific portion of the animal or of the feast is reserved for him and offered to him ceremonially as a public tribute. We have seen that the discharge of obligations and the receiving of benefits are correlatives.' In other words, there is an underlying sense of obligation and a recognition of the principle of *pacta servanda sunt*.

But the first notable proponent of the contrary view was Maine [4] who spoke of the absence of contracts between individuals as due to the regulation of personal relations by the status of the individuals, as well as by the administration and inheritance of property within the family according to customary law. He believed that these adequately account for the lack of detailed rules in so-called ' primitive ' communities. A glance back at the samples of customary rules and standards quoted earlier in the present chapter, taken together with what has already been said in previous chapters about the fallacy of primitive communism, should dispose of this imposing farce regarding the automatic operation of custom and the consequent absence of detailed rules of general rights and duties. We will now attempt to demonstrate its falsity further.

At this stage it seems necessary to take a number of specific customary law situations in which we can observe a contractual element at work, and then to analyse the underlying concept as closely as possible.

Marriage.—It may be as well to start with this very important indigenous institution. Marriage in African societies is a contract

---

[1] Diamond, *Primitive Law*, was cited in support at p. 279 of article, *op. cit.*

[2] In ' Secular Aspect of Ancestor Worship in Africa ', *Jnl. Roy. Afr. Soc.* (Supplement to), Vol. 35, No. 138, Jan. 1936.

[3] Who, of course, knew nothing of Seagle's article.

[4] *Ancient Law*, pp. 325–6, and pp. 378–9.

ostensibly between two families, ' in which the individual interests of the groom and bride, though implicitly or formally recognised, are but a subordinate element of the wider dominating interests of their families '.[1] This may be taken as representing the normal sociological postulate of a customary law marriage in practically all African communities. But, as will be shown presently, it is hardly distinguishable from the marital conceptions which prevailed in England to the end of the Victorian era, or from the French ideas of the marriage tie even to this day.[2]

The importance thus attached by society at large to the creation of the contract of marriage must be due to the fact that, while marriage is like any other agreement to create legal relations between the parties, it differs notably from other forms of contract in that it marks a change of status for the parties. It is this inevitable interdependence of contract and status that accounts for the interest which the European State or the African community (and not merely the two families immediately concerned) takes in the marriage contract.

For purposes of *legal* analysis, however, one must take a closer view of the African marriage. If it is a valid one, it will be seen to consist of two inseparable elements : (*a*) a contract comprising an exchange of promises between the boy and the girl to marry, followed by (*b*) the ceremony of marriage, to which members of the community are invited as witnesses. The first is the *individual* aspect of a marriage, and is the true contractual element in the transaction ; the *communal* aspect is the wider participation of certain members, usually in the last resort the parents or guardians of the marrying couple, in the legalisation of the marriage relationship.[3]

---

[1] Thus wrote J. F. Holleman of the Shona in his *Shona Customary Law*, pp. 73–4. The same has been said of the Basuto by H. Ashton in *The Basuto*, p. 62, and of the Nandi by G. S. Snell in *Nandi Customary Law*, p. 20.

[2] Even in England, members of the aristocratic families still regard marriage sometimes from the standpoint of a selective union between the two families of the bride and groom—Read the recent judgment in *Kremezi* v. *Ridgway* (1949), 1 All. E.R. 662 (where an English naval officer was successfully sued by a Greek woman for breach of promise of marriage no doubt induced by the parents of the man in England).

[3] This point about the parents or guardians of the marrying couple is analogous in principle to the requirement in English law of the consent of the girl's parents or of the court to the celebration of the marriage, if the girl is under 21.

But few students of African law would deny that, at bottom, the actual union is established between the individual husband and wife, who thereby constitute a new family unit within the husband's patrilineage or the wife's matrilineage (in communities where marriage is uxorilocal). Also, most communities have their own peculiar mechanisms for the ascertainment of the willingness or otherwise of the individual parties to a contemplated marriage. Legally, it is not the case, as is so commonly asserted, that the wishes of the intending couple were always brushed aside by their parents (especially, the girl's). One need only look into any detailed description of a typical marriage and its traditional incidents in order to appreciate the chain of interlocking gifts and tokens passing between boy and girl as well as the activities of the inevitable ' go-between ' that almost invariably precede and accompany an African customary union.[1]

Then there is the transfer or agreement to transfer cattle or other *quid pro quo* as a pre-condition of the marriage contract. This element, without which no marriage contract can come into being, is governed by often elaborate rules as to both its initiation and its discharge ; sometimes it must all be paid up before the marriage can take place but, at other times, a deposit is accepted by the girl's parents on condition that the balance is discharged at stated intervals or on the occurrence of a particular event. Also, its recovery, in whole or in part, on the failure of the marriage through the woman's own fault, is again governed by detailed and precise rules in all communities.[2] Considering its place in

---

[1] Let us quote this observation of Dundas as typical of the more enlightened attitude on this point :

' The number of cases in which girls defy all authority, and the futile attempts of the elders to insist on forced marriages being maintained, are proof that the law never provided for such events ; it was not so foolishly designed that it did not recognise that a permanent relationship between men and women must rest on mutual consent.

' To dogmatise on this subject by saying that the girl alone can choose her husband would be unwise. *The proper method is undoubtedly for the suitor to approach the girl first, but after that he must agree with the father.* . . . *After careful observation, I have come to the conclusion that a girl has under native custom as much freedom of choice, and the father as much parental influence, as is customary with us.*' (All italics are mine.) See p. 284 of *Jnl. Roy. Afr. Inst.* (1921), *cit. supra.*

[2] Again, to quote Dundas (*ibid.*, p. 291) : ' It is to be regretted that Europeans have not given sufficient consideration to this subject—in fact, we are apt to regard native marriage as a commercial transaction. So long as we speak of " purchasing wives " we shall probably continue

the whole marital nexus we may say that the transfer or agreement to transfer whatever is the marriage payment in a given community is itself a contract within the wider contract of marriage itself. And if we may make the further inference, an African contract of marriage is in fact a triple agreement. First, there is the primary, *legal* contract between the boy and the girl as the only true partners to the marriage relationship. Then, there is the secondary, *social* contract between the two families of the couple. Finally, there is the ancillary, *socio-legal* contract for the settlement of the marriage payment which puts the seal of enforceability on the entire transaction.

1. *Co-operative labour contracts.*[1]

These arise out of an agreement, which may be *ad hoc* or permanent, between kin-groups or unrelated persons occupying the same, contiguous or sometimes distant territories, for the purpose of assisting by co-operative labour any one or more of their number at a time in tilling, sowing or harvesting farms or in building huts or other dwellings. The one for whom work is being done for the time being acts as host to the rest, supplying them with food and drink and otherwise providing them with free entertainment in the form of drumming and other types of music. This he must do for as many days as the work lasts. He himself is of course an active and not a sleeping partner in the particular labour activity.

The same process is repeated for every member of the team until the previously ascertained needs of all are satisfied. There

to think of matrimony among natives as a matter of sale and barter. I must refer here to the old custom under which cattle received in dowry were not parted with, and this seems to suggest that dowry was considered far more in the light of a pawn or security than as a purchase price. . . . There are very definite rules to make marriage even more permanent than with us. Because we have seen so many cows paid, we have taken their value to be the principal object of a contract, and we have treated marriage and offences against it as matters properly dealt with as civil suits, in which the only question in issue has been a fixed value due from one to the other. So our attitude towards native matrimony has been identical with our manner of treating any other commercial transaction.' See also Pts. I and II of *African Marriage Survey*, ed. by A. Phillips.

[1] For a good example of this type of customary contract, see the account of *Risaga* groups among the Gusii by P. Mayer, *Two Studies in Applied Anthropology in Kenya*, pp. 5–16.

is no actual cash payment for the labour thus pooled, but the feasting and merriment for the duration of an agreed session are regarded as sufficient consideration moving from the one thus benefitted.   But the introduction of money economy seems to be working a change in some areas, and the employer of such labour is beginning to find himself faced with demand on the part of the labourers for cash compensation instead of the customary payment in kind.   This of course must have the effect also of freeing such paid co-operators from any continuing obligation to give their services until all the members shall have been properly suited, as would be necessary under the traditional arrangement.

It seems that, initially, the specific requirements of each must be comparable or at least capable of being quantified on a basis of checks and balances satisfactory to all concerned.   In an arrangement where so much depends on the good faith of the individual members, it is obvious that the penalties for default must rest on the ridicule, the contempt and the social ostracism to which a defaulter—a rare bird in these circumstances—would subject himself.   Economic pressures are also brought to bear upon the defaulter, so that no one would do business with him who has once shown that he would shirk his legal obligations to others.   Clearly, a potent factor underlying the due performance by the individual co-operator of his undertakings voluntarily entered into is the universal recognition of the principle of reciprocity of obligations.[1]

In the final analysis, the elders would look into any reported case and would probably impose a fine upon a defaulter where necessary.   Of course, ample allowances are made for cases of unavoidable illness, or of accident to life or limb, or of some other incapacitating causes not due to a trick or other pretext on the part of an alleged defaulter.

[1] Fortes, *op. cit.*, p. 246, observed of the Tallensi of the Gold Coast : ' . . . a collective hoeing party (pooh kpa' arep) is always made up of co-members of his medial lineage. . . . Distant clansmen only come if they have ties of personal matrilateral kinship with him (i.e. the invitor).   And the motive usually given for responding to such an invitation is " Tomorrow I may need the help of a hoeing party ". Public opinion is critical of those who do not conform to the conventions of mutual assistance, and when they find themselves compelled to call for assistance in collective hoeing or housebuilding or some similar activity, they are left in the lurch.'

L

2. *Contracts of Agistment.*

These are agreements in stock-farming communities whereby owners of cattle, sheep, goat, or even poultry give them into the care and custody of friendly neighbours for the purpose of being reared on a more or less commercial basis. The contract may be for a stipulated period, or it may be made indefinite but determinable at any time by either party should circumstances warrant.

The consideration for the caretaker's trouble varies with the terms on the basis of which the contract was originally entered into. The more usual arrangement is for the owner to have the first young ones produced by a female animal and the caretaker to have the next, and so on till the contract elapses. Other and sometimes complicated networks of profit-sharing are also found, and these usually raise nice problems of adjustment of damages for an unlawful breach of the contract by either party. But we need not enter into these here, as we are concerned more with the concept of this form of contract than with its detailed rules.[1]

3. *Miscellaneous forms of Customary Contracts.*

Other prevalent types of contract are the private engagements of experienced old women as midwives to take delivery of babies, or of practised or professional men and women as surgeons to carry out often delicate circumcision operations on boys and girls. Various forms of presents, more or less fixed in value, are offered and accepted for such services.

Again, short-term as well as long-term ' borrowings ' of land use are common in African communities, the consideration for the lender being a share of the annual produce. Due regard is everywhere had to bad harvests or other agricultural disasters occurring during the continuance of the land loan. Similarly, long and short agricultural tenancies on analogous conditions abound.

Finally, the existence of markets in the vast majority of indigenous African communities, whether these are for internal trade between local members or for external commerce with other tribes or foreigners, indicates a measure of exchange and a species of bargaining to which no one can seriously deny the name

[1] See, e.g., Penwill, *op. cit.*, pp. 107–9, for the Kamba system of Partnership in Cattle ; Ajisafe, *Laws and Customs of the Yoruba* (1924), p. 69 ; H. Cory, *Sukuma Law and Custom*, pp. 468–90 ; Schapera, *Bantu-Speaking Tribes of South Africa*, p. 201.

of agreement in respect of what is being transferred, bought or sold.

Nearly all African communities lacked the art of writing until comparatively recently; accordingly, witnesses played and still play a not inconsiderable part in all categories of customary contracts. The 'borrowing' and leasing of land use, the loan of agricultural implements or of cattle for milking and mating purposes, the transfer or agreement to transfer marriage payments or cattle—all these require for their legal validity the presence of witnesses or other incontrovertible evidence of an alleged contract.

4. Negotiability of certain forms of Property.

Certain African communities like the Ashanti of the Gold Coast and the Yoruba and the Hausa of Nigeria used to employ gold ingots of varying sizes and weights as well as cowries for currency purposes; and the manillas of Eastern Nigeria were only recently abolished as valid currency. There were other forms of customary currencies among other African communities.[1]

It is not generally recognised, however, that certain apparently automatic transfers of the possession of property or of the property itself involves an element of commercial exchange. In the absence of minted coins or paper currencies in most African communities, cattle or farm produce normally serve as accepted media of exchange for normal economic or commercial transactions. It is not always just a process of simple barter of one type of goods for another, as is commonly supposed.

In straightforward economic transactions such as those resulting in the debt of a bull, the creditor may and in fact often does accept a piece of land from the debtor in permanent discharge of the debt. In other cases, also, land is sometimes given in lieu of stock. But it is obvious that only land which is the object of first acquisition [2] by the debtor can be transferred in this way. Dundas records that fields are known to be generally pawned by the Akikuyu as security for debts, often redeemable at double the value of the loan. A little earlier he gave this account:

'Thus if a man owes a cow, the claim stands good for all time despite stock diseases and other risks. This, I think, explains

---

[1] E.g. the Lozi used *mpande* shells as media of exchange: Gluckman, *Essays on Lozi Land and Royal Property*, p. 35.

[2] *Op. cit.*, pp. 284–91. Dundas, in *J.R.A.I.* (1921).

why a creditor generally has to pay something to recover a debt, the debtor being, as it were, paid for his risk. A distinction is, however, made between a debt of an animal placed with a man and a debt consisting only of the value of an animal. If a cow placed with someone or paid in dowry dies, it is sufficient to return the skin and the meat to absolve from any liability for it, but if, for instance, a cow paid in dowry is sold, or a man owes a bull in compensation for something, this can be left over as a debt of undiminished value.' [1]

Should the legitimate occasions arise under customary law for a husband to claim a refund, cattle transferred to his in-laws as marriage payment are not normally returned *in specie*. Other animals of roughly equivalent quality or quantity according to prevailing standards are usually acceptable in place of the ones actually paid in by the claimant. The original animals may be killed or sold by the wife's parents subsequently to the marriage ; however, since it is not regarded as an out-and-out payment but as a security, it must be replaced, if the marriage later breaks down.

If it is proved by the production of the skin and probably of at least a portion of the meat of the animal that it has died through no fault of the in-laws, no form of liability is incurred.

The principles stated in the foregoing paragraphs also hold, whether the medium of exchange adopted for a particular transaction be crops, cattle, or valuable ornaments or jewels.

Another element of this exchange principle is that the cattle received by a father on the marriage of his daughter is not just compensation paid to him for the loss of his daughter to his son-in-law's family ; the father may use the cattle to help his own sons and probably kinsmen with their marriage payments as and when the need arises.

5. *Conclusion.*

The above summary account is meant to illustrate, not to exhaust, the innumerable contractual relationships existing in so-called simple African communities at varying stages of economic development. Many classes of bilateral as well as multilateral agreements have not been included but have rather been left to be inferred from those briefly described.

[1] *Op. cit.*, pp. 284–91.   Dundas in *J.R.A.I.* (1921).

It is clear that the essential nature of mutuality of obligations, of respect for one's plighted word, of the avoidance of fraud or force or unlawful breach of agreement, is present to the African mind. The writer recalls the answer given to him by the judges of the Busoga Central (Native) Court, in the Eastern Province of Uganda, in reply to the question ; [1] What is the legal position if A sues B for cheating him out of his proper share of the spoils of a concerted raid on C's banana garden ? These elders looked at me with evident surprise and almost spontaneously rasped back : We as Saza and Gombolola chiefs would order the immediate seizure of both A and B, the complete restoration of everything stolen, and the payment of a heavy fine by both for their impudence and want of shame. Seeing that our law frowns so much upon theft, how could we be expected to do otherwise ? Even if theft were not the object of their concerted effort, both A and B, provided the joint enterprise is established between them, would be fined for their conduct which must certainly provoke a breach of the peace by causing indignation to other people in the community.

This, in fine, is a fair sample of the indigenous idea that the elders would not hear of an unlawful agreement. In such subtle and indirect ways one chances upon statements of principles of a particular African customary law and, if one's real object is to keep an open mind and to find out what really goes on in the day-to-day, apparently humdrum activities of an African community, one cannot but be convinced that at least the rudiments of what is called contract in English law also exist in African customary law. [2]

It now remains to note briefly one alleged weakness of the African law of contract—the general indifference shown by the customary courts to the enforcement of an *executory* contract. If A agrees to buy a basket or a hoe from B who makes such things for a living and A refuses to pay to or take delivery from B on

---

[1] Which was a slight variation on an actual case they had just tried on the morning of June 13, 1953, when I called there.

[2] If further evidence of this were needed, the reader would do well to consult, e.g., Schapera, *A Handbook of Tswana Law and Custom*, *passim* ; and *Bantu-speaking Tribes*, pp. 200–4 ; Cory, *Sukuma Law and Custom*, pp. 135–50 ; Meek, *Law and Authority in a Nigerian Tribe*, pp. 174, 205, 103–4, 231–4, etc ; Ajisafe, *Laws and Customs of the Yoruba People*, pp. 64–8, 73–8.

completion, neither A nor B can sue for the specific performance, or damages for the breach, of the contract. An action would, however, lie if A's action involved an element of deceit or sharp practice or if B sued A in debt for any expenses he might have incurred in purchasing the necessary materials.

But if the contract involved entails a great deal of expense, in money or labour, it seems that the law will enforce it even if executory. Thus, Gluckman [1] mentions two cases tried by Lozi courts in 1942 in which A ordered a net from a netmaker paying the full purchase price in advance and B ordered a net from another paying only part of the purchase money in advance. Each netmaker later sold the net he had made to the king's *induna* and it was held that A was entitled to the net but B was not. But B was given this curious verdict only because the chairman of the judges over-ruled the unanimous opinion of his colleagues to the contrary. Gluckman records that he was authoritatively informed that B was entitled to the net even if he had paid nothing in advance. These then are clear cases showing that under certain circumstances even executory contracts may be enforced.

Another instance that might be cited to show that executory contracts are not normally enforced at the suit of either party is the non-recognition of actions for breach of promise of marriage. But, in the strict African law of customary marriage, it is not the mere exchange of promises (whether these be those of the boy and girl or of their two families) that brings the contract into being. It is the settlement of the agreed amount of the marriage payment by the prospective husband and, in most if not all societies, the formal handing-over of the girl to him at his parents' home by the girl's parents that conclude the contract of marriage. Until this stage is reached, either party may resile from the more or less social relation to which the initial exchange of promises to marry and the subsequent gifts of presents usually by boy to girl give rise. A jilted young man could in some communities legally recover all substantial presents or their equivalent from the girl's parents, if satisfactory proof were given of all the specific items of his claim.

We see, therefore, that the African does not regard as a legally enforceable contract the mere exchange of mutual promises to marry, since until a contract actually exists there is no bargain to

[1] Gluckman, *Essays on Lozi Land and Royal Property*, pp. 15–16.

which either party can be held in customary law.   Morally, of course, the community looks askance at constituent families suffering their unmarried sons and daughters to change suitors without good cause shown ; public opinion resents it, and invariably demands that as full and fair a recompense as possible must be made to the innocent party.   Cases of breach of promise of marriage were formerly few and far between—a tribute at once to the efficacy of moral sanctions and to the African's love of legal casuistry.   Morally, the standards of right conduct require that the guilty party shall disgorge his or her loot, but only to the extent of the other's material or financial loss ; legally, there is no obligation to compensate for injured feelings or frayed nerves unless an actual contract has come into being before the breach. There is, however, one important qualification to be made to all this : where the boy has had carnal knowledge of the girl he is about to jilt, he can legally be compelled to marry her or pay up her full marriage payment.

It will, therefore, be noticed that this instance of a breach of promise is not really a good one to quote in support of the hypothesis that African law does not recognise executory contracts.

D. LIABILITY FOR TORTS (OR CIVIL WRONGS)

As with Contracts, so it is with Civil Wrongs that are independent of any personal relationship based on agreement.   One person's straying sheep and goats are beaten by another into whose garden they have come, destroying his growing crops.   A may quite negligently drop his cutlass on the bare toes of B, causing him much pain and trouble.   E seduces F's daughter who is under the age of puberty and who is probably already betrothed to G.   If society is to lead an orderly existence, it must clearly have a set of rules to deal with these and similar cases.   And we are fortunate to have to this effect a wealth of illustration from the writings of those who have studied African communities, although most of these were often intended to serve purposes other than the specifically legal.

Thus, according to Penwill, if in former times a man's cattle or goats broke out of his *boma* (an enclosure for animals) by night on to his neighbour's holding which is sown with crops or kept merely for grazing, no compensation was payable for any damage done or crops destroyed. But if the break-out took place by day, compensation was payable. The Kamba argue that the sudden break-out at night could not be helped by their owner ; obviously, the animal's depredations were what, in the English Law of Tort, would be termed ' Act of God ' ; but that when the same thing happened by day, an owner ought reasonably to have done his best to keep his animals off other people's property, since he could then have prevented the eruption by good management. Also, compensation was payable if there was a repetition of the nocturnal trespass by the animals, as that would be evidence of the man's negligence or inadvertence regarding the welfare of his neighbours. ' Now the owner is held responsible for the damage done by his stock, whether there is any particular negligence or not ; and grass must be paid for if trespassed on. Nor is there any difference reckoned between night and day, except as affecting *the degree of negligence* ; some compensation is always expected and paid.' [1]

A man starting a fire which gets out of his control and destroys a neighbour's crops or fences or house or even honey-hives must compensate the latter to the extent of their full value. Should a human being lose his life thereby, full blood-money is payable. The subsidence of another's adjoining holding which has been caused by one person's cultivation of, or excavation on, his land must be fully recompensed. Humans as well as animals falling into a trap set by an occupier of land, even on his own land, are entitled to compensation if any injury should result to them. Penwill thus winds up with an interesting note on damage to property in these words : [2] ' The Kamba hold that a man is always responsible for his actions and cannot evade that responsibility by alleging that another party created the situation that led to his action, by an original act which was itself a breach of Kamba custom.'

A man who sends another person on an errand or journey is normally held responsible for all or part of any harm that may befall his messenger whilst so engaged. Thus, he must bear a proportion of any compensation due to the messenger or his relatives in case of any supervening bodily harm or death ; this would of course be part only of what the injurer or killer might have to pay. But if the messenger's hurt has been caused by his own

[1] *Kamba Customary Law*, p. 104. (Italics are mine.) [2] *Ibid.*, p. 106.

negligence, foolhardiness or other personal fault, his employer is exempt from all blame.[1]

Similarly, Dundas records [2] the case of a man who found a cow in his field eating his crops and who in driving it off struck it so violently that it died in consequence. The *kiama* of the elders made him pay its full value to its owner on the ground that he had used excessive violence in protecting his property.[3] They observed that if the defendant's plea were allowed to justify the killing of the trespassing animal, it might equally well be asserted to excuse the killing of a human being in similar circumstances. In trying to show that intention, accident, and the like are disregarded in homicide cases, the writer gave this hypothetical case : If a man were seized by a lion and his friend, in endeavouring to save him, should inadvertently spear him instead of the lion, that friend would be liable to pay the usual compensation to his relatives for his death.[4] This, it is submitted, would seem to be a doubtful possibility. If such a friend were ever held responsible, however, it might be on the ground that he had allowed his anxious impulsiveness to save his friend to overcome his fair judgment of his own skill in the use of the spear ; by local standards, discretion is also the better part of valour. Had he left his friend alone with the lion and contented himself with merely raising an alarm, either the object of his pity or an abler spearman might have effectively disposed of the animal. At any rate, he need never have hastened his friend's demise by a rash and emotional use of the spear. Be that as it may, it is highly improbable that the elders would have exacted in such a case the full customary penalty for ordinary murder. They would probably have left it to him to make an offer to his victim's relatives out of his sheer contrition of heart.

The writer is, however, interesting when he leaves the tricky realm of conjecture to face the stark realities of African life around him. Thus, he gives[5] these principles of Kikuyu customary law :

[1] Penwill, *op. cit.*, p. 86.

[2] *Jnl. Roy. Anth. Inst.*, Vol. 51 (1921), p. 263.

[3] It is interesting to note in this connexion the similar provision of the Statute of Forcible Entry (1389) in English law. With the actual decision here compare the same one in the case of *Hamps* v. *Darby* (1948), W.N. 313 (pigeons) on similar facts.

[4] See p. 263 and also p. 237 of Vol. 51 (1921) of *Jnl. Roy. Anth. Inst.*

[5] *Ibid.*, p. 267.

A man causing the loss of a leg to another pays about one-third of the full blood-money, which is later deducted from whatever is due to the one so crippled if he should eventually die from the injury. But no such deduction is made from the compensation payable for the death of a person who was crippled or deformed from birth.

These are mere illustrations of types of civil liability in two or three African communities of the segmentary, uncentralised variety. There can be no doubt that other societies, if similarly analysed, would yield the same and even more detailed and developed principles of liability for legal wrongs. But it is unnecessary in a book of theory to analyse them.

As we have seen in the previous chapter, writers on African law have varied in their interpretations from those who only see criminal law everywhere to those who are sure that the African mind is incapable of making any distinction between criminal and civil wrongs—that is, that African law deals solely with civil, in the sense of private, wrongs. We have shown that this view is a false one, but what we may also legitimately infer here is that the latter attitude at least acknowledges the legal fact that African law does recognise a measure of civil responsibility for wrongs. As Thomas, J. put it in the Nyasaland case of *R. v. Robert and Alumani* : [1] ' Native law knows nothing of what we call criminal law ; it knows of wrongs to the individual for which he can in his appropriate native court receive compensation, depending in amount on the nature of the injury and the relative position in the community of the injured party.' [2]

The rationalist conception of liability for tort is that it must be based on fault—that is, that the wrong-doer must have acted intentionally or negligently for him to be liable. [3] This was the general view in developed Roman law, whence it penetrated into Continental law and later into Anglo-American law. [4]

---

[1] (1940), 5 Nys. L.R. 2, pp. 3–4.

[2] It must be noted that the first part of the sentence is incorrect, for the reason already stated. J. Lewin in his *Studies in African Native Law*, p. 105, includes torts as one of the instances of native laws.

[3] E.g. this was on the whole Bentham's view—See *Works*, Vol. 1, p. 292 n. : ' What you have a right to have me made to do (understand a political right) is that which I am liable, according to law, upon a requisition made on your behalf, to be punished for not doing.'

[4] Cf. The Roman law idea embodied in *The Lex Aquilia*.

Now, it is commonly said that in ' primitive ' law the general idea of liability for wrongs done, whether to a human being or to an animal, was that of *Causation*, not *Culpability*. This is sometimes expressed by English writers as meaning that a man acts at his peril.[1] A notable protest was vigorously entered by the late Sir Percy Winfield against this view of early (or ' primitive ') law. He argued [2] that even in early English law, the commission of a wrong was excusable on the grounds of self-defence, Act of God, inevitable accident, necessity, mistake, *volenti non fit injuria*, etc. And although it has been suggested that Winfield did not demolish the general theory of causation but only provided a series of exceptions to it, we are nevertheless, entitled to question whether the modern Continental development of the principle of liability for exposure to risk is fundamentally different from this alleged quality of ' primitive ' law. Owing to the advent of mechanical inventions and appliances, the principle of no liability without fault has had to be altered to allow liability on the condition that he who engages in an activity (e.g. driving a motor-car on the highway) should make himself an insurer for the benefit of those whom his activity may harm.

Also in the English law of tort, the defendant's foresight or state of mind is irrelevant in torts of ' strict liability ' such as liability under *Rylands* v. *Fletcher*,[3] liability for fire, for keeping dangerous animals, for certain types of trespass and for conversion, and vicarious liability of masters for their servants' wrongs. In all these cases, the court merely looks at the act done or omitted, and does not trouble itself about causation. Of course, there is another class of torts in which the defendant's foresight as to the consequences of his act is an essential element in determining his liability ; these are liability for negligence, nuisance, conspiracy, injurious falsehood, malicious prosecution, and defamation. Thus, in the first group, malice in the sense of improper motive is totally disregarded as an element of liability for wrongs, while in the latter it is an ingredient of each species of tort. Finally, it is a fundamental principle of the English law of tort that motive

---

[1] E.g. W. Holdsworth, *History of English Law*, Vol. 2, p. 64.

[2] *Law Quarterly Review*, Vol. 42 (1926), p. 184 ; see also *Law Quarterly Review*, Vol. 55, 450–1.

[3] (1868), L.R. 3 H.L. 330.

is not ordinarily relevant to the issue of personal liability. This is expressed by saying that a good motive will not make lawful an act otherwise unlawful, neither can a bad motive make unlawful an act that is otherwise lawful.

In the light of this comparative evidence it is clear that motive, intention and negligence are not necessarily the invariable attributes of 'European' law. In certain instances under English law they are relevant, in others they are not. The legal position is more or less the same in African customary law. Intention requires both foreknowledge and desire on the part of the individual whose legal liability may be in question. Consequences which are foreseeable are intentional. On the other hand, negligence is independent of intention ; it, however, covers rashness as well as inadvertence, the essence of both being the indifference of the wrong-doer to the welfare of other people.

This is sometimes called the *subjective* view of negligence, meaning that negligence is a state of mind. The objective view is that a person's conduct is negligent or not according as it is reasonable in all the circumstances of the case. The standard is that of the reasonable man. Whichever of the two views we take, the important thing is to find out whether or not there is a guilty mind.

African law is not so mechanical in its operation as to ignore the propriety or impropriety of a wrong-doer's motive in bringing about the unlawful consequence upon which the council of elders or the chiefs are called to adjudicate. To hold otherwise would be to deny all element of rationality to Africans and, therefore, to African law. Custom, as we have been saying all this long while, is neither automatic nor blind in its apparently smooth and leisurely operation. Behind the façade of the chief's visible routine of awarding compensation or imposing fines lie a highly discriminating mind and an accepted scale of values, both of which imply, though they may not express in words, certain underlying assumptions of the whole community. These are understood by the people and so do not require elaboration on every occasion. The outsider is then all too apt to detect in such placid working of the legal order ' the automatic reign of custom ' in African society.

This whole problem of the weighing of motive, intention, and negligence in the circumstances of a wrong-doer's conduct really overlaps the boundaries of the actual administration of justice in African communities. We will, therefore, have occasion to elucidate much of what has been somewhat inadequately expressed here in the chapter on the nature of African judicial process.[1]

[1] See Ch. XII.

CHAPTER IX

AFRICAN CONCEPTS OF OWNERSHIP AND POSSESSION

A CLEAR distinction is everywhere drawn between ownership and possession, particularly of land on the one hand and of all other forms of property on the other.

A. LAND

With respect to land it is interesting to begin our analysis with this notable statement which a Nigerian chief is reported to have made to the West African Lands Committee in 1912 : ' I conceive that land belongs to a vast family of which many are dead, few are living, and countless members are unborn.' The universality of this concept throughout both Sudanese and Bantu Africa has been confirmed again and again wherever indigenous societies have been studied.[1]

Whereas land is corporately owned and normally inalienable (with exceptions to be stated presently), other species of property may be individually owned and alienated either *inter vivos* or on death. Of course, the use of land can be transferred temporarily or permanently, as when immigrant settlers are allowed to settle on family land, at first conditionally upon proving in course of time to be satisfactory components of the host community, and later absolutely upon virtual absorption by and complete assimilation with the landowning group.

It seems that family or group land is regarded as remaining such whether or not continuous physical control (*corpus*) or even active intention (*animus*) to retain such control is in fact exercised or shown. It does not matter for how long the land may be unused by the owning group *as group*, so long as the reputed ' ownership '

---

[1] The present writer was pleasantly surprised when in Nov. 1952, Hosea B. Nkojo, Esq., the then Prime Minister of Toro in Uganda, after reading a few pages of his *Nigerian Land Law and Custom* at random, exclaimed : ' These are the same as our own principles of land rules in Uganda, you know. We can use your book with only minor modifications regarding names, and, perhaps, a few details.'

of it is universally acknowledged by the other members of the community. No one can acquire a title by prescription with respect to it, for customary tenure does not recognise such a title in the particular context. That is why when individuals are attracted away from home to ' whiteman's country ' by paid labour they still regard themselves as owners of their plots left behind in the possession of kinsmen for care-taking ; and they can always assert their claims to them on their return, whenever this might be.

But non-user or ineffectual occupation of his allocated portion by a member for an unreasonably long period (unless for good reason such as the necessities of husbandry like fallow, or un-avoidable flooding or other agricultural disasters), will usually entail a forfeiture of his holding and its re-allocation to another ready and willing to put it to productive use.   So imperative is the need in most African societies for the effective utilisation of land.

1. *Some Special Issues.*

The African conception of land as something that is owned by the group lends itself to a number of interesting sophistications.

Thus, whereas the radical title to the land remains with the family or the community, the individual can have, at any rate in theory, a right only to its use.   In other words, the *ownership* is that of the group, and the individual member has mere *possession*.[1] But this possession is really more than sheer physical control by the allottee of his allocated portion of the land ; he can exclude from it strangers to the group as well as other group members, provided that in the latter event he can show that he has com-mitted no breach of customary rules relative to holdings by group members generally.[2]

We may probably at this stage attempt to deal with the issue of the so-called ' communal ownership ' of land.   The fallacy of so describing the African mode of land-holding arises, partly from the greater fallacy underlying the doctrine of ' primitive com-munism ', and partly from an imperfect appreciation of the exact

[1] That is, using the words ' ownership ' and ' possession ' in their ordinary English senses.
[2] Even then, the other member wanting to usurp the real allottee's right must obtain the prior authorisation of the family head (or chief, as the case may be) to his intended occupation of the neglected piece of land.

nature of the concept in African legal categories. Of the first we have treated, no doubt all too briefly, when we examined the theory of primitive communism.[1] We will now briefly dispose of the second.

What we have said so far as well as what we shall say later will show that the land-holding recognised by African customary law is neither ' communal ' holding nor ' ownership ' (in the strict English sense of the term). The term ' corporate ' would be an apter description of the system of land-holding, since the relation between the group and the land is invariably complex in that the rights of the individual members often co-exist with those of the group in the same parcel of land. But the individual members hold definitely ascertained and well-recognised rights within the comprehensive holding of the group. The chief is everywhere regarded as the symbol of the residuary, reversionary and ultimate ownership of all land held by a territorial community. He holds on behalf of the whole community in the capacity of a caretaker or trustee [2] only ; but he allocates portions of land to family heads according to need, and these in turn re-allocate among their members.[3]

African customary law of tenure has no conception of land-holding comparable to the English idea of a fee simple absolute in possession, or to a theory whereby the ownership of all land in England is in the Crown alone and everybody else holds his land only as tenant of the king.

The African chief or king has no such legal right, even in theory ; [4] he enjoys only an administrative right of supervisory

---

[1] Pp. 83–9, *supra.*

[2] This has been held in a number of Privy Council cases of which these are the most important : *Amodu Tijani* v. *Secretary, S. Nigeria* (1921), 2 A.C. 399 ; *Sunmonu* v. *Disu Raphael* (1927), A.C. 881, at pp. 883–4 ; *Sobhuza II* v *Miller* (1926), A.C. 518, p. 525 (a case from Swaziland Protectorate) ; *Hoani etc.* v. *Aotea District Maori Land Board* (1941), A.C. 308, p. 315 (a case from New Zealand). See also my article in *Journal of Comparative Legislation and International Law*, Nov., 1951, Vol. 33, 3rd Series, Pts. III and IV, pp. 49–55.

[3] See, for further discussion of this problem, my *Nigerian Land Law and Custom* (2nd edn.), pp. 92–4, 155–8. See also Lord Hailey, *An African Survey*, pp. 834 ff. ; Diamond, *Primitive Law*, pp. 269–76.

[4] Gluckman, in his *Essays on Lozi Land and Royal Property*, p. 8, observes in this connexion : ' Untrained students of African peoples have been misled by the idea that in any society people *own* land or things. As a basic concept, this has withstood application in our own

oversight of the land for the benefit of the whole community. If he requires a piece of land, he must beg it of the individual holder of it, if the holder has no immediate use for it.[1] The importance of stressing this point is the tendency of certain African chiefs to assert a wrongful claim to feudal, proprietary ownership to community land whenever European concessionaires wish to acquire it for mining purposes. Any compensation money thus paid to the chief or the king personally as absolute owner would be improper and the title obtained by the purchaser would be voidable, at the best.[2]

On the other hand, a member's right to his holding is in the nature of a possessory title which he enjoys in perpetuity and which confers upon him powers of user and of disposition scarcely distinguishable from those of an absolute free-holder under English law. His title is, therefore, in a sense that of a part-owner of land belonging to his family. He is not a lessee; he is not a licensee; he is not, as is so often said, an usufructuary. He pays tribute to nobody, is accountable to none but himself, and his interests and powers far transcend those of the usufructuary under Roman law.

But a member's portion of family land cannot be sold by him or taken away from him in satisfaction of a debt, though he may pledge the *use* of his own portion for debt. Moreover, he can put his allotment to any kind of productive use he likes, including

culture, though jurists have appreciated that it is not strictly true.' Again, later (at p. 9): ' Many jurists still do not recognise that the ' communal ownership ' of tribal society can often be resolved into clusters of specific rights which groups and individuals hold over a piece of land, its uses, and its products.' For the Lozi the learned author gives details of these rights at pp. 27–34.

[1] Of course, he may, like any other member of the local community, appropriate any previously unoccupied piece of land without asking anyone, since such as yet unoccupied parcels of land are the common property of the community as a whole.

[2] This is because the chief is only a representative of his people and any purchase money he receives really belongs to them and not to him as if he were the true owner. Certain African chiefs had previously pocketed such moneys on the false claim that they owned the parcels of land concerned in their own right. The title passed by the chief, for example, under a mining concession to Europeans, is voidable, not void, since the community can legally upset it on an appeal to the Privy Council that they have neither assented to the particular sale nor received their share of the purchase money from the chief. Such a claim will normally be made through the family heads. The title, however, is absolutely valid if originally passed with the consent of these family heads.

M

the conversion of an agricultural piece of land into a dwelling house ; that is, of course, if his so doing would not adversely affect the legitimate rights of others.   He can, in certain circumstances lease it and, with the consent of the owning group, sell or otherwise alienate his portion.   Again, the individual's holding does not come to an end at his death ; it is heritable by his own children to the exclusion of all others.   In short, he is a kind of beneficial part-owner, with perpetuity of tenure and all but absolute power of disposition.

Another feature of this fascinating concept of customary ownership is the fact that a person can own in the true sense of the word the plants which he has grown and the house or other structure erected on his allotment, while the ultimate title to the land itself remains in the owning group.   If for proper reasons he is ever lawfully ejected from his holding, he is entitled to take away all the superstructure he may have brought on to it.   In some cases, his otherwise conditionally revocable title may become irrevocable in consequence of his having been allowed to build substantial houses or to grow permanent cash crops and other economic trees on his land ;   he is not to be lightly extruded from what is now his own family settlement.

A logical extension of this separateness of bilateral, concurrent ' ownerships ' of the land and of the superstructure on it is the fact that it may be leased, loaned or pledged by its holder to one person while a simultaneous right to reap certain fruits thereon or hunt it for game may be given to another.   Cases are not unknown in which land is permanently given or sold by its owner to another and yet the right to certain economic trees thereon is by special custom reserved solely to the inhabitants of the locality.

2. *Title by Prescription.*

As a rule, customary tenure knows nothing in the nature of a prescriptive claim to land.   The theory is that no land is without an owner.   An individual may, as we have seen above, lose his right to his allotment for unreasonably long non-use, but the family title is indefeasible.   Another member of the family or even a stranger may have such land re-allocated to him on terms by the family, but there is always a right of reverter in the family as the land-owning unit.

It is this ubiquitous ownership that makes any part of the family land that is loaned or pledged to strangers to be recoverable by the original lender or pledgor and his successors from the original borrower [1] or pledgee and his successors *ad infinitum*. There is no Statute of Limitation laying down fixed periods during which recovery or redemption should take place on pain of forfeiture. The result is often that, when all the witnesses to the original transaction (for, in the absence of writing, human witnesses are indispensable to the validity of these oral negotiations) have died out by the time of the second or third generation on either side, controversies arise as to the exact nature of the initial arrangement. Those now in possession of the land might claim it for their own, alleging that the original loan was an outright sale; while the successors of the first grantor might contend, as they may legitimately do under customary law, that the principle is: ' Once a loan (or pledge), always a loan (or pledge) ', and that they can always recover or redeem their land. Nowadays, some kind of limiting period has become necessary, even inevitable.

But it is only fair to add that customary law itself has always had a definite though rudimentary rule that, in the absence of very good reasons, abandonment of one's land for periods varying from three to seven years, according to the locality and type of land, works an automatic forfeiture. Similarly, long and undisturbed possession of a piece of land by another has often been taken to be strong presumptive evidence of abandonment by the owner.

Thus, in a boundary dispute between two divisions of an Akim State on the Gold Coast, the State Council sitting as an appeal court, held that ownership of the disputed land must be presumed in favour of the defendants who admittedly were first on the land.[2] This tendency to prescribe in favour of the adverse possessor has also been noted among the Kamba of Kenya, of whom Penwill wrote: ' Possession of land now implies possession by normal Kamba title, and he who alleges the contrary must prove it.' [3] Similar notions of possession prevail in many other African societies.

Basically, this African way of regarding the entrenched adverse

---

[1] Gluckman, *Essays on Lozi Land Tenure and Royal Property*, p. 33, says that the Lozi recognises the ' borrowing ' of land, but not pledging and sale.

[2] This decision was confirmed by W.A.C.A. in *Ababio* v. *Kanga* (1932), 1 W.A.C.A. 253.

[3] *Kamba Customary Law*, pp. 49–50.

possessor is little different from Von Savigny's idea that ' owner-ship is adverse possession ripened by prescription ',[1] or from the English law doctrine that possession is ' nine points of the law '.[2] Only, in the African condition, a definition of the principles being applied in an actual case is scarcely ever attempted and the theories underlying the rules acted upon are seldom stated.

B.   OTHER KINDS OF PROPERTY

In the case of personal chattels, the mental attitude is quite different.   These are things which men acquire for the purpose of realising social existence through satisfying personal needs and discharging inter-personal obligations.   The relationship between the owner and the thing owned is one of absolute dominium, untrammelled by considerations of the competing claims of the family or of the community which, in the case of land, almost regularly limit the individual's powers of disposition.   Unless the chattels in question are jointly acquired, by inheritance or other-wise, there are no legal fetters of any kind on their owner's power of dealing with them as he pleases.

Customary law invariably allows the individual a free hand with respect to what is self-acquired, and this is why even in the matter of land the person who is first to mark out and clear a piece of land, previously forming part of the community's virgin forest or reserved land, virtually enjoys during his own lifetime the rights and privileges of an absolute owner of property.   When he dies, however, his children succeed to a *joint* inheritance with, until partition or sale, all the customary incidents of tenure.   The principles are the same for inherited cattle, farming implements, crops, or articles of clothing.   There is, of course, nothing to prevent their owner from making such disposition of these in his lifetime as he may choose.   His wishes then are paramount and cannot be set aside.   But, although a man can make a *nuncupative will* of his land to upset the calculations of the customary rules of inheritance, the instances must be rare when his directions are carried out if the effect would be to disinherit some influential but not bad child.   Once the jointly-inherited chattel is divided up, however, each child becomes the absolute owner of his portion,

[1] See Paton, *Jurisprudence* (2nd edn.), Ch. 22 ; Salmond, *Jurisprudence* (10th edn.), pp. 294–5.
[2] See, e.g., O. W. Holmes, *The Common Law*, Lecture VI.

whether such division is carried out by the father before his death or by the children themselves after his death.

1. *Personal Chattels.*

It is sometimes said that the African regards his personal belongings like jewellery, other valuables or even utensils and weapons, as but a mere extension of his own personality, and that this alone accounts for the severity with which theft has always been visited in almost all communities. The death penalty was exacted,[1] particularly in all cases where the culprit had been caught *in flagrante delicto*, because—so the theory goes—it was thought that a convicted criminal was as good as guilty of a diabolical attempt upon the very life of the owner of the property stolen : it was equivalent to an attempt to lop off a member of the owner's body. Driberg, for example, says ' that everything acquires the personality of its possessor ' and that, among the Lango, if A acquires a cow from B in exchange for the equivalent number of sheep, he has in addition to pay B a spear ' for its tail ', because ' B's personality has to be driven out of the animal into the tail, and thence into the spear '.[2]

This may well be the explanation given him by some inarticulate Lango peasant, but one ventures to suggest that few if any of the adjudicating elders would offer this as a rational (as distinct from a *fictional*) account of the customary law principle involved in the exaction of heavy penalties for theft. The true explanation that a sapient African judge would advance is probably that suggested earlier by Driberg himself, to the effect that the thief is so treated ' because he introduces mistrust into the community and by his action invalidates those principles on which the welfare of the community depends '.

If the conjecture about a chattel being regarded as an extension of its owner's personality were the true reason for the exaction of the death penalty for its theft in traditional African law, then it might equally well be applied to explain why, in English criminal law, summary execution of the thief was formerly the penalty for theft of any property of 12 pence or more in value. As late as 1808, a woman charged with the offence of stealing property in a

---

[1] It must not be thought that death was the invariable punishment for theft even in ancient African customary law. Compensation, mutilation and fine were very often the penalties exacted for ordinary cases of theft.   [2] See Driberg's article, *op. cit.*, p. 235, n. 1.

dwelling house was only saved from the gallows by the judges quibbling that a £10 Bank of England note was actually less than 40s.[1]

A similar notion has also been held to underlie the ancient practice found among some African tribes, a practice almost universally shared by other races of mankind, of burying a deceased person's belongings with him. Some say that this practice was due to a belief that the dead person would require these chattels in the next state of existence in the world beyond the grave. Others assert that a person's possessions being mere detachable *addenda* to his personality must be interred with him at death ; otherwise, it is said, the dead man might find his personality incomplete in the next life and might use that as an excuse for his ghost to worry and harass his living relations who would thus be wrongfully keeping back from him these vital parts of his body. It must be said, however, that the protagonists of this theory often admit that at different stages of development the practice ceased and the living started to retain possession of the deceased's chattels on the supposed ground that, since the deceased's own children and family were left behind, his other bodily appendages might also be inherited by the living without running any more risk of ghostly visitations from the grave of the dismembered personality.

Whatever truth there might be in either variety of this ' extended personality theory ', it is at least far from being representative of the general notions of ownership and possession to be found among the majority of Africans. Indeed, the idea that a deceased person's chattels are inherited by his living relations, instead of being buried with him, is certainly widespread in most of their societies known to us.

2. *Debt.*

Debts are, like loan or pledge of land, usually recoverable by the creditor, no matter at what distance of time. A debtor's children, if the debt could otherwise be satisfactorily established against their deceased father, would often pay it off on demand. But it seems that, although there is no period of limitation within which a debt must be claimed or sued for by the creditor, customary law requires that strict proof of its actual existence must

---

[1] See Kenny, *Outlines of Criminal Law* (15th edn.), pp. 208, 249.

be given if recovery is to be obtained. It is submitted that under modern conditions a definite period of limitation, such as we have suggested above in connexion with actions for the recovery of loaned or pledged land, ought to be laid down by statute in this case also.

An obnoxious old practice in some African societies was for the debtor to pawn or pledge himself (or a child or other relation of his under his paternal authority) to his creditor as security for the debt.[1] During the currency of the debt, he or his delegate was expected to render personal service to the creditor, who might and often did allow the pawn to secure his redemption by earning extra remuneration from outside sources. But, until the original debt was repaid, the pawn's services would only count as interest on the capital of the loan and not in reduction of or substitution for the debt. The pawn was, however, legally entitled to demand reasonably good treatment at the hands of the creditor, as the idea was that only a limited use of the pawn's personal services had been transferred and not his person : the pawn as a human individual remained his own master and could not be maltreated like a slave or even a servant.[2] The creditor had only possession of him, not ownership.[3]

However, the system of pawn or pledge of a human being as a guarantee of debt had fallen into desuetude in most places before it was made a criminal offence by the various colonial criminal codes in British Africa.[4]

3. Bailment.

Things that are individually owned, and these may be anything other than family property (i.e. house or land), are often

---

[1] E.g. J. M. Sarbah, *Fanti Customary Laws*, pp. 86 ff. ; Cory, *Sukuma Law and Custom*, § 145 ; Meek, *Law and Authority in a Nigerian Tribe*, pp. 205, 234 ; Ajisafe, *Laws and Customs of the Yoruba People*, pp. 70–2.

[2] Compare the old Roman practice of the *Manus Injectio*. This was the Roman law method by which a creditor was entitled to seize the debtor's body for sale or destruction. The creditor would publicly proclaim the amount of the debt on three consecutive market days. If no one would then ransom the debtor, he was sold across the Tiber or put to death. It was the *Lex Poetelia* of 326 B.C. that provided for the first time that the debtor be permitted to work for the creditor instead of being sold into slavery or put to death.

[3] See pp. 107–8, *supra*.

[4] In medieval English law, a ' pledge ' meant a human surety : see Plucknett, *A Concise History of the Common Law*, p. 592.

transferred by one person or group of persons to another in a variety of ways.   Thus, A may lend or pledge his hoe or cutlass to B either gratuitously or for a consideration in kind, and either for a stipulated period or indefinitely.   Normally, the thing lent or pledged is intended to be used by the borrower or pledgee until the arrangement is lawfully brought to an end, when it is expected to be returned *in specie* to the lender or pledgor.   Due allowance is, of course, made for any reasonable deterioration in the quality of the thing lent or pledged.

There is no doubt at all that African customary law recognises quite clearly that the ownership of the chattel lent or pledged remains in the transferor and that the transferee has merely the temporary possession of it.

If the chattel was originally borrowed for value, the borrower is entitled to retain it until the agreed consideration has run its normal course or until the lender has made a *pro tanto* refund of the balance to the borrower for any loss due to a premature determination of the contract by the lender.   It is doubtful whether the borrower can successfully make such a claim if he is the one who arbitrarily terminates the contract before its normal expiry.   In the case of pledge, the pledgee has a right to retain possession of the thing pledged until the obligation giving rise to the pledge is fully discharged by the pledgor or waived by the pledgee.

Finally, let us suppose that the thing bailed is damaged or stolen by a third party whilst still in the possession of the bailee. The latter can usually obtain compensation for the damage done to the chattel or for its value as determined in accordance with customary law principles.   But it is more usual that the bailor is the one to whom a court would ordinarily award such compensation, as all three parties would have to take part in the proceedings and the eventual award could be mutually divided as between bailor and bailee in suitable proportions.   To this extent, therefore, it may be said that African customary law recognises the possession of the bailee, as distinct from the ownership of the bailor.

C.   OWNERSHIP IN WASTE LAND

As we have stated before,[1] land is never *communally* owned by

[1] Pp. 83 ff, 163-5.

the whole community, except in the sense that certain sacred groves, market places and the as yet unallocated forest land may be said to be so owned. The land-owning unit is normally the family, with the individual adult members each having well-defined portions and usually clearly-established rights thereto. Even where a section of the family land is cultivated jointly by its adult members as a team, the products are often owned in severalty and shared or liable to be shared according to individual deserts. The crops are often garnered separately, or in separate lots, within the common family granary.

In the case of the still unallocated land under the care and supervision of the chief or council of elders, a member of the community is, with the necessary consent, usually as free to acquire a portion of it for himself by right of first cultivation, as he is to enter upon any part of it for the purpose of hunting wild game, tapping oil palms for palm wine, hiving bees and collecting their honey, or just grazing cattle or rearing poultry thereon. And whereas the land thus acquired may be temporarily or permanently owned by the first cultivator in accordance with the rules of customary tenure, the animal or wine or honey or grass thus reduced into possession by an individual is his absolute property,[1] unless any local custom requires him to make a token present out of it to the chief. Of course, this implies that every first cultivator or acquirer of such property must himself acknowledge the right of others to do likewise with respect to other parts of this virgin land. Where there are several concurrent exploitations of parts of such common land, a demarcation of ' spheres of influence ' often becomes inevitable if disputes and friction are to be avoided.

Where the land is wild bush and individual land appropriations have not taken place but only the boundaries marked for the subsequent exploitation of the land's resources, it is easy to find that those possessing such rights do not show the same acquisitive tenacity towards the land itself as they do towards its products which they have reduced into private possession. The attitude is that this waste land belongs to the community and not to the individuals with immediate vested interest in it ; if their supplementary rights are disturbed in a manner over

---

[1] Of course, where the user is continuous the right thus acquired may be heritable by the owner's children *ad infinitum*.

which they have no control, they can always revert to their respective legal allocations in the inhabited areas.

It was ignorance of this fact that must have led Lord Lugard into this oft-quoted but inaccurate remark : ' It is a good example of the simplicity of these ignorant savages, that their sole anxiety was centred in the honey-pots in the trees. " They have no conception of the scope of the question. Here am I wishing to take over a valuable tract of land, and to gain legal possession of the site, on which I wish to build the fort, together with adjoining lands, including the regular camping ground, and the reply is, that there is a honey-pot in the tree on the site : the fact is that waste land in Africa is literally no man's land, and a neighbouring small village headman has no more claim over it than you or I " ' (Diary).[1]

Whatever else Lugard's ' ignorant savages ' in East Africa did not understand it was not their own undoubted right to their bush land. The presence on the land of the honey-farming rights which Lugard failed to appreciate is possibly analogous in its legal implications to the existence of a *profit-à-prendre* on a tract of land in any English countryside to which an intending purchaser's attention would equally well be drawn in the process of negotiation. As for the erroneous assertion that ' waste land in Africa is literally no man's land ',[2] Lugard's own subsequent experience in Nigeria,[3] ought at any rate to have persuaded him into accepting the fact that there is no land without an owner [4] anywhere in Africa.[5]

D. CONCLUSION

Such, in brief, are the main ideas about ownership and possession that are to be found in most African societies. It is

---

[1] *Rise of Our East African Empire*, p. 289.

[2] In the sense that anyone, including a stranger (who might be an Asian, a European or even an African alien to the locality), can equally with the local inhabitants appropriate parts of a local community's land.

[3] Lugard, *Dual Mandate*, pp. 280–353.

[4] ' The natives cannot imagine any tract of land or territory being totally unconnected with a human group. Most tracts of uninhabited bush are " owned " by chiefs, who have ritual jurisdiction over hunting rights '—Fortes, *The Dynamics of Clanship among the Tallensi*, p. 172 ; Lord Hailey : *An African Survey*, p. 745.

[5] I.e. as explained earlier at p. 164.

hardly to be expected that all the aspects here presented would necessarily co-exist in every such community or be expressed in the same way. At any rate, in any African community with a developed legal system, most if not all of these ideas will be found to be generally accepted.

The degree and character of the elaboration of detailed principles observable among a given people must therefore vary with their economic norms and social values. For example, it seems that, amongst the Tswana, to ' show ' an animal to an intending buyer amounts to legal delivery, since failure on the buyer's part to lead it out of the seller's *boma* after such ' showing ' disentitles him from claiming any compensation for the loss or death of the animal not due to the seller's fault. But he is nevertheless entitled to the offspring in due course.[1]   Also, intensive commercial activities within a society or between two or more societies would normally produce varied problems of transfer of chattels as commodities between the vendor and the purchaser, the lender and the borrower, the bailor and the bailee, of the goods. These would in their turn lead to a conscious or an unconscious conceptualisation of the immanent customary notions of ownership and possession in order to make them keep pace with the inevitable changes in the traditional patterns of *intra*- as well as *inter*-group intercourse and commerce.

On the other hand, in societies with less social and economic dynamics, rules tend to follow the placid but by no means static order of simple barter and exchange of chattels, which are a necessary feature of even the smallest human aggregation. The prevailing ideas of ownership and possession will be conditioned by the scope of such economic business as is actually transacted by the members of these societies.

Nevertheless, there is, one strongly suspects, no confusion between the ownership and the possession of chattels, whatever the stage of commercial orientation yet attained by a modern African community. What is owned or possessed may often be insubstantial, but such rights as exist admit of no doubt that the people clearly distinguish the owner from the mere possessor of a thing, whether land or chattel.

[1] Schapera, *A Handbook of Tswana Law and Custom* ; compare the Roman law idea of *Traditio Longa Manu* (Buckland, *A Manual of Roman Private Law*, (2nd edn.), p. 136).

CHAPTER X

LEGAL FICTIONS

A. INTRODUCTORY

EVERY human society is at once static and dynamic. In its relative dependence on its environment it has to be tenacious of the tried and accepted ways of life; but the restless quest of the human mind for adaptation to changing social conditions is irrepressible. When the old standards no longer fit the new demands of existence, the process of adjustment may assume one of two forms : either (*a*) a workable compromise is found between the old and the new, or (*b*) there is a complete breakdown of the existing order. Disintegration only sets in, however, where the rate of environmental change outstrips the society's capacity for adaptation.

The whole course of English legal history shows how often the rigid rules of the Common law, in spite of their being much tempered down by the flexible principles of Equity in a number of ways, have had to be stretched and adapted to new circumstances by the introduction of legal fictions. These have been employed not only in changing the substantive rules of law but also in evolving the rules of procedure.

Other enlightened legal systems have had to make similar use of fictions as a means of effecting necessary adjustments in legal rules. The African legal systems are no exception. It is indeed true to say that many African social as well as legal categories are notional rather than exact. Thus, an African calls a distant and sometimes unrelated head of a village group a ' father ' and his remote cousins are just ' brothers '. It is not until one appreciates that he actually uses these terms on the grounds of politeness and in the interests of group solidarity that one discovers that when the proper occasion arises he does emphatically differentiate between the sociological and the physiological fraternity of the one and the like paternity of the other. One may say that in some ways the whole tissue of his language is figurative,

particularly in his use of relational terms.¹   Care, therefore, must
be taken to obtain the exact sense in which he uses certain terms
of reference if confusion and error are to be avoided.²   In the
sphere of law, this is of especial importance. When changed conditions render such a process necessary he slides easily from the
metaphorical to the fictional if by doing so justice may be done.

As we have seen in the chapter on Status, it is this fictional
use of the word ' brother' that enables the law of the tribe to
be extended to embrace strangers.   By intermarriage, the protection of friends, blood brotherhood, inter-tribal societies, and
the rules of hospitality, foreigners are assimilated with the community as ' brothers ' and are thereby brought within the pale
of the law.   The adoptive family treat them more or less as blood
members and may even go to their rescue in times of social
or economic stress.   The usual help given to members fined for
offences against third parties is normally available to them in
proper cases.   Good fellowship and mutuality of interests are
the abiding features of this sociological fraternity which is so
often misunderstood in many legal considerations.

B.   PARTICULAR SAMPLES OF FICTIONS

Let us now take samples of specific application of legal fictions :
(1) Perhaps we may begin by quoting Driberg who writes : ³
' But Africans are ingenious people and have devised another
and easier way of getting out of an impasse. If any custom or
law begins to feel oppressive, they do not care to abrogate it
at once on account of its religious sanction. But being masters
of legal fiction, they devise a ceremony which in any particular
case will absolve them from the operation of the old law. I
may cite as an example a Thonga ceremony which breaks down
the blood-tie and thus authorises a form of marriage legally
incestuous. In course of time the ceremony becomes an important thing and takes the place of the obsolete law.'

¹ E.g. Ashton, *The Basuto*, pp. 20–1 ; Holleman, *Shona Customary
Law*, pp. 50–4.
² For a general account, see ' African Symbolism ' by E. W. Smith,
in *Jnl. Roy. Anth. Inst.*, Vol. LXXXII, Pt. I, 1952, pp. 13–33, particularly
Section 3 of the article.
³ ' The African Conception of Law ', *Journal of Comparative Legislation
and International Law*, Nov., 1934, pp. 242–3.

(2) Again, if a clan or family member kills another without lawful excuse, legal fiction is invoked in order to avoid the unpleasantness of another member having to lay foul hands on the guilty member. But since the penalty is death for the murderer, his family or clan will employ an outsider—usually a member of the helot or pariah tribes—to carry out the execution, on the theory that the killing of the murderous family member by an alien is no more wrong than if he were killed by an enemy during a battle.

Among the Ovambo, for example, six Bushmen or other tribesmen were usually employed to execute a member found guilty of murder. The Chagga, on the other hand, would arrange a sham fight in the course of which the murderous member would be ' accidentally ' shot by a carefully selected marksman who was a member of the same group. The pretext, of course, was that the whole arranged affair was in fact a mere accident.

(3) There is a curious extension of a legal fiction among the Fangs [1] whereby a wronged person, instead of making a direct demand upon the wrong-doer for redress, goes to another town or to a different district from that in which the offender lives and shoots the first goat he sees or, if he is really incensed, the woman he first meets. The idea is thus to make the original offender doubly liable, first for the initial wrong and then for the second offence committed by his own victim ; the latter will almost certainly cause a stir among both communities or sections of the community thus embroiled. This objectionable practice is said to be intended to make every Fang very chary of committing an offence, since the consequences of his doing so may have far-reaching and often unfortunate repercussions.

(4) A similar but less reprehensible system exists among some other communities. Indirect methods are employed by a complainant in a private suit in order to bring his grievance to the attention of the central authority or council of elders, particularly where notice is taken of public offences only. Such a private suitor may deliberately commit any one of those public infractions of which alone the chief or the elders will take cognisance. In the investigation into this offence, which is very rarely directed against the life or limb of another person, the complainant's real grievance is expected by him to have the chance of being venti-

[1] *Jnl. Roy. Anth. Inst.*, Vol. XXIX, pp. 78–9.

lated.[1] This frequently accounts for the alleged prolixity and irrelevance of certain species of evidence often adduced by litigants at trials in traditional African courts. An observer unaware of this background to the trial would miss the whole point of such a complainant's seemingly inadmissible testimony. We shall deal more with this point in the chapter on the Judicial Process.[2]

(5) Hone, one-time Attorney-General of Uganda,[3] has recorded this interesting account of the process by which the Baganda formerly inflicted the penalty of death upon a male adulterer among the nobility. 'We may pause for a moment to state that, apart from the fact that among the better classes of the Baganda the chastity of married women was carefully guarded, the justification for the exaction of the extreme penalty in such cases of adultery is authoritatively stated to be based on a legal fiction, the very existence of which is, to say the least, remarkable.' He went on to say that at the trial of the case before the chief the adulterer was usually referred to as a 'mussi', meaning a murderer. The point of this mode of address was that, in going about his clandestine business of committing an alleged adultery, a member of the upper class would very presumably carry a spear with which to get rid of anyone discovering him in a compromising situation. Hence arose the fiction that all aristocratic adulterers were potential murderers who would not scruple to kill any interloper and for whom death was considered to be the appropriate penalty. Although heavy fines have since replaced death or mutilation by the gouging out of an eye or by the cutting off of a limb of the culprit, the Baganda still speak colloquially of an adulterer as a 'mussi'.[4]

(6) Even in such matters as the administration of justice we find some African communities employing fictions in an attempt to secure the immunity and the impartiality of the judges. The

[1] Rattray, *Ashanti Law and Constitution*, p. 288.
[2] See pp. 246 ff., *infra*.
[3] H. R. Hone, M.C., K.C., LLB., in an article entitled, 'The Native of Uganda and the Criminal Law' in *The Uganda Journal*, Vol. VI, No. 1, July, 1938, p. 5, the information having been culled from pp. 261–4 of the book entitled *The Baganda* by the Rev. J. Roscoe.
[4] Somewhat similar is the Kamba principle that the same penalty must be paid for the death of a woman following an adulterer's impregnation as for her death resulting from a direct blow with a lethal weapon : Penwill, *Kamba Customary Law*, pp. 72 ff., 82.

Bangala, for example, appoint a chief to act as chief judge in all important cases involving persons in any of the several towns subject to his jurisdiction.   The heads of all families signify their acceptance of his judicial authority by ceremonially cutting down portions of the judge's banana trees in the presence of others. The town in which the judge lives then becomes the one offended by this *casus belli* given by all the people from the offending towns, and since the latter are the offenders they must never be the first to attack the offended town and hence the chief judge. So that, if any of the judge's future decisions should go against any one of these fictional offenders, they cannot raise a finger against the judge so long as the judgment in question is fair and above board and is according to established law.   On the other hand, strong men from the other towns will jointly assist in enforcing the verdict against the party at fault, however much the latter may dislike it.   The fiction consists in the theory that the faulty person has given an offence to the judge by originally cutting down his banana trees and, as it is an accepted principle that no second dispute can be entertained before the solution of the first, the complainant's case against the judge's verdict cannot legally be heard until he has satisfactorily accounted for his initial gratuitous insult to the judge.   In this way, the stability of society is maintained and the immunity of the judge ensured. His own absolute impartiality in arriving at the right decision is guaranteed by the fact that other lesser judges are present at the trial with watchful eyes and are quick to dissociate themselves from an unjust verdict.   The same police force that compels obedience to a lawful decision can equally well cope with a patently unjust judge.

(7) In this connexion it is interesting to note a not very dissimilar arrangement adopted by the Sierra Leoneans of West Africa.   A litigant who felt dissatisfied with a decision of his chief might refer the matter to a neighbouring but friendly chief reputed for justice and character.   This was not intended as an appeal from a Caesar to a better-informed Caesar, since the two chiefs were often of co-ordinate authority ; rather, the reference by the aggrieved litigant to the neighbouring chief was meant to induce the original chief, who alone had jurisdiction to try the case, to do what was right under the well-known rules of customary law governing the case in question.

The process of getting him to do this was usually for the second chief to remit the case back to the trial chief, with a token present —'shakehand'—as a friendly gesture and a polite request for a review of the judgment. The second chief would of course have satisfied himself first of the errancy of the original decision. Such was the moral force of tribal comity that the first chief could only refuse to look again into the matter at the cost of his personal reputation for judicial probity or chiefly rectitude.[1]

(8) In the sphere of substantive rules of customary law, resort to fiction as a means of social adjustment had been no less marked. Among the Matabele, for example, a slave was sometimes allowed to succeed to his master's property on the latter's death, not on any analogy with the Roman institution of *heres necessarius*, but on 'the fiction of adoptive relationship'.[2] A good slave became assimilated with his master's family, and, if he showed the venerated qualities of generosity, intelligence, integrity and leadership ability, there was no reason why he could not become the family head or, indeed, a tribal war-chief.

Again, among the Matabele, a man and his daughter-in-law were (and probably still are) forbidden to eat in each other's presence. When social development rendered it inconvenient strictly to observe this taboo, it became the practice and therefore the law that the man might atone for a breach of the prohibition by the voluntary payment to his daughter-in-law of a token fine.[3] It is possible that, later on, this fine was neither demanded nor paid, and yet both would and did continue to eat face to face.

(9) According to the customary law of the Sesuto 'all children born to a man's wife, whether begotten by him or not, and even if begotten after his death, are regarded as his legitimate issue '.[4] A difficult case may arise where the heir's mother was never legally married to a deceased person, as when a chief or his senior son dies unmarried. The woman is then said to be 'married to the grave' of her deceased husband and, by the *kenela* custom, is taken to wife by the dead man's younger brother in the name of the deceased. ' By a legal fiction, her children

---

[1] J. S. Fenton, *Outline of Native Law in Sierra Leone*, p. 10.

[2] 'Notes on Matabele Customary Law', by H. M. G. Jackson, *Nada*, Vol. 4, 1926, p. 32.

[3] *Nada*, Vol. 6, 1928, p. 7.

[4] Ashton: *The Basuto*, p. 194; the same is true of the Kamba of Kenya (Penwill, *Kamba Customary Law*, pp. 19-21, 23-4).

N

are regarded as the deceased's children and the eldest son should succeed him.' [1]

But when public opinion started to demand that actual paternity alone should determine all issues of legitimacy of children, the courts began to allow a person to disown his wife's illegitimate children who are then awarded to her people for care and sustenance.   Legally, the children belong to their mother's parents.

The practice of the *kenela* (i.e. the levirate) is, however, a dying institution among the Basuto.   What was once regarded as an indispensable scheme of social insurance for aged widows and childless women is now in increasingly bad odour with the rising generation who consider it immoral and retrograde for younger brothers to inherit their deceased seniors' wives. [2]   In the case of chiefs the maintenance of such women is now commonly met from public funds.

(10) Among the Shona of Southern Rhodesia, the law against incest is sometimes circumvented by resort to a fiction.   In remote cognatic or affinal relationships, objections to a proposed marriage on the ground of incest are often overcome by mutual agreement between the families concerned or, in difficult cases, by a fictitious ceremony of ' cutting off the relationship ', particularly where any misfortune befalls one of such families subsequently to the marriage. [3]   Once this ceremony is performed, all legal impediments in the way of the marriage are notionally removed and the distantly related couple may now get married. New social and economic imperatives render some such modification of the old relational pattern of kinship necessary and, indeed, inevitable.

Fortes records that, among the Tallensi of the Gold Coast, matrilineal kinship has a different value for the individual from that of clanship.   Whereas matrilineal kinship confers definite privileges and obligations on an individual in relation to other individuals or to defined groups and has the same value for everybody, clanship is just one of several fictions used to rationalise ties of a particular kind between corporate units. [4]

---

[1] Ashton : *The Basuto*, p. 195.
[2] *Ibid.*, p. 83.
[3] *Ibid.*, p. 184 ; also, Holleman, *Shona Customary Law*, p. 58.
[4] *The Dynamics of Clanship among the Tallensi*, p. 116.   See pp. 115-17 for the author's interesting elaboration of the basic ideas of ' Native Thought and the Realities of Social Structure '.

Where rationalisation breaks down, people would be found prepared to face the issue squarely. Thus, according to local account, the males of Samiit are the sororal nephews of those of Gudaat, but there are no ties of clanship between the two. The Samiit elders, when confronted with this anomaly, frankly retorted : ' That is a long time ago, so now we marry one another.' There is no doubt that this attitude flatly contradicts Tale principle of exogamy which requires that consanguinity, however remote, is always a bar to marriage.[1]

(11) There is a strict rule among the Shilluk of the Upper Nile that a king's daughter may neither marry nor even have any sexual relation with a man. Having carnal knowledge of daughters of reigning or past *reths* (i.e. kings) is therefore entirely prohibited, and an infringement of this rule is a crime against the *reth* himself and all he stands for. Because of this unmarriageability of a king's daughter, the Shilluk invokes the fiction that she is in that sense a male person and that any sexual intercourse with her by (another) male person must be regarded as if it were one of those unnatural offences amounting to sexual perversity, upon which the whole community frowns. But though both parties to this offence formerly suffered the extreme penalty, the punishment has in recent years become compoundable by fine or compensation ; in any case the rule of eternal chastity enjoined upon a king's daughters proved in practice to be but a stupendous farce.[2]

(12) Sometimes what looks like superstition will be found to embody a potent means of attaining social ends. It may take the form of a prohibition designed to discourage sexual immorality. Thus, it is a common Wakamba belief that it is most unlucky for anyone to have sexual intercourse by daytime or when on a journey, since husbands and parents are not then at hand to look after their wives and daughters as they are at nightfall.[2]

Similarly, among the Wachagga, sexual intercourse by an uncircumcised boy with a female of any age was regarded as a heinous crime, punishable by death.[3]

---

[1] *Ibid.*, pp. 96–7.
[2] See P. P. Howell's article, ' Observations on the Shilluk of the Upper Nile ', at pp. 107–8 of *Africa*, Vol. 23, No. 2, April, 1953.
[3] *Jnl. Roy. Anth. Inst.*, Vol. 51 (1921), p. 247, in an article by C. Dundas.

This wide use of fiction may serve to explain a number of apparently curious features of African law.   Just as a man would deliberately commit a major offence as a means of attracting the elders' attention to an entirely unconnected but nevertheless, rankling grievance of his against another person, so another aggrieved individual proceeds to seize the property of a clansman other than the one who is actually liable to him, if such clansman is thought more worth suing.

This is but a short step to a development whereby the issue gradually becomes a stereotyped one as between clan and clan or family and family.   It is not due to any inability on the part of the African to distinguish the individual wrong-doer from the other members of his group.   No, his ' category ' is not so ' savage ' nor so ' confused '.   It has to be viewed as part of the whole mechanism of redressing wrongs by invoking the intervention of those whose neglect of their duty had brought about the guilty individual's original lapse or, at any rate, those whose initial indifference to the complainant's grievance had led him to such desperate measures of self-help.

Similar ironical situations will be found susceptible of explanation on the basis of some underlying fiction, whether in its ordinary or in its extended form.

Enough illustrations have probably now been given of the operation of fictions as means of extending or modifying strict rules of customary law in the light of changing habits of thought and of living.   The slow and often imperceptible processes of these legal fictions are apt to elude the vigilance of all but the initiated in African law.   Their subtlety is heightened by the vagaries of the transition from rural to urban life through which many of the African societies are passing today.

Maine has defined a ' legal fiction ' as ' any assumption which conceals, or affects to conceal, the fact that a rule of law has undergone alteration, its letter remaining unchanged, its operation being modified '.[1]   He is right when he says that fictions satisfy the desire for improvement without at the same time offending their ' superstitious disrelish for change '.   But while it is true that they are invaluable expedients for overcoming the rigidity

[1] *Ancient Law* (1927 edn.), pp. 30–1.

of the law, it is not wholly accurate to assert that they necessarily cease to be of importance so soon as a society has ' escaped from its swaddling-clothes and taken its first steps towards civilisation '. One need only scan the pages of A. L. Polak's *Legal Fictions* and *More Legal Fictions* in order to appreciate how vigorous but deft legal fictions still are even in the very highly developed English society of today.

Jones, after criticising the opinions of those who say that ' the season of fictions is now over ' and after showing the vigour and continuing usefulness of fictions, concludes : ' Instead of being an odd anomaly, it takes its place as the type of a mental process which is indispensable if thinking of any sort is to be possible.'[1] A little later he adds :

' The fictions of Jurisprudence are therefore assertions about rules of law and not about the facts to which these rules apply, although they often take the form of attaching to new groups of facts consequences formerly following other groups. In essence, they are metaphors of speech, terminological devices, and not distortions of the truth.'[2]

The writer points out that even Bentham, who in his *Comment on the Commentaries*[3] had charged that lawyers ' can no more speak at their ease without a fiction in their mouths than Demosthenes without his pebbles ', later admitted that the abstract concepts of ' right ', ' duty ', ' obligation ', ' power ', and so on, unlike the ancient fictions of the writ of Latitat, Common Recovery, etc., are necessary and indispensable fictions without which ' the matter of language could never have been formed, nor between man and man any converse carried on other than such as hath place between brute and brute '.[4]

In the African situation, legal fictions continue and will continue to help on the course of rapid adaptation of traditional legal concepts to meet the needs of changing economic and social values. As relationships become more artificial and stereotyped, and therefore less natural and intimate, fictions tend to multiply in order to fill the resulting gaps both in the substantive rules themselves and in their operational processes. Without the use of legitimate fictions the legal transition from tribal into marginal

---

[1] J. W. Jones, *Historical Introduction to the Theory of Law*, pp. 164-6.
[2] *Ibid.*, p. 177.   [3] *Ibid.*, p. 75.
[4] Bentham, *Theory of Fictions* (ed. Ogden), p. 137.

society and from marginal into urbanised (or industrial) society, would be haphazard and non-synthetic.

But since fictions alone cannot effect the necessary change-over, every known legal system has always supplemented the process by resort to direct and open declaration of change in existing rules. This is the method of legislation, and we shall examine in the next chapter the part played by it in both ancient and modern African customary law.

CHAPTER XI

LEGISLATION UNDER CUSTOMARY LAW

ACCORDING to Maine, the order of precedence among factors of legal development is in the chronology of fiction, equity, and legislation.[1] *Fictions* come first in tempering the rigidity of traditional rules which, through centuries of repetition, tend too often to be conservative in their jealous regard for social stability and orderliness. The old rules continue to bear their pristine names and well-worn features but, in their practical operation, inconvenient and harsh aspects are being continually toned down and adapted to new circumstances. When this subtle process becomes too slow or too inadequate, there follows a further stage in the reform of the law by means of *equity*. What the pretence of fiction cannot achieve indirectly, an appeal to natural justice and objective reasonableness ought to ensure directly. Therefore, all outmoded legal rules and reactionary customs may be disregarded as contrary to what is ordinarily accepted as fair and just. The final and most *conscious* stage of legal change is reached when old rules are specifically altered in order to make them accord with the changed situations of life and thought. This is the era of *legislation*, which Maine equates with an advanced stage of a society's legal evolution.

Now, as other writers have shown, Maine's order is neither universally valid nor scientifically accurate. Many ancient codes clearly antedate the emergence of equity or fiction, while the principle of natural justice in the form of a higher (i.e. eternal) law has been acknowledged in *themistes* (i.e. judgments), which are said to precede even customary rules themselves.[2] The truth

---

[1] At pp. 26 and 29 of his *Ancient Law*. See also his *Lectures on the Early History of Institutions*.

[2] Far from preceding equity, fiction has often been prompted by it, for it is the equitable instinct for change in the existing law which has almost invariably given rise to the creation of some fiction or other in order to circumvent its iniquity. Coke expressed a truism in his famous epigram : ' in fictione juris semper aequitas existit ' (3 Blackstone, *Commentaries on the Laws of England*, 43).

is that the three factors, which it is to the credit of Maine to be the first to bring out so lucidly and so well, sometimes occur in the order he has suggested, but are more often found working together at almost every stage of legal development in most human societies.

In the sphere of African law, fiction, equity and legislation seem to be concurrent influences making for legal change. The king, the chief, and the village headman are each in his turn regarded as the father of his people and the fountain of justice, or at least should be; he is also the head of the deliberative assembly or council of notables. In chiefless communities, the inevitable interplay of counterbalancing segments which are so regular a feature of all their social and cultural activities renders the free application of equitable considerations of fairness and impartiality absolutely necessary among these highly equalitarian peoples. The elders of such communities come together in varying composition depending upon individual competence and skill in certain groups of matters of traditional law and custom, although a hard core of these elders frequently recurs in most of these shifting bodies. The result, accordingly, is that whether an African society has or has not a chieftaincy system, the legislative, the judicial, and the administrative functions tend to overlap,[1] with consequent elasticity in the technique as well as the interpretation of rules of customary law. Equity and fiction naturally form part of such a judicial process, and legislation is an indispensable adjunct to (not merely a last resort in) the whole system of traditional administration of justice.

We may now proceed to consider in some detail the nature and methods of legislation under African customary law. It is of course necessary to remember that the absence of writing rules out the existence of documentary codes of law such as are the enviable possessions of the Assyrians, the Babylonians and their imitators and successors in the art of codified law. This makes it inevitable that our discussion of the African efforts in legislation has to be limited to more recent times of which we have some

---

[1] Dr. C. K. Allen writes of England : ' Even in the fourteenth century, when the constitutional form of Parliament has become settled in essentials, there is no invariable line of demarcation between the legislative, judicial, and administrative functions ' (*Law in the Making*, 4th edn., p. 359).

record. But it does not follow that their legislative enterprise is only of recent date. What we do know of it is in itself sufficient as a testimony to what must have been going on centuries earlier : it is, as someone has aptly described it, a 'concentrate of past experience'. In this connexion a very salutary reminder was given nearly forty years ago in these words :

'Customary law is the experiences of generations which successively have cast this and that aside, tried many methods and found them to fail, until at last some course remained open which proved itself the most workable and acceptable, not because it met merely one requirement, but because it fitted into all other circumstances. *Therefore it is a deeply-thought-out code, and the experience and intellect of generations have worked to make it one link in a chain of usages and ideas.* For the law as approved by custom is but part of the mechanism of society.' [1]

We see then that the absence of ancient codes or of early records of written laws in Africa does not necessarily presage a static condition of the customary law, nor are we justified in refusing the name of legislation to such processes of legal change as are to be found operating in African societies at various stages of their legal life.

It is easy to argue that the legislative and the administrative are two different processes and that the latter more aptly describes the method of legal change in African societies, seeing that the judicial and other functions are not institutionalised in some of them. While there is some truth in the charge that clear demarcation of functional boundaries is not a noticeable virtue of certain African communities, it must be remembered that the vice of imprecision afflicts all systems of law *in esse*. It is certainly not about African law that John Austin wrote these words :

'So far as political powers can be described by the words legislative and executive in any determinate meaning, that meaning must be this. Legislative powers are powers of establishing laws, and issuing other commands ; administrative powers are powers of administering or carrying into operation laws or other commands already established or issued. If this be the meaning of the words, they cannot accurately describe two opposed classes

[1] Dundas, 'The Organisation and Laws of some Bantu Tribes in East Africa', an article in the *Jnl. Roy. Anth. Inst.* (1915), Vol. 45, pp. 234–306, at pp. 305–6.

of sovereign powers. For a great part of the *administration* of existing law consists in *making laws*.'

Accordingly, Austin quite rightly proceeds to give this warning: ' That the legislative sovereign powers and the executive sovereign powers belong, *in any society*, to distinct parties, is a supposition easily shown to be false. . . .' [1] And it is Austin's opinion that : ' Of all the larger divisions of political power, that into *supreme* and *subordinate* is perhaps the only precise one, and is possibly sometimes the one really present to the minds of those who speak of the distinction between *legislative* and *executive* powers as if it were a precise division.' [2]

Even in England, after the establishment of parliamentary legislation both judges and councillors took a hand in the business of law-making. Thus Plucknett says : [3] ' The great concern of the government was to govern, and if in the course of its duties legislation became necessary, then it was effected simply and quickly and without any complications or formalities.'

Salmond defines legislation as ' that source of law which consists in the declaration of legal rules by a competent authority '.[4] This has the great merit of including all methods of law-making. And Professor Plucknett insists : ' It must be remembered that the repeal of existing law is just as much legislation as the introduction of new law.' [5] He adds : ' . . . whether it is established by the King in Council, or in a Parliament of nobles and commons as well, is completely immaterial. It is equally immaterial what form the statute takes, whether it be a charter, or a statute enrolled and proclaimed, or merely an administrative expression of the royal will notified to the judicial authorities by means of a letter *close*. . . . There is, however, no legal difference whatever in the effect or authority of statutes produced in these different ways.' [6]

---

[1] J. Austin, *Lectures on Jurisprudence*, p. 98. (The italics are mine).

[2] *Ibid.*, pp. 99–100.

[3] *Concise History of the Common Law* (3rd edn.), pp. 304–5.

[4] *Jurisprudence* (9th edn.), p. 206. Cf. Austin's citation, with approval, of Hobbes's statement that ' The legislator is he (not) by whose authority the law was first made, but by whose authority it continues to be law.' *Ibid.*, p. 141.

[5] Plucknett, *op. cit.*, p. 302.

[6] *Ibid.*, p. 304.

A. CUSTOMARY LEGISLATION

Considered, then, as a mode of law reform, legislation under African customary law may take many forms. It may issue (1) as the personal decree of a reigning king or chief, or (2) as the joint resolution of the king's advisers in consequence of deliberation in executive council, or (3) as the *ad hoc* proclamation by spokesmen of certain internal bodies or associations, such as secret societies and market guilds, or (4) as the authoritative declaration of specific regulations arrived at after due debate at a public concourse of chiefs, elders, and commoners summoned together for the purpose, or (5) as the judicial modification of old rules in the course of settling disputes arising out of new circumstances.

It is clear that (1), (2) and (4) are principal types of legislation binding either a section or the whole of the people, according to the legislative intendment or the extent of effective legislative power ; while (3) can only be a *subsidiary* type of law-making, is enforceable only against those legally subject to its sway and, even then, only in so far as the chief or chief-in-council has expressly authorised it or has not forbidden it. If it is considered high-handed or contrary to customary norms of social behaviour, etiquette or decency, it will be largely ignored by the people and may sooner or later fall into desuetude. In the case of judicial law-making, the limits of the changes introduced into customary rules will be set as much by the authority and prestige of the individual judge as by the apparent conformity of the newly initiated rule with established standards and usage. Fiction, analogy and equity are all prayed in aid by the judge who would secure popular approval for his measure. But he must be careful not to give the impression that he is thereby consciously sanctioning a definite departure from an accustomed rule of traditional law.

Let us now consider in detail each of the listed types in turn :
(1) Legislation by Chief's Decree.
(2) Legislation by Chief-in-Executive-Council.
(3) Institutional Legislation.
(4) Legislation in Public Assembly.
(5) Judicial Legislation.

1. *Legislation by Chief's Decree.*

This form of altering existing rules of customary law or of laying down new ones to meet the changing needs of society was neither normal nor popular.   Only autocratic rulers whom the pomp of political power or the pride of military conquest had corrupted would make laws by mere personal decrees, without the consent of the people expressed through the usual channel of consultation with the elders of the community.   Laws thus made were by the ordinary people more often broken than obeyed, whatever pressure might be exerted by the lawgiver to enforce them.

On the other hand, a popular king or ruler might come to be so regarded as the father of his people that he could by common consent be credited with the power to amend the laws or lay down new ones on his personal responsibility alone.   But, even so, one finds that the very fact of his popularity almost invariably meant that he would scarcely embark on a course of altering the law or of making a new rule unless he had previously ascertained the wishes of the people in the matter.   Such a decree would also prove generally acceptable if the changed rule had clearly become so obnoxious to the public that no one would regret its abolition, or if the newly declared rule seemed manifestly to supply a long-felt social need.   None the less, it is hardly conceivable that a good king or chief would proceed on mere personal initiative to make and unmake laws without going through the due process sanctioned by the established usage of his particular society.

If, therefore, we regard legislation by the personal decree of a king or chief as an exception rather than as the rule in African customary law, we shall be nearer the truth.   In this connexion it must be noted that such references to royal laws (e.g. a law of Lewanika, or of Lerotholi) as one sometimes comes across in the literature on this subject, must be understood only as relating to those enacted by the traditional legislative procedure *during* the reign of the monarch whose name it bears.[1]   The ascription of the particular law to such a ruler was as much an acknowledgment of his sovereign power as a means of enhancing the authority of the law itself.

---

[1] Of course, even an irregularly decreed law by an unpopular ruler might equally well be thus designated.

2. *Legislation by Chief-in-Executive-Council.*

Where there was a regular system of government, the traditional mode of African administration was through a king assisted by his important chiefs operating as the territorial executive.   There was, under the hierarchical arrangement of chieftaincies, a fair measure of devolution of legislative power, so that the village chief assisted by the family heads could often pass laws on local matters and even publish and enforce applicable central laws.

In this way, what the autocratic ruler would seek to do with such undesirable results, the ideal king or chief often secured by democratic discussion in executive council.   The twin principle of the paramountcy of the king and of legislative devolution will be seen to characterise such highly organised confederacies as those of the Yoruba or of the Ashanti.

Among the Yoruba,[1] the king with his capital at Oyo ruled over a considerable number of chiefdoms at the heads of which were his appointed representatives, who formed ' the council of chiefs ' to advise the king at court.   Johnson gave this instance of a change in the law of royal succession that was thus made about a century ago at Oyo.   To enable the king's eldest son to acquire the necessary education in the duties of kingship which he would one day assume, it was customary for him to be gradually associated more and more with the daily performance of important royal functions.   The *Aremo* (i.e. heir apparent) virtually reigned with his father and, in the later days of the Yoruba Empire, he was sometimes suspected of having encompassed his father's death so as to accelerate his own succession to the throne.   In Johnson's words :

' It was therefore made a law and part of the constitution that as the Aremo reigned with his father, he must also die with him. This law had the effect at any rate of checking parricide.   It continued to take effect up to the last century when (in 1858) it was repealed by Atiba, one of the later kings, in favour of his Aremo Adelu.' [2]

While the king continued to make laws on national matters with the advice and consent of his chiefs the latter were given a free

[1] For an account of the Yoruba system of government, see Forde, *The Yoruba-Speaking Peoples of South-Western Nigeria*, pp. 19–24 ; Dennett, *Nigerian Studies*, Ch. IV.

[2] *History of the Yorubas*, pp. 41–2 ; also pp. 57, 69.

hand over purely local affairs : ' But in every case the ruling of the local chiefs and their councillors must necessarily be the law for that tribe since the fundamental laws are not violated.' [1]

The position is very much the same among the Ashanti. Rattray states that the chief was ' expected to do little or nothing without having previously consulted his councillors, who in turn conferred with the people in order to sound popular opinion ' ; [2] again, that ' a good Chief was scrupulously careful to rule through his Elders and to allow all lesser chiefs to manage their own affairs . . . he dealt with the matters that arose outside the sphere of his direct control through the proper channel.   Decentralisation alone made good government possible.' [3]

In such highly developed political societies we naturally want to know how desired changes in the law were brought about. The movement for reform of the law often arose from the felt inadequacy of certain traditional rules as applied to the settlement of specific cases, sometimes by the village court and sometimes by the highest tribunal.   But in societies of this type the king rarely set the ball rolling.   Thus Rattray observes : ' In Ashanti it (i.e. *the Sovereign Power*) is apparently embodied in an oligarchy, and its functions were seldom, and are not even now to initiate new legislation.' [4]   When the need as well as the desire for change had become sufficiently widespread and the unwanted rule could not be got round by the invocation of a legal fiction or equity, then the king or head-chief would be apprised of the matter so that he might summon his chiefs or sub-chiefs to a legislative assembly.

We have this interesting account of the actual process of law-making in Ashanti : [5] ' The King is the President of the Legislative Board, but he seldom, if ever, initiates any legislative act.   It is the province of the people through their representatives, the Councillors, to introduce legislation, and say what law shall direct their conduct.   Hence, when a law is to be promulgated, which

---

[1] *History of the Yorubas*, pp. 96–7.
[2] *Ashanti Law and Constitution*, p. 87.   [3] *Ibid.*, p. 88.
[4] Rattray, *op. cit.*, p. 2 ; Also Danquah, *Akan Laws and Customs*, pp. 61–4.
[5] Casely Hayford, *Gold Coast Native Institutions*, p. 42 ; also p. 66, as to the summoning of the chiefs as councillors to the State Council of the King to enact laws ; and, pp. 73 ff., as to the chiefs' functions and importance generally.

is done by the " beating of the gong-gong ", the formula, in the mouth of the Linguist is, " The King and his Councillors and Elders say I must inform you——" ; then follows the particular command and the words " Par Hi ", an emphatic, exclamatory phrase, and a loud rattle of the gong, by way of a general proclamation. Such a law, once thus promulgated, lives from generation to generation, within the memory of the community, and the command is never without its sanction. Any other way of enacting laws for the people is not in accordance with the Customary Law of the people.'

This statement of Ashanti legislative procedure equally well describes what anyone will see, or used to see until probably recently, all over Yoruba country. The present author has personally witnessed this process, as the bell-men of successive *Obas* (kings) of Lagos went their rounds proclaiming new laws.[1]

We need hardly stress that by far the commonest form of lawmaking in African societies of the centralised type is this one by the king or paramount chief in executive council, or by a regular session of the council of elders. The main interest of this phenomenon for purposes of legal analysis lies in the fact that it constitutes a bridge across the vale that separates the old order from the new. Indeed, it is more than a bridge and, if we may mix our metaphors, it forms the bedrock upon which the modern administrative authorities have been built in Africa. We shall have occasion to recur to this point presently.[2]

For legislation among societies less highly organised than those of the Yoruba or Ashanti but nevertheless having a chiefly system, we may take the Tswana of Bechuanaland Protectorate so ably described for us by Schapera.[3] He states that, before the advent of the Europeans, Tswana law could be changed by (i) a decree by the chief, (ii) court decisions, and (iii) the influence of the laws of neighbouring peoples. All the five tribes discussed in the monograph proceeded at different paces in their legislative

---

[1] In many tribes there are annual or other periodic promulgations of major laws, together with an announcement of new legislation. The Barotse are said to resent changes effected in this way, sometimes to the point of becoming estranged from their ruler.

[2] See under the sub-heading, ' Modern Legislation ', below.

[3] Schapera, ' Tribal Legislation among the Tswana of the Bechuanaland Protectorate : A Study in the Mechanism of Cultural Change' (1943), pp. 101. A *London School of Economics* Monograph. The Appendix to the book contains a list of the legal codes of the Tswana.

changes. Thus, the Ngwato abolished both the marriage payment (*bogadi*) and the initiation ceremonies before either the
Tswana or the Ngwaketse, the remaining two tribes being the
Kwena and the Bakgatla. These changes were effected, we are
told, by the chief acting either on his own or with the support of
one of his councils ; he, however, describes the chief's powers as
varying in proportion to whether he was exercising them as a
ruler who consulted his inner council, his council of headsmen,
or both these councils and the popular assembly.

The writer describes the instance of a written code of 60 laws
among the Ngwaketse in 1912, listing the items of land tenure,
family law, livestock and other economic activities as coming
within the scope of legislative change. The sale and consumption
of liquor and certain religious ceremonies such as the practice of
initiation, have all been abolished by legislation—mainly to prevent the splitting up of the tribe into its Christian and non-
Christian elements. Through legislation traditional tributes have
now been replaced by present-day taxes.

The chief issues administrative decrees such as those relating
to the grazing of cattle and the reaping of crops ; he also determines questions of the validity of certain customary law rules—
whether, for example, Christians should be compelled to observe
the practice of the levirate. The chief can abolish, as once did
the Ngwaketse, the ceremony of circumcision ; also, he can
regulate the current rate of the *bogadi* (marriage payment), or
even abolish it, as was done in 1820, when there was a scarcity of
cattle because of disease and, when conditions improved, it was
revived. If the chief might abrogate he could also create institutions by means of laws, as when Kgama II once instituted a
regular police force for the tribe.

Schapera reaches the conclusion that the Sotho have a more
developed mechanism of changing the law by legislation than have
the Nguni-speaking peoples, and that this might be due to the
differing impact of the indirect system rule upon each Protectorate,
or the comparative neglect of the latter peoples by social scientists.

The Basuto speak of ' the Laws of Lerotholi ', at the head of
which stands this law (Declaration No. 2) regarding succession :
' Succession to the chieftainship in Basutoland shall be by right
of birth, that is, the first-born male of the first wife. If the first
wife has no male issue then the first-born male of the next wife

in succession shall be heir to the chieftainship. Provided that if a chief dies leaving no male issue the chieftainship shall devolve upon the male following according to the succession of wives.' With the support of Lerotholi, the then Paramount Chief, the Basuto National Council was established in 1903 and was given an official constitution in 1910. Its first important function was the reduction into writing of the principal customary laws of the Sesuto which was published as *The Laws of Lerotholi* in 1907.

Under the traditional system, legislation was the business of public meetings known as *pitsos*, of which more will be said later. On this score this passage deserves attention :

' No native chief is despotic in the sense that he can carry out any measure in opposition to the will of his people, and of all the chiefs known to us at that time, Moshesh was one who could least afford to disregard the inclination of his subjects. He was merely the head of a number of clans, each with very large powers of self-government. Every one of his sub-chiefs expected to be consulted in matters of importance, and if his advice were neglected gave no support to his superior.' [1]

3. *Institutional Legislation.*

By this is meant that body of subsidiary or delegated legislation which is usually enacted by certain well recognised institutions operating within a given community. Such bodies are the so-called Secret Societies, so regular a component of African communities, certain trade associations [2] which exist for the regulation of internal trade as well as inter-regional commerce, and the innumerable craft guilds of blacksmiths, artists and the like. All these and more of their kind exercised and still do exercise varying powers of delegated legislation for the guidance of their own members.

Johnson has this to say of the Ogboni Secret Societies among the Yorubas : ' Amongst the Egbas and Ijebus, the Ogbonis are the chief executive, they have the power of life and death, *and power to enact and to repeal laws* : but in the Oyo provinces the Ogbonis have no such power ; they are rather a consultative and advisory body, the king or Bale being supreme, and only matters

---

[1] Quoted from Theal, ' Basutoland Records ', p. 48, at p. 216 of Ashton's *The Basuto* (1952). See also pp. 18–22, *supra*.

[2] E.g. the *Parakoyi* of the Yoruba.

O

involving bloodshed are handed over to the Ogbonis for judgment
or for execution as the king sees fit.'[1]   It would therefore seem
that the Ogbonis sometimes acted as the executive authority over
the whole community—in which capacity they made and unmade
laws, and sometimes they were employed to enforce laws passed
in the king's council.   In either case, their influence extended
beyond the boundary of their immediate membership.   But this
does not seem to be the case with most African autonomous institutions within the community and under the aegis of the kingly
or chiefly power.   The normal exercise of their authority in
institutional legislation is limited to their own members.

However, to the extent to which their enacted measures do not
infringe a rule of customary law nor any of the royal or chiefly
laws, they are enforceable in the traditional courts, though only
as between parties properly subject to them.   Very often, these
institutions themselves set up their own domestic tribunals to
enforce the societies' codes.

Of probably the same order of importance are the laws passed
from time to time by the ubiquitous African institution of the
age-grade association.   These correspond to the various boys' and
girls' social clubs of Western societies and, like them, they make
laws and often unmake them for the regulation of their members'
conduct, even beyond purely associational activities.

What we have been discussing under the name of ' institutional
legislation ' is usually styled as _autonomous legislation_ in works on
jurisprudence.[2]   It is claimed to be autonomous in the sense that
it comprises the formal utterances of persons or bodies of persons
not forming an organic part of the normal legislative machinery
of the State.   Examples are Railway Bye-Laws and University
Regulations.   Such enactments, it probably need not be emphasised, are neither binding on the traditional courts nor are they
entirely free from the control of the king or chief in executive
council.[3]

4. _Legislation in Public Assembly_.

Either in addition to or in substitution for legislation by a king
or chief in executive council, we have this method of law-making

[1] _Op. cit._, p. 78.   (The italics are mine.)
[2] Salmond, _Jurisprudence_ (7th edn.), pp. 175–6 ;   Allen, _Law in the
Making_ (3rd edn.), pp. 449 ff.
[3] Cf. J. C. Gray, _The Nature and Sources of the Law_, p. 149.

by public discussion. Public assemblies are usually held for the express purpose of a full-dress debate on the public affairs of the community, with a view to making the various laws accord as far as possible with the facts of daily life. Participation in the deliberations is not limited to the chiefs or elders of the community and anyone present who has something useful to say can do so.[1] The sense of the meeting is ordinarily ascertained more by the preponderance of expressed opinions than by a formal vote for or against a proposed law or change in the law.

This manner of law-making is rare among African societies with strong, political organisations and instituted hierarchies of chiefly councils. Thus it has hardly ever been employed among, for example, the Yorubas, the Ashantis and the Baganda, while it seems to be customary among, for example, the Ibos, the Kamba, and the Basuto.[2]

In one such community, the Ibo, a group of people would use the occasion of a market gathering or of a social meeting (e.g. a second burial ceremony) to discuss public affairs.[3] We are

[1] All this seems similar to the English 'County Meetings' of the eighteenth and early nineteenth centuries, recently described in an interesting article entitled 'County Meetings' by B. Keith-Lucas in *The Law Quarterly Review*, Jan., 1954, pp. 109-14. We may quote here the concluding paragraph (p. 114):

'Reading the accounts of these meetings one is struck by the fact that they constituted a part of democracy which is lost today. Here, in an official assembly, peers and farmers, rich men and poor men, met to discuss the affairs of their county or of the nation. Exempted from all the restrictions which bound other public meetings, opinions were freely expressed, and the sheriff, presiding as the traditional head of the county, allowed both sides to speak their minds. Some sheriffs were of course less fair than others, and some meetings degenerated into rowdyism. But on the whole their decay was a real loss to the people.'

[2] The position of the Basuto, with their established chiefly system, is in this respect somewhat anomalous.

[3] Cf. Plucknett's account (pp. 302-3 of his *Concise History of the Common Law*, 3rd edn.) of the enactment of a statute in thirteenth-century England—e.g. :

(i) 'The Provisions (or Statute) of Merton', 1236, probably the earliest English statute, begins thus :—' It is provided in the King's Court on Wednesday after the feast of St. Vincent in the 20th year of the reign of King Henry, the son of King John, at Merton in the presence of the Archbishop of Canterbury and the other bishops and the greater part of the earls and barons of England there present for the coronation of the said King and of Eleanor, the Queen (for which purpose they were summoned), after discussion of the common good of the realm upon the articles underwritten : Wherefore it was provided and granted. . . .'

(ii) If the occasion of a coronation could be used to discuss public

warned by Miss Green that ' if specialised institutions are hard to discover this is not to say that an Ibo community, far from resting on immemorial custom, seems always ready for new departures even to the extent of discussing, as Owerri was doing, the altera- tion of such apparently fundamental conditions as the rules govern- ing exogamy '.[1]   For example, on one market day was altered the existing rule about the right of Umueke villagers to cut palm nuts.   The old law was that only the members of a land-owning group could legally cut palm nuts growing on such land.   As this arrangement favoured the old men at the expense of the young by limiting the area to what the former could effectively cope with, but which did not give scope to the stronger young men to obtain enough income for marriage and other purposes, the age-group of the adolescents of the village had made representations to the village elders to alter this law.   The old strictness was in effect relaxed so that the young men had greater latitude of cutting palm nuts on common land than they previously had ; but the new law did not grant their sweeping demand for a free-for-all exploitation of the palm trees.

Sometimes, a cluster of related villages [2] will entrust the business of changing the law, which affects the group as a whole, to their elders who are assisted by a body of men with something like a professional organisation.[3]   An assembly, thus constituted, once enacted that all men and women of Agbaja must go to the central market regularly on pain of payment of a fine and that no palm-oil work must be done on certain market days, the aim of this regulation being to satisfy the universally-felt desire to enlarge the market.   Since this law was of general application, the consent of all powerful groups or institutions in the community was also sought : there were prior consultations by the *Nde Dibea*, first with the eleven court members who were hereditary holders of certain socio-spiritual offices, and next with eleven senior women from the principal villages of Agbaja ; finally, a panel of young

affairs with a view to legislation, equally well could be any other social gathering.   Thus we are told that the Statute of Marlborough (1267) was 'entollred' in the presence of ' several distinguished foreigners ', including King Henry of Rome and his son, and the then Papal Legate. This fact was recited at the beginning of the Statute.

[1] *Ibo Village Affairs*, p. 132.
[2] There were sixteen villages in the group making up Agbaja.
[3] In this case, it was the *Nde Dibea*—a guild of doctor-magicians.

men was set up to ensure obedience to the new law.[1] But the ultimate consent of the council of elders—the *nde ama ala*—was indispensable to its validity. Accordingly, the formal declaration of the law would be made at a village assembly summoned for the purpose, possibly by a beating of drums.

But, for such joint legislative assembly to yield any valid regulation, the various village segments must have some common identity, ethnic or other. Co-ordinate village groups, even if related, do not usually owe any duty of obedience to one another's laws, unless it be the result of mutual agreement reached at a tribal conclave of elders of all the groups concerned. Consequently, any attempt by one village to foist on its neighbour laws that have been passed within its own borders and according to its own needs would prove abortive, if not dangerous. Thus, village A passed a law forbidding cattle owners to allow their cows to eat other people's crops anywhere within the village and giving power to the owners of the crops to kill any trespassing cow found eating the crops. Their emissaries trading in the cosmopolitan market of village B tried to impose this law on the inhabitants of the latter, and a big fight ensued until the court intervened. Village B naturally resented the impertinence of Village A in thus attempting to dictate to them what they should do. On the other hand, village C members who also were in the habit of trading at village B's market thought well of the proposed regulation, and the women brought back news of the proposed law to their own village for due consideration and adoption by the village elders : they too had for long been plagued by the depredations of cows, sheep and goats on their farms.[2]

Among the Kamba, there were always one bull, two cows and a certain number of goats in their marriage payment. While the number of goats varied according to specific agreements between the parties, that of bull and cows was constant. In recent times, sheep or cash are more commonly substituted for goats for agricultural reasons. In 1926, at the instance of the then District Commissioner, a large *baraza* [3] held that sheep or goats should be

[1] *Ibid.*, p. 135.   [2] *Ibid.*, pp. 210–11.

[3] The Wachagga's name is *Njama* for the assembly of the chief assisted by a council of persons who are not necessarily elders but are in the majority elderly men as well as seniors of the clans.   The Wakikuyu call it *Kiama*, while the Wakamba word is really *Nzama*.   See Dundas, ' Native Laws of Some Bantu Tribes of East Africa ' in *Jnl. Roy. Anth. Inst.*, Vol. 51, (1921), p. 222.

interchangeable and that, wherever possible, the cash equivalent of the market price of a goat be accepted instead of the goat. It was not agreed, however, that a claimant should invariably be able to demand money instead of a goat.[1]

Similarly, an established rule of customary law may be modified by the ' utui ' elders. An old and impotent man, after the usual marriage payment, took a young girl to wife ; but, as he was unable to have the children he so much desired, two of his stepsons by his senior wives' previous husbands had each a child by the girl. She later tired of this anomalous position and ran off with her two children to her father's place. The elders held, contrary to established law, that she could nevertheless keep the children who undoubtedly belonged to the old man and that the marriage payment be refunded by her to him. This decision received the backing of a substantial body of local opinion but, to set all doubts at rest as to this deliberate change in the law, the following law was laid down (in 1943) by an assembly of the elders : [2]

' Where a father of a girl is dissatisfied with his son-in-law, he may approach the " utui " elders and advise them of his intention to repay to his son-in-law the full bride price received. If the " utui " elders agree that he has good grounds for his action, they will assist him to do this, and the husband of his daughter will thereafter have no claim to the woman or the children born of her. Until such time as the bride price has been returned the husband retains a right to the children.'

Again, the customary compensation for certain cases of homicide used to be twelve cows. But when the Supreme Court took the jurisdiction in capital cases away from the native courts, the practice quickly grew up among the elders of ordering the culprit, on his eventual release from prison, to pay half of the traditional amount of penalty, having due regard to the punishment he had just undergone. If he was executed or if he died in prison, there was of course an end to the matter ; otherwise, he must pay the further compensation to his victim's relations even if he obtained his release after remission of a life imprisonment. A civil action of debt was normally brought against the killer to recover such additional compensation. The Local Native Council (Minute 6/1937) finally ruled thus :

' After discussion it was decided that if a man were hanged the

---

[1] Penwill, *Kamba Customary Law*, p. 3.   [2] *Ibid.*, pp. 20–1.

relatives of the murdered man should have no claim to blood-money as the crime had been expiated by the murderer's death. If he were only imprisoned but died in prison, they would likewise have no claim as he had been punished by God. If he were sentenced to a term of imprisonment, then on his release he should be sued for half the customary amount of stock by the deceased's relatives. It was decided that the offender be sued in person and that it would be conducive to the peace of the district if this were done, as otherwise there was a risk of vendettas occurring.' [1]

In Basutoland, customary legislation took place at public meetings called *pitsos*, to which all adult males were summoned and over which the chief or his representatives presided. The councillors, with whom the subjects for consideration would already have been discussed by the chief, introduced the matter with prefatory remarks and then threw it open for general discussion. The final decision, based on the sense of the meeting as a whole, was then announced by the chief or his senior councillor. Thus, Mokhachane called a *pitso* in 1841 to protest against the spread of Christianity, and Letsie I called another in 1888 to prohibit the practice of *bohali* (marriage) cattle payment. Moshesh, too, similarly abolished in 1840 the death penalty for theft and the legal execution for sorcery. [2]

According to Philip Mayer, [3] there was no national, tribal or even clan authority among the Gusii and, therefore, no regular system of general councils or meetings of the people at large. But when changes were deemed necessary by the Getutu tribe, special meetings were arranged on the authority of the *abagambi* (i.e. judges), ' who publicly voiced the necessity for reduction and pronounced sanctions against transgressors '. This example was soon followed by the remaining six tribes in Gusii country. The writer's comment on the legislative process of this chiefless society is as follows : ' While they believe the fluctuations of the bride-wealth rate to be associated with economic conditions, Gusii do not think that equilibrium always re-establishes itself automatically.

[1] *Ibid.*, pp. 80–1. During my research tour of East Africa in 1953, I found this a universal problem in the administration of justice in the traditional courts.

[2] Ashton, *The Basuto*, pp. 216, 252.

[3] See his ' Two Studies in Applied Anthropology in Kenya ' (1951), *Colonial Research Studies*, No. 3.

Deliberate measures of control were undertaken from time to time, in days before the advent of British administration. Indeed, bridewealth control seems to have been the sole field in which the Gusii people as a whole ever united under semi-legislative measures—an indication of the importance attached to it in the traditional society.' [1]

Notable legislative reductions of marriage payment are those initiated by—

(1) *Bogonko*, a famous warrior and elder of the Getutu in the early 1890's. Elders from other parts were invited to a *baraza* to discuss the matter, but they demurred to his suggested reduction of the number of cows from 18 to 10. Thus his proposed change in the marriage law failed for lack of popular support.

(2) *Ogeto*, a grandson of the great Nyakundi (founder of the Getutu tribe) and a respected *Omogambi* (i.e. judge), effected (c. 1903) a popular reduction shortly before his death in 1906. This was before the British administration of the territory. Elders and men of all ages from all over Getutu as well as stranger clans attended the legislative assembly (*baraza*) which was held at the traditional open space for inter-tribal peace conferences. An elder's suggestion to establish a lower rate for immigrants was shouted down on the principle that ' all people should be equal in price '. Then Ogeto and his wife, who was a priestess, pronounced the usual public curse which was regarded by the Gusii as essential to the final authority of a newly-enacted law. The words used ran somewhat like these : ' Let us all now agree to three cows. May any man die who disobeys these words.' [2]

(3) *Ichwara*, a great grandson of Nyakundi, summoned a similar meeting to the same spot in 1930, that is, during the British administration which, however, had no hand in the matter. The assembly unanimously acclaimed his proposed reduction, *which was also made retrospective in its operation*. Although the retroactive aspect of the new law occasioned some difficulties, many refunds of excess cattle payments were in fact made.

The writer then draws the conclusion that these three elements were necessary to the efficacy of the legislative reforms in Gusii

[1] *Colonial Research Studies*, No. 3, p. 22.

[2] For a similar use of this conditional curse among the Akan of the Gold Coast, see 'The Supreme Court and the Customary Judicial Process in the Gold Coast ', an article by J. N. Matson in *The International and Comparative Law Quarterly*, Vol. 2, Pt. I, pp. 47–59, at p. 50.

society : (1) authoritative action by the most eminent powers that then existed ; (2) democratic consent, expressed by acclamation at large public meetings ; and (3) powerful sanctions (magical) voiced by authority.

It will thus be seen that in every type of legislative activity studied under this head, the public proclamation which invariably accompanies changes in the law ought to ensure cognoscibility to all and sundry. It is, however, not quite clear whether a new piece of legislation passed at the top of a tiered system of political organisation and handed down to subordinate chiefs to publicise and enforce in their areas, would become effective there from the date of its original enactment at headquarters or only from the date when actually proclaimed in such areas. One gathers the impression that the actual practice was more akin to the French system, which prefers the latter date, than to the English system,[1] which adopts the former.

This fascinating theme offers full scope for speculation as to what the exact position might have been in the heyday of the old Yoruba kingdom under Oyo, or of the Ashanti Confederacy centred in Kumasi, or of the Zulu suzereignty under King Shaka, or of the far-flung Bunyoro Empire based on Hoima. In the absence of written record of such theoretical problems it is difficult to be sure how far modern attempts at a hypothetical reconstruction of the past can be regarded as possible and how far as plausible. But such remnants (or *relics*, it does not really matter which) as have been vouchsafed to us would seem to support the suggestion offered in the foregoing paragraph.

5. *Judicial Legislation.*

Gray's definition of legislation is, it will be remembered, that it is ' the formal utterances of the legislative organs of the society '.[2] This limited view of the matter clearly excludes judicial legislation. But we have Holland's words for the view that ' the making of

---

[1] Up to Henry VII's reign the Sheriff of every county had to promulgate and enforce throughout his bailiwick all newly enacted laws passed at Westminster. But the first attempt at systematic promulgation of new enactments was made in 1796, when it was formally laid down that, immediately after their due enactment, they should be distributed throughout the country. (Allen, *Law in the Making*, 4th edn., pp. 389–90.)

[2] *Nature and Sources of the Law*, p. 145.

general orders by our Judges . . . is as true legislation as is carried on by the Crown and the Estates of the realm in Parliament '.[1] The two learned writers appear to have taken up rather extreme positions in what is ultimately a controversy about the nature of the judicial function.[2] The true view would seem to lie between the two opinions. While it is true that judges do make law by developing existing rules so as to cope with new situations in conformity with the general principles of law operating in a given society, they cannot as true legislators consciously innovate laws ; their proper function is to make additions and developments, not innovations.[3]

Changes in the law through judicial decisions are often introduced imperceptibly in response to new ideas currently accepted by society at large. Others constitute innovations which sometimes shock public opinion and usually affect the reputation of their declarants. To gain a measure of acceptance, such abrupt changes can only be made by the most important courts ; that must certainly be the case if they are to be followed at all by other and lower courts.[4]

Nadel says that changes in the law are keenly followed throughout Nupe, not out of any enthusiasm for the spread of true knowledge of what the new law is, but out of ' suspicion and fear of a biased jurisdiction and legislation. Whole sections feel themselves tricked and threatened by this dangerous law and reject co-operation with its agents and the groups which it seems to favour.' [5] When a politically-backed law seeks to extend a uniform jurisdiction and legislation over new social domains, one of two things is bound to happen : *either*, the indigenous law reacts against the imposed rule so successfully as to force it to adjust itself to meet local ideas, *or*, a process of mutual assimilation takes

[1] *Jurisprudence*, p. 76.

[2] Cardozo has admirably discussed, in Lecture III of ' The Nature of the Judicial Process ', the function of the judge as legislator.

[3] For a narrow conception of the term ' judicial legislation ', see Keeton, *Elementary Principles of Jurisprudence*, p. 56 : ' Judicial legislation comprises those general rules governing the procedure of the courts which the sovereign power allows them to make and to enforce ; they should be distinguished from the rules which the courts formulate through judicial decisions.' This means that judicial legislation consists only of Rules of Court—civil and criminal Procedure, and has no relation to changes in substantive rules of law.

[4] See, generally, Ashton, *The Basuto*, pp. 252–3.

[5] *A Black Byzantium*, p. 137.

place resulting in the common acceptance of the new legal ideas. The first hypothesis is true of Nupe where Islamic law is being forced, as elsewhere in Northern Nigeria, to adapt itself to the traditional notions of family law and of kinship rights and obligations. Nadel observes : [1]

' The knowledge of the more important changes (e.g. in the treatment of seduction and adultery) has spread throughout the country and the changes remain linked in the memory of the people with the names of the judges who were their originators. Some changes are regarded as good, others as bad, and accordingly, judges have earned or forfeited the reputation of being " wise men ". The lawgivers themselves have been aware of the necessity of bringing their extraneous legal machinery into at least partial harmony with existing conditions and conceptions.' [2]

B. MODERN LEGISLATION

The only direct link between the past and the present of legislative machinery in Africa is the chief-in-council type. Even its alternative, the council-of-elders variety, has had to approximate to this pattern under the practice of the British Government to create non-traditional, ' warrant ' chiefs. The resulting confusion has led to the recent introduction of the English system of local government into those African societies which formerly knew no traditional chiefs. More recently still, even the chief-in-council has undergone modifications especially where the false claims of autocratic tradition has misled the British administration into the error of establishing certain kings and chiefs as Sole Native Authorities. [3] True councils, the majority of whose

[1] *Ibid.*, p. 172.

[2] These Nupe judges (*Alkalai*, as they are called) invariably belong to the ruling families of the Kingdom at Bida and are usually out of touch with local rules and practices of customary law.

It is also significant that formal legislation has not been enacted on such matters at the Etsu's Council (p. 102) or at the Council of Elders (p. 45). It would be inconceivable if such were not the case, in view of the elaborate devolution of authority in the Nupe Confederacy so ably described by the author at pp. 115–22.

[3] Even now, one sees relics of a vanishing era in the provisions of the Northern Nigeria *Native Authority (Definition of Functions) Law, No. 3 of 1952*, according to which *a chief in council* is distinguished from *a chief and council*. The former may act otherwise than in accordance with the advice of his council, but the latter must act only with the council's consent.

members are elected while the continuity of tradition is maintained by the retention within them of traditional personages, now flourish in many territories.

These councils legislate on a large number of purely local matters, but they are often given the power to administer certain Ordinances of the Central Government, with or without modification.   Sometimes, the reconstituted chiefly council may pass bills obviously based on Central Government Ordinances and these, when enacted, are claimed to be part and parcel of current customary law.   Thus, in Buganda, the African Chief Judge of the Lukiko Court wrote, *inter alia*, under the title of *Buganda Customary Law* :

' New laws are added to Buganda Customary Law from time to time.   An example of this is forgery.   A hundred years ago there was little or no writing in Buganda, so forgery did not exist. Now writing is general and forgery occurs.   This offence is punished as being contrary to Buganda Customary law.'

A preceding sub-section runs : ' The Kabaka's laws which have been passed with the approval of the Lukiko and His Excellency the Governor.' [1]   Sometimes, power is expressly reserved to Local Authority Councils to declare from time to time what particular rules of ' native law and custom ' really are and to amend or abolish obsolete ones.[2]   These statutory councils have both an *original* and a *subordinate* legislative power over certain categories of subjects.   The various Local Government Councils in Uganda are given power in their warrants to enforce Protectorate Ordinances relating to Poll Tax, Witchcraft, Sleeping Sickness, Public Health, and Diseases of Animals.   Original legislative enactments of the Kabaka's Lukiko (i.e. Great Council) include the Adultery and Fornication Law, 1917 ;   The Cotton Cultivation Law, 1919 ;   The Busulu and Envujo Law, 1927 ;   and The Liquor Law, 1938.   Subordinate legislation usually takes the form of re-enactments by Local Government Councils of Central Government Ordinances, with or without suitable modifications

---

[1] Para. 13 on p. 28 of ' Directions issued by the Chief Justice under s. 20 of the Buganda Courts Ordinance, No. 4, of 1940—Part I, Criminal Cases '.

[2] See, e.g., (the Nigerian) Native Authority (Amendment) Ordinance, No. 3, of 1945 ; Native Law and Custom (Ashanti Confederacy Council) (Repeal) Ordinance, No. 2, of 1953, together with State Councils (Ashanti) Ordinance, No. 4, of 1952.

to suit local circumstances ; it may also be the making of local regulations or orders giving effect to some provisions of an applicable Central Government Ordinance.[1]

If we turn to an African society with a more or less simple political structure, we discern other features of the present legislative process. For example, we notice the weakening of the legislative authority of traditional institutions among the Basuto : the protection given to chiefs by the British Government had made these chiefs less dependent on the consent and support of their people, and *pitsos* are now rarely held, except ' to announce orders that have been promulgated by the Administration or the Paramount Chief '.[2] They were used for such purposes as vital meetings between the chiefs and the British or Boer officials to discuss the disarmament proposal of the Cape Government (1874), peace terms after the Gun War (1883), and raising the tax so as to dispense with the grant-in-aid of the Cape Government (1898).[3] Because no longer needed for such purposes, the customary legislative assembly is now declining in importance.

This dependence of the chief or quasi-chief upon the recently-established British Government has also been noted elsewhere, and the result is the same with regard to the diminished lustre of the chiefly crown, at least in legislative matters. There is a noticeable ambivalence in the attitude of the common people towards customary legislative institutions on the one hand, and the new statutory councils on the other. Thus, although the Gusii elders [4] regarded the legislative process from Bogonko's days and beyond (under indigenous rule) to Ichwara's times and later (under British rule) as one continuous development of customary law, the younger generation are sceptical. With the institution of non-traditional Government-sponsored chiefships and the omission of the publicly-pronounced magical sanction from modern legislative activity, these younger men now require that for a new law to be really effective, it must be given the clear blessing of the currently recognised authority—the Local Native

[1] We have given here the instance of Uganda only as a type of the modern legislative problems in centrally organised African societies. Much of what is described applies also to similar or even better organised communities elsewhere.
[2] Ashton, *op. cit.*, pp. 217–20.
[3] Ashton, *op. cit.*, p. 216.
[4] Philip Mayer, *op. cit.*, pp. 26–7.

Council, backed by the British Administration. One chief expressed this new attitude in these words : ' At my barazas I threaten people who pay more. . . . I can call the offender to my baraza, but if he refuses to listen, I shall be forced to give up. This is the position at present. In the end the reduction will have to go to the Local Native Council. . . . Without the L.N.C. it is not law. . . . I don't believe that even the District Commissioner or the Provincial Commissioner could make law at a baraza, without the L.N.C. If they want it to become real law, they will refer it to the L.N.C.' [1]

Now it is to be noted that, although the Local Native Council is a Government-established body, it has nevertheless gained such general acceptance among the people as to make them regard it as the only true symbol of authority denoted by the British Government itself. Thus, the direct democracy of the traditional Gusii *baraza* must be effectively combined with the representative democracy of the statutory Local Native Council in order to give authority to legislative enactments. This dualism will no doubt disappear when the Local Native Council has itself achieved a truly representative status both in composition and function.

Finally, a theoretical argument has been advanced and partly refuted by a learned writer on the legal effect of the advent of the British Administration on laws previously laid down by customary legislative institutions—e.g. the Laws of Lerotholi. Since 1907 these laws have been revised and added to from time to time.[2] Several were new laws which took account of prevailing social changes, and others were Government statutory laws (proclamations) which were thus incorporated into Basuto law.

Ashton therefore argues that these laws cannot strictly be regarded as really statutory since neither the Paramount Chief nor the Basutoland Council had been given express legislative authority by the British Government. ' But,' counters the writer, ' they had the effect of law, were legally binding in the native courts and were consulted and quoted by litigants and by the courts.' Surely, orders of the chiefs issued and enforced before the Native Administration Proclamation of 1938 must be

---

[1] Philip Mayer, *op. cit.*, p. 26.
[2] A new version of The Laws of Lerotholi was published in 1946. It consisted of four parts—Pt. I is strictly customary law but Pts. II–IV are strictly statutory.

valid in so far as they were based on the chief's traditional authority, and must in due course form part of the accepted body of customary law in general ? [1]

It is probably needless to warn the reader against the inference that our all too brief survey of modern legislation under African law is calculated to show that British influence on African legislation is pernicious. It must suffice to say that no account has been included of legislation in other than a purely customary law setting, nor has our analysis been directed to advancing any negative estimate of a complex and delicate issue of African law and administration.

[1] Ashton, pp. 250 ff.

CHAPTER XII

THE CUSTOMARY JUDICIAL PROCESS

THERE are a few popular fallacies that must be disposed of here if a true picture of the customary judicial process is to emerge. As we have seen [1] some writers deny that African law *is* law and, therefore, that the traditional tribunals *are* courts; others, again, while they are inclined to grant the name of law to African law, insist that there is no conception in the latter analogous to the modern distinction made in English law between civil and criminal, although a group of these writers would admit a possible distinction between public and private law. We have already shown the thinness of either view [2] and would not have mentioned it again here but for its immediate relevance to the problem of methods of customary adjudication of disputes. For, the all too common assumption that African judicial process recognises only *arbitration*, but no judgment, may be traced to both these erroneous attitudes to African law.

When it is said that arbitration is the essence of the customary judicial process, it is not usually clear what meaning is to be attached to the word in the context of African law. Is it arbitration according to the English common law and the Arbitration Act, 1889, where parties to a dispute agree at the outset to be bound by the award of the chosen adjudicator(s)? Or, is it one of the many African customary modes of referring a dispute to the family head or an elder of the community for a compromise solution based upon subsequent acceptance by both parties of the suggested award, which becomes binding only after such signification of its acceptance, and from which either party is free to resile at any stage of the proceedings up to that point? A third sense, which is really a hotchpotch of these two, is that which has been developed by, for example, the Supreme Court of the Gold Coast and called ' arbitration according to native customary law '; the essence of this is the prior agreement of the parties to be bound by the award, followed by its publication —both being elements of an English common law arbitration.

[1] See Chs. III and IV.   [2] See Ch. VII.

Now this strange brand of arbitration requires no writing ; the award cannot be enforced (as can its English common law proto-type) as a judgment of a court, but may serve only as a defence by one of the parties as a case of estoppel by *res judicata*.[1] It seems also that neither party can lawfully resile *after* the award has been made.[2] We need not emphasise that this synthesis of the two English and African legal ideas is a curious amalgam, partaking of the nature of neither pure common law arbitration nor customary law arbitrament (which, by the way, seems a better word than ' arbitration ' to describe customary adjudication).

Of these three separate processes generically called arbitration it is not always easy to ascertain which is meant when African customary judicial process is so described. But one suspects that it is not so much a *process* as a *concept* that is the underlying assumption of the majority of writers who say that traditional settlement of disputes is all arbitration, and not the judging of a case followed by enforcement of any consequential award. This attitude entirely ignores the fact that African law distinguishes between criminal and civil wrongs, between offences affecting the whole community as likely to disrupt its corporate existence and those left to the private arbitrament of the individuals con-cerned. As will be seen presently, the procedure of bringing the culprit to book naturally differs in the case of offences of the former type from that for offences in the latter category. Those who predicate of the customary judicial process a system of wholesale arbitration, therefore, overlook the clear distinction that is in fact made by customary law between the two types of process.

But even some of those who recognise a distinction into ' public ' and ' private ' in African law appear to imply that it is possible to characterise the procedure adopted in trying ' public ' offences as properly judicial while that employed in ' private ' suits is best regarded as arbitration. Thus Driberg wrote : ' In his adminis-tration of the public law, the chief, or whatever the legal authority may be, sits as a judge and awards the appropriate sentence ;

---

[1] *Mensah* v. *Takyiampong*, 6 W.A.C.A. 118 ; see on this matter the interesting article by J. N. Matson, entitled ' The Supreme Court and the Customary Judicial Process in the Gold Coast ', in *I.C.L.Q.*, Jan. 1953, pp. 47–59 (Vol. 2, Pt. I, 5th Series).

[2] *Kwasi* v. *Larbi and ors.* (1953), A.C. 164 ; see A. N. Allott's note on this case in *I.C.L.Q.*, July 1953, Vol. 2, Pt. III, p. 466.

P

but it would be more correct to call the inquiry into a private
suit an arbitration rather than a trial, and very often no judgment
is pronounced, the general opinion of the court being obvious
to everyone.' He cited in support of this view an authority on
the Akamba who made a similar distinction by arguing that ' we
speak of " trial " before a *kiama* (legal council), the natives speak
of a consultation ' and that it is clearly ' not the business of the
elders to enforce their decisions '. If the last clause is true, it
is not easy to see why Driberg added : ' Everyone knows the
law and the law is universally accepted. Only questions of fact
are in dispute, and once these have been established by arbitration
their legal sanctions are normally sufficient to secure compliance.' [1]
Now, while there are large elements of truth in these somewhat
incoherent statements, they do not present the whole picture.
We must, however, defer further consideration of this matter
till the end of this chapter when we shall be better placed
to appraise the true aim and purpose of the customary judicial
process. It is sufficient here and now to state that, although
the maintenance of the social equilibrium is the prime objective
of African as indeed of any legal system, its judicial process is
not best described as consisting mainly of arbitration,[2] a much
misused word in nearly all the contexts in which it is usually
applied to African legal procedure.

Having pointed out these preliminary misconceptions about the
nature of the judicial process in African customary law, we can
now proceed to describe its main features, also pointing out
incidentally other errors at the appropriate stages. In doing so
we must bear in mind three factors :

(i) That the mode of settling disputes largely depends upon
whether the society in question belongs to our Group A type
(i.e. whether it has a strong, centralised political authority), *or*
whether the particular society is of our Group B type (i.e. whether
it is a segmentary, uncentralised political community) ;

(ii) That, even within a hierarchically-graded, centralised
society, differences both of emphasis and of procedural formalities

---

[1] Driberg's article ' African Conception of Law ', *op. cit.*, p. 242.
[2] Matson, *op. cit.*, p. 49 : ' In particular it is incorrect to distinguish two different kinds of customary judicial process, one that of a
" court ", based on compulsive power, and one that of " arbitrators "
based on a prior agreement of the parties to accept the award to be
pronounced. The agreement came after, not before, the decision.'

may often exist as between the king's or paramount chief's court, on the one hand, and the village headman's, on the other ;

(iii) That whether the society in question is of Group A or Group B type, the procedure for dealing with criminal (or public) wrongs is different from that for dealing with civil (or private).

With these points in mind, let us now turn to a full but by no means exhaustive discussion of the main steps in customary judicial procedure.

A. HOW AN ACTION IS BROUGHT

The modes of commencing a suit vary considerably, depending on whether the alleged wrong is civil or criminal, and also on whether the society is chiefly or chiefless.

In a society with a kingly or chiefly system, all matters tending towards the disruption of the social order—that is, those which are denoted by the word ' crimes ' in English legal language— must be reported to the king or chief, or to one of his sub-chiefs or councillors in the locality where the crimes have been committed. It is the duty of everyone in the community to assist in bringing a culprit to justice, and it would be regarded as morally reprehensible for anyone to oversight a known and obvious disturber of the social equilibrium in which everybody has so inevitable a stake ; such oversight might in certain circumstances implicate the person known to have so shielded the culprit. If a grave offence, such as theft of another's goat or hoe or bananas,[1] has been committed openly, all present are expected to raise a hue and cry,[2] with a view to apprehending the criminal and taking him before the local chief or councillor.

If an offence committed by an accused person is so grievous as to excite the crowd or the injured party into instant retaliation, the offender may usually escape summary justice by beating a hasty retreat into any nearby sanctuary, such as a sacred grove or king's palace, chief's or councillor's residence, pending the hearing of the case against him. Driberg is quite right in observing

---

[1] But it depends on the quantity taken, especially where banana is the staple food (as in East Africa).

[2] Compare the old English common law process of pursuing, with horn and with voice, all felons and such as have dangerously wounded another—see Plucknett, *A Concise History of the Common Law* (4th edn.), p. 406.

that this is ' the chief social function of sanctuaries in African societies '.[1]   Once a supposed or even an actual criminal has sought the refuge of a sanctuary—be it ever so ramshackle as a flimsy grove of bare thatch—none of his pursuers dare touch him.   Such is the universal reverence for established institutions in practically all African societies, whether the traditional political authority is central or horizontal.   The whole thing is a device against free or frequent indulgence in vendetta by the populace. Of course, it is otherwise if the criminal were caught by the injured party and/or his sympathisers before reaching the security of a sanctuary.

In addition to this general responsibility of members of the community for the due apprehension of a criminal, many African societies with strong political organisations, administrative machinery and military force have developed a system of public functionaries who perform a variety of police duties, including the forcible production of recalcitrant offenders before the king or paramount chief.   Such societies were the pre-British kingdoms of Ashanti in the Gold Coast, the Yoruba and Benin kingdoms of Nigeria, the Bunyoro and Buganda kingdoms of Uganda, the Confederation of King Shaka of the Zulu and the Matabele chiefdom of Southern Rhodesia.   These all had certain characteristics in common : the revered power and influence of the ruler, a well-ordered and regular system of courts with a personnel of judges, linguists or griots, court orderlies, messengers and even town-criers, to announce—*inter alia*—fixtures such as the dates and times of important trials of public interest.   Members of the standing armies are freely employed in many of these capacities particularly in times of peace.   Either of their own motion or through report made to them or in consequence of express orders from higher authorities, any of these court officers but in particular the court orderlies could enforce the appearance of an offender before a court to stand his trial.

Some communities having the institution of secret societies —like the Ogboni of the Yorubas of Nigeria or the Poro of the Mende of Sierra Leone, to mention only two—employed these

---

[1] *Op. cit.*, p. 241.   Dundas has also noted, (p. 236) the same attitude towards sanctuaries by the Wakikuyu, Wakamba, Watheraka, etc., of East Africa.   For a similar function of sanctuaries, ' cities of refuge ', in the England of Henry VII, see Plucknett, *A Concise History of the Common Law* (4th edn.), pp. 406–7.

powerful organisations for the administration of a kind of Star Chamber justice in certain categories of political offences. This is to be expected, seeing that these societies usually comprised most of the influential dignitaries in the local community and were closely allied with the ruling dynasties.

It will be noticed that, so far, we have been discussing the indigenous mode of prosecuting a criminal, one who has offended against the public code in a way that threatens the stability of the whole fabric of society. We must not forget that there is another class of wrongs to which the courts of a kingly or chiefly African society give equally patient attention. The normal procedure in these civil or private suits is for the injured party to make a complaint to a neutral elder, who is usually the head of the family or lineage, where both parties to a dispute belong to the same household or lineage. If the subject-matter of the complaint is of sufficient merit to warrant his intercession, he will summon the other party to his presence so as to acquaint him with the case stated against him. Should he want the matter gone into by his particular elder, both of them are then invited to attend together at a time and place considered convenient for the hearing and settlement of the case. In two cases, however, such an elder may refuse to deal with the complaint: (1) Where the subject-matter is too trivial to worry about and the complainant is deemed to be merely raising a storm in a teacup, for the principle of throwing a case out of court on the ground that it is *de minimis non curat lex* is as much true of African legal procedure as of the English ; little patience is spared for the mere grouser or the slow-witted ; (2) Where the elder considers that the issue involves an important legal principle or a great subject-matter such as a land dispute. These are normally for the chief's court, to which the matter must be reported, either by himself or by the parties themselves.

In a dispute between two family or village headmen or between two sub-chiefs, the first step is to approach a third with the complaint which he would proceed to settle if both parties agree to his hearing the case, but which he or they would report to the chief or head-chief if the disputants should so desire or if their refusal to submit the dispute to adjudication is considered likely to lead to a worsening of the relationships between them and their respective families. The local chief then has a clear duty to report the matter to the paramount chief or king at head-quarters.

Inter-boundary disputes or those relating to intercommunal dereliction of duty (such as when members of one community default in the seasonal joint clearing of a common thoroughfare), are ordinarily heard by delegates from both sides, with those of a neutral third community acting as presiding judge. The pre-liminary step is taken by the chief of the complaining community sending his emissaries to the chief of the defaulting community, drawing the latter's attention to stated grievances and requiring these to be remedied in the interests of inter-tribal comity. If no satisfaction is forthcoming or if relations have already become strained in consequence of a previous grievance, the first step in the matter might be the direct invitation of the third party to intervene, without any preliminary overtures being made to the other side.

The foregoing represent most of the customary modes of com-mencing the prosecution for crimes and of instituting proceedings for the settlement of civil disputes in a society with a kingly or chiefly system of political organisation.

Let us now consider the practice in societies where authority is dispersed rather than concentrated and where, because of the absence of traditional kings or chiefs, judicial and administrative organs are far less formal and institutionalised than they are in the societies we have just been discussing.

As representative examples of this type of African society and its indigenous methods of instituting proceedings we may take those of the Ibo of Eastern Nigeria and of the Kamba of East Africa. Of the Ibo Miss Green,[1] and of the Kamba Mr. Penwill,[2] have in their respective spheres shown how even these atomistic systems of political organisation follow fairly distinct procedures according as the offence in question is regarded as disruptive of the social order (or likely to be so) or is one of which the lineage headmen need take no cognisance until their intervention is expressly invoked. There are no permanent traditional tribunals with institutionalised judicial officials for the production of offenders before the council of elders, who act as the ultimate

---

[1] Green, *Ibo Village Affairs.*

[2] Penwill, *Kamba Customary Law* ; see, also, Snell, *Nandi Customary Law*, pp. 79–83.

guarantors of the social order and the preservers of the public weal.

In this capacity the Kamba elders constitute, as often as necessary, the ' king'ole ' for the trial of flagrant murderers, habitual criminals like incorrigible rogues, and even occasional perpetrators of shocking acts of moral depravity, such as the man who was executed for violently raping a mother and her daughter in circumstances of aggravation.[1] The procedure is for the ' utui ' elders, where they felt that a crime was too serious to be atoned for by the fine of a bull or by driving the culprit out from the ' utui ', to accuse him before the elders of the ' kibalo ' and those of the neighbouring ' ibalo '. It is most interesting to record the very significant fact that this so-called chiefless society also had a definite mechanism of enforcement in such cases, as we are told[2] that ' they would summon the young men with their weapons to a certain place at a certain time—the " king'ole " would gather '. Similarly, the Ibo council of elders would ultimately delegate picked men to ' go out at night to kill the man ' who had committed incest[3] or other heinous offences against ' ala '. The procedure is for the entire village to be summoned by a drum, which ' indicates that there is some notion of the community being concerned in these breaches of the law ' ; also the commission of a serious public offence, such as the placing of a piece of ' bad medicine ' on a valuable tree useful in house-building which stood near the place in the stream where people drew drinking water, would entail ' a general, rather than an individual, taking of action '. Anyone who saw or knew of such a crime should report it to the various family or extended family heads, who would then arrange a trial. ' There was, however, no special person to whom recourse must first be had. There is in fact no special, judicial machinery, but things are done in a recognised and ordered way.'[4]

With regard to the institution of proceedings for the redress of *private* wrongs Miss Green has in different places described[5] for the Ibos of Umueke Agbaja a number of alternative modes, of which we may list the following six :

(1) As we have seen in the case of chiefly societies, this chiefless

---

[1] Penwill, *op. cit.*, pp. 75, 89.   [2] *Ibid.*, p. 89.
[3] Green, p. 100.
[4] *Ibid.*, pp. 111–12.   [5] *Ibid.*, pp. 106 ff.

society also employs the mechanism of two disputants calling in a few individuals in the first instance to settle their dispute for them. If they are dissatisfied with the verdict they can take the case before a more influential elder or group of elders for whose impartiality and wisdom the disputants entertain a higher regard. As a last resort, a case, if of sufficient public importance, may be taken before an *ad hoc* council of elders constituted by the various family or lineage heads of the local community.

(2) Another expedient that a complainant may adopt is the beating of a drum up and down the village announcing that he has a grievance which he desires to be investigated. The elders will then foregather to judge the case on the spur of the moment or within a few days thereafter.

(3) A party with a grievance may, on the other hand, go straight to the elders and tell them that he has a case against another party. The latter is then summoned by such elders before them, either directly or to a specially convened meeting a few days later. This short cut to the informal authority of the elders has the merit of by-passing either of the first two forms of procedure.

(4) A similar approach to elders is involved in the arrangement whereby a complainant requests a member of *nde dibea*—a professional organisation of certain spiritual elders—to summon a meeting of the fraternity for the purpose of judging his case. The organisation almost always enjoys considerable influence, not only within a local community, but also over widely scattered neighbouring villages. It is obvious that any intending litigant will be able to gain the hearing of such an august body only if his case has an importance which compels its attention. For small disputes, therefore, this procedure would seem clearly unsuitable.

(5) ' Invoking the sacred spear of the important yam spirit ' is another mode of starting a case. It entails the rather curious procedure of the complainant placing a ' sacred ' spear outside the alleged offender's house or that of his parents if he is a minor. This, in Ibo eyes, is equivalent to putting black magic or poison on the offender or his parents—in itself a public outrage on the whole community. The elders would thus be goaded, as they were in fact intended by the complainant to be, into taking immediate steps to hear the matter in dispute.

A second feature of this act of placing the sacred spear outside an offender's house is that, since its presence in the owner's house (or village, where this is different from the offender's) is indispensable at the advent of the annual new yam fertility ceremonies, the annual planting might be held up in the village as a whole or in the two or more villages involved if no early steps were taken by the elders to secure the return of the sprar to its owner by the prompt settlement of the dispute.

Where the shrine of the god of a sacred spear is in a village different from that of its owner, an unpopular complainant often seeks to avoid local prejudice in his own village by invoking the supernatural intervention of a distant spear, thus transferring the dispute from the plane of the purely village jurisdiction to that of an independent village or inter-village adjudication.

(6) Grievances or other sources of dispute that are not pressing may be left to one of the important ceremonial occasions, e.g. kinship gatherings such as those connected with a second burial, for an accusation by the offended before those present. If the alleged offender is also present and the matter in dispute admits of being summarily disposed of, the case is dealt with there and then. Otherwise, a later day is fixed for the hearing.

There are three points to note here. The first is that the six methods above described operate when the offender is known or suspected. But where he is unknown, and since there is no regular police or detective system, resort is more directly had to the supernatural in order to divine the culprit. A *Dibea* (i.e. a diviner) is normally consulted as he is expected to have wide local knowledge, whether this is obtained by natural or supernatural means. Frequently, a group of suspects will then be made to swear their innocence. The one who refuses to swear then runs the risk of being held as the likely offender. In many cases, the victims of theft or other undiscovered crimes would not trouble to consult a *Dibea*, since they might consider the game not worth the candle. This *Dibea* procedure may therefore be regarded as a *seventh* method of starting a case.

Secondly, it is probably worth remarking that resort to divination is almost entirely confined to attempts to discover unknown criminals ; it is hardly, if ever, employed in ordinary cases of civil or private disputes, as the offender will almost certainly then be known or be reasonably ascertainable.

The third point is that the six methods are not claimed to be of universal application in all societies that have no strong centralised political organisation, nor are they restricted to such societies. Indeed, any or all of the six methods (including the consultation of a diviner) may be found employed in a chiefly as in a chiefless African society ; in the case of chiefly ones, at least at the lower levels of adjudication of disputes.

Thus, Rattray records how an Ashanti who has a grievance may deliberately commit a public offence in order to induce the elders to enquire into his present action as well as the real case he wants investigated.[1]

Again, we learn [2] that, among the Akans of the Gold Coast, in addition to the private settlement of ' house matters ' by the calling in of the elders, another mode of commencing litigation is by either of the parties to a dispute, concerning, e.g. the ownership of property, swearing reciprocal oaths claiming the property to be his. Both would then go, or be made to go, before the particular chief whose oath has been sworn, as the parties are deemed to have indicated by the sameness of their oaths the chief whom they want to judge the case.[3] This obtains in Ashanti. In the Fanti area, an oath in similar circumstances, even if not reciprocated by the other party, is sufficient to initiate an action, it being then the duty of either party to report to the chief whose oath has been sworn.

B.   TYPES OF TRIAL AND MODES OF TRYING THE CRIMINAL

When by any, or a combination of any, of the eight or nine modes of commencing a suit, the chief in a chiefly society, or the council of elders in a chiefless one, has thus been acquainted with the occurrence of a cause of action, a day is fixed for judging the case. The character of the subsequent trial differs according to whether a *criminal* or a *civil* wrong is in question ; for, contrary to what one is often told by some writers, a clear distinction

[1] *Ashanti Law and Constitution*, p. 288.

[2] Matson's article, *op. cit.*, p. 51.

[3] This is not unlike the Roman law procedure of the *legis actio sacramenti*, when the parties before the *praetor* appoint a *judex* in a similar fashion. Of the same character is the Ibo trial procedure by Oath and Betting, presently to be described below under ' Types of Trial and Modes of Trying the Criminal '.

is made by African societies even in the matter of procedure at
a trial. ' Akan customary law ', observes Matson,[1] ' recognised
two classes of acts giving rise to judicial proceedings : those
causing danger (spiritual more often than mundane) to the community, either as a whole or in the person of its head ; and those
causing harm only to individuals.' This, as we have shown
again and again,[2] can be predicated of practically all types of
African societies. We are, however, concerned, in the present
section, with the trial of a person accused of a crime or a public
offence which constitutes an outrage on the community.

The treatment of the criminal, whatever the society, can be
swift and summary in the case of certain types of offence.[3]
Minor crimes such as petty pilfering, simple assault or innocent
breaches of market regulations may be, and are in fact often,
dealt with on the spot, provided that the offender is known
and especially when he is caught in the act. In the case of
minor thefts, the recovery of the article from the thief on the
scene of the crime is usually followed by a formal accusation of
him before the chief or council of elders sitting as a court to
try the case.

But grave offences are normally attended by often elaborate
but sometimes indirect trial procedure. Two main lines of
approach may be distinguished on the basis that (1) the offender
is known and (2) the offender is unknown.

(1) *Known Offenders* : The procedure adopted is stricter in a
chief's than in a ward headman's court,[4] and again in a chiefly
society system than in a chiefless society one ; the essentials are,
however, seldom dissimilar.

As an illustration of the procedure for the trial of a murderer,
an incorrigible robber or other habitual criminal in a chiefless
society, we may take the Kikuyu practice of the ' king'ole ' and

---

[1] *Op. cit.*, p. 48. The writer clearly admits a distinction between
criminal and civil proceedings when he writes : ' Even when it (i.e. a
" house matter ") got to the chief, however, the attitude of the adjudicators was not, as in the case of punishable acts, that of an angry chief
seeking to impose retributive and deterrent punishment on a wrong-
doer. . .'

[2] See Ch. VII.

[3] This must have misled some observers into thinking that African
criminal procedure has contributed little to the development of substantive or adjective law—see, e.g., Matson, *op. cit.*, p. 48.

[4] Holleman, *Shona Customary Law*, p. 17.

the ' mwinge ' described by Dundas.[1] When a person has become such a notorious criminal that his guilt is not in doubt, the local elders invite the elders from the remoter parts to witness the trial. The case against the criminal is then fully explained to these. Also, the consent of a father or brother or other living close relative must be obtained to the intended trial and execution. If this relative decides to withhold his consent, the killing cannot be carried out and only compensation is payable.[2] The dissenting relative must, however, swear by the *kithitu* (a sacred symbol) that, should the culprit repeat his crime or be again guilty of another serious one, he would not then withhold his consent. But if he agrees to the execution of the criminal relative, he must commence the hunting down of the offender by throwing earth at him—a sign that he abjures the wrong-doer for ever. All this takes place in a secluded spot in the bush. The relative is normally expected to kill the culprit by strangulation but, if he wilts on the ground of sentiment, certain armed youths who have been specially summoned for the purpose will be ordered to spear the culprit to death. By this device it is ensured that, when a father freely consents to his son's death or a man to his brother's, the punishment must have been fully deserved by the culprit. The presence of the invited elders similarly serves to guarantee the fairness of the proceedings besides ensuring the guilt of the accused according to the accepted standards of inter-tribal law and comity.

Nevertheless, this description of the ' king'ole ' and ' mwinge ' procedure would have been more valuable if it had included an account of the preliminary process of the accusation, of the evidence adduced in support of it, and of the accused's defence (if any). Some such steps must surely have preceded the actual trial and execution, since the virtual veto of the relative or (presumably) of one or more of the invited elders would have had no possible basis of acceptance by the trial elders. It must be either the inadequacy of the evidence or the non-compliance with certain settled rules of customary law as to guilt that buttresses

---

[1] In his article ' The Organisation and Laws of Some Bantu Tribes in East Africa ', in *Jnl. Roy. Anth. Inst.* (1915), Vol. 45, pp. 234–306, at pp. 258–9 ; see also, Penwill, *op. cit.*, pp. 89–91, for the Kamba.

[2] But this compounding of the death penalty by compensation is permitted by the assembled elders only where a homicide was not cruel or grievous or disruptive of the social equilibrium.

any such effective objection to the original course proposed by the trial elders.[1]

(That this apparently summary procedure is an abridged version of the normal process of customary trial should be clear when we turn from the case of a persistent or notorious criminal to that of lesser offenders.)

Again, if we take the case of the public execution of a witch or wizard, we are likely to see it as just another peremptory dispatch of the accused without prior adduction of evidence to ascertain his innocence or guilt. A very careful investigation into the circumstances of the whole event should reveal to the outside observer that what he has witnessed represents only the last stages of what is in fact a long and, by local standards, painstaking assessment of the unfortunate victim's evil ways over the years. The consensus of local public opinion has gradually built up against him : he was the notorious maker of ' bad ' medicine, known by many to have brewed concoctions secretly for various persons who had administered these to their supposed enemies, often with fatal consequences ; or he might himself have put dangerous poisons in some rival neighbour's *boma*. In several cases, his agents in mischief would not reveal the mastermind behind a complicated network of intrigue and systematic poisoning of often apparently unrelated or unconnected persons —all is carried on behind the cloak of complete anonymity, rendered all too easy by people having to live cheek by jowl in a closely-knit kinship group.

When, therefore, accusations are eventually made against this Fagin, the outsider is apt to dismiss the whole thing as based on a mere suspicion of an innocent man, but the elders of the community have by long experience of such practices acquired remarkable skill in their detection, even if they have to wait many years to accumulate irrefutable evidence of the culprit's guilt. By the time this stage is reached, at least the majority of the local people will have known of his nefarious activities.

[1] In defence of the whole procedure of this apparently summary punishment of major criminals, see Dr. Wagner's uncritical remark at p. 219 and Radcliffe-Brown's useful corrective in his Preface at pp. xv–xvi of *African Political Systems* (1940), where the latter shows effectively that the *king'ole* of the Kamba and Kikuyu and the *injoget* of the Kipsigis and Nandi were always held ' by an orderly procedure directed by men in authority '.

It is when the storm finally breaks that all and sundry are summoned to hear the recitation of his past criminal record. He is
closely questioned about each of the deaths or other misfortunes
previously associated with his name, and some of his partners
in crime are also made to testify to what he has made them do
at one time or another. Thereafter, his execution is simple and
summary. There are, of course, occasions where the chief claims
the monopoly of dealing with cases of witchcraft, and others where
local elders deal with such cases themselves. But in every instance, it would on proper enquiry be found, *firstly* that the
administration of some noxious medicine by or through the
accused was at the bottom of the majority of cases of public
execution for so-called sorcery or witchcraft, and *secondly* that
this serious offence commonly designated witchcraft is really a
matter of cunning and clandestine poisoning through a variety
of physical contacts.[1] In this respect we may take Dundas's
percipient suggestion : ' The justice of this (i.e. the public execution of a wizard) appears to us, of course, extremely doubtful,
but the native spares no means to obtain proof, which to him is
conclusive, and it is certain that many cases of so-called sorcery
are real instances of poisoning.'[2] The evidence here seems to
be reinforced by this testimony of two reliable social anthropologists with respect to the Nyakyusa : ' Supernatural sanctions
were believed to be effective only against kinsmen, neighbours,
and those with whom a man was in personal contact. No one
feared witchcraft from outside the chiefdom.'[3]

So far we have been considering cases of major public offenders
and the seemingly unceremonious mode of trying them. We have
been at some pains to explain something of the background
against which to assess what looks like a short-circuiting process
of condemning such offenders. That this apparently summary
procedure is an abridged version of the normal process of cus-

---

[1] This is not to deny the undoubtedly widespread belief in the supernatural powers of witches or wizards usually embroidered upon this
intricate and abstruse working of the astute practitioner's art and wiles
by ordinary and unsuspecting members of the community. What they
fail to fathom they naturally attribute to super-human agency. But few
of the knowledgeable elders, it is suspected, really subscribe to this
common view of the culprit when they decide to execute him in public.

[2] *Jnl. Roy. Anth. Inst.* (1915), Vol. 45, pp. 234–306, at p. 278.

[3] Wilson, *The Analysis of Social Change*, p. 16 ; see also G. Wilson,
' An African Morality ', in *Africa*, Jan., 1936, p. 91.

tomary trial should become clear when we turn from the case
of a persistent or notorious criminal—whether he be a wicked
murderer, a habitual criminal or a sullen wizard, for all are to
African eyes ' of imagination all compact '—to that of lesser
offenders. We have shown earlier that certain species of robbery
and adultery (in some societies) were formerly punished with the
extreme penalty.[1] The procedure for trial in such cases affords
a striking illustration of the special care normally taken by the
chief or council of elders to obtain clear proof of the accused's
guilt. Writing of the Kikuyu, Dundas stated : ' I am therefore
convinced that the killing of an adulterer was not permitted under
any circumstances ; in fact, it is often said, though not rigorously
adhered to, that if a man had not been an eye-witness to the
adultery of his wife he could claim nothing.' [2] This requirement
of proof of an accused's guilt within the context of life as lived
in a local African society will be found to be a recurrent *motif*
in the African administration of justice, whatever the offence
being judged.[3]

In most West African states with their powerful ' secret '
societies [4] it seems fairly true that serious political offences are
dealt with by a method that smacks very much of Star Chamber
justice. As we have shown,[5] the leaders of these politico-judicial
bodies often wield very wide powers in matters of ' Church and
State ' : they can make and unmake kings, they supply most
of the king's councillors, they organise and supervise trade and
markets, and it is often they who control the spiritual activities
of the community. These oligarchies, as conservators of the
public weal, take care of such recalcitrant or disloyal nobles as
might otherwise prove unamenable to the ordinary procedure
of the trial of an accused person. The commonest types of
offence, of which important personalities are accused in this way,
are treason against the king or paramount chief and probably
adultery with a wife of one of his ' fellow peers of the realm '.

---

[1] See Ch. VII, *passim*.   [2] *Ibid.*, p. 274.
[3] Talbot, *The Peoples of Southern Nigeria*, p. 619, wrote : ' On the
whole it may be said that, as in the Roman Empire, at any rate in the
time of the Antonines, a man was regarded as innocent until he was
proved guilty, with the proviso that the amount of evidence required
might be considered insufficient in an European court.'
[4] See, generally, Butt-Thompson, *West African Secret Societies* (1929).
[5] See pp. 197–8 earlier.

The trial itself takes place behind closed doors with, of course,
the king's permission thereto or presence thereat. While what
actually goes on there is never reported except the verdict, we
gather from reliable sources [1] that the assembled notables would
no doubt do their utmost to satisfy themselves in most cases
about the innocence or guilt of an accused by such means of
doing so as are open to them.[2] The judges at purely political
trials might not, however, be so nice about strictly legal details
of guilt.[3]

But in those African communities which have no such powerful
' secret ' societies, there are often to be found certain spiritual
functionaries whose role differs but little from that fulfilled by
' secret ' societies in chiefly communities.

(2) *Offenders Unknown* : Having considered the modes of trying known criminals, we may now examine the position when
the offender is unknown.

It is obvious that no trial can take place where the wrong-doer
has yet to be identified and brought before the chief or council
of elders. To aid in the difficult task of identification, various
expedients are resorted to by different African communities.
Ordeals, oath-swearing and divination are the three principal
modes of appeal to the supernatural, employed in the detection
of crime. At this point, it cannot be too strongly emphasised
that trial by ordeal is not necessarily the universal or even the
chief method of determining the guilt or innocence of a person
accused of serious wrongs. All generalisations based upon its
incidence in certain categories of undetected crimes have failed
to take account both of its *raison d'être* and of the extent of its
prevalence.

Frequently, the preliminary step taken in the investigation of
a crime whose perpetrator is unknown is for the victim or his
relation to consult one of a recognised class of diviners to be
found in almost all African communities. Partly from his own

[1] Forde, *The Yoruba-speaking Peoples of South-Western Nigeria*,
pp. 17–18 ; Talbot, *The Peoples of Southern Nigeria*, p. 756 (secret
societies were bulwarks against tyrannical chiefs); Dennett, *Jnl. Roy.
Afr. Soc.*, Vol. 16 (1916), pp. 16–29, particularly pp. 25–6 ; also
Dennett, *Nigerian Studies*, pp. 41–2.
[2] Talbot, *ibid.*, p. 634 : ' In Egbaland, all serious matters were judged
by this association.'
[3] See *Jnl. Roy. Anth. Inst.*, Vol. XIX, pp. 160–4 (1890), an article
by Mrs. R. B. Batty.

extensive local knowledge of men and affairs throughout his district and partly from what by careful questioning and logical inferences he may gather from the consultants' own stories and expressions of opinion, this deft and crafty practitioner can often indicate a circle of suspects from among whom it is probable the real culprit will be found. Of course, his superior intelligence enables him to hoodwink the unwary majority into a belief that this essentially intellectual effort of his *is* in fact of magical or supernatural origin. All sorts of *mumbo jumbo* are produced in the process—cowrie shells, bowls of water, sands in a sack, etc.—and these are manipulated to yield an answer to coincide with the diviner's personal predilections, largely if not entirely induced by his nice balancing of probabilities for or against certain suspected individuals. It will thus be seen that divination as employed in the detection of crime by African societies has no *juridical* character but is only an extra-legal prelude either to the ordeal or the oath-taking, which are both legal.[1]

When none of those named as suspects is prepared to confess to his guilt, or sometimes if particular individuals have been taxed with the commission of an alleged crime by the victim without any prior consultation with a diviner, the assembled elders or the chief will then subject each in turn to the form of ordeal considered appropriate in all the circumstances of the case. The ordeal might take the form of the juice of a tree (e.g. sass-wood) mixed with water, or a burnt powder made from it and dissolved in water; a knife or other piece of iron might be heated in a fire; the culprit might be taken to a nearby pond or stream. The guilty one is he who should drink the water and become sick,[2] handle the red-hot knife and get burnt, or sink when immersed in the water. We are assured by Penwill for the Kamba that ' these ordeals are mostly used in what English law would classify as criminal cases—often theft or murder when the culprit is unknown '.[3]

For the same purpose is the use of the oath. As an alternative

---

[1] See Lowie, *op. cit.*, pp. 392, 407–8.

[2] Penwill, *op. cit.*, p. 69, says these poison ordeals are not usually fatal.

[3] Penwill, *op. cit.*, p. 67. To the same effect was the evidence of G. Lindblom, *The Akamba*, p. 165; this writer also listed other forms of ordeal, e.g. of the needle, the axe and the bead—see pp. 175–9.

to the ordeal, the Kamba attempt to determine guilt by means of the *kithitu* oath or, in family or inter-group disputes, the *ndundu* oath. Each oath is sworn on a sacred object which might vary from a curious mixture of ' the teeth of a hyena, the teeth of a dead man, pieces of a porcupine quill, special roots and plants, earth from the hearth in the hut of a dead woman, a piece of an earthen food-pot, certain special small stones, and so on '—all wrapped up in a long binding and carried in a woven basket-like covering. The *kithitu* to be used in a particular case is brought to the place of trial by its guardian at the invitation of the party, who is not required to swear on it as to the facts in dispute, except to say that the *kithitu* contains no poison or other harmful substance which can injure the accused when he comes to swear on it. He swears this three times and also strikes the *kithitu* three times, repeating each time : ' If I lie, may this *kithitu* seize me myself.' He also swears that, if the accused should, after the ceremony, follow him secretly to his house to offer him bribe, he would never accept it and that, if he should, ' may the *kithitu* seize me myself '. After the accuser has taken these preliminary oaths, the accused steps forward and, before the assembled elders who prescribe the particular form and phrasing of the oath he is to take, swears the principal oath touching the crime charged or the issues in dispute. A goat is then killed, the stomach contents being scattered about the spot symbolically to cleanse the place of trial, while the flesh is cooked for the trial elders. Then the trial proper ensues.

The only difference between the *kithitu* and the *ndundu* is that the latter is less potent than the former in that whereas a false oath by the former affects not only the swearer himself but certain close relations like his wife and children, a false oath by the latter affects only the swearer and no one else. Women can neither be guardians of a *kithitu* nor are they allowed to swear on it, because their ' intelligence is limited ' and they might lightly swear in a manner that would probably wipe out their entire family. They are usually allowed, however, to swear, e.g., by striking their earthen cooking pots, or to swear on their loin-cloths.

As guilt cannot be quickly shown by either the *kithitu* or the *ndundu*—for each requires for showing its effect a specific period ranging from a few days to about six months from the oath-taking—resort may sometimes be had to one of the many forms of the ordeal for the purpose of getting quick results. Of course, an exception exists where the accused refuses to swear when called upon to do so ; his refusal to swear is usually taken as sufficient evidence of his guilt.[1]

Evans-Pritchard has shown that the oath is only used among the Azande for cases of so-called witchcraft and adultery because of the absence of witnesses or other evidence.[2] Among the Bantu of North Kavirondo, the late Dr. Wagner witnessed the actual return of stolen property after the uttering of imprecations by the owner.[3]

Another use of the oath is as a curse. Driberg says that Chagga witnesses are solemnly cursed by the chief before being allowed to give evidence at a trial, and that if an Ashanti witness dies soon after the trial he is held to have been guilty of perjury and the judgment may consequently be reversed. ' The expedient by which witnesses are put on oath,' adds Driberg, ' vary considerably. They may even be subjected to the ordeal together with the parties to a suit, but more commonly they are sworn, if an oath is administered, on some sacred symbol, such as a spear, the presumption being that the supernatural sanction invoked would automatically punish any perjury.'[4]

Some African societies are known to be content with the swearing of an oath, without recourse to a poison ordeal of any kind. The Ibo of Umueke Agbaja believe that a false oath is as bad for the swearer as is a poison ordeal and is not as likely to kill so many people as the latter, should the accused be proved false.[5] A supernatural object, associated with the spirit of thunder, can be invoked against an unknown offender. There is a special class of people to whom application is made if its services are

[1] For this account see Penwill, op. cit., pp. 56–68.
[2] Witchcraft, Oracles and Magic, pp. 33–4, 63 ff.
[3] See his ' Bantu of North Kavirondo ', p. 201 of African Political Systems.
[4] Op. cit., p. 240.
[5] Green, op. cit., p. 95. On the other hand, some other tribes like the Bemba of Northern Rhodesia do not believe in the swearing of oaths ; rather, witnesses are solemnly cautioned by the chief at the commencement of the trial, and there is no provision for penalising perjury.

required. Its invocation in a case of theft is held to be capable
of harming not only the thief but all those who have even inno-
cently shared in the stolen goods. This is widely believed to
be responsible for cases of otherwise unaccountable illness. It
seems, therefore, to be an elaborate means of securing a wide
measure of sanctity for private property by discouraging not only
the thief but also any accessories. The Ibo, being inveterate
traders, naturally want buyers of goods to beware of what they
buy and so maintain strict and honest dealings. Recourse to
the supernatural is thus had for the purpose of achieving practical
results and social objectives.[1] The *psychological* basis of it must
not be under-rated.

An interesting type of Ibo trial procedure is that of *Oath and
Betting*.[2] The accuser and the accused each bet a named stake,
say 5s., and must then produce a token (a flute or a knife) in
lieu of it. The tokens are handed to an elder, who acts as stake-
holder. If, ultimately, either party fails to produce the amount
of his bet, the elder is held responsible for it. Thereafter, the
accused swears his innocence on an *agbara* (i.e. another sacred
object [3]) of the accuser's choice. If within the appointed time

[1] Green, *op. cit.*, p. 115.
[2] *Ibid.*, p. 127.
[3] English witnesses in English courts swear on the Bible, and can ask
for the particular version or portion, e.g. the New Testament, of it that
they regard as binding. Roman Catholics usually swear on the Douai
version. Although many people believe it is still necessary to ' kiss the
Book ', yet this practice was on hygienic grounds abolished some years
ago. The Quakers believe that it is wrong to take any oath. Like
atheists and agnostics they simply affirm solemnly and sincerely to speak
the truth. The Jews swear on the Pentateuch, with their heads covered.
Mohammedans swear silently on the Koran. The Buddhists swear by
Buddha, asking for punishment for their migrating souls if they do not
speak the truth. The Chinese Confucians swear by breaking a saucer
or by blowing out a candle, saying that if they do not tell the truth
may their souls be smashed like the saucer or snuffed out like the candle.
In the Isle of Man, the oath is that the swearer promises to be impartial
as ' indifferently as the herring's backbone doth lie in the midst of the
fish.' The Hindu swears ' facing the Ganges ', while the Nagas of
Assam chop a fowl in two as a symbol of what will happen to them if
they do not speak the truth. Other examples of oath-taking at a judicial
trial could be given, but those listed must suffice. It is abundantly clear
that most oaths are based on the universal idea of supernatural sanction
and that history records the human reliance on one sanctified, even
mystic, source of authority after another which are regarded as sacred
and all-powerful.

English law, on the authority of *Omychund* v. *Barker* (1748), 2 Eq.

—a year, six months, or any other period fixed for the *agbara* to act—the accused dies, the accuser gets his 5*s*. back and the other 5*s*. is divided among the judges of the case. If the accused does not die, he gets his money back together with half that of the accuser, the other half going to the people who judged the case. This Ibo procedure of declaring an individual, who survives the prescribed period after the oath-taking, free of his oath has been shown to be a feature of the Kamba and Ashanti procedures and will be seen to be a *leitmotif* in the judicial process of all the African societies employing the oath as a mode of discovering guilt.

Where a judicial system like that of the Ibo still relies largely on the supernatural method of swearing and has yet to develop an advanced technique of sifting evidence, it may be that the oft-quoted weakness of the indigenous procedure does serve to stave off a possible miscarriage of justice by a not too rigorous insistence on the judgment being executed immediately. The purpose of consulting a diviner is often aimed at lessening the social tension by affording a temporary mitigation of any bitterness felt by the aggrieved—an important device among an excitable people living cheek by jowl. This is more usually the case when positive evidence of guilt is lacking or the verdict seems to be against the weight of such evidence as was available when judgment was given. But where public opinion is more or less unanimous against a criminal, or where a culprit has been caught red-handed or with no reasonable chance of denial, sentence is usually executed on the spot, often in a swift and summary manner by those who have decided the case or those appointed to do so by the judges.[1]

In cases where resort has been had to the ordeal as a mode of determining guilt, it will often be observed that the principle is based upon a presumption of the innocence of the person or persons subject to it. It must be granted, however, that the element of chance which trial by ordeal involves is too great to

Cases Abr. 401, and the Perjury Act 1911, recognises this and therefore permits any witness to swear by anything in which he believes. But, also, the Act does not leave anything to chance and provides up to seven years' imprisonment for breaking an oath, irrespective of any future punishment with which divine wrath may visit a perjurer.

[1] Green, *op. cit.*, pp. 113–14, 125.

make it judicially desirable or socially just. But, in the absence of a developed alternative technique for discovering an unknown criminal, nearly all human societies [1] have at one stage or another of their legal evolution employed the ordeal for the judicial determination of guilt.[2] Thus, to go no farther than English law, trial was (a) by various forms of ordeal (e.g. of the hot iron, of boiling water, of cold water, and of the cursed morsel), (b) by the oath of oath-helpers (usually twelve men friends or relatives of the accused) called ' compurgators ' who had only to swear that an oath sworn by the suspect was clean but who were not required to swear to the facts of the case : this is also known as ' wager of law '; (c) by battle (introduced into England by the Normans) which in civil cases was not fought between the parties themselves but between their respective champions who later became professionals fighting for litigants up and down the country ; in criminal cases, the battle was fought between the accuser and the accused personally and, if the defeated defendant escaped being slain in the battle, he was instantly hanged on the gallows specially prepared nearby for the purpose. Thus, a judicial duel between two contradictory witnesses was allowed to decide the rights of the parties.[3] It was thought that appeals of felony and trial by battle had been abolished in England until the case of *Ashford* v. *Thornton* [4] early in the nineteenth century came to English lawyers as a surprise. An Act of Parliament [5] was hastily passed definitely abolishing both modes of trial.

Regarding the ordeal, Maitland wrote : ' . . . if of two litigants, the one contradicts the other flatly, if the plain " you did " of the one is met by the straightforward " you lie " of the other, here is a problem which man cannot solve. He is unable yet to weigh testimony against testimony, to cross-examine

[1] One recalls that the Athenians handed Socrates a cup of hemlock in the belief that his influence on Greek youths was, on the whole, pernicious. And we have Lord Russell's recent reminder in his *What is Democracy ?*, at p. 32 : ' Hobbes was befriended by Charles II when Parliament decided that Divine wrath at his impiety was the cause of the Plague and the Great Fire.'

[2] See also, V. C. Sarkar's article, ' Aspects of Indian Law ', in the *International and Comparative Law Quarterly*, Vol. 2, Pt. 3, July, 1953, pp. 410–15.

[3] Plucknett, *op. cit.*, pp. 111–16 ; also, *English Historical Review*, Vol. 16, p. 730.

[4] (1818), 1 Barn & Ald. 405.   [5] 59 Geo. III, c. 46.

witnesses, to piece together the truth out of little bits of evidence. He has recourse to the supernatural. He adjudges that one or other of the two parties is to prove his case by an appeal to God.' [1] This proved so obviously unsatisfactory that Pope Innocent III had, at the Fourth Lateran Council in 1215, to forbid the clergy from performing their hitherto traditional religious ceremonies in connexion with ordeals ; and although the ordeal was thus robbed of its accustomed religious ceremony, it lingered on in many parts for a long time afterwards until its ghost was finally laid in 1819.[2]

The ordeal is, therefore, not the exclusive invention of African societies, nor is it universal among them. Some that formerly used it had ceased doing so before the British advent ; a good many others had, however, retained it until abolished by British legislation. Miss Green, in spite of her account of the various modes of appeal to the supernatural among the Ibos of Umueke Agbaja, can still write thus of them : ' Of practical activity, technical knowledge and hard common-sense there is no lack among this go-ahead intelligent folk, but an apparent lack of weakness in that social structure can often be explained by the use of a supernatural device where a practical one would normally be used by a European society.' [3] Basing himself upon his East African judicial experience, Roberts emphasised : ' Even among primitive tribes where trial by ordeal is still practised, the decisions arrived at are not necessarily unfair.' [4]

[1] Pollock and Maitland, *History of English Law*, pp. 62–3.
[2] See also Hanbury, *English Courts of Law*, pp. 36–7.
[3] *Op. cit.*, p. 131 ; she adds in another place, at p. 56 : ' . . . a particular diviner will often be tested before consultation. He may be asked, for instance, to divine the number of seeds in an unopened fruit.' With respect to the Yoruba of Southern Nigeria, Prof. Bascom recently wrote : ' A second factor, probably operative in many other systems of divination, but which is of special importance for the Yoruba Ifa, is that in spite of the numerous occasions when diviners are consulted, obvious decisions are made by the individuals themselves '.—*Jnl. Roy. Anth. Inst.*, LXXI, 1941, pp. 43–54, at p. 44. Compare Lowie, *op. cit.*, p. 391 : ' As Prof. Hobhouse has pointed out, archaic procedure frequently revolves not so much about the exact determination of guilt or innocence as about the prevention of internecine strife. Nevertheless, even in the ruder cultures, methods are employed to ascertain the truth of an accusation or the merit of a dispute, but usually the means used are shot through with the magico-religious notions prevalent among the people. Under this head two sets of usages demand attention, oaths and ordeals.'
[4] Roberts, *Tangled Justice*, p. 79.

It should therefore be remembered that societies employing the ordeal or the oath are not so irrational or trustful of mere supernatural sanction, even in the special case of unknown offenders to discover whom the ordeal and the oath are principally employed, that they do not seek to supplement it wherever possible with some practical organisation and technique of discovering the criminal and punishing him. Thus we notice the very interesting practice among the Kamba and several other tribes of East Africa of carrying out a *post mortem* examination of the corpse of a deceased in order to find the cause of an unknown or otherwise inexplicable death. The elders hold an inquest and attempt a careful review of the deceased's life to discover whether he had at any time been struck or injured by another, in earnest or in jest. ' In some cases,' wrote Dundas, ' the proof will be that, ever since the deceased was damaged in such and such a way, he had been known to be ailing. If there is no such proof, or the injury was of recent date or showed external symptoms, elders are summoned and the corpse is dissected. *They do this with considerable skill, and undoubtedly by long practice they are often able to detect an injury to some organ.* On the other hand, ignorance results often in the most absurd diagnosis.' [1]

If such a *post mortem* examination yields no evidence of any discoverable internal injury to an organ, the elders might put an otherwise sudden and mysterious death down to witchcraft. This, as we have seen, is often another way of saying that the deceased might have been secretly poisoned by someone with whom he had had a quarrel or even a dispute over some property or a wife. Dundas adds elsewhere [2] that, during the process of dissection by the professional surgeons of the tribe, ' although they may be deceived by the effects of a disease, they will very quickly detect any real abnormality. I do not doubt that the like is done among many other tribes.' [3]

---

[1] *Jnl. Roy. Anth. Inst.* (1915), Vol. 45, pp. 234–306, at p. 277. (Italics are mine.)

[2] *Jnl. Roy. Anth. Inst.* (1921), Vol. 51, pp. 217–78, at p. 240.

[3] It is interesting to recall in this connexion the following excerpt from a report on the Wellcome Historical Medical Museum exhibition in London on ' The Medicine of the Aboriginal Peoples in the British Commonwealth ', culled from *The Observer* of Sunday, Aug., 16, 1953, p. 3 :

Penwill has confirmed this *post mortem* procedure among the Kamba,[1] adding that the site of a personal injury occurring during an individual's lifetime, if considered likely to result in his death, is marked by some witnessing elder making four or six cuts on the place so as to facilitate future identification. This precaution renders easier any later inquest or dissection. The practice of marking is confined to the trunk or the head since injury to these, the most delicate parts of the human body, is most likely to prove fatal. Finally, we may note that some African societies adopt other practical measures for the purpose of ascertaining hidden or otherwise unknowable truth regarding the commission of a crime. Thus Lowie records that in addition to other means such as the ordeal, ' Uganda law recognised torture for the purpose of extracting information' from an accused person.[2]

But Lowie does not describe the means or method by which such torture was carried out. Was it, for instance, similar to the English common law procedure of the *peine forte et dure* which involved the extraction of a confession (or an agreement to be tried by jury) from an accused person who would not speak in court, by patiently crushing him to death between two boards and under a growing pile of weights? It was abolished in 1772 by 12 Geo. III c. 20, which provided that such a refusal to plead amounted to the accused's conviction.[3]

A modern form of the ordeal in the United States of America

' If aboriginal medicine is primitive and naïve, some of its feats of surgery win the unstinted admiration of more orthodox surgeons. Its practitioners are masters at the art of trephining, one skull on view showing no fewer than eight different trephine holes " in various stages of healing ". The holes were made for recurring headaches.

' Perhaps the most impressive exhibit, for the skill attending its use, is a foot-long, wood-handled, curved knife which its donor, a British doctor, has actually observed employed in the performance of a Caesarean operation. The woman in labour was made drunk on banana wine and tied to the bed. Two hours after the operation she breast-fed her baby, and was herself up and about on the eleventh day. A tribute both to native skill and native stamina.'

Dr. E. A. Underwood, the Director of the Museum, was thus commenting apparently on the Yorubas of Nigeria, concerning whose cult of Shopono, God of Smallpox, he was reported as having talked to visitors a little earlier in the report.

[1] *Kamba Customary Law*, pp. 83–5.
[2] *Op. cit.*, p. 411.
[3] Plucknett, *op. cit.*, p. 122.

is the increasing use of so-called 'truth serums' to extort confessions in criminal investigations. Drugs like sodium amytal and sodium pentothal are commonly employed in the process, and a recent Yale University report says that some people under the influence of these drugs were able to confess to 'crimes' they did not commit while others were able to cover up their guilt with ingenious lies.

C.   METHODS OF SETTLING DISPUTES

From our study of the indigenous ways of dealing with the criminal at a trial, let us now turn to a brief consideration of the respects in which the settlement of private suits differs from such a trial.

The first point to note is that, although ordeals are largely employed in criminal trials, yet they may also be invoked in certain civil disputes where witnesses are unavailable; the extent of their use is, however, necessarily far more limited. But whatever the preliminary steps taken to acquaint the chief or elders with a complainant's cause of action, the case has to be judged in traditional fashion. Sometimes, the judges' seating arrangement is casual and unordered; sometimes it is semi-circular, with an inner arc of the senior elders to the front while an outer arc of the junior elders guards the rear; at other times and in other parts, especially in chiefly societies, it is horseshoe in shape, in the centre of which is the chief's dais flanked on either side by his councillors while the other officials sit in a row to the right and left along the parallel but opposite walls of the courtyard. In the second and third types of seating arrangement, the open end lets in the parties to the case who stand or sit in the well of the court, in the full view of all those present at the trial.

As an instance of the first type of uninstitutionalised judicial trial we may take this account given by Miss Green[1] of the ceremonial opening of an Ibo hearing. After the complainant has, on the day appointed for the judging, brought his case to the attention of the elders in one of the modes previously described, the elders forgather under a big tree in the middle of the village and the litigants produce the customary court fees in the form of

[1] *Ibo Village Affairs*, pp. 120 ff.

palm wine or cooked food. As many other villagers as are interested in the case may also turn up, for the Ibo saying is : ' A case forbids no one.' Among the assembled elders must be a fixed number of traditional holders of certain spiritual offices (called *Ofo* holders), the number being normally four. The four *ofo* symbols were on the occasion in question produced and placed on the ground near a big stone at the foot of the tree. Then the elders drank the palm wine, the most senior pouring some of the wine on his own *ofo* while the one next in seniority dripped his with the blood of a small chicken. As each did that, he uttered some such imprecation as this : ' Let the guilty one be found out. Whoever sees the truth in this case and does not say it, may *ofo* kill him. Whoever tells a lie, may *ofo* kill him. Whoever does not say what he has heard about this case, may *ofo* kill him. Whoever does not judge aright, may *ofo* kill him.' Then all the four *ofos* were knocked on the ground, and this gesture was mimicked by all present at the trial. (This had the effect of introducing an atmosphere of awe and solemnity into the situation.) After this rite was over, the people, who had stood up whilst the imprecations were being uttered, sat down again and the defendant began to state his case. Ordinarily, the plaintiff has the right to open a case, but in this instance the case had previously been heard by a small group of adjudicators and the present trial was an appeal from that earlier decision. When both sides had stated their cases, witnesses to the facts of the case were called. One of the witnesses ' was interrupted by a fellow villager and told to keep to the point, and to remember that they had brought *ofo* and that it would kill anyone who did not speak truly '. Another man, an *osu* (i.e. one of a class formerly despised as a sub-citizen), spoke a good deal during the hearing. He seemed to be a kind of court orderly who was ' calling people to order now and then to get silence for speakers '. Finally, certain of the elders withdrew to consider the verdict. When they returned they demanded palm wine, after consuming which one of them declared the decision. As the verdict outraged both parties, a retrial was accordingly demanded for another date.[1]

There was a litigious character among this audience who, although not a party to the case, held a brief for one of the

[1] Green, *op. cit.*, pp. 120–4. But see also pp. 108–9, *supra*.

litigants with considerable skill and knowledge of customary law niceties ; indeed, he was known to have been a recurrent figure at nearly all important trials in the village. It is important to make this brief note of him here, as we shall come across him elsewhere in similar situations in other African societies.

The semi-circular arrangement of judicial seating occurs, for example, among the Theraka, the Kikuyu and the Kamba. Dundas tells us [1] that the Theraka had the curious procedure of allowing a plaintiff or defendant to state his or her case through a proxy. A, a plaintiff, would address his remarks and refutations to B, who had nothing to do with the case, and C, the defendant, would similarly address D. But both A and C addressed B and D by the names of A and C respectively. The reason for this roundabout procedure is, we are told, that the Theraka are remarkable for their hot temper and that it was more than likely that, if the parties addressed each other directly, they would end up in blows.

It is probably appropriate at this stage to deal shortly with the constantly recurring phenomenon of legal representation at African judicial trials. The origin of this widespread practice may possibly be traced to the indigenous principle that the head of the family alone is responsible for the wrongs of members of his household *vis-à-vis* third parties. A wronged person would consult his elder brother in minor cases and his father in major ones ; in either case, it is the head who will take the matter up with the village elders. For the same reason, it will be noticed that in all chiefly societies, the chief it is who represents his community in all dealings with other communities. Driberg has noted the interesting Chagga practice according to which, besides the recognised spiritual leader of the clan, there is someone called ' The Great One in Legal Matters '. It is his duty to represent the clan, not as a paid advocate of an independent litigant, but as a legal guardian. ' It is a small step ', wrote Driberg, ' from this to the direct representation by fee'd counsel which we find as an established custom over wide areas in the Congo, and in Sierra Leone where (according to Dapper) pleaders wore masks to avoid recognition.' [2] These champions-at-law are in fact to

[1] *Jnl. Roy. Anth. Inst.* (1915), Vol. 45, p. 250.
[2] *Op. cit.* (article), p. 233 of *Journal of Comparative Legislation*, Nov., 1934.

be found in almost all African societies, from the most highly centralised down to the most segmentary.[1] This explains why in every Native Court Ordinance enacted by the British Administration in Africa one invariably finds provision for voluntary legal representation of a litigant before a Native Court by the husband, wife or other relation (though never by a qualified advocate).

We may now give the Ewe judicial trial procedure as an illustration of that of a chiefly society. Lowie says [2] that suits are normally tried by a chief in council, which body when so sitting is designated in the vernacular as ' the old woman '. The plaintiff and the defendant each take the floor in turn, the witnesses of each are examined, the judges later withdraw and finally return to announce their verdict, not directly to the audience, but to the Speaker or Linguist [3] of the court. It is the latter who proclaims the decision by rubbing white earth on the arm of the successful litigant. The loser must pay all costs and, in addition, the compensation awarded to his opponent. Lowie adds : ' Both the style of the pleading and of the procedure are remarkable. The utterances of every witness are repeated by the official speaker, through whom alone the judges are apparently expected to take cognisance of testimony.' This device requires a little elaboration which we shall attempt later. For the present it only remains to refer to the use of the oath—private, tribal, royal, and religious—by swearing which an accused person declares his innocence and invites an official examination of the allegation made against him. The formula for each type of oath is usually associated with some private or public calamity ; in the case of a public catastrophe, once the king has specifically designated it as the subject of a judicial oath, no one should refer to it in any other connexion ; the same is true of well-known private oaths.[4]

---

[1] See pp. 239–240, *supra*, for the Ibo character mentioned before in this connexion.

[2] *Op. cit.*, p. 407.

[3] Compare the similar role performed by the linguist—a walking encyclopædia—at the courts of the Ashanti chiefs : Hayford, *Gold Coast Native Institutions*, pp. 68–72, 94. The name by which this official is called in Delafosse, *The Negroes of Africa*, is the *griot*.

[4] For the same practice among the Akans of the Gold Coast, see Rattray, *Ashanti Law and Constitution*, pp. 288, 370, 389.

All this is more or less true also of the Akan peoples of the Gold Coast who, as we have shown,[1] employ the oath in similar fashion. A successful litigant, and not (as in the Ewe trial just described) the losing party, was expected to pay the adjudicators *aseda* (i.e. thanksgiving), although other irregular fees were sometimes paid. The unsuccessful party would for his part indicate his preparedness to accept the verdict by repaying the *aseda* to his opponent ; any other compensation or restitution would, of course, also be paid there and then. That settled the matter in dispute. On the other hand, either party could, if he considered it unfair, flout the compromise decision, when the case would be tried all over again by another and more influential person or group of persons. The final act was the formal reconciliation of the parties by making both swear reciprocal oaths that they had forgiven and forgotten.

The pre-British Uganda process may be noted here on account of its advanced judicial organisation and technique. A well-graded hierarchy of courts ranges from those of the village *miruka* chiefs, through the higher district *gombolola* chiefs, again through the still higher county *zaza* chiefs, to the central court of the great Lukiko presided over by the grandee who in former times combined in his office the functions of a Chief Justice with those of a Prime Minister until the two posts became separated and were occupied by two different dignitaries. The Central Court was the final court of appeal for practically all cases except that occasional ones of great public importance might be heard by the same court presided over by the *kabaka* or *mukama* (i.e. the king) himself. Formerly the plaintiff paid a fee of twenty cowrie-shells when stating his case to the *muruka* or the *gombolola* or a barkcloth as a condition of the chief summoning the defendant, who must himself pay a goat and a barkcloth. A successful plaintiff received two goats and a barkcloth in addition to any actual award. An appeal to the central court usually involved the high initial fee of ten goats and five barkcloths, and the unsuccessful party might, in addition to refunding all court dues, also pay to the presiding judge a quarter of any fine paid. All this is reminiscent of the reason assigned by Lambard for similar payment made to English justices in the Tudor period—that ' the laws do now and then cost them a trifle, rather to let them know

[1] See p. 222, *supra*.

that they do not behold their well doing than that themselves
do stand in need of any recompense '.[1]

D. MODES OF ADDUCING EVIDENCE

We may now consider how, during a trial, evidence is adduced,
weighed and considered. While it is true that, in African judicial
process, there is no fiction of judicial ignorance, it does not follow
that judgment is based ' not on evidence but on pre-knowledge
and agreed adjustment or assessment following public argument '.[2]
The personal knowledge of some or all of the judges is not a disadvantage, as it normally is in English trial procedure, except that
African judges have been known to decline service on a Bench
before whom a near relation of theirs is appearing as a litigant.[3]
Also, ' *Audi alteram partem* ' is as much a principle of African, as
it is of English, legal procedure ; [4] a popular Yoruba saying is :
' Wicked and iniquitous is he who decides a case upon the testimony of only one party to it.' Nor is the presence of both
parties required for the mere purpose of ' public argument ' of
' pre-knowledge and agreed adjustment or assessment '. Assuredly
the tariff of fines and compensations is common knowledge and
will be applied in the judgment *after* all the merits of the case
have been gone into according to the due process of customary
law. It is not just to debate the measure of punishment that the
trial is held, but rather to marshal the facts with a view to establishing applicable points of legal rules.

Probably the most important means of adducing evidence in

[1] In his ' Eirenarcha ' (1581), cited at p. 142 of Dr. C. K. Allen's
The Queen's Peace (1953), Dr. Allen tells us that ' the " trifle " consisted of a few fees for certain formal duties and apparently the right to
retain a proportion of goods stolen and recovered.' (*Ibid.*)

[2] H. E. Lambert in his *Kiambu Guide*, cited by Phillips in his *Report
on Native Tribunals in Kenya*, p. 245.

[3] Rattray has described the elaborate arrangement in Ashanti to
obviate the possibility of the chief being judge in his own cause or of
being accused of nepotism—*Ashanti Law and Constitution*, p. 90.

Green records, *op. cit.*, p. 128, that when two disputants approached
a senior third, the latter ' objected, saying that he was a near relative
to both and ought not to hold their tokens '. It must be added, however, that when no one else could be found willing to discharge the
obligation, this man had to undertake it ; but the case itself was heard
by neutral elders.

[4] So held by Pollard, ag. J., in the Nigerian case of *Thomas* v.
Ademola II (1945), 18 Nig. L.R. 12, p. 33.

practically all African societies is the calling of human witnesses as to disputed issues of fact. The chief sits with his supporting judges, the court remembrancer (or linguist or griot) takes his position on a lower pedestal to the right of the judges, and the court crier or orderly tirelessly appeals to the audience to keep calm and quiet as witnesses give their respective testimonies. The complainant begins by stating his case, unless the cause is being heard on appeal, when (as we have seen [1]) the defendant begins. After the plaintiff has finished, he is called upon to substantiate important allegations with definite proofs. This he may do by calling witnesses who would testify to the truth of such statements. The defendant then takes the floor, states his defence and may call his own witnesses. Examinations and cross-examinations of and by the several parties and their witnesses next ensue, with one or the other of the judges (except the chief who must maintain a kind of dignified aloofness until judging time arrives) interjecting queries designed to clarify issues and to keep the parties and the witnesses to the salient points in the case. Any member of the audience who has something to say that is valuable may ask to be permitted to tender his own evidence touching the case.

In uncentralised political societies, less precision in the division of functions may be noticed, as also the apparently casual manner in which witnesses often give their evidence from their positions as members of the audience. Formalities as to the matter and manner of the testimony thus given are usually discounted by the elders judging the case ; what is important is that anyone and everyone who knows about the case should be allowed or encouraged to testify—we have shown [2] how imprecations are uttered at the opening of a case by some four elders, enjoining people to come forward and speak on disputed issues between the parties to the case. To a casual observer, however, this elasticity in procedure often appears to be an unregulated invitation to all and sundry to join in the battle of words raging around them. It would be quite unfair to take the occasional sparring matches, into which the verbal arguments sometimes degenerate before order is once again restored, as representing the general pattern of trial procedure among a people with a flair for verbal fireworks but with a tenacity for the ultimate reign of immemorial custom. To

[1] See p. 239.   [2] P. 222.

those who have tried to understand the subtle workings of indigenous judicial process, the general picture at such gatherings is one of order, not chaos.[1]

Human witnesses, then, are the primary sources of information at a trial in which vital points are in dispute between the parties.[2] The chief and his assistant judges or the council of elders give the highest regard to the testimony of an eye-witness, particularly if he enjoys a reputation for veracity and integrity. Stories told at second-hand are listened to with suspicion and are, as likely as not, lightly regarded. The litigant who stands a good chance of winning his case is the one who can produce the most convincing evidence in support of his case, and this is frequently a person with direct knowledge or rare opportunity of knowledge of the facts in dispute. If the dispute concerns an alleged debt, the defendant must produce eye-witnesses, since ' debts are not paid except in the presence of elders, or before a council '.[3] If A alleges that B steals his goat or necklace or whatever tangible, movable object it may be, each must be produced before the elders or positive proof given of its whereabouts so that they may be identified by the court. Even in matrimonial cases, wives and children over whom two men are suing each other for a refund of precedent marriage payment are often to be seen in court as human exhibits. The Shilluk hold that cattle which are legally returnable as ' bridewealth ' on the death or divorce of the wife are not, if they die whilst in the possession of the wife's parents, expected in practice to be returned, but the hides must be produced as evidence of the animals' death through no fault of the wife's parents.[4]

Among some tribes, means are adopted to record the various points made by the parties and their witnesses. Thus, the Kikuyu elders are accustomed to require witnesses each to produce a bundle of sticks, each of which is about two feet long ; these sticks, like an abacus, act as tallies to count scores made by either side of relevant points in the course of often windy speeches.

---

[1] See, e.g. Green, *op. cit.*, pp. 78, 112, 114.

[2] The insistence on human witnesses is obviously inevitable in pre-literate communities, such as were African societies until recently, in the legalisation of many transactions.

[3] Dundas, *op. cit.*, Vol. 45, p. 293.

[4] P. P. Howell, in his article, ' Observations on the Shilluk of the Upper Nile ', in *Africa*, Vol. 23, No. 2, April, 1953, p. 102.

R

On the final number of sticks piled up before each of the two parties to the dispute the issue of the case often depends.[1] In this connexion it is useful to recall this evidence of Dundas's : ' Not the smallest item is ever allowed to go by. It appears to us often ludicrous that the elders should sit in solemn conclave about some trivial claim of remote origin, but the Mkamba in particular is persistent beyond belief. He seems actually to take a delight in litigation, in the pursuit of which he will expend his last penny. We can conceive that when this is protracted through generations, and that so long as a claim is not settled there will be no peace for either party, a wise man will always pay his liabilities. Even between the best friends and nearest relations, compensation is paid which one might otherwise expect would be waived.' [2]

This brings us to another sore point in the African judicial process—the often over-exaggerated charge of tedious prolixity and apparent irrelevance of testimony.[3] There can be no doubt that many African witnesses relish a taste for oratorical display and that their audiences—and which audience anywhere in the world does not ?—enjoy good talk.[4] The freer rein so noticeably given by African judges to parties and witnesses each to say his say in his own way does not mean that these judges are undiscriminating in their reception of evidence. Though there are no strict rules against hearsay evidence, yet there are indigenous modes of applying checks and balances, such as the use of counting sticks or other symbols already noted, the periodical clapping of hands by members of the audience in approval of telling points of law or custom made by a speaker, the occasional interruption from a member of the bench to bring a loquacious and erring witness back to the points at issue—all these and more are employed if and when considered necessary. It is nevertheless the case that African judges are anxious to let a litigant have his say, seeing that they, too, like Lord Hewart, L.C.J., appear to believe that it is not enough that one should do justice, but that one must let

[1] See Phillips, op. cit., pp. 39 ff ; and John Bull, Oct. 20, 1951, p. 26.
[2] Dundas, op. cit., p. 294.
[3] See p. 179, supra.
[4] As Lowie has said, op. cit., p. 404 : ' . . . the Negroes have almost everywhere an orderly method of procedure before constituted tribunals. They display a remarkable taste for juridical casuistry and a keen enjoyment of forensic eloquence.'

it be manifestly observed that one is doing justice. They, too, do not like irrelevancies. Hence some societies have developed (i) firstly, the system of representation of a litigant at a trial by a blood relation with a tried aptitude for eloquence and clarity of exposition ; these can more easily be restrained from obscurantist digressions, not only because they ought to know better than ordinary members of the community the finer points of procedure, but also because they are each worth a number of such persons as witnesses, literally as well as metaphorically ; (ii) latterly, the system of champions-at-law serves as an indigenous answer to the problem of unlearned parties or their lay representatives having to present cases which, from the point of view of the learned judges, is often done in the worst possible light ; the appearance of this class of professional advocates in an African community marks, as we have said earlier, an advanced stage of legal development.

Where there is no legal representation, it seems that African judges tend to act like European (or Continental) judges, and the procedure partakes of the nature of an *inquisitorial* enquiry, with the judges asking almost all the questions from the Bench. Where there is legal representation, African judges act more or less like Anglo-Saxon ones, the procedure being *accusatorial* in character and there is far less interruption from the Bench— whether the case being tried is civil or criminal.[1] The role of the ideal African judge in this connexion has been well put by Rattray, with reference to the Ashanti : ' In court, his role was and is that of a judge who sits and permits others to do most of the talking, he himself only interfering at times to correct some irregularity or to guide the case. An *Ohene Okyeame*, i.e. a chief

---

[1] Strictly speaking, however, we ought not to use the term ' accusatorial ', in as much as the system of trial it connotes requires an arraignment before a jury by means of a written accusation known as an indictment. The increasing complexity of English society led to statutes being passed to empower justices to deal with small offences not involving any direct injury to life or property ' out of sessions ' and to convict offenders ' on sight '. This required no written accusation of any kind. It soon became the practice for justices to hear such cases in the home of one of their number or sometimes in the local inn. Anthony Trollope in his *Last Chronicle of Barset*, truthfully records as typical the trial of a Mr. Crawley in the large room at ' The George and Vulture ' at Silverbridge. The increase in such trials led to the passing of the Indictable Offences Act, 1848. (See Whiteside, *Lectures on Magistrate Courts* (1951), p. 10.)

who takes upon himself the duties of his *Okyeame* (Spokesman or Prosecutor) was and is a term of opprobrium all over Ashanti.'[1]

It is interesting to observe the obvious similarity between this conception of the ideal African judge and that contained in this dictum of Lord Green, M.R., in *Yuill* v. *Yuill* :[2] 'A Judge who observes the demeanour of the witnesses while they are being examined by counsel has from his detached position a much more favourable opportunity of forming a just appreciation than a judge who himself conducts the examination. If he takes the latter course he, so to speak, descends into the arena and is liable to have his vision clouded by the dust of the conflict. Unconsciously he deprives himself of the advantage of calm and dispassionate observation.'

It is, therefore, this desire of the African judge to maintain absolute impartiality (or at least not to appear to be taking sides by a too meticulous disallowance of witnesses' testimonies where these look irrelevant) that must explain the wide latitude usually given when hearing cases. But it is not all the running commentaries of litigants and witnesses that can properly be described as irrelevant testimony. Thus Lowie has caught something of the spirit of the thing when he writes :[3] ' In the deliverances of the witnesses and litigants wise saws, long-drawn-out similes and parables abound. " Listen ! " the speaker exhorts his audience, " we need not quarrel in today's assembly. If we calmly discuss one point after the other, we shall discover who is to blame and shall know what to do in the case. If little birds are swarming together and a stone is cast among them, usually none is struck ; but if a particular one is aimed at, it is sure to be hit." A chief complains of being involved in frequent litigation by his opponent in these words : " The mouse boxed the cat's ears, the mouse said that the cat was seeking a quarrel." Indeed, whole folk-tales are recited in illustration of a point.' Such analogies and anecdotes, based as they commonly are upon the intellectual and moral values acknowledged in the society of which they are an expression, are no more irrelevant than are, say, Lord Simon's similar citation of part of Milton's poem on his blindness—' They also serve who only stand and wait '—in the course of his judgment in *Century Insurance Co.* v. *Northern Ireland Road Transport*

---

[1] *Ashanti Law and Constitution*, p. 81.
[2] (1945), 61 T.L.R. 176, p. 178.   [3] *Op. cit.*, pp. 407–8.

Board [1] (concerning the liability of employers for the tort of their servant who, in delivering petrol to one of his employer's customers, carelessly caused a big fire by throwing off a match which he had used to light his cigarette while standing by during the unloading) ; or the same learned judge's reference to Shakespeare's *Othello* when, in the course of a brilliant judgment in *Holmes* v. *D.P.P.* [2] (where a man was on trial for having killed his wife on a sudden confession of adultery), His Lordship observed—' Even if Iago's insinuations against Desdemona's virtue had been true, Othello's crime would have been murder and nothing else.'

The English Law Reports abound in such judicial references to literature, science, mythology, and the like, whenever the learning and inclination of particular judges so dispose them to employ these either for the illustration of a point or for the edification of their hearers in court. In the African condition, there is no written literature or other material embodiment of the accumulated treasures of bygone ages. This gap is filled by the old chiefs and elders of the community who are the walking libraries of the unwritten folk-lore of the community, and who are invariably entrusted with the settlement of important disputes on this ground among others. Simmons, the well-known American sociologist, sums up the situation well when he writes :

' Among the preliterate peoples memories have been the only repositories of knowledge, skills and rituals. Where writing and records have been unknown—where all that was worth knowing had to be carried in the head—a lucid mind, a good memory, and a seasoned judgment, even when housed in a feeble frame, have been indispensable and treasured assets to the group. Those endowed with the art of writing and surrounded by printed documents can scarcely appreciate the inestimable value of an aged person possessing more knowledge than any other source within reach. There are unlimited examples of the role of the aged as custodians of folk wisdom.' [3]

Amidst what seems at first prolix or platitudinous will often be found nuggets of ' folk wisdom ' and moral precepts which when embodied in publicly proclaimed judgments of the chief or of the elders may profit both litigants and spectators. When litigants or witnesses put forward their sometimes abstruse or cumbrous

[1] (1942), A.C. 509.   [2] (1946), A.C. 588.
[3] L. W. Simmons, *The Role of the Aged in Primitive Society*, p. 131.

testimonies, we can usually rely on the judge with ' a lucid mind, a good memory, and a seasoned judgment ' to separate the grain from the chaff and to seize upon the essentials of the arguments in order to reach the right conclusion thereon.

The absence of strict rules for the exclusion of inadmissible evidence is not the unmitigated evil it is often alleged to be.   There is no system of trial by jury, upon which have been gradually built up in English law the various technical rules of evidence, including the Hearsay Rule, by which certain species of inadmissible testimony are excluded.[1]   But the assembled fellow-villagers or neighbours at an African trial constitute, if we may say so, the best possible body of jurors to determine the guilt or innocence of one of their number.   Certain of the presentees can and often do express opinions bearing upon the issues involved, in a free and impartial manner, which are open to cross-examination and/or rebuttal there and then (in contrast with the English jury of twelve men who argue the case out *in secret* and must be unanimous in their verdict).[2]   It is also important to note that, even then, the rigid rules of exclusion of inadmissible evidence only operate to prevent bias on the part of the jurors, not on the part of the judge who, like his African counterpart, can usually be

---

[1] It should be remembered that the Rule of Exclusion of Hearsay Evidence does not obtain on the Continent of Europe or in Scotland, because the introduction of the Jury system into these countries was much later than it was into England : See J. W. C. Turner, *On Kenny's Outlines of Criminal Law*, p. 403 n. 3.

[2] See also Ch. XIII, *passim*, later.   Thus, Lord Hewart, in *R.* v. *Armstrong* (1922), 2 K.B. 555 : ' It may be that some jurymen are not aware that the inestimable value of their verdict is created only by its unanimity, and does not depend upon the process by which they believe that they arrived at it.   It follows that every juryman ought to observe the obligation of secrecy which is comprised in and imposed by the oath of the grand juror.'   We should add here that grand juries were abolished in 1934 on the ground that they were obsolete, expensive and virtually useless.   The petty jury, which has always been the jury that tries the cases, itself swears no oath of secrecy—though the jury bailiff, before conducting the jurors to their retiring room, swears in open court that he will neither speak to them himself nor allow anyone else to do so in the jury room.

Juries in Scotland need not be unanimous in their verdict ; in fact, they frequently decide by a majority verdict.

The English Jury derives from the institution of the Frankish Inquest which William I first employed in the compilation of the Domesday Book and which Henry II adopted and extended as the starting point of the modern jury (see Plucknett, *op. cit.*, pp. 106–10).

trusted to discount irrelevant testimony in his final appraisal of the case as a whole.　In England, where the more natural channels of information about an offender had been dammed both by the rules for the exclusion of inadmissible evidence and by the growing complexity of social life, it became necessary to reopen them by the appointment of Probation Officers.　These officers collect information concerning the mode of life and family antecedents of the offender, information which under the judicial processes of African customary law is obtained from the testimony of the offender's fellows on the spot.　It is not being suggested that the African judicial process is on this account superior to the English judicial process, but only that, given its particular context, it is not without its own redeeming features.　We would do well to heed Sir Frederick Pollock's warning : ' Rules of evidence and procedure are largely determined by national and historical conditions which, though not really arbitrary, cannot be accounted for by universal principles.' [1]　An understanding of this should dispel the illusion current among some European writers that the African judicial process is unjust merely because it is not modelled in certain respects on European procedure.

This observation holds good also in the case of the familiar allegation, upon which we have touched only lightly so far, that there is no fiction of judicial ignorance in African judicial process. When regard is had to some often forgotten factors, it will be appreciated that African judges in judging a case do not make use of their personal knowledge to any greater extent than do English judges.　When an African judge is charged with using personal knowledge, a sufficiently clear distinction does not appear to be made between his probable knowledge of the character and antecedents of the offender (based upon the ground of living in a common locality) and his knowledge (or, more frequently, lack of knowledge) of the special facts of a case involving the offender and a third party who may or may not be also known to him. Both may be known to the judge, but more often than not, the facts surrounding their dispute are outside his ken.　For example, both parties may have quarrelled on the farm and injured each other, the one may have stolen the other's knife or hoe, adultery with his wife may be alleged by the one against the other —in these and innumerable other instances he would be a

[1] *A First Book of Jurisprudence*, p. 113.

very inquisitive old fool and a notorious busybody who could claim foreknowledge of these events even in the least complex village community. The fact of foreknowledge alone, if no other, would automatically disqualify such a character from ever being appointed a judge by anyone—so high and lofty is the indigenous conception of a judge and his role in an African society.

Again, if the alleged 'pre-knowledge' of the judge of which we hear so much is that which he may have gleaned from one of the parties or an officious interloper before he comes to sit as judge over a case, it is doubtful whether he can really do much havoc during the subsequent public trial at which he himself is as much under the critical surveillance of the audience as are the parties themselves. The applicable rules of customary law are fairly well-known to all present and it is inconceivable that they would tolerate any manipulation of the facts or of the law that is patently contrary to established usage. In any case the aggrieved party would almost certainly appeal to one higher authority after another until the king and his councillors have to judge the case. A perverse judge of first instance runs the risk, in a highly organised judicial system such as is the Ashanti's, of being mulcted in heavy penalties by the king if the appeal should ultimately be successful ; [1] or, in a decentralised one like that of the Kikuyu or Ibo, of public ridicule and popular opprobrium for even a single oblique decision.

Any knowledge, therefore, with which a judge may thus be properly credited is the general one, current in the local community and accordingly known to nearly all present at the judging. When we come to think of it, the English judge is ordinarily in no better position on this score. He is permitted by law to *take judicial notice* (i.e. to require no proof at all) of a large and miscellaneous category of matters during his hearing of a case ; e.g. points of constitutional law such as the relation between England, Scotland, Wales and Northern Ireland, and that between Great Britain and other countries of the Commonwealth and the Colonies and of foreign countries—the administrative divisions of England and Wales into counties and boroughs, etc.—everything published

---

[1] Cf. The Roman law principle of *judex qui litem suam fecit*, i.e. the judge who 'made the cause his own' by giving an unjust decision through negligence, bias, incompetence or corruption was guilty of a quasi-contract and accordingly liable to pay damages to the unsuccessful litigant who should subsequently succeed (Buckland, *op. cit.*, p. 331).

in The Gazettes of London, Edinburgh and Belfast—Official Seals and Signatures of State functionaries, Government Departments, etc.—the rules of the English Common Law, Procedure and Customs either established in judicial decisions or certified to the High Court—and notorious facts, such as that the streets of London are narrow, that children are naturally mischievous, that the sun rises in the East and sets in the West, that human beings are different from the lower animals, etc. Similarly, an English judge may in this and other respects *refresh his memory* with the aid of books like dictionaries, almanacs, encyclopaedias, calendars, text-books, etc., by reading them up himself and using any such knowledge at the trial without requiring the parties to give any evidence thereof. If all else fails, he can on matters too specialised or technical for him to understand by himself, summon experts to explain these to him in court and to be questioned as to their testimony, but so that the judge may disregard any such evidence in whole or in part and decide the matter entirely on his own view of the case. Even in certain non-technical matters such as identification of persons or of handwriting or of other matters of daily occurrence, ordinary members of the public may be invited to give evidence of their private opinions touching the case being tried. In basic essentials this procedure is like the African judicial process by which all these different classes of persons would all be present from the start or as the case proceeds and could be called upon to express their opinions on particular issues in the case. It is very often when this is being done that the casual observer jumps to the inevitably erroneous conclusion that any and everybody can attend an African trial and take part in the talking as and when he likes, without regard for order or decorum, without let or hindrance. If, when he were faced with a specific African law case, he knew or could recall accurately the way in which English law works in its procedural aspects, his error would be the less and his understanding deeper.

One more point we should dispose of here is the use and extent of presumptions, both of law and fact, in African judicial process. In addition to the taking of judicial notice of certain categories of matters, refreshing his memory by means of books or other documents, and receiving the expert as well as the opinion evidence of witnesses, an English judge is entitled to, and frequently does, make rebuttable as well as irrebuttable presumptions of innumerable matters of law and of fact respecting cases he happens to be trying.   For example, he takes it for granted that an infant under eight years of age is *doli incapax* (i.e. incapable of conceiving a criminal intent) and cannot therefore be tried for any alleged crime ;   also, a boy of fourteen cannot commit rape, just as a husband cannot be indicted for rape on his wife ;   again, a man and a woman living together and notoriously regarded as husband and wife by their friends and neighbours are presumed to be a lawfully married couple and all their offspring as legitimate, though for purposes of divorce strict proof of the marriage is required ; finally, where two persons die in circumstances rendering it uncertain which of them dies before the other, there is a conclusive presumption that the elder must have preceded the younger.   These are elementary instances and do not pretend to exhaust the long list of facts and situations as to which the English judge does not require witnesses or any other evidence or mode of proof.   As in English law, so in African law, the judges make extensive use of presumptions, rebuttable as well as irrebuttable, in the course of judging cases.

It is this use of presumptions that most observers of the African judicial process so frequently omit to take into account when they accuse the judges of employing their private knowledge of the litigants (and of the facts stated by these) in their adjudication of disputes.   Naturally, the advantage (or disadvantage) of a small community is that the judge has unusual opportunities of observing his fellows' behaviour and nuances ;   he is thus able to draw a variety of inferences from bald or even garbled statements of the parties to a dispute which only those who partake in the particular cultural milieu can make.   To this extent, it is quite possible that the African judge tends to notice rather more facts and to presume wider issues of law and fact than would an English judge.   The types of presumptions must in the last resort depend upon the social and psychological norms accepted and observed in the community whose judges are expected to make them.   If these observations were constantly borne in mind, much confusion could be avoided.   Thus, a writer, otherwise usually fair, fell into the error of assuming that African law does not base liability on fault in homicide as in other cases, and gave this example among the Kikuyu :   ' Thus a woman, going to her hut to get some liquor for a man, fell down on the way, cutting her leg severely. According to her account she had been knocked down by the man and kicked on the leg. We might suspect that the truth of one or other of these stories would be material to the case, but the elders waived this point altogether and held that whether she had been knocked down or whether she fell was immaterial, since the man was liable for the damage in either case.' [1]

The foregoing illustration is a very unsatisfactory basis for the kind of inference drawn by the writer. In the first place, we have shown [2] how among the Akamba, the Akikuyu and related tribes, a person who sends another on an errand may be held liable for any injury to his person or property whilst the messenger is lawfully engaged upon the task assigned, provided the messenger has had a due regard for his own safety or that of his property. But that does not seem to have been the case here, as the very charge and counter-charge between the woman and the man show; nor was there any such claim made either by the woman or by the judges. It is on this principle alone, if proved, that the elders could be taken to have ' held that whether she had been knocked down or whether she fell was immaterial, since the man was liable for the damage in either case '. In the second place, the writer seems to have expected the elders to demand evidence as to which of the two conflicting stories was correct, even though in the circumstances of the case no human witness was available at the material time. In the third place, the writer's remark— ' We might suspect that the truth of one or the other of these stories would be material to the case, *but the elders waived this point altogether* ' [3]—misses the point of the judge's decision. The fact is that the elders, like the writer himself, regarded the truth of one of the two stories as material; what in fact they did *not* do was to waive ' this point altogether '. As seasoned judges of local matters, they simply preferred the evidence of the woman to the man's. And they seem to have drawn from this the presumption, which the man failed to rebut, that the woman must have been tripped by the man. Into this conclusion other collateral factors may have entered, such as the previous course of conduct between the two, the possibility that the request for liquor was only a pretext for the man to get her into a place suitable

[1] Dundas, *op. cit.*, p. 293.
[2] See pp. 156–7, *supra.*   [3] Italics are mine.

for the assault, the nature of the severe cut to her leg may have been inconsistent with the type of injury which in the elder's experience could have been accidental or self-inflicted. It is suggested that, if the case were properly probed, the basis of the elders' decision would be found to be a rebuttable but unrebutted presumption of fact against the man. Other similar instances of so-called disregard by African judges for evidence of fault will doubtless occur to the reader and can usually be explained on this hypothesis.

E. USE OF PRECEDENTS

It is not clear to what extent African judges can be said to make use of previous decisions in determining current cases before them. Some writers have denied that African customary law ever makes use of previous judicial decisions ; they argue that what African judges do when they refer to earlier cases is that they are merely looking for repeated evidence of established custom. There is some truth in this, but the assertion is not true of African customary law in general. African customary law is no doubt more like English common law, at least until the establishment of the principle of binding judicial precedents between the sixteenth and the eighteenth centuries, than any system of codified law. But it suffers from the absence of the written records on which alone a proper system of judicial precedent can develop in the sense in which the theory is commonly understood in English law. In preliterate African societies, the living and flexible character of indigenous law makes it constantly necessary for the adjudicating chief or council of elders to refer to previous cases decided by themselves, by their predecessors, or by other notable contemporaries, especially if such cases have become notorious through frequent citations or through having been connected with well-known public events or personalities or places. But, since human memory is naturally limited in its range of recalling unrecorded details of events which happened ' long ago and far away ', the precedents cited are often comparatively recent. Thus, Godfrey and Monica Wilson observed of the Nyakyusa : ' Legal decisions are made in accordance with precedents, but since there are no written records the cases cited are necessarily comparatively recent.'[1]

Even so early an anthropologist as Hartland,[2] whom one might expect to agree with those who deny the conception of judicial precedent in African law, is emphatic that the principle is recognised among Bantu tribes in the south-eastern corner of Africa.[3] Miss Green, with her usual insight into the Ibo mind and institutions, has discovered the extensive use made of the concept of judicial precedents by so uncentralised an African society as that of the Ibos of Umueke Agbaja. Thus she writes : ' Then came the usual references to other cases ' ; [4] again : ' The putting of it (nshi) was, he said, a correct judicial procedure and he quoted precedents for it. Later in the case precedents were in fact invoked and it was clear that the method was a regular, if not a very frequent one ' ; [5] further on : ' Her suggestion was hotly discussed, both sides in the usual Ibo fashion quoting many other cases as precedents in support of their own points.' [6] It would be pointless to reproduce the many other references of the author to the same effect.

We will conclude our brief list of illustrations by citing this observation of Dundas on the judicial process of the Kamba, the Kikuyu and other tribes in East Africa : ' It may well be that there is a certain amount of confusion in these rules, and it must be remembered that such cases are so rare that the elders generally can only go by what has been done in some previous case *which they recollect*.' [7] The last clause in this quotation probably expresses the limiting factor of the application of the principle of judicial precedents in African customary judicial process. It is significant in more ways than one : (*a*) it shows how comparatively recent must be the African judge's citations if they are only made of cases ' which they recollect ' or of which the litigants and witnesses remind them ; and (*b*) it leads to the inevitable inference that such precedents as are cited and accepted are followed more from reverence for the authority of the judges

---

[1] *The Analysis of Social Change*, p. 29.
[2] *Primitive Law*, p. 207.
[3] Kafir law recognises the same distinction : see ' Maclean on Native Law and Custom ', Pt. I, in *African Studies*, Vol. 12, No. 4, Dec. 1953, pp. 181–8, at p. 181.
[4] *Op. cit.*, p. 128.   [5] *Ibid.*, p. 109.   [6] *Ibid.*, p. 204.
[7] *Op. cit.*, p. 266 (*Jnl. Roy. Anth. Inst.*, 1915). (Italics are mine).

who formerly pronounced them or from a desire for conformity with established usage than from any legal recognition of the binding force of judicial precedent.[1] African judges do not, as modern English judges do, regard themselves as being under a legal obligation to follow previous cases, except that they would be loath to disregard well-established ones for fear of seeming perverse or recalcitrant.

It is worth noting that in those African societies which have evolved a regular system of court officials, precedents are more constantly employed than we have so far indicated. This is rendered possible by the presence of the court remembrancer or linguist or griot whose duties include the tracing of the genealogies of litigants as of notable cases. Through long practice, patient study and constant application, they have come to be unfailing reservoirs of knowledge of family histories, court decisions and social norms. By carefully and methodically memorising such details as they occur in and out of court, they supply the want of written records, and the cases they recall to the judges' attention often go back as far as the tenth generation.[2] A somewhat startling measure of the constant change taking place in the English theory of judicial precedent is indicated by this *obiter* of Lord Wright in *Haseldine* v. *Daw* : [3] '. . . reported cases, with comparatively few exceptions, become obsolete in fifty years'.

F. DECLARATION OF THE VERDICT

When the litigants or their representatives and witnesses have been heard, persons and objects involved in a dispute have been seen, and the linguist or court remembrancer has drawn attention to precedents, the chief in council or the council of elders (as the case may be) would retire to consider their verdict. If all the necessary fees [4] have been paid by either or both of the parties as prescribed for the specific type of case by the law of the par-

[1] Strict French legal theory does not recognise Judicial Precedents. See Allen, *Law in the Making* (4th edn.), p. 171.

[2] The writer has himself witnessed this first in a Native Court at Oshogbo in Southern Nigeria in 1938 ; later, in other places in Nigeria, Gold Coast and Uganda at different times between December, 1951, and July, 1953.

[3] (1941), 2 K.B. 343, p. 345.

[4] If not, the judges may insist on outstanding fees being paid *before* judgment is announced.

ticular community, then, in the case of a chiefly society with a linguist, the judgment is announced by this official ; but, in the case of a chiefless society, the announcement is normally made by the most senior of the adjudicating elders, although the task is sometimes performed by any more competent member of the panel specially delegated for the purpose where the traditional titular head is considered otherwise unable or incompetent.

In some societies, more judgments than one are delivered. Each of the participating elders, sitting so to speak *de banco*, gives his own view of the case according to a strict order of seniority or rank, and the final decision is usually by a majority. This practice is not peculiar either to a chiefly or to a chiefless society.

But whether the judgment pronounced is single or multiple, one can scarcely fail to be struck by its essentially practical aim and social purpose. Of course, African judges do not spin out theories or enunciate principles in as articulate a fashion as do English ones, but most of their intellectual and moral assumptions are implicit in the prevailing legal norms which are the common property of all and sundry. They do reason these out in their appropriate context, though never in abstraction from the social and cultural milieu of the particular community. Rather, theirs is a pragmatic approach to the ideal of justice as conceived and accepted in the society of which the judges no less than the litigants form a part.

Every legal system evolves a judicial process, the primary and inescapable task of which is to find a solution to every dispute or problem presented to it. The evidence may be insufficient but, as long as there is forthcoming some evidence, a kind of decision must be reached. Of course, any judicial process would dismiss a case not *supported* by a jot or tittle of evidence. Wherever the parties are able to provide some measure of evidence, however, a judgment has to be given one way or the other. As Judge Cardozo has so pertinently remarked : ' Law must be satisfied to test the validity of its conclusions by the logic of probabilities rather than the logic of certainty.' [1] Absolute certainty is an ideal which is as desirable as it is unattainable in the vast majority of cases. A judicial process can only achieve an approximation to certainty based upon the ascertained facts as presented to the judges. The determination of the issues must depend in any

[1] *The Growth of the Law*, p. 33.

given context upon the nature of the facts and of the means of ascertaining them available to the judges.   Once the facts are ascertained in the manner appropriate to the case in hand, the often definite and well-known customary rules are applied in order to reach a solution.   With reference to the judicial process of the peoples of Southern Nigeria, Talbot has truly said what is of general application to most African peoples in these words :   ' Considerable intelligence is displayed by the average judge, and, in those cases in which no element of witchcraft or other belief repugnant to modern feelings enters, it is probable that the right decision is given with as much certainty as in an European Court.' [1]

G. FORMS OF PUNISHMENT

(1) In *civil* disputes, judgments are often flexible in form so as to enable the penalty to be adjusted as nearly as possible to the type of injury inflicted by the defendant upon a successful complainant.   In the absence of special circumstances, the decisions given are not regarded as being *ipso facto* inexorable.   The determining factors are the capacity of the guilty party to pay the amount fixed as fine or compensation to his opponent, the latter's readiness to accept a lower or substituted assessment (e.g. payment of five sheep in place of a cow), the possibility that the judges' estimate of the reparation deemed to be due from one party to another might be erroneous either because the guilty party could turn out later to be richer than they knew or because their own view of the actual harm done to the other party might prove to be unfair or unreasonable.   All these tend to make the judges wary of imposing inflexible and inexorable amounts as fine or compensation.   An appeal by the aggrieved party against an award would often lead to a reassessment in the light of fresh points disclosed as to the relative circumstances of the parties.

This flexibility, if viewed against the background of the general pattern of the African judicial process, is not so strange as it seems at first sight.   Some writers have seized upon it as clear evidence of the imprecision of customary law ;   indeed, one critic has averred that ' the justice which pre-British courts administer

[1] Talbot, *The Peoples of Southern Nigeria*, Vol. III, p. 619.

cannot be regarded as a body of laws '.[1]　This is, however, written in ignorance of an analogous practice in English legal procedure, in which appeals against awards of damages and/or costs from a lower to a higher court may and often do result in reduction or variation of the original sum fixed by the lower court.　In the African judicial process the parties often try to avoid appealing on the mere ground of the award being excessive or inadequate by arguing it out there and then before the trial judge(s).　It is only if no satisfaction is obtained that the case is taken to a higher court or before a different panel of adjudicating elders.　Nor must it be forgotten that inflexibility, rather than looseness, will be found to characterise verdicts given in certain classes of case : (i) where restitution has been ordered of a party's chattel or parcel of land, together with any reparation that may be ordered to be paid for consequential loss or damage to such object ; (ii) when a definite tariff of fines and compensations exists and there are no extenuating circumstances to justify any special variation ; (iii) where the parties had sworn at the outset to abide by whatever is the award in the case.　It is thus only in borderline cases that flexibility prevails.

(2)　In *criminal* cases such as sorcery or witchcraft, wilful murder and the like, the penalty is death by shooting, spearing, hanging, drowning or impalement of the convicted person.　These penalties also avail for treason and certain types of political offences. For lesser crimes as well as for cases of compoundable murder, fines and other composition payments are normally decreed. These tend to be rigidly enforced and exacted, and there is little disposition either on the part of the elders or of the parties to compromise on the fixed rate of penalty payable.　The picture is generally that of an angry chief or council of elders peremptorily decreeing what must be paid to assuage injured feelings or physical

---

[1] P. 121 of *Akim Kotoku*, by M. J. Field, cited by J. N. Matson, *op. cit.*, p. 49, where the latter affirms : ' Firm rules of law do exist, but they leave room for a great deal of give and take.'　An instance was later given, at pp. 52–3, of a woman who was found guilty of assaulting a man and who was asked to pay 30s. as compensation to him.　The man complained that the award was too small and the court raised the amount to 80s., which he accepted with some reluctance.　It is submitted, however, that the difficulty of African judges in this type of case is to find an acceptable method of quantifying damage in so intangible an offence as an assault.　We shall say more on the point in the next chapter.

S

impairment or loss of a blood relation. Young offenders are often flogged or whipped.

There seems to be no widespread use of imprisonment as an indigenous institution for punishing a criminal. The practice nearest to it in East Africa, of which we have record, was the Uganda system of confining a convicted person in the stocks : this consisted of boring a hole through a heavy log of wood, thrusting the culprit's foot into it, and tying to the leg a rope by lifting which the criminal could walk about in a limited area. But escape was rendered impracticable both by the presence of human guards and by the fact that the log was constantly rubbing against his foot as he walked. In the case of desperate criminals, both arms as well as one leg were put into stocks.[1]

But among the Yoruba of Nigeria there seems to have been in pre-British days an established practice of imprisonment. According to Talbot, the Yoruba employed several devices for securing repayment of their debts and ' resort is sometimes had to imprisonment, but this rarely cancelled the debt, and was only a way of exacting interest '.[2] He added a little further on[3] : ' Every chief or big man had a prison or cell in which he kept his own criminals for such offences as disobedience, drunkenness, etc. ; those who had committed any serious crimes were, however, usually detained in the prison of the Ogboni Society where this held sway.' Temple also states that serious criminals were usually detained in the Ogboni Society's prison-house.[4] Ajayi Crowther, himself a Yoruba, is reported as having recorded that, in 1853, three criminals who had previously been detained were executed by one Jaguna in the Ogboni's Council House at Abeokuta.[5]

It is possible that similar instances of the use of imprisonment could be found among some other African societies. It is by no means certain, however, whether and, if so, when prison became a customary means of punishing offenders.

To what extent amputation or disfigurement of a vicious recidivist may have been practised in some societies we have no

[1] Lowie, op. cit., p. 411.
[2] The Peoples of Southern Nigeria, Vol. III, p. 632.
[3] Ibid., p. 634.
[4] ' Notes on the Tribes, Provinces, Emirates and States of the Northern Provinces of Nigeria ', p. 1, 378–9.
[5] See Dennett, Nigerian Studies (1910), Ch. IV.

exact information besides, that is, such an occasional reference to the practice as we find, for example, in Hone's account that among certain Uganda tribes ' the punishment for theft was mutilation or the payment of compensation. . . .'[1]

H. EXECUTION OF JUDGMENT

If after the declaration of the award by the judges, the guilty party complies with the terms of the judgment, there is of course no more to be done in the matter. But if he defies the verdict and refuses to pay the fine or compensation, or to make restitution as decreed, then the issue of enforcing his compliance arises. In centralised societies with institutionalised military and administrative machinery, law enforcement by appointed officials is the rule. The chief, with the weight of authority that comes from the consensus of his councillors and of the public, can usually ensure that the guilty one does not bilk his obligation to his injured opponent or flout the concerted will of the community as expressed in the judgment. But the usual complaint that there is no organised and regular system of police is truer when applied to chiefless societies. When one comes to examine the facts closely, however, one does not find that the execution of the judgment of the council of elders presents the spectacle of ineffectiveness that is often painted by some writers.

We have seen in the procedure of the ' mwinge ' and of the ' king'ole ' among the Kikuyu and the Kamba respectively how the adjudicating elders invariably arm themselves with a *posse* of youthful warriors equipped with all necessary implements for putting a condemned murderer to death. Regarding the Ibos of Southern Nigeria, Miss Green has described how offenders against the codes of conduct enjoined upon members of certain associations, or even against what have been publicly decreed as binding rules at meetings in market-places, are brought to book through the machinery of a band of local ' police ', deputed for the task by the elders of the community; and here, again, an *ad hoc* brigade of stalwart lads is normally pressed into the service.[2] Even women are known to have taken a hand against some of their own sex in enforcing the payment of fines, or otherwise securing a compliance

[1] See Hone's article in *Uganda Journal, op. cit.*, p. 7.
[2] See p. 74 n. 2, *supra*.

with accepted social norms. Ordinary cases between two or
more women are usually heard by women judges, especially where
breaches of market or club regulations are in question. In any
event, women generally act as the watch-dogs of their community against antisocial behaviour.[1] The writer has also
discovered [2] that the dual division of the Agbaja village, in addition
to promoting the quick performance of communal work, serves
to supply a kind of police system for the enforcement of laws and
regulations as between the two exogamous halves of the village.
Each half acts as a watchman against the conduct of the other in
a spirit of mutual, inter-group rivalry. The personal possessions
of an offender are seized by the picked men of either side, if a fine
duly imposed is not promptly paid.[3] These arrangements are
rendered possible in a society in which the ties of kinship are so
heavily underlined by the bonds of common locality.

The Fanti of the Gold Coast, like the Yoruba of Nigeria, have
a system of self-help whereby the creditor has the right personally to beset the house of his debtor or to employ others to do so
on his behalf, and to follow the latter about in and out of season
and generally to make such a nuisance of the whole thing as to
impel the debtor to pay up and be rid of his creditor's persistence
and importunity.[4] Until a final settlement is made, the debtor is
under a legal liability to feed and accommodate his unwanted
guest, who enjoys an unlimited licence to interrupt his conversa-
tions with third parties, to obstruct his work or movement as
and when he likes, and to plague him in every way. All this
might be dispensed with if, on arrival at the unfortunate debtor's
house, the creditor descries anything of value he can seize either
in partial or in total satisfaction of the debt. If only a proportional abatement is thereby secured, the creditor is entitled to

[1] Green, *op. cit.*, pp. 101, 111–12, 143, 226–30. See, also, Penwill,
op. cit., p. 64, where neighbours, especially women, are said to have
descended upon a defaulter's house for failure to pay up the customary
goat after the elder's decision had been announced.

[2] *Ibid.*, pp. 142–3.

[3] Cf. Dundas, *op. cit., Jnl. Roy. Anth. Inst.* (1915), pp. 292–3 : ' It
seems that a creditor is entitled to take anything from his debtor, but
not until his claim has been awarded by the elders. In Ukamba it
has been asserted that wives and children may be taken in this way, but
this was denied again by a large assembly of elders.'

[4] For the identical Yoruba practice see Talbot, *The Peoples of Southern
Nigeria*, Vol. III, pp. 632–3, 698.

distrain on any other article of property or to resort to the tactics already described,in an effort to obtain satisfaction for the balance.[1]

Various other modes of indigenous law enforcement exist in other African societies, depending upon the kind of arrangement made locally for effecting compliance with the judgments of the chief in council or of the council of elders. Some are naturally more elegant than others, but the African judicial process everywhere attempts to offset the disadvantage of a delicate mechanism of enforcement by supplementing its functioning by a reliance on the general law-abidingness of those whose ideal of justice it represents. Dr. Allen recently observed concerning English law that ' the most admirable laws are nugatory without the means of implementing them, and that the best means of enforcement is to forestall the very necessity of enforcement.' [2] This, if we may say so, is no less true of African customary law. So germane to this aspect of the judicial process are the learned author's observations,[3] that the present writer must be forgiven for quoting him here at length :

' For the greater part of our history we have attempted to make the community responsible, by various means, for policing itself. There have been from the earliest times certain accredited peace officers, of whom the most important were, anciently, the shire reeve, the bailiff, the town reeve, and the petty constable. But for the general maintenance of order and the pursuit of malefactors the traditional method was the very ancient and primitive one of constituting each man his brother's keeper, in the sense that another and more powerful individual, or else a group of his neighbours, was answerable for every person's good behaviour. . . . The most common example was that of the magnate who was held responsible for those within his *mund*. In the Middle Ages this liability seems to have shrunk to the circle of the lord's household, the members of which were in his *mainpast*—the domestic dependants fed and maintained by him.'

The group-pledge, which imposed liability on kindred members for an erring brother, also gave them the right to take vengeance or accept composition (*wergild*) for the shedding of his blood. This system soon developed into the territorial units of the *borh*,

---

[1] Sarbah, *Fanti Customary Laws*, pp. 86, 94-5 ; Ajisafe, *The Laws and Customs of the Yoruba People*, pp. 70-2.
[2] C. K. Allen, *The Queen's Peace*, p. 125.   [3] *Ibid.*, pp. 69 ff.

the *tithing* (= a tenth of a hundred), and the *hundred*—all designed to ensure the good order of their members by the concerted action of all.   The Frankpledge was the culmination of these earlier institutions of social insurance and legal suretyship for the law-abidingness of its members.   Again, the hue and cry imposed another type of group liability in county and hundred by requiring all to follow the trail of a felon, especially a cattle-thief, until he was apprehended, on pain of the pursuers bringing upon themselves heavy penalties if the felon were ever allowed to escape. Then, there were the watch and ward, the approver, and the common informer, ' who has incurred the odium of the tell-tale with less risk and more profit than the approver ' until the Common Informer's Act, 1951 substituted for his customary financial rewards prosecution by summary procedure or on indictment and a fine not exceeding £100 for any of the offences forbidden by law.   It was not until 1829, by the Metropolitan Police Act of that year, that the modern system of regular police was established in England.   Allen concludes : [1] ' Our constables are still "kin-police", men and women with more disciplinary duties but few greater powers than any of their fellow-citizens ; they are legitimate descendants of the old pledges and watchmen and constables of the people—but with one vast difference.   It took us a thousand years to discover that the effective guardianship of the peace is a " whole-time job " for highly qualified and disciplined officers. . . .'   They are not what Reith [2] has called ' ruler-appointed police ' who are agents of terror in modern totalitarian countries, nor have they the power of certain of their Continental counterparts who can impose ' on-the-spot ' police fines for minor, e.g. traffic, offences.

Apart from the modern British development of the system of a regular police force, therefore, the arrangements in most African societies to ' forestall the very necessity of enforcement '

[1] C. K. Allen, *The Queen's Peace*, p. 118.
[2] C. Reith, *The Blind Eye of History*, Pt. III.   Of the nine principles of police action which the writer lists as inherent in the discipline origin-ally enjoined by the first Commissioners, Rowan and Mayne, the seventh runs :
' To maintain at all times a relationship with the public that gives reality to the historical tradition that the police are the public and that the public are the police ; the police being only members of the public who are paid to give full-time attention to duties which are incumbent on every citizen, in the interests of community welfare and existence.'

of the law were roughly equivalent to these ones formerly employed by English law. Great store is set on the prevention of breaches of the law; and the clan head, the lineage or family head, the institution of the age-grade and other associations—all these are saddled with the responsibility for the good behaviour and general law-abidingness of their members. Fear of ridicule, opprobrium or social and economic ostracism act as powerful deterrents to crime and, where the society is still culturally homogeneous, these mechanisms of the vicarious liability of the lineage or household head and of personal abhorrence of crime by the individual himself serve in a large measure to preserve the equilibrium of society. But as the community grows unwieldy through internal fecundity or external admixture so that it loses its homogeneity, the old sanctions tend to become inadequate to the new needs of maintaining law and order. It is at that stage that the more developed African societies have been hard put to it to evolve new ways and means of ensuring law-abidingness and social stability. Hence it is that we find in centrally organised societies with a definite hierarchy of political authorities, judicial institutions and administrative machinery, the emergence of a *militia* which can be used for purposes both of external aggression or civil defence and of internal security, including law enforcement. But we have also seen that even in uncentralised African societies variants of this *militia* exist for more or less the same purpose: reference has already been made to the ' king'ole ' and ' mwinge ' of the Akamba and of the Akikuyu, and a similar organised use of sections of the community for the welfare of the whole has been noted in the Ibo employment of a *posse* of sturdy lads or of a bevy of young women in the execution of judgments and the enforcement of regulations; even the two halves of an exogamous community serve, as we have shown, the purposes of a village police force.

J. THE JUDICIAL PROCESS IN PERSPECTIVE

The above does not pretend to be an exhaustive or even an adequate account of the African judicial process. It is rather a survey of what has seemed to the writer to be the most significant features of African legal procedure and a cross-section of its most common attributes. The discussion of some of the controversial aspects of this judicial process has sometimes had to be more sketchy and summary than we should have made it in a more ambitious treatise on the subject. It is thought, however, that the treatment will be found to be not unsuited to the limited, immediate objective of a concise analysis of basic legal concepts of a highly interesting subject. We may now conclude with a brief review of the African judicial process as a whole.

As we have said very often, the general opinion of writers is that the aim of African law is the maintenance of the social equilibrium. While this is true enough as a statement of principle, the implied suggestion that ' European ' law has a different aim is not valid. What African law strives to achieve is the solidarity of all those subject to its sway by repairing, as far as possible, all breaches that tend to disturb society. In other words, its basic assumption is neither more nor less than the ideal of Jeremy Bentham's eudae-monistic philosophy—namely, that the justification for law in society must be ' the greatest happiness of the greatest number '. Kant has expressed the same idea in his definition of law as ' the aggregate of the conditions under which the arbitrary will of one individual may be combined with that of another under a general inclusive law of freedom '. Von Jhering considers that the function of law is the determination of the legal interests of the members of a given community in such a way as to avoid friction or collision therein. And Roscoe Pound, as we have seen, seizes upon this to set for law in human society the task of ' social engineering ', by which he means in effect the due regulation of the conflicting claims of the several citizens in the eternal effort to realise social justice.

We may therefore say that the ultimate purpose of law in a society, be it African or European, is to secure order and regularity in the conduct of human affairs and to ensure the stability of the body politic. Where there is a divergence in the approach is that whereas African law strives consciously to reconcile the dis-putants in a law suit, English law often tends to limit itself to the bare resolution of the conflict by stopping at the mere apportion-ment of blame as between the disputants. Arthur Phillips [1] reports Lambert as having written in his *Kiambu Guide* : ' It was, therefore, a judgment by agreement intended to restore and pre-serve the social balance, and differed materially in principle from

[1] See his admirable *Report on Native Tribunals in Kenya* (1945) Ch. IV, paras. 188–92. Especially interesting are paras. 497–500.

a judgment in European Courts, which is a judgment by decree intended to enforce the legal rights of one party to the complete and permanent exclusion of the other, whatever the effect on the social equilibrium may be.' But this is only a matter of emphasis in the judicial mechanism, and the degree to which a society can afford to arbitrate without at the same time feeling the necessity for calling a truce must depend on the extent of the intensity of social relations among its members.

In the conditions obtaining in many African societies, the margin of social security is often too narrow for peremptory, unilateral penalties to be fashionable. That is why the judges often follow up the payment of fines or compensation with a cere-monial reconciliation of the parties, so that personal rancour and clan feud might not have free rein to the detriment of the social order. Matson, in an article to which we have referred before, observes : [1] ' The object of the elders was not punishment, but settlement of the dispute ; not a declaration of strict legal rights, but reconciliation. The tender of amends (mpatse) by the wrong-doer implied an apology for the wrong done ; its acceptance meant forgiveness and forgetting.' Miss Green records of the Ibos that the guilty was often required to take palm wine and oil beans to the innocent party so that they might eat together and thus make peace.[2] But it is suggested that only the smallness of the scale of social organisation renders this possible, desirable and, indeed, inevitable.

If we may quote Lambert's *Kiambu Guide* [3] once more : ' The native method would tend to adjust disturbances of the social equilibrium, to restore peace and goodwill, and to bind or rebind the two disputing groups together in a give-and-take reciprocity. The European method would tend to widen the gulf between the two groups by granting *all the rights to one of them to the exclusion of the other*, because it would in general concern itself with facts and legal principles and take no cognisance of social implications.' [4] Had Robert Browning been minded to see something of the African judicial process, as he certainly did see something of the

---

[1] Matson, *op. cit.*, p. 48.
[2] Green, *op. cit.*, p. 110.
[3] Phillips, *op. cit.*, p. 39, where another Memorandum of one Mr. S. H. Fazan, describing the indigenous procedure for the hearing of cases, was quoted by the learned author.
[4] Italics are mine.

Italian during his long sojourn there, equally well might he have applied these lines to it:

> *. . . Thus*
> *Was justice ever ridiculed in Rome :*
> *Such be the double verdicts favoured here*
> *Which send away both parties to a suit*
> *Nor puffed up nor cast down,—for each a crumb*
> *Of right, for neither of them the whole loaf.*[1]

Let us hasten to add that, although the difference between the English and the African (or, in this instance, the Italian) approaches to the problem of justice would have caused him understandable surprise, he would nevertheless have found, by probing the issue and pondering its implications, that justice was never in fact ' ridiculed ' merely on the ground of a divergence in method. When one comes to think seriously about the matter, one soon realises how utterly unsatisfying it must be that in a case where neither all the rights nor all the wrongs of the case are on one side or the other, one of the parties should be made to carry away ' the whole loaf ' while the other retires embittered and disgruntled, but is powerless to show his exasperation only because of the State force behind the judges. Confidence in the judicial process cannot but be slightly undermined by such happenings and the general impression of the layman is that the State's ' law is an ass '. Society becomes increasingly estranged from this type of ' lawyer's law ' as argued and interpreted by professional Bench and Bar between them. The litigant is often a mere bewildered onlooker in court.

But how different is a system in which the twin elements of cognoscibility and publicity are present, in that everyone or nearly everyone knows the main rules of customary law, and the arguments as well as counter-arguments are publicly marshalled and weighed one against the other, sometimes with the aid of symbols such as sticks or stones or handclaps, and sometimes by the preponderance of evidence. The judgments take the form of apportioning blame and praise for particular acts or omissions of the litigants as they unfold their stories and buttress them by witnesses or other evidence. It is the one who, on balance, has more points against him that finally gets mulcted in fine or compensation for

[1] *The Ring and the Book,* I, 11. 747–52.

the benefit of the other. Restoration of the parties to the *status quo ante* is the keynote of the judicial process, and nothing must be left in the possession of the one which legitimately belongs to the other.[1] Even where the final point is scored by only one party so that fine or compensation is imposed on the other, the latter goes away at least satisfied by the open-handed way in which the various aspects of the respective rights and wrongs have been acknowledged and appraised in the course of the judgment(s). The verdict, where it goes against him, does not strike him as the command of an all-powerful judge laying down an inexorable law which he hardly understands, or which can hardly be regarded as the expression of the common consciousness of the community.

In the vast majority of cases the general atmosphere of the African judicial process is not one of enforced awe or sullen resentment but is, as Krige has said of the Lovhedu system,[2] one of peaceful debate of the issues dividing the litigants in the sure belief that some kind of acceptable solution will be found out of the elder's fund of wisdom and sense of justice. The criminal is similarly made to pay compensation for his misdeeds if such a composition will be adequate to the damage done to his victim. Banishment, hanging, drowning and the other indigenous modes of getting rid of the outlaw and the recidivist are resorted to only when all other means have been exhausted of re-incorporating such in society as useful members thereof. Only in these few cases is the judicial process prompt, definite and inexorable.

Generally, African judges are wont to indulge in end-of-trial judicial homilies to the parties.[3] In these they attempt to state

---

[1] Thus, no adjustment is possible where it is the full restoration of a chattel or a parcel of land that is decreed, for it is not a ' crumb of right ' but ' the whole loaf ' that in such cases properly belongs to the rightful owner. Additional payment in kind may be ordered for illegal detention or occupation. Of course, if it is shown that the one party has some property of the other in his own care or possession, nice issues of adjustment might arise.

[2] See J. D. Krige, ' Some Aspects of Lovhedu Judicial Arrangements ' —*Bantu Studies*, XIII, 2, June 1939, pp. 114–15.

[3] Someone has written recently of Lord Goddard, the Lord Chief Justice of England : ' No judge has made greater use of the end-of-trial opportunity for a judicial homily. It is in his address to convicted prisoners and unsuccessful litigants, in his Divisional Court strictures on the conduct of erring J.P.'s, that he is at once most pontifical and most news-worthy. Some may question the value as well as the propriety of the prolonged sermon to a prisoner awaiting sentence. . . . But it is

and enunciate the norms of social behaviour expected of right-minded members of the community, to condemn departures from these objective standards, and to praise such acts as tend to maintain and enhance the general well-being of the community. The delivery of these sermons in the course of judgment often affords the listeners a measure of vicarious pleasure. It would be superfluous to add that they are invariably as instructive as they are edifying.

All this very well accords with the character of the African judge as a peace-maker anxious to effect a reconciliation, if necessary by making one to pay fine or compensation to the other or to restore such other's property being illegally withheld, but always by the gentle process of argument and persuasion leading gradually and inevitably to a verdict that is at once clear and fair. The judge's reasoning and statements are punctuated at appropriate stages with allusions to the legal principles involved and to wise saws and apt aphorisms intended to elucidate his meaning.

But running through it all is his transparent duty to reconcile the disputants with each other, to re-incorporate the minor criminal in society at large, and to show the necessity for elimination of the malefactor and the antisocial. In this often difficult task the judge or judges must apply the law to the facts as found and do so in such a way as to command the respect and approval of the overwhelming majority of the people. All technicality is eschewed in his earnest endeavour to do justice, fair play, and equity. It is this motive of the judge to do equity that is the most persistent characteristic of the African judicial process. Did not Aristotle in his *Rhetoric* [1] write? :

' It is equity to pardon human failings, to look to the lawgiver and not to the law . . . to wish to settle a matter by words rather than by deeds ; lastly, to prefer arbitration to judgment, for the arbitrator sees what is equitable, but the judge only the law, and for this an arbitrator was first appointed, in order that equity might flourish.'

It remains to conclude that only in this sense is the African judge an arbitrator.

in these homilies, and other similarly *ex cathedra* pronouncements, that the Lord Chief Justice has revealed his qualities and his prejudices to the world.'—an article, entitled ' His Majesty of the Law ', in the *New Statesman and Nation*, Jan. 2, 1954, p. 16.

[1] 1.13.1374b, Grant's Translation, *Apud Eth. Nic.*, note to v.10, 1.

CHAPTER XIII

IMPACT OF ENGLISH LAW UPON AFRICAN LAW

A. GENERAL CONSIDERATIONS

THE brief survey of the main principles underlying African legal theory, which we have just attempted, naturally prompts the enquiry as to how much of it is of contemporary relevance and what prospect it has for survival in its contact with outside influences.

English law has impinged upon African law in two main respects : (a) in its modifying influence on those aspects of indigenous customary law which have so far survived the impact of British legal and cultural invasion; and (b) in its creative role of supplying the deficiencies of the traditional law and usage brought about by the new commercial and economic values. The first category relates to such phenomena as changes in property law (e.g. corporate and inalienable ownership becoming gradually individual and alienable), the growth of landlord and tenant relationship as rents become payable in lieu of traditional dues, the increasing though gradual break-up in the customary ties of family and lineage with a consequent narrowing in the individual's sense of obligation towards his kin. The second embraces the introduction of criminal law and procedure, mercantile law (e.g. banking, insurance, negotiable instruments and bills of exchange), and industrial law regulating the relations between the new class of wage-earners—an unknown quantity in indigenous society—and the equally new aristocracy of employers of labour.

In its earlier encounter with English law under comparable auspices, the Roman-Dutch law of Ceylon and South Africa has undergone a similar transformation, as have Hindu, Mohammedan and Burmese laws of India, Pakistan and Burma. Julius Lewin has suggested [1] that the spread of Christianity in Africa might ' help to inaugurate an era of uniformity of European ideas among Europeans and Africans alike '. While a greater degree of

[1] P. 10 of his *Studies in African Native Law* (1946).

assimilation seems likely in the case of African than in that of Asian law, it is at least doubtful whether complete uniformity will ever be achieved by it with English law. A kind of legal *tertium quid* is the most likely phenomenon to emerge from the impact of English upon African legal ideas. If we discount the Scandinavian legal invasion of Anglo-Saxon England which culminated in the reforms of King Cnut as too transient to leave any lasting impression, we can say that the Norman Conquest importation of the French legal conceptions of contract, debt, jury, court, etc., did not lead to a wholesale supersession of the existing Anglo-Saxon tribal laws. Indeed, the developing English common law proved eventually capable not only of absorbing the new ideas and practices (including trial by battle and subinfeudation), but also of evolving along its own particular lines. It would seem that African law bids fair to making a similar absorption of English law.

B. SPECIFIC ASPECTS OF THE IMPACT

Let us now consider some specific aspects of the impact. Probably the first obvious feature to be noted is that the various traditional tribunals have been substantially adopted as instruments of legal administration by being recognised and re-organised by statute. The procedure in these statutory Native Courts is in theory based on simplified versions of English rules, but the old customary judicial procedure still largely predominates therein. Thus, it will be seen that the former practice of litigants being legally represented at a customary trial by a relation or other champion-at-law has in most instances been retained by the Administration ; one accordingly finds it as an almost invariable provision of a Native Court Ordinance that permission shall be given by judges thereof ' to appear for a plaintiff or defendant any duly authorised husband or wife, guardian or servant, the master or inmate of the household of any such plaintiff or defendant '. Again, while there has been express statutory abolition of sorcery or witchcraft, trial by ordeal and slave-dealing, other traditional practices like the customary use of oaths in litigation, which we have previously described,[1] have been retained —e.g. the oath method of instituting legal proceedings on the

---

[1] Pp. 229–233, *supra*.

Gold Coast has been adopted and regulated by the Native Courts (Ashanti) Procedure Rules of 1949, v. 6, as amended by Rule 6 of 1951 and Reg. 6 of the Native Courts (Colony) Procedure Regulations of 1945.

But even into these statutory Native Courts there have been imported a few innovations. Each court is enjoined to keep a number of books for recording cases tried and important judgments delivered. This work is carried out by the court clerk who shares with the court interpreter a prestige in the eyes of illiterate litigants that is out of all proportion to their really humble status in the new judicial set-up. It is not that similar functionaries were absent from the previous traditional arrangement, as witness the role as well as the dignity of the court remembrancer or griot or spokesman among certain African societies, to which we have before referred.[1] The novelty largely consists in the arming of such subordinate officials of the statutory court with the new magic wand of the record book and of spoken English ; especially is this the case among societies which were formerly without any formalised system of court officials but which have thus been newly endowed by the Administration. The innovation tends to clothe such functionaries with an aura of exaggerated respectability which they are all too often prone to exploit to their private advantage, at least in the early stages of British Administration.[2] The court clerk and the court interpreter have at one time or another been sometimes regarded as more important than even the judges, particularly in statutory British-established courts like the Magistrate's or Supreme Court where so much depends upon the interpreter's handling of his delicate task. He it is whom the illiterate litigant hears and understands ; it is he who is interposed between the litigant and the judge and who has to render to the latter the substance of the former's case ; surely, so the illiterate litigant believes, it is the interpreter's duty and privilege to sway the ultimate verdict of the judge for or against him.

Then, there is the widespread use of African elders and others with knowledge of local customary law as *assessors* in the British-established courts. These assessors are as much witnesses to facts—for a disputed point of customary law is normally a matter

---

[1] Pp. 241, 258, *supra*.
[2] See, for example, my *Groundwork of Nigerian Law* (1954), p. 108.

of fact to be established by evidence—as they are judges of facts, since they are often called upon to pronounce upon issues involving other than purely customary rules.[1] Legally, they do not constitute a body of jurors and, therefore, the presiding judge is not bound to accept their opinion on any point he may have referred to them for determination. Otherwise, they are frequently useful to the judge, particularly if he is foreign to or unacquainted with the local law or society. Their usefulness will no doubt vary with the extent of their grasp of the point at issue and their general appreciation of the whole tenor of the case which they are to assess.[2]

Another noteworthy modification of customary usage is the regulation of the number of those entitled to sit in a statutory Native Court as judges. Imperfect acquaintance with the actual legal situation in traditional African judicial process has produced the oft-repeated generalisation that there is no limit to the number of those who could take part in the adjudication of a dispute, just as there is no bar to the number who could be present at the hearing. We have shown how, even in the less organised communities where proceedings appeared informal, there was usually a recognised order of precedence in speaking at a trial and an equally established circle of persons entitled to participate in the pronouncement of the verdict. But when, at the British advent, people saw that appointment to a statutory Native Court membership meant an accretion of prestige and an opportunity for earning easy money in the way of salary and other perquisites, unqualified persons began to assert a bogus claim to entitlement to serve as judges of these courts, invoking a non-existent rule of customary law in order to justify their pretensions. It is to the credit of the British Administration, however, that such claims, whether or not they were well-founded, were resisted to some extent by laying down in every warrant constituting a statutory

[1] E.g. they are frequently employed in criminal trials under the colonial Criminal Codes.

[2] Of the somewhat similar difficulty which sometimes arises with English juries, let us take this observation of the Rt. Hon. Sir Travers Humphreys, in *A Book of Trials* (1953) : ' It was useless to institute criminal proceedings unless the fraud was one which could be readily understood by the average juryman. So far as the £20,000 was concerned, we were unable to advise any criminal prosecution.' The famous English criminal lawyer and judge wrote this of the Hooley frauds, even when convinced that a jury's verdict ' is almost invariably right '.

Native Court, a definitive provision for the composition of the court.[1] The tendency in recent years has been progressively to whittle down the number of members wherever this has proved too large and unwieldy in practice. It is naturally to be expected that mistakes would be made in the appointment of suitable and qualified personnel in a situation where false claims proliferate. Nevertheless, the result has often been as satisfactory as could have been expected.[2]

Yet one more source of anxiety about the impact of English law upon African customary law is the investment of the lay judges of the statutory Native Courts with the power to apply and interpret certain categories of legislation, central as well as subordinate. It may be the case that the species of enactments which they are normally called upon to deal with is not as complicated as that of those with which trained lawyers and judges have to grapple in the British-established courts primarily applying English law. But, even so, the judges must have been not infrequently irked by the niceties no less than the seeming facetiousness of some of the more technical aspects of certain Ordinances such as the Criminal Code. If the portions of such central legislation as they may have to apply bear any relation to similar offences under customary law, or if the enactment is itself the product of the local council on familiar topics, then the judges' task is not formidable : they either apply the provision of the former as if they were dealing with a customary offence in a new setting, or they deal with the latter in the light of the need felt for a change in, or a regulation of, the existing legal arrangement. Either way, the compromise solution might be unhappy if only because precarious and unpredictable. The District Officer's or Commissioner's supervisory oversight might succeed in correcting such errors, but it would be better for it to have been able to

[1] For an example of the problems of selection and composition of members of Urban Courts in Northern Rhodesia, see A. L. Epstein, *The Administration of Justice and the Urban African* (1953), pp. 10-16, H.M.S.O.

[2] In dealing with the need for reform of the various Benches in England, Mr. J. A. Joyce, in his *Justice at Work* (1953), has suggested that the best way to ensure fairness would be to appoint two J.P.'s each from the Right and Left, respectively. He questioned : ' What chance has a younger person who appears before a Bench of half a dozen local politicians in their sixties and seventies who rely almost entirely on the police for their facts and the clerk for their law ? ' This seems, however, to be a slightly exaggerated picture of the English Petty Sessions.

T

prevent them. A device for securing this is the practice of requiring these officers to tour their districts with the text of a new applicable enactment, explaining its purport and mode of application to those concerned. Although this is a help, yet it is obvious that the enactment in question might still be subsequently misapplied or misconstrued. Only a kind of systematic training of either, or preferably both, of the presiding judges and the court clerk in such modern processes would ensure a reasonable measure of accuracy and efficiency. In the analogous situation of English lay justices, the institution of solicitors as clerks of courts is a redeeming feature, though it too stands in need of reform. In the sphere of legislation, the statutory local councils have been given powers (*a*) to issue Rules and Orders defining or modifying the application of local customary law, e.g. land tenure rules ; (*b*) to regulate and provide for purely local government functions by means of rules dealing with market organisation, assessment and collection of Poll Tax, Local Rate, Forestry and Fisheries, or the brewing and selling of liquors ; (*c*) to implement and, where necessary, to supplement Central Government Ordinances, and other measures relating to general administrative, judicial, health, and social matters. In this last capacity, a local council may sometimes find itself saddled with the task of adopting and incorporating a Central Government Ordinance (or portions of it) like the Criminal Code Ordinance into its own statute book ; sometimes, such adoption is not mandatory but is merely permissive, as when the local authority is given a free hand, as to whether and if so, which to adopt in whole or in part, of the central enactments, since social and economic conditions in one part of a territory might warrant it while those in another part of the same territory might not.

In these ways, as in many others, rules and practices of English law have been in varying degrees incorporated substantially or in modified form into the modern African customary law as administered in the statutory Local (or Native) Courts. The process of such assimilation is often so subtle and imperceptible that, in many respects, the imagination of the judges of these courts sometimes ' becomes suspicious of its offspring and doubts whether it has created or adopted '. It seems, therefore, perfectly natural to the African Chief Justice of Buganda, in his handbook for the guidance of local courts, to classify an offence like forgery as part of the traditional customary law, remarking : ' A hundred years ago there was little or no writing in Buganda, so forgery did not exist. Now writing is general and forgery occurs. This offence is punished as being contrary to Buganda Customary Law.' [1] This is as direct a case as any of the conscious incorporation of an English legal concept into a dynamic body of customary law which, in this instance, seems to regard the transition from an *oral* to a *written* lie [2] as a natural and spontaneous legal development. It may be granted, however, that the highly technical ingredients of the offence of forgery in English law might not necessarily be required in its Buganda offspring, at least in the early stages of its adoption. But this is no valid argument against its assimilation with customary law.

Another way in which the customary law is being virtually but perhaps unostentatiously affected is the recent tendency of appointing as Native Court judges or assessors African individuals who have acquired a nodding acquaintance with some elements of English law and procedure by reason of previous employment with the Central Government in the judicial or administrative branches. Some of these may have seen service in a Provincial or District Commissioner's office, or in a Magistrate's or even the Supreme (or High) Court. The growing administrative policy to separate the chiefs as early and as much as possible from purely judicial work and to leave them free to pursue the actual task of local government administration has encouraged the process of secondment of these junior officers from the central government to the statutory Native Courts. When they are thus entrusted with the delicate work of administering customary law in these courts, they cannot be expected to be entirely innocent of the English legal ideas and practices of which they have heard and read or with which they have dealt. It is not an easy matter to know how far their views of the customary law, as this unfolds itself from day to day in the local courts, can be regarded as undiluted and evolving versions of the native genius and how far they are a mixture, conscious or unconscious, of African and English strains.

[1] Chief Justice's ' Directions ', Pt. I, Criminal Cases issued under the Buganda Courts Ordinance No. 4, of 1940, s. 20, p. 28.

[2] For has not C. S. Kenny said that ' a forgery is a document which not only tells a lie but tells a lie about itself ? ' *Outlines of Criminal Law* (15th edn.), p. 298 ; also *Select Cases*, p. 188.

This indirect impact of English upon African law is, however, more likely to be noticed in the sphere of substantive than in that of procedural law. The reason is that, although in theory the various Native Courts are to be allowed to carry out their work uninhibited by technical rules of evidence and procedure, nevertheless, as fair an approximation to the English ideal as possible is everywhere being encouraged, though no doubt in a simplified form. Whatever preconceptions about English procedure these recruits to the Native Court Bench might bring with them could therefore be more openly revealed than could be a deliberate importation of English substantive rules into a wholly indigenous aspect of customary law. Yet this must be happening subtly and probably unconsciously all the time, with little or no protest from the more orthodox and often more knowledgeable members of the court who have not had the chairman's advantage of prior central government service and who are sometimes too timid to challenge suspected departures from the traditional law by these, to them, agents of the central authority. But the instances must indeed be few in which even such unorthodox darlings of the Administration would deliberately fly in the face of solid opposition from these redoubtable upholders of the entrenched ' mores majorum '. Rather than court unpopularity for an attempt to manipulate customary law to his own purpose, an aspiring innovator would yield his ground to the local legislative council. Minor modifications dictated by expediency or supported by commonsense are still possible, whether these proceed from changes in current public opinion or from the judge's earlier intercourse with the ways and standards of English law. It is normally difficult to tell in such cases which is the inducing cause of legal change.

C. EFFECTS ON THE CIVIL AND THE CRIMINAL SIDES OF AFRICAN LAW

Having thus indicated both the *adoptive* and the *additive* aspects of the impact of English law upon African customary law, we may now point to another important feature of the same phenomenon. This is the differing effects of the impact in the *civil* and in the *criminal* spheres of law. We may note, for instance, that a greater degree of assimilation of English legal concepts by African customary law has taken place in the law of contract and tort than in the law of crime and other statutory, technical offences. Again, the marriage between both English and African laws is less happy in the field of *procedure* and administration than it is in that of *substantive* rules. But this administrative problem is probably inherent, to some extent, in the basic divergence between certain aspects of the two systems of substantive rules sought to be merged together. It is now necessary to examine these problems in some detail with a view to discovering in what important particulars and to what degree English law has affected African customary law.

In the chapter on the general principles of legal liability,[1] we have described the nature and scope of group as well as individual responsibility for civil and criminal wrongs in African societies. Now, one result of the impact of the new economic and technical ideas upon the African has been the loosening up of kinship ties and obligations and, hence, the widening of the ambit of customary rights and the narrowing of the extent of the traditional duties of the individual. Cash economy and wage labour have increased the individual's self-reliance to a point that makes him often less solicitous of the welfare and economic stability of other members of his family or lineage towards whom he would in former times have felt at least a strong sense of moral obligation. The joint basis of the ancient patrimony, of which the members of an autonomous household used to be sharers according to individual needs and deserts, is rapidly yielding place to one of personal self-assertion and economic self-sufficiency, out of all regard to the claims of the kin. All these seem to be a logical development of the traditional African conception that a person should be free to do what he likes with his own so long as social solidarity is not thereby endangered : we see this, for example, in the premium placed on the unfettered right of the first cultivator of a parcel of virgin land or common forest to treat the property virtually as an absolute estate of freehold, since such an acquisition has been the result of his personal exertion. But this lasts for only the term of his natural life ; for, once he dies and his children inherit, they have a corporate interest in the inheritance. This interest is, however, subject to all the qualifications imposed upon the use and enjoyment of such family land by customary law, seeing that they have obtained something not

[1] See Ch. VIII.

the outcome of personal effort. Nevertheless, what each grows
on or excavates from his portion of family land—as being the
product of his individual exertion—belongs to him or her absolutely. Other instances of the halo with which customary law
surrounds the go-ahead individual, even under the system of
subsistence economy, might be multiplied ; the conception of
the right of such a one to dispose of his property as he chooses is
widespread in African societies.

It is therefore but a short step from all this to the modern
assertion, by the African wage-earner or trader or professional,
of the rugged individualism of Western man. The relevance of
this development to legal theory is the correspondingly decreasing
disposition of the urban African to hold himself legally, or in
many cases even morally, bound to contribute towards or indemnify a relation who has been cast in damages to a third party
by the courts and whom he might at least have felt obliged to
succour in similar circumstances in the past. This tendency of the
African towards an apparent nonchalance in these matters has
also been hastened by his daily contact with European social and
economic ideas and habits, which seem to be bringing out of him
the less sociable traits in his indigenous culture but which he is
powerless to resist in modern world conditions.

The result, then, of this culture contact is that, in the domain
of *civil* law, there is increasing individualisation of the legal
liability of members of the average African household ; or, to be
more accurate, a growing assertion of the often latent but always
existing right of the individual to refuse legally to answer for the
defaults or wrongs of another by being made to contribute towards
the compounding of these. As we have shown, in nearly all the
instances usually cited in support of the so-called theory of
collective responsibility of the clan for its member's misdeeds to
others, there was never any doubt that the wrong-doer was himself
primarily liable in law and that the vicarious responsibility of his
group, if any, was only secondary. But it is this secondary
aspect of the matter that has usually been given most emphasis on
the ground, no doubt, of the practical operation of the sanction
of enforcement against certain group members which is observable
in many societies. If the urban African, therefore, tends to ignore
his accustomed kinship obligations by refusing to indemnify, or
make contribution on behalf of, a relation held legally liable to

others, he thereby also releases such a one from similar obligation should a like misfortune befall him in future. This is perhaps inevitable in communities where family or village members are already ceasing to be their 'brother's keeper' and where the pressure of new economic needs is working a relentless disintegration of the old joint patrimony.

The basic notions of the English law of torts, such as negligence, nuisance, trespass, detinue, defamation, liability for animals, vicarious liability and seduction, are, like the general defences of Act of God, inevitable accident, mistake, self-defence and self-help, conceptions with which the African was already familiar under his own customary law. They do not, therefore, strike him either as exotic in their impingement on him or as esoteric in their practical operation in regard to him. It must be admitted, of course, that some of the technical refinements of tortious liability, e.g. the artificial distinctions regarding the liability of an invitor for injuries to an invitee, of a licensor to a licensee, and of an owner of premises to trespassers, are to the African often bewildering. But, then, these are by no means every English lawyer's meat, let alone every layman's. On the other hand, the closely related concept of the *Rylands* v. *Fletcher* type of liability (whereby an owner of property is liable for any dangerous animal which he may bring, either by himself or through an agent, on to his land and which escapes to injure a neighbour) does not seem to occasion the African any trouble.

Similarly, in the field of contract, English legal ideas are being absorbed, particularly in the introduction of writing in the legalisation of transactions that previously required the evidence of human witnesses. Considerations of English public policy which forbid actions based on illegal or immoral agreements are not essentially different from the African customary law requirement, that the social solidarity of the community must be maintained at all costs and that the elders must set their face against all antisocial activities which would disturb that solidarity. For an alleged breach of a lawful agreement to be countenanced by the judges, the complainant has to satisfy them that he has done his own part towards it or given some value for it and that it would be unconscionable for the other party to break his plighted word. Witnesses must also be produced both as to the agreement itself, to the *quid pro quo* already given or promised, and to the alleged breach. Compensation for any damages suffered or specific performance of unfulfilled but outstanding obligations may be ordered by the elders, who may also take into account such factors as frustration, impossibility of performance, fraud or mistake of one or both parties. The legal incapacity of minors, of certain classes of married women, and of lunatics is also tolerably familiar to customary law. But, again, here as with the law of tort, some refinements of the English rules governing contract could prove abstruse to the African litigant—e.g. aspects of the English rules as to offer and acceptance by post or as to cross-offers, or the subtle distinction between unilateral, mutual and common mistakes, or the niceties of an infant's contract for ' necessaries '. Mention should also be made of the surprising ingenuity currently displayed in the employment of all kinds of scraps of paper as evidence in such transactions as contracts for the sale of land, and worthless conveyances drawn up by semi-literate letter writers. In many instances, the sanctity attached by the sophisticated African illiterate to such documents and others in lawsuits can only be paralleled by the somewhat similar enthusiasm that greeted the advent of contracts under seal in England.[1]

On the whole, therefore, we see that the English concepts of civil law obligations are paralleled by similar notions in African customary law. The impact in this sphere is neither abrupt nor dissonant. It is not as if two entirely dissimilar and irreconcilable bodies of thought are being thrown together into an unassimilable mass. Rather is the process one of easy but gradual integration of the one with the other. Far otherwise, however, is the situation when we turn to the sphere of English criminal law and its administration in Africa.

Thus, no easy matter to the average African is the modern English law of larceny [2] with its bewildering variety of embezzlement, larceny by a servant and by a bailee, and fraudulent conversion ; or the subtle and often perplexing distinction between larceny by trick, obtaining by false pretences, obtaining credit by fraud, and common law cheating. These and other similar instances it is that render the criminal side of English law so unlike its civil side in the total impact it makes upon African law. It is

---

[1] See pp. 595–6, 598–600 and 55–6 of Plucknett, *op. cit.*
[2] As embodied in the Larceny Acts, 1861 and 1916.

not at all that the idea of larceny or theft is alien to African conception, as indeed our earlier account [1] of the severity of the penalty with which its incidence is everywhere visited under customary law will have shown.   What is baffling to the African, as also to the vast majority of Englishmen, is the wealth of detailed rules and subtle distinctions by which the English criminal law in particular is characterised.   It is this feature also that marks it off from the Continental Code system with its broad and generally not over-subtle provisions for the classification and definition of offences.

To the extent to which many of the technical rules of English criminal law bear little relation to the norms of social behaviour, as understood and practised in a given African society, will their application to individual offenders therein seem artificial and probably also unjust.   That a blatant criminal might and sometimes does go scot-free on the ground that the particular offence charged in the indictment has been called by the wrong title, or that he is sometimes discharged on a technicality of substantive or procedural law, or again, that an innocent person should occasionally be punished for an offence of which he might only technically be held guilty, serves merely to widen the gulf between the African and ' the white man's law '.

If we turn to the actual administration of criminal justice similar difficulties arise.   The first and perhaps the most obvious one is the predominance of imprisonment as an almost invariable mode of punishing nearly all types of criminals.   As Major G. St. J. Orde-Browne has rightly remarked : ' European penology is still dominated by incarceration as the best, indeed almost the only way of dealing with the offender ;   medieval ingenuity afforded alternatives of varying ghastliness, but these have been abandoned ; capital punishment grows rarer, and the use of the lash is increasingly deprecated.   Reformation rather than retribution becomes the goal of the magistrate . . . nevertheless, these are modifications of the jail system and detention in some form is the usual specific for crime.' [2]

Now, there are two inadequacies about the institution of imprisonment as a major penal sanction : the one proceeds from

---

[1] See Ch. VIII, *passim*.
[2] *Jnl. Roy. Afr. Soc.*, Vol. 32, No. 127, April, 1933, pp. 148–59, at p. 158.

the point of view of the African and the other is a more general indictment of the system. As regards the first, where a person has been found guilty of, for example, manslaughter of another and is thrown into gaol without at the same time being made to pay the blood-money to his victim's surviving relations as required by customary law, not only such deprived relatives but also the general public are infuriated by the procedure. Imprisonment benefits the British Government by thus providing it with another servant, while it does nothing to assuage the personal grief or satisfy the legal expectations of the bereaved family. And it seems that it is not only the Africans who have been piqued by this aspect of the problem.

Jeremy Bentham, among other thinkers, once argued thus. If a person were to set fire to his neighbour's house, he ought to be punished so as to serve as a lesson to him and to others. Imprisonment would normally be resorted to in such a case. But, in Bentham's view, it should be juster and simpler to fine the offender a certain sum which should then be made over to his victim so as to achieve the additional aim of compensation to the wronged : ' . . . the best fund whence satisfaction can be drawn is the property of the delinquent, since it then performs with superior convenience the functions both of satisfaction and of punishment. But if the offender is without property, ought the injured party to remain without satisfaction ? No, for satisfaction is almost as necessary as punishment. It ought to be furnished out of the public treasury, because it is an object of public good, and the security of all is interested in it.' [1]

While it is true that in certain circumstances English law has now made provision under a scheme of compulsory insurance for the payment of compensation to one damnified by an impecunious offender, there is no additional provision for the punishment of the culprit for involving not only his victim but also the rest of the community in financial loss.[2] This is still the case in matters

---

[1] *Theory of Legislation* (ed. Ogden), Ch. 18, entitled ' Principles of the Penal Code ', p. 317.

[2] An offender may of course be ordered to make a restitution of stolen property or pay compensation of up to £100 under certain statutes —e.g. Larceny Act, 1916, s. 45 ; Criminal Justice Administration Act, 1914, s. 14(1) ; Forfeiture Act, 1870, s. 4 ; Criminal Justice Act, 1948, s. 11(2). All these statutes assume that the culprit is able to restore the stolen property or to make the compensation.

of civil liability. Punishment of the offender and a corresponding satisfaction of the offended are two distinct questions that must be faced if real justice is to be achieved. Hence in many statutory Native Courts persons sentenced for offences like manslaughter are sent to prison as prescribed by the Criminal Code, but for only half the stipulated period ; either before or after serving their sentence they are made to pay the customary compensation to their victim's surviving relatives.

Another objection to the widespread use of imprisonment as a form of punishment in African societies is that it does not frequently carry, at least on its first introduction, the same kind of social stigma as it does in English or any other society which has acquired a proper appraisal of its aim and purpose. Indeed, instances have often been quoted to show how prisons have at one time or another been regarded among certain African communities as worthy of being patronised on account of their superior living amenities and the easier opportunities they often offer to their inmates to learn a trade than are available in their own homes. Persons have been known to go out of their way deliberately to commit offences and parents have been reported as having incited their sons to do so, with the sole purpose of achieving such (to them) worthwhile ambitions.

Again, the work prisoners do for the Government outside the prisons consists mainly or necessarily of public services like making or repairing roads, keeping certain public buildings clean and tidy, and so on. These undertakings are by customary usages those always regarded as honourable and public-spirited for all able-bodied male members of the local community. It is, therefore, not surprising that those whose only punishment for important crimes is the participation in these praiseworthy public duties should take pride in their membership of a co-operative labour unit that after all provides the traditional beer-drink in the new guise of food, living accommodation and, to cap it all, a vocation. Looked at in this way, imprisonment in such African societies would be seen to defeat its own ends and to serve the very reverse of the purpose for which it is intended.

Fortunately, this complacent attitude towards the penal institution of imprisonment is not characteristic of all African societies, nor is the general condition of the prisons so attractive as to invite public patronage. In all African communities in which the aim and purpose of a prison sentence have been grasped, people are anxious to avoid the opprobrium and obloquy with which those who have undergone it are invariably regarded. Because the living standards of many members of such communities do not compare too unfavourably with those obtaining in the prisons, there is no inducement for the generality of people to covet a life therein ; while participation in the public side of prison work, even for one day, is dreaded as worse than a year's confinement on much harder work within it, however appalling internal conditions might be. Even here, however, imprisonment does not meet the fundamental objection that it is not a satisfactory substitute for other forms of penalty recognised and appreciated under African customary law.

In the various attempts to state what the object of criminal punishment should be, five different views have been put forward : (1) to punish the criminal for his wrong-doing ; (2) to reform him and so turn him into a useful member of society ; (3) to deter others from wrong-doing by showing him up as a bad example ; (4) to make him atone for his iniquity by a process of moral retribution ; and (5) to protect the public against an evil-doer.[1] Although there may be a bias in favour of one or more of these alternatives, nevertheless, no modern system of government adopts any one criterion to the exclusion of the others. That being so, it follows that imprisonment cannot be the only or the best penalty for the criminal.

Hardly any indigenous African society has evolved a hide-bound system of imprisonment as a comprehensive mode of dealing with the criminal.[2] Death for certain types of killing, compensation for other types of homicide as well as for a variety of lesser offences, fines for general offences and other private wrongs, banishment or exile for certain forms of antisocial behaviour, whipping and flogging for other forms of wrongs especially by young boys (but never inflicted on women), restitution to its true owner of property illegally held—all these are recognised by customary law as legitimate and rational modes of dealing with an offender, but not imprisonment. It is difficult, however, to see

[1] It is easy to show that all the five might be reduced to only the three clear alternative theories of the Punitive, the Reformative, and the Deterrent.

[2] But see the exceptions mentioned at p. 262.

how modern African communities in contact with English law and administration can escape the bane of imprisonment as a form of penalty for crime. But while it will be agreed to be such a necessary evil, it is eminently desirable that its use be confined within limits far narrower than those usually permissible under pure English law and practice.[1] This should be possible if fuller use is made of the various traditional alternatives just listed and of a few others to be mentioned presently.

The unsatisfactory nature of imprisonment as a form of penalty for many types of offences led to the institution of the Probation System in Massachusetts in 1878. It was nearly thirty years later that it was fully adopted in England [2] under the Probation of Offenders Act, 1907, as a result of which many offenders who would formerly have been cast in gaol are now placed under an officer of the court for general supervision and report during a stated period when such offenders are put on their good behaviour. On a breach of any of the conditions of his recognisance, an offender may be tried and punished in any manner considered suitable by the court. Sometimes, a first offender might be tried but, before being sentenced, a Probation Officer might be asked to acquaint the court with the offender's character and antecedents, which information he would have had to collect before or during the pendency of the trial. This helps to bring in part at least of the sociological background of the offence and of the offender which the strict English doctrine of judicial ignorance has all but shut out for centuries from the judge's purview.[3]

If told about this probation procedure, an orthodox African judge could be trusted to murmur a retort that he would have done just that with far less ceremony and greater enjoyment as one who is but part and parcel of the offender's cultural and social

---

[1] There are very many other criticisms of the prison system into which it is not proposed we should enter here. We are now concerned primarily with those of immediate relevance to the African situation in its relation to English law.

[2] See Turner, *On Kenny's Outlines of Criminal Law*, p. 528 (§ 792). Continental European countries have since 1945 made increasing use of the ' parole system ', and the ' suspended sentence '. They have yet to adopt this Anglo-American probation system.

[3] As we have shown in the preceding chapter (at pp.251–5 ff), English judges have, however, never in fact been as judicially ignorant as this high theory would at first seem to suggest. But the limitation is still there.

milieu and, therefore, better placed to make a more correct, because personal, appraisal of the offender under trial.

Transportation to some penal settlement used to be another English mode, besides imprisonment, of punishing the criminal. This afforded him an opportunity of making good later, while depriving him of the society of his relatives and friends at home. For example, Australia and New Zealand might never have been founded but for such transportation.[1] It is, of course, the very age-old custom, practised by nearly all human societies from the dawn of time until today, of banishing into exile those who defy the collective *mores* and the social *ethos* of their community in a manner not admitting of their local punishment and re-incorporation in any other way. This is no innovation of English law and its proper use does not, therefore, dismay the African.

Similarly, the introduction of the Jury System is not unfamiliar to the African in so far as it embodies the principle that an offender ought to be judged by his fellows instead of by a judge, who under the English theory of judicial ignorance might not know enough about the circumstances of the offender and of the offence in question. Under the customary law procedure an accused person is exposed to the full rigour of public examination and debate in the presence of his fellow villagers or townsmen whom he cannot easily hoodwink with false stories, since he can so much more quickly be contradicted by other evidence on the part of those who know his circumstances well.

What is not so easy for the average African to appreciate is the English rule that all the twelve jurors must be unanimous in their verdict and that this verdict must be reached in secret, without an opportunity for the debate among the jurors being heard by all concerned, so that doubts and errors in the mind of any juror might be resolved or corrected in the process. Nor is the exact role of the foreman of the jury clear to Africans when they learn that he often has to use his best endeavours to get all recalcitrant jurors to agree with the view of the majority so as to be able to present a united front when asked by the presiding judge about their verdict. Is the foreman a sub-judge or just

---

[1] With very few open spaces now unoccupied in the world today, transportation *en masse* is no longer practised or practicable ; it seems, however, that individuals (especially in the colonies) may still be so dealt with in English law.

another layman whose view of the case under consideration may be as erroneous or as prejudiced or as fair as that of any other dissentient juror ? Of course, if the majority fail to persuade a single juror, the verdict falls to the ground. But this one juror might be wrong as against the remaining eleven ? How much better would it be if the whole matter could be argued out in open debate so that the rights and wrongs could be publicly canvassed and the better view of the majority be allowed to prevail ? These and similar anxieties seriously disturb the confidence of the African offender in the justice of English law. Perhaps it is as well that the Jury System does not operate in the statutory Native Courts or the junior British-established courts like the Magistrates' Courts. It is chiefly employed in Supreme or High Court cases and, even then, mostly in serious criminal offences. Nevertheless, whenever these affect an African offender the repercussion on the local community is no less disturbing.

It would be easy to go on in this way listing specific aspects of English law in its general impact upon African law. Enough indication has, however, been given of the broad issues of law and administration that still await solution. It is perhaps permissible to suggest in retrospect that many of the new developments, e.g. Probation System, Jury Trial, Police, are more or less elegant, modern European adaptations and refinements of the old but often rudimentary methods of administering justice in African societies. The only difference is that the maintenance of social order was often incomparably easier in these societies than it is in the more complex urban communities of today. As Lowie has well put it with such pungency :

' Of course it is true that social organisations differ in complexity, but that difference fails to provide a criterion of progress. . . . If our enlightened communities coped as successfully with, say, the problem of maintaining order as ruder peoples in a simpler environment, then it might be conceded that our complex administrative machinery represents an intellectual advance. But the condition is contrary to fact, and our cumbersome method of preserving the peace and the more elegant solution of the same problem in simpler circumstances remain incommensurable.' [1]

One can only add that, even in Africa, the old sanctions no longer prove adequate to the needs of modern life with its rapidly

[1] *Primitive Society*, p. 426.

changing concepts of social and economic values. For better or for worse, British Colonial Africa is bound to tread a path of legal and administrative development which may be very similar to, if not always identical with, that already trodden by Great Britain. It may also have to face sooner or later the same types of problem which beset the path of legal evolution everywhere.

We shall try briefly to indicate the general line of this development towards the end of the next and final chapter.

CHAPTER XIV

SUMMARY AND CONCLUSIONS

WE shall now proceed to make a brief recapitulation of the main analyses made and arguments advanced in the preceding chapters. Before we go on to that, however, it cannot be too strongly emphasised here, as we did at the beginning, that this study has not been conceived in the spirit either of a legal polemic or a sociological critique. The aim throughout has been rather the marriage of anthropological research data on African societies to the juristic technique of analysing specific concepts and basic institutions. Naturally, in such a process, many time-honoured puerilities about African law have had to be jettisoned to the extent to which they have failed to bear precise analysis. Wherever the evidence about any particular theory has been glossed over, distorted or imperfectly appreciated, an effort has been made objectively to put the issue in its proper perspective. And it will be clear to the reader that the opportunity has very rarely been missed of confirming or supporting the views of those writers who happen to have made a correct or useful appraisal of specific African legal ideas.

In this wise we began by classifying African societies into the three broad categories of :

(*a*) Those that have no centralised political authority but are mainly segmentary kinship groups in which authority tends to be dispersed, rather than concentrated. In this rudimentary political organisation, authority is hardly yet institutionalised and the essential mechanism for securing the social order are rules, rather than rulers.

(*b*) Those that have a strong centralised political authority, a military organisation, and an administrative and judicial machinery. These possess the traditional chieftaincy system and are frequently strong kingdoms with a regulated hierarchy of royal and chiefly authorities.

(*c*) Those that are usually loosely-knit confederacies composed of a number of semi-independent chiefdoms, the heads of which recognise the supremacy of one king as being the fountain and highest example of *divine* kinship. These societies are hardly distinguishable from those in (*b*) except that they are normally homogeneous, theocratic states, often of the autocratic type of Moslem political system. For purposes of practical exposition, we have decided to exclude purely Islamic societies of this order and to use only the first two groups as our terms of reference.

We have considered, all too briefly perhaps, some of the various opinions that have been entertained of African customary law, ranging from such extreme position as that it is all fetish and irrational superstition to such half-way house as that it is all custom : custom is king. It should be added that we have of course noted the opinion of the few judicious and fair-minded students of the subject who see in African law a rational system of social control which once ' studied and understood are hardly less enforceable than rules under English law '.

This leads inevitably to the posing of the perennial question of jurisprudence : What is Law ? Do Africans distinguish between *law*, in the sense of a body of obligatory rules of conduct, and *custom*, which is a mere principle of social conformity the breach of which does not entail any form of penalty ? In an attempt to answer this question we have had to review and assess the more noteworthy definitions of law so far propounded both by jurists and by social scientists : we have had to reject, in common with European and a few English jurists, the Austinian theory of law as the command of a political sovereign over political subordinates, not indeed because African societies are in Austin's ' state of nature ', i.e. unorganised, warring communities based on the Hobbesian conception of *homo homini lupus*, but because to the African, as to von Savigny, law is *Rechtsüberzeugung*—an expression of the common consciousness of the people—to the end that, in the vivid phrase of Roscoe Pound, it may serve the purposes of ' social engineering '. Thus conceived law has been shown to be clearly distinguished from custom in African societies ; the drumming and feasting that often accompany a customary marriage have been misunderstood by some writers as forming part of the legal requirements, whereas the discharge of, or promise to discharge, the marriage payment by the prospective groom is alone of the essence of the contract.

Another popular fallacy about African law, which we have felt obliged to analyse and reject, is the attractive theory of the unity of the clan in its relation to group status and collective responsibility. We have shown, we hope successfully, how neither the ' peacock ' theory nor the ' sheep ' theory about the African conception of the individual fits in with the evidence thrown up by patient and careful sociological fieldwork. To take one example, we have Gluckman's authority for the view that the Barotse have no clan system as commonly understood. We have, therefore, tried to explain that, far from being a slave of custom and far from being bogged down disconsolately by kinship ties and obligations, the individual in African society has his definite rights and duties within the framework of the group. And the often exaggerated responsibility of the group for the individual has been shown to be no more and no less than the principle of vicarious liability so familiar to English lawyers. Of course, the extent and nature of this are naturally wider in the African context. Finally, we have also emphasised that those who identify the individual with his group have not sufficiently appreciated the distinction between *legal responsibility*, which African law attaches personally to the individual at fault, and *moral liability*, which African custom imposes on certain but not all of his kin.

Next, we have, by random but careful selection of African notions about certain wrongs, shown that it is possible to distinguish between criminal and civil offences, as these are understood in English law ; and this, despite Radcliffe-Browne's warning against the application of Western concepts to ' primitive ' notions. The great anthropologist's substitution of ' public ' and ' private ' delicts has been shown to be open to at least the same objection as is usually levelled against the well-known dichotomy of criminal and civil. If, then, we regard the *essence* rather than the *form* of the matter to be classified, we must distinguish between those offences that affect or are likely to disrupt the entire social equilibrium of a given community, and those that are better left to private arbitrament. What is put in each category must, however, be different in the African legal context from what it is in the English.

From this we have passed on to a fairly detailed examination of the general ideas of legal responsibility in African customary law. This is an aspect of the individual-versus-group-status theory previously considered, but here we are immediately concerned about the actual content of such concepts as criminal

U*

responsibility and the various grounds of exemption therefrom, tortious liability and defences thereto. Also, we have had to face the question that some sceptics have often asked : Does African law recognise anything in the nature of a contract ? Put in another way, is there any notion in African societies that agreements are binding and ought not to be broken at will ? Again, is there a conception analogous to the *quid pro quo* necessary to support a simple contract under English law ? We have answered these and related questions in the affirmative, citing such familiar instances as the marriage contract (which we have shown to be really a *triple* contract in one), the traditional ' borrowing ' and ' leasing ' of land, the co-operative labour and economic units, whether lineal or territorial, and so on.

No study of African customary law could be considered adequate or helpful which did not include an account of the indigenous concepts of ownership and possession of property—land as well as chattels. We have accordingly examined what is often loosely termed ' communal ownership ' or, more loosely still, ' community usufruct ' of land and tried to demonstrate that there is no such thing. There is, however, a corporate holding and occupation of particular parcels of land by the several families in any given village or town ; such parcels may have been acquired by right of first cultivation by the family founder or through allocation by the village head or chief among the component lineage heads. Howsoever acquired, these family allotments are in fact held in clearly-defined, individual ownership which, though inalienable without family permission or consent, is nevertheless heritable by the children of each holder and transmissible down his line *ad infinitum*.[1] The African owner-occupier of family land is thus seen to be ' a strange bed-fellow ' of the Roman usufructuary with whom he is popularly identified but who had no kind of proprietary interest in his purely temporary holding, and who was often hedged about by numerous conditions restrictive of its user.

Again the universal African idea of land-holding is that ' no land is without an owner ' : desert, swamp or jungle, every piece

[1] See Lord Hailey's *Native Administration in the British African Territories* (1951), Pt. IV, p. 55 : ' African custom has always recognised the " individualisation " of land-holding, in so far that the occupier or his kindred have a heritable right to a holding so long as it is " occupied " in the sense which local usage attaches to that word.'

of land is the property of the neighbouring community which can show effective and prior control over its boundaries as against all others. This dormant, reversionary ownership remains in the chief or council of elders, in whom rests the ultimate power to allocate and re-allocate fallow or unused parcels of land among members of the community according to need. With regard to chattels, the customary view is that they are freely alienable by their owners and may be pledged, loaned or exchanged at will and without the necessity to consult anyone about it. Finally, we have indicated the scope of the use of cattle or farm produce as media of exchange—e.g. as negotiable instruments in such matters as customary marriage payments, contracts of agistment and the like.

One of the means whereby formerly rigid rules, e.g. that of non-alienability of family land, have been modified, e.g. into one of conditional alienability, has been the use of legal fictions. Such is the symbolic and figurative nature of the African judge's imagery that, seizing upon the essentials of his customary legal principles, he quickly transfers inconvenient or outmoded concepts to a new plane, rationalising the process on the ground of expediency or utility. But if a desirable extension or modification of an old rule is not possible, he desists from attempting a violent wrench of it out of context and beats a hasty retreat to the legislative council hut. Finally, we have noted the modern use made of these customary legislative institutions as instruments for passing local government laws and the consequent weakening of the old traditional sanctions.

Having dealt with these basic problems of the African ideas of law we turned, almost inevitably, to a somewhat clinical analysis of the customary judicial process. With most societies, especially of the uncentralised type, lacking a system of institutionalised police and other law enforcement officers, not less than nine different modes of bringing an action have been described. This has been followed by an account of the varying types of judicial trial in both criminal and civil matters, the use and place of oaths, divination and ordeals in the judicial process, the trial itself and the legal representation of litigants by champions-at-law and the position of the linguist or griot both in the giving and taking of evidence and in the declaration of the verdict. Again, we have explained why and the extent to which there is no theory of judicial ignorance in the traditional type of procedure ; we have explained the requirement of proof by the production of witnesses and objects involved in litigation, and how some societies carry out *post mortem* examinations for the purpose of discovering physiological causes of sudden, unexplained deaths ; we have also noted the use of objects like sticks, pebbles and other symbols as tallies to count scores of legal points made by either party in the course of stating his case. We have, moreover, considered the use made of precedents in the customary process, the mode in which the judges declare their verdict, the various forms of punishment known to customary law and, incidentally, the absence therefrom of imprisonment and probation. We showed the methods of execution of judgment to be hardly less effective in the strong centralised societies of Africa with administrative machinery and military organisation than they are in a modern state. Indeed the problem of law enforcement might even be easier ; we also showed that in many uncentralised societies, lacking uniformed police or bailiff, the duties were effectively performed by the two halves of exogamous communities or by more or less regular bands of youthful warriors belonging to a particular age-set and acting under the direction of the elders.

Looking back on the customary judicial process in perspective we have noticed how, in the less organised African societies as well as in some organised ones, *processes* rather than *institutions* are the things upon which attention must be concentrated. Often in the midst of the apparent casualness of the proceedings is enacted an important phase in the human drama of the local community. The judges are more intent on the maintenance of the social equilibrium than on a strict declaration of legal rights and duties of the litigants without regard to the social consequences of their verdict. Instead of spinning out abstract theories of law, their aim is usually the pragmatic one of removing the causes of social tension, of binding or rebinding the estranged parties in a give-and-take reciprocity, of the re-incorporation of an erring member in the social structure. Only where the activities of a member are antisocial and disintegrative of the social solidarity is there a resort to banishment or death by impalement, shooting or hanging. But in the generality of cases tried under the customary process the conscious purpose is reconciliation of the parties by a fairly just apportionment of blame or deserts. Hence the normal atmosphere is one of peaceful debate and argument of the pros and cons of the issues in dispute ; the litigants do not approach the court awed by a sense of majesty or fear ; they go there in the spirit of respect for the chief's or elders' authority to decide what is best, amidst the fanfare of publicity, of open debate and of well-known rules of customary law.

Finally, we have briefly sketched in some of the highly intriguing problems of the relationship between African customary law and English law. Our analysis in the preceding chapters has shown that there is no intrinsic opposition between the two and that the extrinsic divergencies of form and content of some basic principles have been occasioned as much by historical and geographical factors as by commercial and technological considerations. It is probably not too much to say that, given its specific context, each system is valid for the type of society and the species of task for which it is designed, at least so long as the process of acculturation has not resulted in a disruption of the African society by the European impact. But when the latter has in varying degrees of effectiveness introduced extraneous elements such as cash economy, machinery, and the art of writing, the old corporate sense of tribal loyalty and family obligation begins to disintegrate and the traditional mechanisms for securing the order and stability of society become gradually inadequate. The new ideas and practices of an industrial society impinge upon those of an agricultural one in a manner affecting not only the substantive rules of customary law in many respects but also the traditional rules of procedure. In the field of penology imprisonment is as normal to the English system as are fines and compensation to the African one.

The African litigant is naturally bewildered by many aspects of the British judicial innovations. For example, an illiterate African offender was once brought before a Nigerian magistrate and asked to plead ' Guilty or Not Guilty ' to the charge of riding his bicycle, after sunset, without a lighted lamp. He grinned at the magistrate, shook his head, and retorted somewhat acidly : ' What a question ! Is that not what I have been dragged before you to find out ? ' We may laugh at him for his ignorance of English criminal procedure but, on second thought, logic will not be found to be entirely on our side. Again, a man negligently killed another by running him down with his limousine car, and a Tanganyika judge sentenced him to six months' imprisonment for man-slaughter. The deceased man's relatives went away more disconsolate and embittered than before, as they were told that that was all English law could do for them.[1]   One of them was heard to shout as he walked out of the court-room : ' He may work for the Government, but he has yet to pay us the usual compensation as blood-money. Until that is done we are unrequited.' How much more satisfying to these persons the customary judicial method would have been ! Compensation to the bereaved, not imprisonment by the authorities, would have been ordered by the elders.[2]   Of course, as we have seen, the modern statutory Native Courts everywhere have their own way of avoiding this piece of English legal humbug by first sentencing the offender in such a case to prison and then, on his coming out, making him pay a reduced rate of compensation according to the tribal tariff schedule of penalty.

To quote a third instance, it often happens in the case of technical offences under some Ordinance that a sophisticated offender employs a lawyer to defend him, in a frame of mind which seems to imply that the white man's law ought to be confronted with the white-man-trained lawyer (they should understand each other better). Then, after long and often protracted arguments back and forth, the African offender is let off on a technicality, substantive or procedural. He breaks out irrepressibly into protestations of his guilt ! And he is hustled away—an innocent man—even though he admits his guilt and is ready and willing to pay for it.[3]

Nevertheless, a good many changes for the better have taken place in African law. As we have shown, cases of so-called witchcraft, trial by ordeal and similar obnoxious practices, have been prohibited by legislation. The traditional tribunals have been re-organised and improved, especially from the point of view of

---

[1] The extent to which they could have brought another civil action under F.A. Act, 1846, for damages according to Tanganyika law is not clear, nor was the point ever mentioned to them by anyone during the trial. The appropriate statutory Native (or Local) Court would probably supplement this verdict with an award of the customary blood-money compensation.

[2] In this case, it was later learnt that a Local Court ordered the culprit, on his release from imprisonment, to pay half the customary blood-money to his victim's surviving dependants.

[3] See, e.g. G. W. B. Huntingford, *The Nandi of Kènya* (1953), p. 101.

procedure, civil no less than criminal. But the endowment of illiterate chiefs with powers to apply and interpret certain Ordinances and Regulations sometimes of a complex character cannot be said to be a particularly happy feature of the new legal order ; for, whereas the English lay justices perform a similar function, they are often not only well-educated people but also assisted on legal points by solicitors acting as their clerks. The spread of education and a system of legal training should, with the passing of the years, remove most of these defects.

Finally, we may say that though attempts might be made to produce monographs, handbooks or even codes of particular communities, the lines along which African customary law in the various British Colonies is likely to evolve would appear to be that of the English common law, not that of the Continental Code. Both its dynamic character and present prospects would seem to indicate that it should do so. A closer degree of assimilation with English law is forecast, but it does not seem that the two will ever entirely coalesce.[1] America, and the other countries of the Commonwealth, retain the common law system whilst pursuing their several and independent developments along local lines. The customary law of each African territory with its many facets should in its turn evolve into a common law on the English model, capable of absorbing the shock due to alien contacts and new ideas and of meeting the ever-present challenge of rapidly changing social needs.

[1] As Bryce has shown in his *Studies in History and Jurisprudence* Vol. I, p. 83, we must remember that assimilation between two legal systems does not generally prove effective in strong, national aspects of life such as marriage and the family, land tenure, inheritance and succession, etc. Indeed, these matters are in almost all British Colonies now normally left in the exclusive jurisdiction of African courts.

BIBLIOGRAPHY

Abraham, R. C., *The Tiv People*. Lagos : Govt. Printer (2nd ed., 1933).

Ajisafe, A. K., *Laws and Customs of the Yoruba People*. London : Routledge ; and Lagos, Nigeria : C.M.S. Bookshop (1924).

Allen, C. K., *Law in the Making*. London : Oxford University Press (4th ed., 1946).

— — *Legal Duties and Other Essays*. London : Oxford University Press (1931).

— — *The Queen's Peace*. London : Stevens (1953).

Aristotle, *Rhetoric*, Grant's translation, *Apud Ethi. Nic.* London : Dent (1953).

Ashton, H., *The Basuto*. London and New York : Oxford University Press (1952).

Austin, J., *Lectures on Jurisprudence or the Philosophy of Positive Law Vol. I*, ed. R. Campbell. London : John Murray (5th ed., 1885).

— — *Lectures on Jurisprudence*. Students' Edition. London : John Murray (13th impr., 1920).

— — *The Province of Jurisprudence Determined*. See Preface to first item under this head (1832).

Bentham, J., *Collected Works, Vol. I*. London : Bowring (1843).

— — *Limits of Jurisprudence Defined*. U.S.A. : Columbia University Press (1945).

— — *Principles of Morals and Legislation, Vol. I*, in Bowring Edition of Collected Works (see above).

— — *Theory of Fictions*, ed. C. K. Ogden. London : Routledge & Kegan Paul (1932).

Blackstone, Sir W., *Commentaries on the Laws of England, Bks. III & IV*.

Bryce, Lord James., *Studies in History and Jurisprudence*. London : Oxford University Press (1901).

Buckland, W. W., *A Manual of Roman Private Law*. London : Cambridge University Press (2nd ed., 1939).

— — *Some Reflections on Jurisprudence*. London : Cambridge University Press (1945).

Burke, E., *Reflections on the Revolution in France, 1790*. London : Dent (1953).

— — *Thoughts on the Cause of the Present Discontents (1770)*. London : Dent (1953).

Busia, K. A., *The Position of the Chief in the Modern Political System of Ashanti*. London and New York : Oxford University Press (1951).

Butt-Thompson, F. W., *West African Secret Societies*. London : Witherby (1929).

Cardozo, B. N., *The Growth of the Law*. New Haven : Yale University Press (1924).

Caton-Thompson, G., *The Zimbabwe Culture : Ruins and Reactions.* Oxford : The Clarendon Press (1931).

Cory, H., *Sukuma Law and Custom.* London and New York : Oxford University Press (1953).

—— and Hartnoll, M., *Customary Law of the Haya Tribe.* London Lund, Humphries (1945).

Culwick, A. T., *Good Out of Africa.* Rhodes-Livingstone Paper No. 8. Livingstone, N. Rhodesia (1943).

Danquah, J. B., *Akan Laws and Customs.* London : Routledge (1928).

Delafosse, M., *Negroes of Africa.* Washington, D.C. : Associated Publishers Inc. (1931).

Dennett, R. E., *Nigerian Studies.* London : Macmillan (1910).

Diamond, A. S., *Primitive Law.* London and New York : Longmans, Green (1935).

Driberg, J. H., *The Lango : A Nilotic Tribe of Uganda.* London : T. Fisher Unwin Ltd. (1923).

—— *The Savage as he really is.* London : Routledge (1929).

Duguit, L., *Law in the Modern State.* Translation by H. J. Laski. New York : The Viking Press (1919).

Durkheim, E., *L'Année Sociologique, Vol. I.* Paris : Librairie Felix Alcan (1896).

—— *De la Division du Travail Social.* Paris : Librairie Felix Alcan (5th ed., 1926).

—— *The Division of Social Work* or *The Division of Labour in Society.* Translation of *De La Division du Travail Social.* Glencoe, Illinois : The Free Press (1947).

Ehrlich, E., *Fundamental Principles of the Sociology of Law.* U.S.A., Cambridge, Massachussetts (1936).

Elias, T. O., *Groundwork of Nigerian Law.* London : Routledge & Kegan Paul (1954).

—— *Nigerian Land Law and Custom.* London : Routledge & Kegan Paul (1951).

Epstein, A. L., *The Administration of Justice and the Urban African.* Colonial Research Studies. London : H.M.S.O. (1953).

Evans-Pritchard, E. E., *The Nuer.* London : Oxford University Press (1940).

—— *Witchcraft, Oracles and Magic Among the Azande.* London : Oxford University Press (1937).

Fenton, J. S., *Outline of Native Law in Sierra Leone.* Freetown, Sierra Leone : Government Printer (1951).

Forde, C. D., *The Yoruba-speaking Peoples of South-Western Nigeria.* London : International African Institute (1951).

Fortes, M., *The Dynamics of Clanship among the Tallensi.* London : Oxford University Press (1945).

Fortes, M., and Evans-Pitchard, E. E. (editors), *African Political Systems.* London : Oxford University Press (1940).

Frank, J., *Law and the Modern Mind*. New York : Coward-McCann. London : Stevens (1949).

Freeman, K., *The Paths of Justice*. London : Lutterworth Press (1954).

Friedman, W., *Legal Theory*. London : Stevens (3rd ed., 1953).

Gluckman, M., *Essays on Lozi Land and Royal Property*. Rhodes-Livingstone Paper No. 10. Livingstone, Northern Rhodesia (1943).

Goyet, M. F., *Précis de Droit Pénal Spécial*. Paris : Recueil Sirey (6th ed., 1948).

Graveson, R. H., *Status in the Common Law*. London : Athlone Press (1953).

Gray, J. C., *The Nature and Sources of the Law*. New York : Columbia University Press (2nd ed., 1921).

Green, M. M., *Ibo Village Affairs*. London : Sidgwick & Jackson (1948).

Grotius, H., *De Jure Belli ac Pacis* (1625). Translated by Whewell. Cambridge University Press (1853).

Hailey, Lord, *An African Survey*. London : Oxford University Press (1938).

— — *Native Administration in the British African Territories, Pt. IV*. London : H.M.S.O. (1951).

Hanbury, H. G., *English Courts of Law*. London : Oxford University Press (1953).

Hartland, E. S., *Primitive Law*. London : Methuen (1924).

Hayford, C., *Gold Coast Native Institutions*. London : Sweet & Maxwell (1903).

Hives, F., *Justice in the Jungle*. London : John Lane (1932).

Hobbes, T., *The Leviathan*, reprinted from the edition of 1651. London : Oxford University Press (1909).

Hobhouse, L. T., *Morals in Evolution*. London : Chapman & Hall (5th ed., 1925).

— — *The History of Social Development*. London : Allen & Unwin (1920).

Holdsworth, W. S., *History of English Law, Vol. II*. London : Methuen (4th ed., 1938).

Holland, T. E., *The Elements of Jurisprudence*. London : Oxford University Press (13th ed., 1924).

Holleman, J. F., *Shona Customary Law*. London and Cape Town : Oxford University Press (1952).

Holmes, O. W., *The Common Law*. Boston, U.S.A. : Little, Brown & Co. (1948 impression).

Howell, P. P., *A Manual of Nuer Law*. London : Oxford University Press (1954).

Hughes, E. R. (Ed.), *The Individual in East and West*. London : Oxford University Press (1937).

Humphreys, T., *A Book of Trials*. London : Heinemann (1953).

Huntingford, G. W. B., *The Nandi of Kenya*. London : Routledge & Kegan Paul (1953).

Ibn Battuta, *Travels in Asia and Africa (1325–1354)*. London : Routledge & Kegan Paul (1929).

Jennings, W. I. (editor), *Modern Theories of Law*. London : Oxford University Press (1933).

Johnson, S., *History of the Yorubas*. London : Routledge (1921).

Jones, J. W., *Historical Introduction to the Theory of Law*. London : Oxford University Press (1940).

Joyce, J. A., *Justice at Work*. London: Chapman & Hall (1953).

Kaberry, P. M., *Women of the Grassfields*. London : H.M.S.O. (1952).

Keeton, G. W., *Elementary Principles of Jurisprudence*. London : A. & C. Black (1930).

Kelsen, H., *Society and Nature : A Sociological Inquiry*. London : Kegan Paul (1946).

Kenny, C. S., *Outlines of Criminal Law*. London : Cambridge University Press (15th ed. 1936). (16th ed. revised Turner, 1952.)

Lambard, *Eirenarcha* (1581).

Leakey, L. S. B., *Mau Mau and the Kikuyu*. London : Methuen (1952).

Lewin, J., *Studies in African Native Law*. Cape Town : The African Bookman (1947).

Lindblom, G., *The Akamba in British East Africa*. *Archives d'Etudes Orientales*, vol. 17. Uppsala, East Africa (2nd ed., 1920).

Locke, J., *Two Treatises of Civil Government, Bk. II*. London : Dent (1953 ed.).

Lowie, R. H., *Primitive Society*. London : Routledge (1921).

Lugard, Sir Frederick, *The Dual Mandate in British Tropical Africa*. Edinburgh : Blackwood (2nd ed., 1922, 4th ed., 1929).

— — *Rise of our East African Empire*, two vols. Edinburgh and London : Blackwood (1893).

Lugard, Lady Flora Louise, *A Tropical Dependency*. London : James Nisbet (1905).

MacIver, R. M., *Society : Its Structure and Changes*. New York (1932). Now republished as *Society : An Introductory Analysis*. London : Macmillan (1949).

MacMillan, W. M., *Africa Emergent*. London : Faber & Faber (1938).

Maine, H. J. S., *Ancient Law*, ed. Sir F. Pollock. London : John Murray (1906).

— — *Lectures on Early History of Institutions*. London : John Murray (3rd ed., 1880).

— — *Village Communities in the East and West*. London : John Murray (1907).

Mair, L. P., *Native Policies in Africa*. London : Routledge (1936).

Malinowski, B., *Crime and Custom in Savage Society*. London : Kegan Paul (1926).

— — *The Family among the Australian Aborigines*. London : Hodder & Stoughton (1913).

Mayer, P., *Two Studies in Applied Anthropology in Kenya*. Colonial Research Studies, No. 3. London : H.M.S.O. (1951).

Meek, C. K., *Law and Authority in a Nigerian Tribe*. London and New York : Oxford University Press (1937).

— — *A Sudanese Kingdom*. London : Kegan Paul (1931).

Melland, F. H., and Young, T. C., *African Dilemma*. London : United Society for Christian Literature (1937).

Morgan, L. H., *Ancient Society (1877)*. London and New York : Henry Holt (1907).

Nadel, S. F., *A Black Byzantium*. London and New York : Oxford University Press (1942).

Paine, T., *The Rights of Man* (1789). London : Dent (1953 ed.).

Paton, G. W., *A Textbook of Jurisprudence*. London : Oxford University Press (1951).

Penwill, D. J., *Kamba Customary Law*. London : Macmillan (1951).

Phillips, A., *Report on Native Tribunals in Kenya*. Nairobi, Kenya : Government Printer (1945).

— — (ed.), *Survey of African Marriage and Family Life*. London and New York : Oxford University Press (1953).

Pigafetta, F., *History of the Kingdom of Congo* (Rome, 1591). London : John Murray (1881).

Plucknett, T. F. T., *A Concise History of the Common Law*. London : Butterworth (4th ed., 1948).

Polak, A. L., *Legal Fictions*. London : Stevens (1945).

— — *More Legal Fictions*. London : Stevens (1946).

Pollock, Sir F., *A First Book of Jurisprudence*. London : Macmillan (6th ed., 1929).

— — *Introduction to History of the Science of Politics*. London : Macmillan (1911).

— — and Maitland, F. W., *History of English Law before the Time of Edward I*. Cambridge University Press (2nd ed., 1898, 2 vols.).

Pound, R., *Interpretations of Legal History*. London : Cambridge University Press (1923).

— — *Justice according to Law*. New Haven : Yale University Press, London : Oxford University Press, (1952).

Radcliffe-Brown, A. R., and Forde, C. D., *African Systems of Kinship and Marriage*. London : Oxford University Press (1950).

Rattray, R. S., *Ashanti Law and Constitution*. Oxford : The Clarendon Press (1929).

Read, C. H., and Dalton, O. M., *Antiquities from the City of Benin*. London, British Museum : Longmans, Green (1899).

Reith, C., *The Blind Eye of History*. London : Faber & Faber (1952).

Rivers, W. H. R., *Social Organization*. London : Kegan Paul (1924).

Roberts, C. C., *Tangled Justice*. London : Macmillan (1937).

Robson, W. A., *Civilization and the Growth of Law*. London : Macmillan (1935).

Roscoe, J., *The Baganda*. London : Macmillan (1911).

Rousseau, J. J., *Du Contrat Social*, in translation *Social Contract*. London : Dent (1953).

Russell, B., *What is Democracy?* London : Batchworth Press (1953).

Salmond, Sir J., *Jurisprudence*, ed. by J. L. Parker. London : Sweet & Maxwell (9th ed., 1937).

Sarbah, J. M., *Fanti Customary Laws*. London : Clowes (2nd ed., 1904).

Savigny, F. von, *System, Vol. I.* (Holloway's translation), (1840–1849).

Sayre, P. (editor), *Interpretations of Modern Legal Philosophies, Essays Presented in Honour of Dean Roscoe Pound*. London and New York : Oxford University Press (1947).

Schapera, I., *Bantu-speaking Tribes in South Africa*. London : Routledge (1937).

— — *A Handbook of Tswana Law and Custom*. London : International Institute for African Languages and Cultures (1938).

— — *Tribal Legislation among the Tswana of the Bechuanaland Protectorate*. London : Lund, Humphries (1943).

Seligman, C. G., *The Cult of the Nyakang and the Divine Kings of the Shilluk*. Khartoum : Welcome Tropical Research Laboratories, Gordon Memorial College (1911).

Simmons, L. W., *The Role of the Aged in Primitive Society*. U.S.A. : Yale University Press (1945).

Stammler, R., *Theory of Justice*. Trans. by I. Husik in Modern Legal Philosophy Series. New York (1925).

Stone, J., *The Province and Function of Law*. Sydney : Associated General Publications Pty. (1946).

Talbot, P. A., *The Peoples of Southern Nigeria*. London : Oxford University Press (1926).

Temple, O., *Notes on the Tribes, Provinces, Emirates and States of the Northern Provinces of Nigeria*. Cape Town : Argus Printing and Publishing Coy. (1910).

Thurnwald, R. C., *Black and White in East Africa*. London : Routledge (1935).

Vinogradoff, P., *Common-sense in Law*. London : Oxford University Press (1913).

Wade, E. C. S., and Phillips, G. C., *Constitutional Law*. London : Longmans Green (3rd ed., 1946).

Westermann, D., *The African Today and Tomorrow*. London : Oxford University Press (1934).

Westwood, G., *Society and the Homosexual*. London : Gollancz (1952).

Wilson, Godfrey and Monica, *The Analysis of Social Change*. London : Cambridge University Press (1945).

INDEX

Abandonment of land, 165, 166, 167–8

Abraham, R. C., 23 n. 2

Accident, relevance of in African law, 136, 139, 140, 142, 178

Actions, methods of commencing, 218–22

Adat law, comparison with African law, 31

Adultery, Baganda treatment of, 179; as a civil offence, 102, 128; as a criminal offence, 123, 227; as a crime under French law, 122

Advocates, customary professional, 247

African democracy, 18–22, 98–9, 192–4, 197, 210

African Dilemma, by Melland, F. H., and Young, T. C., 27 n. 3

African empires and civilisations, 9, 14 n. 1

African laws, existing studies of, 6; in opposition to European laws, 34, 106, 110 ff., 130; reason and logic in, 28–34; self-contradiction among critics of, 36; similarities between several systems of, 2–4; those subject to, 6–7; various attitudes towards, 5, 25 ff.

Age, importance of, 102, 104–5, 249

Age-grades, 86, 103, 105, 198, 267

Age-sets, 74 n. 2, 103, 105

Agistment, contracts of, 150

Ajisafe, A. K., 153 n. 2, 171 n. 1, 265 n. 1

Akan chiefs, constitutionality of, 19

Akim Akotoku, by M. J. Field, 261 n. 1

Aliens, incorporation of, 106

Allen, C. K., 77, 79, 126, 188 n. 1, 198 n. 2, 205 n. 1, 241 n. 1, 243 n. 1, 258, 265, 266

Allott, A. N., 213 n. 2

Amazons of Dahomey, 100

Ancestor, myth of the original, 14–15

Anglo-American legal system, 110, 114, 122, 158, 289 n. 2

Anthropologists and African law, 27–34, 48–55

Arbitration, African judicial process as, 212–15, 272

Arbitrator as judge, 272

Aristotle, idea of 'mutual service', 92, n. 1; on justice and equity, 272; on Greek law, 30 n. 3

Ashanti, distinction between murder and manslaughter, 142; kingdom of, 205, 216; matrilineal system of the, 101; treatment of crimes, 113

Ashton, H., 104 n. 3, 123 n. 3, 146 n. 1, 177 n. 1, 181 n. 4, 182 n. 1, 197 n. 1, 206 n. 4, 209 nn. 2 and 3

Assessors, use of in judicial proceedings, 275–6

Associations, law-making by, 197–8

Assyrians, ancient law codes of the, 188

Austin, J., similarity to Kelsen, 42 n. 1; theory of law, 54, 37 ff., 294; view on legislation, 189–190; on sanction, 56–7; on status, 76–7

Azande, Nebeli and Ngobo societies of the, 86; witchcraft among the, 231

Babylonians, ancient laws of the, 34, 188

Baganda, centralised kingdom of, 14, 216; Queen dowager among the, 101; treatment of adultery by, 179

Bailment, of chattels, 171–2

Bamenda, status of women of, 101 n. 4

Bantu, distinction between intentional and unintentional wrongs by the, 133; law, contrasted with British law, 128; treatment of homicide and similar crimes, 113; use of oath among the, 231

Banyoro, treatment of accidental homicide by, 136

Barton, R. F., 32 n. 8

Basoga, Central (Native) Court of the, 153; conquest of by the Baganda, 23; penalty for murder among, 135–6

Basutos, age of marriage among, 104 n. 3

Battuta, I., 9 n. 7

Batty, R. B., 228 n. 3

Bayankole kingdom, 11

Bekri, El, 9 n. 7

Belgium, adoption of Code Napoléon in, 44

Bemba, cultural homogeneity of, 11; no oath-swearing among the, 231 n. 5; status of being a, 95

Benin, art of, 10

309